WHAT ARE THOSE CRAZY AMERICANS SAYING?

(WHEN THEY PUT WORDS TOGETHER)

**An Easy Way to Understand
Thousands of
American Expressions**

by

Jarold Kieffer

3rd Edition

KIEFFER PUBLICATIONS
© Copyright 1998

**9019 Hamilton Drive
Fairfax, Virginia 22031 USA
Phone: (703) 591-8328
FAX #: (703) 359-4244**

THIRD EDITION

This 3rd edition results from active buyer responses to five printings of the 2nd edition (1990). A purse/pocket-size book cannot be encyclopedic in its coverage of American expressions. However, a small, low cost, easy-to-use book proved to be very popular. Now, a small enlargement of page size and format changes made possible the addition of many more expressions to the book. These changes plus new categories of expressions make the 3rd edition even more useful as an inexpensive tool for people who wish to understand the language Americans use in the workplace, on the street, in newspapers and movies, and on radio and television.

Library of Congress Catalog Card Number: 98-91488

Kieffer, Jarold A.
 What are those crazy Americans saying?: (when they put words together): an easy way to understand thousands of American expressions / by Jarold Kieffer.
 pp 472 cm. 11x17.5
ISBN 1-877627-02-X
 1. American-Dictionaries. 2. English language-United States-Terms and phrases. 3. English language-United States-Conversation and phrase books. I. Title.

10 9 8 7 6 5 4 3   CIP

 Copyright © 1998 by Kieffer Publications. All rights reserved. No part of this book may be reproduced in any form by any means without written permission from Kieffer Publications.

TABLE OF CONTENTS

Table of Contents (Continued)

DEDICATION

As with the 1st (1989) and 2nd (1990) editions of "What Are Those Crazy Americans Saying?," I dedicate the 3rd edition of this book to my longtime colleagues at Senior Employment Resources (SER). The able volunteer and paid staff of this not-for-profit organization, based in Fairfax County in northern Virginia, encourages the continued productivity of older people and has found paying jobs for thousands of them over 15 years. The whole idea of such a book arose directly from one of SER's programs that helped older refugees and immigrants gain paying jobs. Their difficulties in understanding the slang and other American expressions used by their bosses and fellow workers caused me to think about an easy-to-use little book that they could refer to for quick help with their problem.

The popularity of this book world-wide, especially the 2nd edition, which, without any marketing program, went through five printings, confirmed my belief that an American expressions book that was small in size, had an easy-to-use format, and was low cost would be attractive to an expanding number of people from other cultures who wish or need to interact effectively with Americans. Slight page size and format changes in this 3rd edition made possible the inclusion of several thousand more expressions and their meanings, which will make the book even more helpful.

The intensive editorial work incidental to fitting the thousands of expressions and their meanings into a small book took a lot of effort, and I thank many friends and family members whom I pestered by asking for their sense of the exact meanings of particular expressions and how best to word both the expressions and their meanings for accuracy and simplicity.

I reach back also to thank George Fahham from the Sudan,
who, in 1988 was a neighbor in Fairfax, Virginia while in
America on a student visa. During our frequent conversations,
I unwittingly used many American expressions that baffled him
despite his razor sharp mind and good grasp of English. He
was very polite and did not wish to embarrass himself or be
impolite by asking me to clarify what I was saying. However,
he overcame his reluctance to appear uninformed and regularly
asked me to explain more clearly what in the world I was saying. Far from resenting his frequent questions, I sensed the
problem I was creating for him and took pains to find the right
words or example to explain what each expression I used meant
to Americans. That discipline of searching for words and
examples that had meaning to him was invaluable to me as a
guide to the editorial effort that led to "What Are Those Crazy
Americans Saying?" in 1989 and it successive editions.

Finally, I thank my very patient wife, Frances, who, while
wishing I would relax more at age 75, recognized the function
of the book and supported my long preoccupation with preparing each of the three editions and with managing the affairs of
the publishing company that sells the book.

INTRODUCTION

The motivation for writing the first edition of "What Are Those Crazy Americans Saying?" (1989) grew directly from observations of a felt need. America's population always has been augmented by immigrants and refugees. Today, millions of people from other cultures live in America and must interact with Americans as neighbors, and on the job, in shops, banks, government offices, or on the street. Some come with a working knowledge of English, but most need help from others to teach them or to interpret what is said to them. Over time, most acquire a sufficient stock of words and their meanings to enable them to function reasonably well, but American slang, idioms, and other peculiarly American expressions are a special problem to them.

Even those who have a good grasp of English are baffled when they hear or read American slang or other expressions. They may understand the meaning of many English words, but when Americans combine these words in expressions or give them unexpected meanings, the result is confusion and puzzlement. As is often the case, not wishing to appear uncomprehending, they also feel embarrassment. Some would like to show their ease with English by trying to use American expressions, but they fear that they will use them the wrong way and be embarrassed. Such people also struggle for comprehension when they encounter American slang in American newspapers and magazines, or when they go to movies or listen to programs on radio and television.

The increasing internationalization of the world's economies has added further communication difficulties. Year by year, more Americans are interacting with non-Americans in expanding commercial, educational, and government relations. American executives often now report to bosses in other countries, or they may be interacting with their staffs or professional colleagues in other countries. Teams involved with product development, marketing, and scientific research commonly are made up of people from a number of countries.

As English has become more popular as the common language (written and spoken) in these enterprises, American expressions tend to be a special challenge to people from other cultures. The challenge is made even more difficult by the tendency of Americans to give new and strange meanings to words (Example: "Not" is now used as a way of saying: "No," or "I won't do it!") Then, Americans often use the same expression to mean totally opposite things. (Example: That's just great!" means both "Wonderful!" and "That's awful!") The reverse also is true. Totally opposite words can mean the same thing. (Example: "Close down" and "Close up" mean the same: ([Cease operations]).

Understandably, English language instruction courses often focus on teaching elemental or "survival" English. However, even with more advanced courses, time does not permit much teaching of American expressions. While teachers are well aware of the communications importance of such expressions, they commonly note the lack of easy-to-use, low cost sources that they could recommend to their students for self-instruction.

Several excellent encyclopedias of American expressions exist or are in preparation that are very useful for persons studying their origins and usages. However, they are expensive, multi-volume, and bulky. Also, by their nature, their style is scholarly, historical, and very detailed. Often, the user must wade through several paragraphs to discover the meaning of an expression. Smaller American expressions books also can be found, but they tend to be selective in the types of expressions covered and do not include whole ranges of expressions that commonly baffle people from other cultures. Some focus on regional or humorous expressions; others group them in categories relating to animals, colors, parts of the human anatomy, or emotions.

Small, paperback English dictionaries are of little help in understanding American expressions, because they focus on meanings for individual words. Larger, high quality dictionaries include meanings for some expressions, but the reader must search intensively for them among all the other uses for the words involved. Also, they are too big to be carried by people to help them in their daily communication efforts.

A study of the utility of each of these types of publications, when the first edition of "What Are Those Crazy Americans Saying?" was being developed in 1988, as well as other books on this subject published since, reaffirmed that the new third edition should, as did the earlier editions, continue to (1) have the single purpose of helping readers learn the meaning of American expressions; (2) be small, easy to carry, and low cost; (3) use an alphabetical approach to organizing the expressions; and (4) focus on the meanings of such expressions.

What is Included and Excluded?

Therefore, this book does not include the history of American expressions. While that is a fascinating and often controversial subject, the sole purpose of this work is to enable readers to find expressions quickly and learn what Americans mean when they use them. Inclusion of expression histories would have made it impossible to keep the book small and low cost.

Some expressions were used in England during America's colonial period or before and are still are used there. However, if they are commonly used by Americans today, they are included in the book. Another guideline for inclusion is that the expressions are commonly used and well-understood by Americans <u>generally</u> rather than primarily by a particular ethnic or regional group. However, regional expressions that have come into common use are included.

Expressions whose meanings are self-evident are excluded. (Example: "Like looking for a needle in a haystack") Foul language and ethnic slurs are excluded. The few swear words or expressions included are in such common use as to be almost sanitized. (Example: "The hell you say!" ([Is that true?]))

Most expressions are worded in the male gender or are neutral. While it could be alleged that this practice reflects a bias, its purpose is exactly the opposite. If both genders had been used, questions could be asked as to why male gender was used in one case and female gender in another, and whether such use implied bias or encouraged stereotypes. However, female gender is used where it is natural or essential to the proper meaning. (Example: "She's my better half." ([My wife]))

Also, expressions appear in the form that Americans ordinarily use them, which in some cases means that letters are dropped or added. (Examples: "Hi'ya all!" ([How are you?] [Hello everybody!]), a friendly greeting, and "Byee!," an unfriendly way of telling someone to leave).

Expressions are worded in the present tense, except where their commonly used form is in the past tense. (Example: "He's **HAD** it." ([Been beaten] [Lost his patience]))

To help readers focus quickly on particular alphabetical chapters, the capital letter for each chapter is located in the lower right margin of each page. Key words for each of the special chapters are similarly located.

HOW TO USE THE BOOK

<u>Key Words are Arranged Alphabetically</u>

Expressions are arranged in the alphabetical order of their key word, which is shown in **BOLD** type and capital letters.

Example: It doesn't **ADD** up

The meaning of each expression appears below the expression in brackets and then parentheses. While brackets are used both in the expressions and their meanings statements, parentheses are used <u>only</u> to indicate meanings.

Example: It doesn't **ADD** up
       ([It makes no sense])

<u>Expressions With More Than One Key Word</u>

Expressions that have more than one key word are repeated with their meaning statement at the alphabetical location of each of the key words involved.

Example: I'll be with you in two shakes of a lamb's tail
       ([Very quickly])

In this case, the expression has three key words, which, in alphabetical order, are: "**LAMB'S**," "**SHAKES**," and "**TAIL**." Hence, the full expression and its meaning are found in Chapter "L" with the key word "**LAMB**" highlighted in **bold** type and capitalized. Next, it is found in Chapter "S" where the key word "**SHAKES**" is highlighted. Lastly, it appears in Chapter "T" where the key word "**TAIL**" is highlighted. This repetition arrangement lengthened the book a little, but it speeds the process of finding expressions and their meanings.

For example, a person may have heard the above-mentioned expression but can remember only one of its key words, say the word "TAIL." If the expression appeared alphabetically only under "LAMB," and the listener had not remembered that word, no clue would exist for finding the expression and its meaning. Also, even if the expression was read rather than heard, the reader doesn't have to guess and flap pages to see which word was chosen for the alphabetical position of the expression in the book. Any of the three key words could be used to start the search for the expression and its meaning.

Asterisk (*) Used to Mark Beginning of a New Expression

Expressions are arranged in alphabetical order from left to right on each page. Expressions on the right side are set apart from those on the left by an asterisk (*)

Different Words Mean That Mean the Same Thing

Often, different words can be linked to a key word with each linkage producing the same meaning. Note that each of the different words set off by brackets [.....] could stand alone with the word "AIR" to produce the same meaning.

Example: I'll [dance] [float] [walk] on AIR
([Be very happy])

These variations are also presented in the book at the alphabetical location of each of the bracketed words involved, that is, the "dance," version of the expression is found in Chapter D, and the "float" and "walk" versions are found in their alphabetical chapters. However, they are presented in a combined way with "AIR" in Chapter A, to give the reader an instant sense of the various options available. Such combination presentations are used for this purpose throughout the book.

Extra Words Used to Clarify the Meanings of Expressions

In many cases, the reader is helped to understand better the meaning of an expression by showing several ways its meaning could be explained. Where these added explanations are given, they are shown separated by a semicolon (;).

Example: He's **ACTING** up
   ([Causing problems; misbehaving])

Expressions That Have Various Meanings

Many expressions have several meanings. For example, the expression: "All fired up" may be used to describe someone who is very angry. However, it also means that someone is very enthusiastic. Usually, the context of the conversation or writing in which the expression is used quickly identifies which meaning is intended. In the book, the different meanings are presented in brackets in parentheses ([....] [....]) under the expression.

Example: All **FIRED** up
   ([Angry] [Enthusiastic])

Added Words That Change Meanings

The meaning of an expression can change with the addition of one or more words. For example, "I'll get away" means: "I'll take a vacation." It also means: "I'll escape." These variations are shown in brackets. However, when the words "with it" are added to this expression, its meaning now includes the idea that "I won't be caught or punished." This type of modification of the expression is shown in brackets [.....], and its impact on the meaning statement is shown by adding the bracketed words in its second line, as follows:

Example: I'll get **AWAY** [with it]
    (I'll [take a vacation] [escape]
    [not be caught or punished])

Alphabetical Arrangement of Second Key Words

Certain words such as "TAKE" or "UP" are commonly used in American expressions. Indeed, expressions that include the word "Take" require over six pages in Chapter "T." To help speed location of expressions that include such heavy-use words, they are arranged in the alphabetical order of their **second** key word. For example, on the bottom of Page 386, where the "Take" expressions start, it can be seen that "the expression: "**TAKE** it into account" is followed by "**TAKE** after him!," followed in turn by "**TAKE** him apart!" and so on, according to the alphabetical order of the **second** key word in each expression.

However, in many cases expressions may have more than two keys words. Example "**TAKE** the bull by the horns." In such case, the word "bull" is used for placing this expression alphabetically among the **TAKE** expressions listed in Chapter T. It is suggested that readers remember these arrangements when they encounter many pages of expressions that include the same key word. Also, recall again that where expressions have more than one key word, they and their meanings can be found in most cases by starting the search at the alphabetical location of any of the other key words.

A Further Suggestion for Readers

"**TAKE**," "**UP**" and certain other words are used in many expressions. That means that the search for the meaning of an expression including such words may take more time and patience. Readers, therefore, are urged to take a moment to look over a whole page or two of expressions including such words before trying to find the particular expression being sought. That quick review will help the reader understand the alphabetical arrangement of the "**TAKE**" expressions, for example, and help speed location of the expression being sought. This process also will help the reader learn more about how such a word is used in a variety of expressions.

Split Words

Persons struggling to understand other languages commonly focus on certain words they become familiar with over time. When dealing with languages such as English and German, that tend to run words together to make other words, the learner may focus on only familiar parts of run-together words.

To help such persons cope with American expressions that have run-together words, the book includes an unusual feature. For example, the run-together word "Bonehead!" is shown in divided form with the "**BONE**" part of the word highlighted in **bold** and capital letters in Chapter B, but in Chapter H, "**HEAD**" is the part highlighted. This feature is used to give the reader more options for identifying a key word and using it as a place to start searching in the various alphabetical chapters, to discover the meaning of expressions.

Example: In Chapter B   In Chapter H

Examples: **BONE**head!   Bone**HEAD**!
                  ([Ignorant fool!])

Expressions and Meanings With Words Left out

Some expressions and meaning statements could be completed in several ways. For example, the expression: "I'm crazy

ABOUT... could relate to girls, certain foods, horses, etc.. Rather than use book space to list all the possibilities, the editorial way of showing missing words, namely dots instead of words (...), is used.

Contractions

As is the case with some other languages, English makes broad use of contracted words in its ordinary spoken and written modes. Typically, such contractions involve making two words into one and leaving out one or more letters. In this book, contractions are used in ways that Americans normally use them. While some long word contractions were avoided, the test always was how to word an expression without making the usage stilted, awkward, or untypical of the way Americans actually use the language. As a guide to the reader, the most common contractions found in the book are:

Contraction	For the Words
Don't	Do not
He'll	He will
He's	He is
How's	How is
I've	I have
I'm	I am
I'll	I will
It's	It is
She'll	She will
They'll	They will
We'll	We will
What's	What is
Who's	Who is
You're	You are

SPECIAL FEATURES

To be of further help to readers, the book concludes with a
number of special chapters that are not alphabetical and have
other purposes.   These special chapters are considerably
enlarged over those found in the 2nd edition. They focus on
expressions Americans use when they are amazed or frustrated
(See pages 464-465); when they say hello or goodbye in friendly or unfriendly ways (See pages 458-460); when they express
agreement or disagreement (See pages 461-463); or when they
wish to avoid or soften swear words (See pages 468-469).

Generally, other than for these purposes, many of these expressions have no other purpose. They are included because
people from other cultures hear Americans utter them, or they
are seen in print. How can they be other than puzzled when an
American says: "I'll be a monkey's uncle" or tells someone to
"Butt out!"?   In the Special Feature sections, the reader can
discover that when an American says: "I'll be a monkey's
uncle" he or she is simply expressing surprise or amazement at
something. Or, when he or she says "Butt out!" someone is
being told "Goodbye" in a very unfriendly way.

Also, Americans and many other people, following the biblical
commandment against using the name of God in vain, have
evolved alternatives. Examples: "Holy smokes!" or "For goodness sakes!" (See pages 466-467). Finally, Americans have
many alternative ways of referring to jails or prisons (See page
470), to toilets (See page 471), and to money (See page 472).

PART I
Alphabetical Chapters

PART I
Alphabetical Chapters

Chapter A

An **A-1** fellow
(An excellent person)

It's **A** O.K.!
(It's all right!)

I'm taken **ABACK**
(Surprised; offended)

Learn the **ABC'S**
(The fundamentals)

From **A** to Z
(Everything)

[Be] [Get] **ABOUT** it!
(Start!)

Don't beat **ABOUT** the bush
(Say what you are thinking)

I'm crazy **ABOUT**...
(I admire...very much)

I [gad] [knock] **ABOUT** with...
(Associate; travel with...)

He harps **ABOUT**...
(Talks continuously about...)

Keep your [head][wits] **ABOUT** you!
(Think carefully!)

How **ABOUT** that?
(I'm amazed!)

I'm not **ABOUT** to...
(I have no intention of...)

He's on [and on] **ABOUT**...
(Talks [continuously] about...)

I'm out and **ABOUT**
(I'm active)

I set **ABOUT**
(Began; started)

He'll storm **ABOUT**
(Move wildly; in a rage)

Tell me **ABOUT** it!
(I already know it!)

A

I'm up and **ABOUT**
([recovered]
[I'm awake and active])

* I know what I'm **ABOUT**
([My purpose is clear]
[I have experience; knowledge])

It's what I'm **ABOUT**
(My nature; purpose)

* What is it **ABOUT**?
(What is its character?)

Open and **ABOVE** board
(Correct; proper)

* It's a cut **ABOVE**...
(It's better than...)

He's **ABOVE** the salt
(An important person)

* I'm **ABOVE** that
(I wouldn't behave that way)

ACCORDING to Hoyle
(According to the rules)

* A no-**ACCOUNT**
(A bad person)

On **ACCOUNT** of...
(Because of...)

* Take it into **ACCOUNT**
(Consider it)

I'll **ACE** a deal
(Make an agreement)

* **ACE** [it] [them]
([Complete it] [Win it]
[Outperform them])

My **ACE** [in the hole]
[up my sleeve]
(My secret advantage)

* The **ACID** test
(The critical proof needed)

All over hell's half **ACRE**
(Everywhere)

* A wise**ACRE**
(A sarcastic; bothersome person)

It's **ACROSS** the board
(Applies to everything)

* Come **ACROSS**!
([Give it to me!]
[Do what you promised!])

A

I'll come **ACROSS** as...
(Be perceived as...)

       * I'll [come] [stumble]
        ACROSS it
       (Find it [by chance])

Get **ACROSS** that...
(Communicate that...)

       * I'll run **ACROSS** him
       (Meet him)

It's a class **ACT**
(High quality)

       * Clean up your **ACT**!
       (Reform yourself!)

Get your **ACT** together
(Organize yourself better)

       * I have my **ACT** together
       (I'm confident; well organized)

A high wire **ACT**
(Very risky)

       * Read him the riot **ACT**!
       (Give him a strong warning!)

He'll **ACT** up
(Cause problems; misbehave)

       * How does he get off
       ACTING that way?
       (Why does he behave that way?)

I want a piece
of the **ACTION**
(A share of the activity)

       * Where is the **ACTION**?
       (Where is the key activity?)

He **ACTS** funny
(He behaves strangely)

       * I don't know him from **ADAM**
       (He's a stranger to me)

It will **ADD** insult to injury
(Make things even worse)

       * It doesn't **ADD** up
       (It doesn't make sense)

It **ADDS** up to...
(The result is...)   * A cozy **AFFAIR**   * An off/on **AFFAIR**
       (Intimate)   ([Occasional] [Uncertain])

A

A splashy **AFFAIR**
(An extravagant party)

I went far **AFIELD**
(I wasn't focused)

Go like a house **AFIRE**!
(Very fast)

Something is **AFOOT**
(Is happening)

He's **AFRAID** of his shadow
(He is fearful; timid)

I'm **AFRAID** so
(Unfortunately, it's true)

[Get] [Go] **AFTER** it!
([Try to] Do it!)

He's a person **AFTER**
my own heart
(We share similar interests; values)

He's **AFTER** her
(He's wooing her)

Look **AFTER** him
(Care for him)

Take [out] **AFTER** him
(Chase him)

He's **AFTER** me
(He's trying to find and punish me)

I take **AFTER** him
(I resemble him)

He's at it **AGAIN**
(He's doing it again)

Come **AGAIN**?
(Repeat what you said)

There you go **AGAIN**!
(You [did] [said] it again!)

Now and **AGAIN**
(Occasionally)

You can say that **AGAIN**
(That's true; I agree)

Time and **AGAIN**
(Repeatedly)

It goes **AGAINST** my grain
(It violates my nature)

I'll hold it **AGAINST** you
(Blame you)

AGAINST all odds   * I'm up AGAINST it
(Despite many obstacles)   (I'm in trouble)

AGAINST the wall   * I'm AHEAD of the game
(Trapped)   (I have an early advantage]
    [I'm well-prepared])

Go AHEAD!
(Do it!)   *   Full steam AHEAD!
    (Move vigorously!)

I'm a step AHEAD of him
(I anticipate his actions)   *   AHEAD of time
    (Earlier than expected)

I AIM to...
(I intend; plan to...)   * I have a lot of balls in the AIR
    (I'm working on many things)

Come up for AIR
(Stop work for a while) * I'll [dance] [float] [walk] on AIR
    (Be very happy)

Give him the AIR
(Abandon; jilt him)   *   He's an AIRhead
    (He's not smart)

It's hot AIR
(Exaggerated talk)   *   It's in the AIR
    (It's widely discussed)

Vanish into thin AIR
(Disappear)   *   Up in the AIR
    (Uncertain; undecided)

Put on AIRS
(Act overly important)   * An ALBATROS around
    my neck
A smart ALECK   (A troublesome burden)
(A bright but annoying person)

A

6

I'm **ALIVE** and kicking   *   Look **ALIVE**!
(I'm well and happy)   (Be alert!)

He'll [eat] [skin] you **ALIVE**   *   **ALL** along I...
(Punish; overwhelm you)   (From the beginning, I...)

ALL atwitter   *   The be-**ALL** and end-**ALL**
(Excited)   (The best version of something)

That beats **ALL**!   *   You'**ALL** come back!
(I'm amazed!)   (Goodbye!)

Dang it **ALL**!   *   **ALL** in a day's work
(A softened swear expression)   (Normal; routine)

I'm **ALL** ears   *   In **ALL** events,...
(I'm listening carefully)   ([Anyway,...] [However,...])

What's so **ALL**fired important?   *   **ALL** fired up
(What is so critical?)   ([Angry] [Enthusiastic])

I'm **ALL** for it   *   On **ALL** fours with...
(I strongly support it)   (In complete agreement with...)

A free-for-**ALL**   *   ...as **ALL** get out
(Everyone is fighting)   (Energetically; fast)

Give it your **ALL**   *   Go **ALL** out!
(Make a maximum effort)   (Make a full effort)

It's **ALL** for the good   *   He's **ALL** heart
(It's helpful)   (He's [generous] [stingy])

A

7

7

Hi'ya **ALL**!
(Hello, everybody!)

*

ALL in **ALL**
(Considering everything)

I'm **ALL** in
(Exhausted)

* For **ALL** intents and purposes
(In every sense)

For **ALL** I know,...
(I'm not sure, but it is possible)

* In **ALL** likelihood
(Probably)

ALL by my lonesome
(It's me, alone)

* By **ALL** means!
([Yes!] [I agree!])

It's **ALL** I need
(I don't need more trouble)

* By **ALL** odds,...
(In every way,...)

ALL at once   * Once and for **ALL**
(Suddenly)   (For the last time)

* Go **ALL** out!
(Try very hard!)

It's **ALL** over
(Completed; finished)

*

He was **ALL** over me
(He overwhelmed me)

ALL over the [lot] [map] [place]
([Everywhere] [Without focus])

* **ALL** the rage
(Very popular; stylish)

ALL right!
([Yes!] [I agree!])

*

ALL the same,...
(Nevertheless,...)

If it's **ALL** the same to you,...
(If you don't object,...)

* **ALL** set?
(Are you ready?)

ALL of a sudden
(Without warning)

* He's not **ALL** there
(Not fully alert; not sane)

A

8

Of **ALL** things!
(I'm amazed; puzzled)

ALL in good time
(Eventually)

ALL told,...
(Counting everything)

For **ALL** the world,...
(In every way,...)

A blind **ALLEY**
(It goes nowhere)

I **ALLOWED** as how,...
(I admitted; explained that...)

[Leave] [Let] me **ALONE**!
(Don't [bother] [hurt] me!)

Let well enough **ALONE**!
(Don't disturb things!)

Barreling **ALONG**
(Speeding)

He'll come **ALONG**
(He'll finally agree)

When you get **ALONG**
(Get older)

*   I'm **ALL** thumbs
(Very clumsy)

* I have it **ALL** together
(I'm well organized)

*   He's **ALL** wet!
(He is misinformed; wrong)

*   For **ALL** it's worth
(For its full value)

* It's right [down] [up] my **ALLEY**
([I'm very qualified for it]
[It's perfect for me])

*   Go it **ALONE**
(Act independently)

* [Leave] [Let] it **ALONE**!
([Don't touch it!]
[Don't say another word!])

*   All **ALONG**, I...
(From the beginning,...)

*   I'll be **ALONG**
(I'll join you soon)

*   It's coming **ALONG**
(Progress is being made)

A

[Get] [Run] **ALONG** [with you!]
([Leave!] [Stop your nonsense!])

* I get **ALONG**
([I relate well to others]
[I support myself])

Go **ALONG** [with it] [for the ride]
([Concur] [Share the experience])

* I'm [humping] [inching] **ALONG**
(Moving slowly)

Play **ALONG** with...
(Appear to cooperate with...)

* Run **ALONG**!
(Leave now!)

I'll run **ALONG**
(Leave now)

* String him **ALONG**
(Keep him in doubt)

I'll string **ALONG** with you
([Go with] [Support] you)

* Tag **ALONG**
(Go with me)

Tool **ALONG**
(Cruise; move easily)

* [All right] [Enough] **ALREADY**!
([Stop it!] [Expression of impatience])

I'm **ALWAYS** there in a clutch
(I help when it is needed)

* He's **ALWAYS** crabbing
(Complaining)

It's a serious **AMOUNT**
(A large amount)

* In the final **ANALYSIS**
(Considering everything)

AND how!
([Yes!] [I agree!])

* No if's, **AND'S,** and but's
(Without reservations)

Our **ANGEL**
(Our benefactor)

* What is his **ANGLE**?
(His agenda; objectives)

A

What is he **ANGLING** for?
(What does he seek?)

He's off on
ANOTHER kick
(A new adventure; enterprise)

Somehow or **ANOTHER**
(By some means)

It's a flip **ANSWER**
(Casual; unthoughtful)

He's a penny-**ANTE**...
(An unimportant...)

He has **ANTS** in his pants
([He is agitated] [Impatient])

He's **ANTZY**
(Nervous; restless)

In **ANY** event,...
([Anyhow,...]
[Whatever happens,...])

ANYTHING goes
(No rules apply)

ANYWAY you [cut] [slice] it
(However you calculate it)

Take him **APART**!
(Punish him!)

I upset the **APPLE**cart
(Foiled the plan)

The **APPLE** of my eye
(My favorite person)

A good **APPLE**
(A likeable, fine fellow)

In **APPLE**-pie [order] [shape]
(In fine condition)

A sad **APPLE**
(A person who always loses)

What do you think
of those **APPLES**?
(What is your reaction to...?)

Tied to his mother's
APRON strings
(Dependent on his mother)

Right you **ARE**!
(You are correct!)

There you **ARE**!
(See, as I predicted!)

A

11

A tight **ARGUMENT**
(A carefully reasoned position)

I have a bum **ARM**
(My arm is in bad condition)

A shot in the **ARM**
(Something that renews spirit; strength)

Strong-**ARM** him
(Force him)

Busier than a one-**ARMED**
 paperhanger
(Extremely busy)

My knight in shining **ARMOR**
(My hero)

Don't beat **AROUND** the bush
(Say what you are thinking)

I've been **AROUND** [the block]
(I'm experienced)

He'll come **AROUND**
(Finally agree)

Just **AROUND** the corner
(Near)

* [Bend] [Twist] his **ARM**
Put the **ARM** on him
(Force him to [do]
[not do] something)

* It cost an **ARM** and leg
(Very expensive)

* He'll talk an **ARM** and leg off you
(He won't stop talking)

* **ARMED** to the teeth
([Very well-prepared]
[Carrying many weapons])

* Up in **ARMS**
(Angry; aroused)

* He's **AROUND** the
[bend] [corner]
(He's crazy)

* Bring him **AROUND**
([Gain his support]
[Restore him to consciousness]
[Invite him to visit])

* Don't [fool] [goof] [horse]
[monkey] [play] **AROUND**!
(Don't [flirt] [be funny!]
[have sex] [waste time])

A

12

I [go] [knock] **AROUND**
with ...
(Associate with...)

* We go **AROUND** and
AROUND
(We argue)

Green **AROUND** the gills
(Nauseated)

* [Hang] [Stick] **AROUND**!
(Don't go away!)

I hang **AROUND** with...
(Associate with...)

* Don't jerk me **AROUND**!
(Don't tell me one thing
and mean another)

Kick it **AROUND**
(Consider it)

* It's been kicking **AROUND** for...
(It has a long history)

He'll lead him **AROUND** by the nose
(Control him)

* Don't mess **AROUND**
(Act quickly)

Don't mess **AROUND** with...
(Don't get involved with...)

* He's nosying **AROUND**
(Examining; questioning)

Pad **AROUND**
(Go for a walk)

* He's pussyfooting **AROUND**
(He's very [cautious] [stealthy])

Run rings **AROUND** him
(Outperform him)

* Until that day rolls **AROUND**
(Until that time,...)

A run-**AROUND**
(Deceptive tactics that
mislead and waste time)

* Don't screw **AROUND**!
(Don't waste time!)

See you **AROUND**!
(A goodbye expression)

* Don't shillyshally **AROUND**
(Be decisive; forthright)

A

Throw your weight **AROUND**
(Use your influence
to gain your objectives)

* Turn it **AROUND**
(Make it more successful)

* Turn-**AROUND** time
(Time needed to [do the job]
[be ready again for action/service])

Work him **AROUND**
([Punish him]
[Change his thinking])

* It's dead on **ARRIVAL**
(It has no future)

He has **ARRIVED**
(He is successful)

* A straight **ARROW**
(An honest person)

State of the **ART**
(Best technology in use)

* The genuine **ARTICLE**
(Authentic)

I would **AS** soon...
(I would prefer...)

* Take it **AS** is
(In its present condition)

AS far as I'm concerned,...
(With regard to my interest,...)

* **AS** for me,...
(With regard to me,...)

..., **AS** it were
(..., as if it were so)

* **AS** you were!
(Keep doing what
you were doing!)

He's **ASKING** for it
(He's looking for trouble)

Fast **ASLEEP**
(In deep sleep)

* **ASLEEP** at the switch
(Not alert)

Rest **ASSURED**
(It's certain)

* He's **AT** it again
(He's doing it again)

A

What is he driving **AT**?
(What is his objective)

Have **AT** it!
([Do it!] [Try it!])

He's **AT** large
(He hasn't been caught)

AT [long] last!
(Finally!)

I'm **AT** sea
(Confused; lost)

He **ATE** my head off
(Severely criticized me)

No strings **ATTACHED**
(No limiting conditions)

He's all **ATWITTER**
(Excited)

AW, come on! [now!]
([An expression of impatience]
[I don't believe it!]
[You're joking!])

It will blow you **AWAY**
(Amaze; stun you)

*   Get **AT** him
(Reach and punish him)

*   I'm **AT** home with it
(I'm comfortable with it)

*   Elected **AT** large
(By a vote of the
whole electorate)

*   **AT** [the] least
(The minimum)

*   That's where it's **AT**
(Where the action is)

*   **ATTA**boy!
(An expression of praise
to encourage someone)

*   Pay **ATTENTION**!
(Listen carefully!)

*   He's an **AVERAGE** Joe
(An ordinary person)

*   Blow them **AWAY**!
([Kill] [Overwhelm] them!)

*   It will carry you **AWAY**
(You will become enthusiastic)

A

Do **AWAY** with it!
(Destroy; get rid of it!)

Make a get**AWAY**
(Escape)

A give**AWAY**
(A thing of value given/
sold at little or no cost)

I won going **AWAY**
(Very easily)

He'll pass **AWAY**
(Die)

I can put it **AWAY**
(Eat a lot)

Shy **AWAY** from...
(Avoid...)

Square it **AWAY**
([Fix it!] [Get it done!])

He's carrying on
something **AWAY**
(He is very agitated)

He has an **AXE** to grind
(He has his own agenda)

*   A get**AWAY**
(A vacation place)

* I'll get **AWAY** [with it]
([Take a vacation] [Escape]
[Not be caught or punished])

* It's a [dead] give**AWAY**
(It betrays; reveals
what is hidden)

* Make **AWAY** with it
(Steal; take it)

* Put him **AWAY**!
([Knock him unconscious!])
([Defeat] [Jail] [Kill] him!])

* Right **AWAY**
(Immediately)

* Spirit him **AWAY**
([Hire] [Kidnap] him)

* [Salt] [Sock] [Squirrel] it **AWAY**
([Hide] [Save] it)

* Give him the **AXE**!
(Fire; remove him!)

A

Chapter B

A **BABE** in the woods
(An untested, naive person)

He's a cry **BABY**
(He complains a lot)

Don't **BABY** him
(Don't coddle him)

Don't throw out the
BABY with the bathwater
(Don't let small problems
defeat larger goals)

It's your **BABY**
(You are responsible)

Behind my **BACK**
(Without my knowledge)

He has **BACK**bone
(Courage; resolve)

The straw that will break
the camel's **BACK**
(The decisive factor)

[Break] [Bust] your **BACK**
([Try] [Work] very hard)

It's on the **BACK** burner
(It has a low priority)

You'all come **BACK**!
(Goodbye!)

BACK him into a corner
(Leave him no good options)

By the **BACK** door
(Indirectly; secretly)

BACK down!
(Concede; withdraw!)

BACK to [the drawing board]
[go] [square one]
(Start from the beginning again)

It's like water off a
duck's **BACK**
(It has little impact)

It's a fall**BACK** position
(A position to retreat to if needed)

I'm **BACK** on my feet
(I [am well] [have resources])

I'm flat on my **BACK**
(Ill and in bed)

He's doing **BACK**flips
(He's very excited; happy)

* I'm **BACK** on my game
(I'm playing well again)

Get **BACK** at him
(Gain revenge against him)

* Get off my **BACK**!
(Don't nag me!)

I'm **BACK** to go
(I must start again)

* Don't go **BACK** on me
(Don't break your promise)

BACK to the [old] grind
(To my regular work)

* The **BACK** of my hand to you
(I'm angry with you)

I know it like the **BACK**
of my hand
(I'm very familiar with it)

* In the **BACK** of my head
(In my deep memory)

* Hold **BACK**
(Don't make a full effort)

Keep **BACK**!
(Keep your distance!)

Knock **BACK** a glass of...
(Have a drink of...)

* My **BACK** will kick out
(Become painful)

* He's laid **BACK**
(Reserved; relaxed)

He's on the **BACK** of his lap
(On his buttocks)

* The monkey is on my **BACK**
(It's my responsibility)

BACK off!
([Move away!])
(End your [attack] [effort]!)

* He's on my **BACK**
(He is pressuring me)

He'll **BACK** out
(Not keep his promises)

* A pat on the **BACK**
(A compliment)

Pin his ears **BACK**!
(Beat; humiliate him!)

* He's in my **BACK** pocket
(I control him)

Put your **BACK** into it!
(Use your strength)

* I'm [**BACK**] in the saddle
(I'm [at work] [in control] again)

BACK to the salt mine *
(Back to work again)

We'll scratch each other's **BACK**
(Help meet each other's needs)

Take a **BACK** seat *
(A lesser position)

A set**BACK** *
(A disappointment)

It set me **BACK**...
(It cost me...)

Cover your **BACK**side!
(Maneuver to avoid blame)

* No skin off my **BACK**
(It means nothing to me)

Take it **BACK**! *
(Apologize!)

He'll talk behind your **BACK**
(Speak about you, not to you)

Don't talk **BACK**!
(Don't argue!)

* It's **BACK** on track
(Moving again as planned)

Don't turn your **BACK** on... *
(Don't reject...)

BACK him up!
(Support him)

He's our **BACK**-up
(Our person in reserve)

* His **BACK** is up
(He's angry)

My **BACK** is to the wall
(I have no good options)

* Bend over **BACK**wards
(Make a special effort)

I'm **BACKED** up
(Behind in my work)

* He's **BACKING** and filling
(Making excuses; evasive)

GreenBACKS   *   Bring home the BACON
(Money)   (Get [income] [results])

Save his BACON   *   There is BAD blood between them
(Rescue him)   (They hate each other)

Off on a BAD foot   *   It's a BAD hair day
(A poor beginning)   (I have many problems today)

I [got] [have] it BAD   *   It's not [half] BAD
(It controls me)   (It's really good)

I look BAD   *   BAD-mouth him
(I have a poor image)   (Say bad things about him)

What's the BAD news?   *   He's BAD news
(What do I owe?)   (He causes trouble)

I'm BAD off   *   He's a BAD sport
(I'm [distressed] [poor])   (He reacts badly to losing)

It leaves a BAD taste in my mouth   *   Too BAD!
(It troubles me)   ([I'm sorry!] [Who cares?])

I'm in a BAD way   *   It's going from BAD to worse
(I'm [sick] [in trouble])   (The situation is deteriorating)

The cat is out of the BAG   *   [Put] [Tie] on the
(The secret is revealed)   [feed] [nose] BAG
                            (Eat!)

He's gone BAG and BAGGAGE   *   A grab BAG
(He left with all his things)   (It contains many things)

B

I'm holding the **BAG**
(I'm blamed; held responsible)

* It's in the **BAG**!
(Success is assured)

BAG it! *
([Finish] [Stop] it!)

I'm the **BAG** man
(I carry money to others
for illegal purposes)

It's a mixed **BAG**
(It's good and bad)

* It's [not] my **BAG**
([Not my style; interest])
(It's my responsibility)

He'll sand**BAG** us
(Try to [coerce] [trick] us)

* **BAG** them!
(Capture them!)

He's a wind**BAG**
(He talks too much)

* **BAIL** out!
([Escape] [Go] [Leave]!)

BAIL him out
([Rescue him]
[Pay to get him out of jail])

* Fish or cut **BAIT**!
(Produce or quit!)

I'll wait with **BAITED** breath
(Anxiously)

* He's half-**BAKED**
(Silly; unsound)

It's a **BALD**-faced...
(A totally false...)

* It's a **BALL**
(It's [easy] [wonderful])

Carry the **BALL**
(Take responsibility)

* I must play catch-up **BALL**
(I'm losing and must
work hard to win)

He's a [corn] [goof] [odd] **BALL**
(A silly; strange person)

* The **BALL** is in my court
(The next move is mine)

B

Don't drop the **BALL**   *   Behind the eight **BALL**
(Don't lose the opportunity)   (In a difficult situation)

Eye**BALL** it   *   It's eye**BALL** to eye**BALL**
(Go look at it)   (A tense confrontation)

He's a **BALL** of fire   *   It's a new **BALL**game
(He has great energy)   (A new [situation] [start])

He [has a lot] [is] on the **BALL**   *   Low**BALL** it
(He is able; effective)   (Show it with a very low cost)

Play [hard] **BALL**   *   Keep the **BALL** rolling
(Cooperate) ([Be ruthless])   (Keep things active)

A screw**BALL**   *   A sleaze**BALL**
(An odd, strange person)   (A dishonest person)

I **BALLED** up * It's **BALLED** up * It will go over
(Made errors)   (It's a mess)   like a lead **BALLOON**
   (The response will be bad)

It's a trial **BALLOON**
(A test to get first   *   A **BALL**park estimate
reactions to an idea/plan)   (A quick judgment,
   without careful analysis)

I have a lot of **BALLS** in the air
(I'm working on many things)   *   I'm [in hock] up
   to my eye**BALLS**
[Great] **BALLS** of fire!   (My credit is exhausted)
(Expression of amazement)

    *   He's full of **BALONEY**
   (He's wrong)

B

It's a hulla**BALOO**
(An uproar; a noisy affair)

*

He'll **BAMBOOZLE** you
(Take advantage of; fool;
swindle you)

The top **BANANA**
(The boss)

*

I'm going **BANANAS**
(Crazy)

…,to beat the **BAND**
(Enthusiastically)

*

I'll make out like a **BANDIT**
(Profit greatly)

It had a **BAND**wagon effect
(It caused many people to
change their thinking)

*

It's a **BANG**
(A lot of fun)

More **BANG** for the buck
(More cost-effective)

* I get a **BANG** out of it
(I enjoy it)

A **BANG**-up job
(Excellently done)

*

A whiz**BANG**
(A remarkable person)

It will break the **BANK**
(Make me poor)

*

I'll cry all the
way to the **BANK**
(Complain about something
but profit from it)

Knock off the **BANK**   *
(Rob it)

* It's money in the **BANK**

BANKnotes
(Money)   * **BANK**roll him
(Finance his activities)

(Its success is certain)

*   **[BANK** on it]
[You can take it

Belly up to the **BAR**
(Confront the matter)

to the **BANK]**
(It is very reliable; worthy)

B

He's a **BAR** fly
(He drinks a lot in bars)

..., **BAR** none
(With no exceptions)

BAREbones   *   **BARF**
(Plain; simple)   (Vomit)

He **BARGED** in
(Pushed his way in)

He'll **BARK** up the wrong tree
(Waste time on the wrong thing)

All around Robin
Hood's **BARN**
(A lengthy process)

No holds **BARRED**
(No restrictions apply)

Scrape the bottom
of the **BARREL**
(Use the poorest quality)

Cash on the **BARREL**head
(Actual cash)

* Clear out lock, stock, and **BARREL**!
(Go and take your things!)

Like shooting fish
in a **BARREL**
(Very easy to do)

He's a **BARREL** of fun
(He's humorous)

I'm over a **BARREL**
(My options are not good)

BARRELING along
(Speeding)

Give him both **BARRELS**!
(Make a strong attack on him!) * I won't get to first **BASE**
(I'll fail)

I'm off **BASE**   *   Touch **BASE** with...
(I'm behaving badly)   (Communicate with...)

A **BASH**   *   Cover all **BASES**   *   **BASKET** case
(A big party)   (Prepare well)   ([Very sick] [Hopeless])

B

24

Don't put all your   *   Going to hell in
  eggs in one **BASKET**   a hand**BASKET**
  (Don't rely too much on   (To ruin and fast)
  one factor or option)

        *   I didn't **BAT** an [eye][eyelash]
Go to **BAT** for him   (I [showed no surprise]
(Help him)   [was very casual])

Going like a **BAT** out of hell   *   Right off the **BAT**
  (Very fast)   (Immediately; quickly)

An old **BAT**   *   **BAT** out a...
(An old, unpleasant person)   (Prepare quickly a...)

I'm up to **BAT**   * ,...to **BAT**   *   I'll take a **BATH**
(I must perform now)   (,...also)   (Lose a lot of money)

Don't throw out the baby   *   A **BATTLE** royal
  with the **BATH**water   (A big fight)
  (Don't let small problems
  defeat larger goals)   *   [He's **BATS**]
          [He has **BATS** in his belfrey]
BAWL him out   [He's gone **BATTY**]
(Criticize him)   (He's crazy)

BE about it!   *   The **BE**-all and end-all   *   Could **BE**!
(Start!)   (Best version of something)   (It's possible!)

BE done with it!   *   Far **BE** it from me,...
(End it!)   (I wouldn't think of it)

                *   **BE** my guest!
              (Take what you want)

B

How **BE** you?
(How are you?)

          *   Let it **BE**!
         ([Say nothing more about it!]
         [Don't touch it!])

Let me **BE**!
(Don't bother me!)

   *   **BE** that as it may,...
   ([Anyway,...[However,...])

So **BE** it!
([All right]
[That's the way it will be])

   *   I'll **BE** there for you
   (I'll support you)

BE in touch with...
(Communicate with...)

   *   Draw a **BEAD** on...
   ([Aim at] [Focus on])

He's [off] [on] the **BEAM** * **BEAN** * **BEAN** him!
(He's [wrong] [right])   (Head)   (Hit his head)

He's off his **BEAN**
(He's crazy)

   *   A **BEAN** pole
   (A very tall, thin person)

He's full of **BEANS**
(He's wrong)

 * Not worth a hill of **BEANS**
   (Worthless)

He knows **BEANS**
(He knows nothing)

   *   Spill the **BEANS**!
   (Tell what you know!)

It's a **BEAR**
(It's very difficult)

   *   **BEAR** [down] [up]!
   ([Try hard!]
   [Endure!] [Persevere!])

Loaded for **BEAR**
([Well prepared]
[Carrying a heavy load])

   *   **BEAR** me out!
   (Confirm what I say!)

B

26

A **BEAR** by the tail
(A very difficult problem)

* **BEAR** with us
(Be patient)

* **BEAT**
(Very tired)

...,to **BEAT** the band
(Enthusiastically)

* Don't **BEAT** [about]
[around] the **BUSH**!
(Say what you are thinking!)

Don't brow**BEAT** me!
(Don't bully me!)

* **BEAT** the bushes for...
(Search hard for...)

He's a dead **BEAT**
(He doesn't pay debts)

* **BEAT** him at his own game
(Defeat him in what he does best)

He **BEAT** me hands down
(Easily)

* Don't **BEAT** a dead horse
(It's useless;
don't waste time)

BEAT it!
(Go away!)

* It's off **BEAT**
(Unusual)

* He didn't miss a **BEAT**
(He never hesitated or paused)

BEAT them [off!] [out!]
([Defeat them!]
[Get there before they do!])

* **BEAT** his pants off!
(Overwhelm him!)

BEAT him to the punch
(Act before he does)

* **BEAT** the [stuffing]
[tar] out of them!
(Really punish them!)

BEAT his time
(Court his girlfriend)

* **BEAT** up
(Hurt)

* Up **BEAT**
(Confident)

Off the **BEATEN** path
([Not easily found]
[Remote])

* He's **BEATING** his gums
(Talking uselessly)

B

That **BEATS** all!
(I'm amazed!)

*

BEATS me!
(I don't [know] [understand])

[It's a **BEAUT!**]
[**BEAUTIFUL!**]
(It's excellent; wonderful!)

*

An eager **BEAVER**
(An energetically
ambitious person)

What's **BECOME** of him!)
(What happened to him?)

*

It's [not] [un]**BECOMING**
(It's [not good manners]
[unsuitable] [poor taste])

It **BECOMES** you
([It fits your style]
[You look well in it])

*

BED down!
(Go to sleep!)

Get in **BED** with them
(Join with them)

*

You made your **BED**,
now lie in it
(Suffer the results
of your decision)

It's between me and the **BED** post
(It's a secret)

*

Put it to **BED**
([Settle the matter]
[Complete; finish it])

It's no **BED** of roses
(It's difficult; not easy)

I should have stayed in **BED**
(Better that I should
have done nothing)

*

Don't get up on the
wrong side of the **BED**
(Don't be in a bad mood)

Put a **BEE** in her bonnet
(Give her an idea)

*

Busy as a **BEE**
(Very active)

It's the **BEE'S** knees!
(It's wonderful!)

*

Mind your **BEES**wax
(Don't interfere in other's affairs)

B

Raise a **BEEF**   *   Take your **BEEF** out on...
(Complain)   (Focus your complaint on...)

BEEF it up   *   What's the **BEEF**?   *   Where's the **BEEF**?
(Strengthen it)   (The complaint)   (The important part)

Make a **BEE**line for...   *   He's a has-**BEEN**
(Move straight to...)   (He is no longer famous)

BEEN there [; done that]   *   He's crying in his **BEER**
(I had that experience)   (Depressed; telling his troubles)

Here's egg in your **BEER**!   *   **BEG** off
(A drinking toast)   (Refuse to help or serve)

BEHAVE yourself!   *   He'll talk **BEHIND** your back
(Act in a proper way!)   (He'll speak about you, not to you)

BEHIND my back   *   He's not dry **BEHIND** the ears
(Without my knowledge)   (Young and inexperienced)

I'm **BEHIND** the eight ball   *   **BEHIND** the scene
(In a difficult situation)   (Out of public view)

[I'll fall] [I'm way] **BEHIND**   *   Get it **BEHIND** you
([Lag] [Lagging] in my work)   (Move on with your life)

For the time **BEING**   *   He has bats in his **BELFREY**
(For the present time)   (He's crazy)

You better **BELIEVE** it!   *   Seeing is **BELIEVING**
(It's true!)   (If I see it, I may believe it)

B

BELL the cat   *   Clear as a BELL
(Get someone to agree   ([Very understandable]
  to do something)   [Unambiguous])

Ring his BELL   *   Saved by the BELL
([Get his attention; interest]   (Rescued at the last moment)
 [Hit him in the head])

                               *   Hell's BELLS'S
Be there with BELLS on   (Expression of
(Be there on time)   amazement/frustration)

It doesn't ring any BELLS   *   With BELLS and whistles
(I know nothing about it)   (With fancy things added)

He's a BELLYacher   *   I have a BELLY full
(He always complains)   (I can't tolerate more)

BELLY up to the   *   I went BELLY up
[bar] [problem]   (Bankrupt)
(Confront the matter)

                               *   He hit BELOW the BELT
He's BELOW the salt   (He acted unfairly)
(A less important person)

                                   *   BELT him one!
I have a lot of experience under my BELT   (Hit him!)
(I learned a lot)

                                   *   Tighten your BELTS
BENCH him!   (Economize)
(Take him out of action)

                               * BEND [his arm] [him out
He's around the BEND   of shape]
(He's crazy)   (Force him to [do] [not do] something)

B

BEND over backwards
(Make a special effort)

*

He'll **BEND** my ear [off]
(He'll talk and talk)

BEND the rules
(Be less strict)

*

He's on a **BENDER**
(He's drunk)

Give him the **BENEFIT**
of the doubt
(Doubt him but don't argue)

*

Hell-**BENT** for leather
(Moving very fast)

*

Give him wide **BERTH**
(Avoid him!)

I'm **BESIDE** myself
(Very anxious)

*

It's **BESIDE** the point
(It's irrelevant)

You **BEST** be...
(You should...)

*

Our **BEST** bet
(Our most favorable option)

My **BEST** bib and tucker
(My best clothes)

*

Put the **BEST** face on it
(The best appearance)

Put your **BEST** foot forward
(Show yourself to your
greatest advantage)

*

Give it your **BEST** shot
(Make your best effort)

The **BEST** of both worlds
(A gain either way)

*

I'll **BET**!
(I doubt it!)

Our best **BET**
(Our most favorable option)

*

I'll **BET** my [boots]
[bottom dollar]!
(I'm certain)

BET the [farm] [house] [works]
(Commit everything)

You **BET**! [your life!]
You **BETCHA**!
([That's a fact!] [I agree!]
[You can be sure of it])

All **BETS** are off
(The outcome cannot
be predicted)

You make a **BETTER** door
than a window!
(You're blocking my view!)

I hadn't **BETTER**
(I shouldn't do it)

Build a **BETTER** mousetrap
(Improve the product)

I'm **BETTER** off
than he is
([I have more money]
[My situation is better])

The **BETTER** part of
valor is to...
(It would be smarter to...)

He'll think **BETTER** of it
(He'll change his views)

* He doesn't miss a **BET**
(He's alert to opportunities)

* **BET** you even money
(Let's wager dollar for dollar)

* You **BETTER** believe it!
(It's true!)

* Get the **BETTER** of him
(Dominate him)

* I'll go you one **BETTER**
(I have a better...)

* My **BETTER** half
(My wife)

* I'm **BETTER** off [this way]
(My situation is more favorable)

* The **BETTER** part of it is...
(Most of it is...)

* I want a **BETTER** shake
(A more favorable share)

* It will take turn
for the **BETTER**
(It's condition will improve)

It's **BETWEEN** me
and the bed post
(It's a secret)

* **BETWEEN** the devil and
the deep blue sea
(There is danger on all sides)

It hit me **BETWEEN** the eyes
(I saw it at once)

* Few and far **BETWEEN**
(Rare)

I'm the go-**BETWEEN**
(I help the parties
relate to each other)

* There is no in-**BETWEEN**
(Nothing in the middle)

BETWIXT and **BETWEEN**
(In the middle)

* I'm **BETWEEN** a rock
and a hard place
(I face hard choices)

He's in the far **BEYOND**
(He's dead)

* It's **BEYOND** me
(I don't understand it)

He's **BEYOND** me
(I can't control him)

* **BEYOND** the pale
(Outside of normal society)

My best **BIB** and tucker
(My best clothes)

* **BIFFY**
(Toilet)

* It's **BIG**
(Popular; in demand)

Act like a **BIG** boy
(Behave more like an adult)

* One of the **BIG** boys
(A person of high rank)

He's too **BIG** for his britches
(He acts more important
than his capacities justify)

* **BIG** bucks
([A lot of money]
[High cost])

BIG [cheeze] [shot] [wheel] [wig]
(A high ranking person)

* **BIG** [deal] [thing]!
(Nothing to get excited about)

B

A **BIG** [deal!] [to do]　　　　*　　　　They had a **BIG** do
([It's exciting!]　　　　　　　　　　　　　　([A bad argument]
[An important event])　　　　　　　　　　　　　[A big party])

Make a **BIG** do about it　　*　A **BIG** fish [in a little pond]
(Cause great excitement)　　　　　(A high ranking person
　　　　　　　　　　　　　　[in a small organization or place])

The **BIG** [guy] [man]
(The boss)　　　　　　　　　*　　　　It will go over **BIG**
　　　　　　　　　　　　　(People will [like] [not like] it)

Give him a **BIG** hand
(A lot of applause)　　　　　*　　　　He has a **BIG** head
　　　　　　　　　　(He is very impressed with himself)

He's **BIG**-hearted
(Very generous)　　　　　　*　　　　　The **BIG** house
　　　　　　　　　　　　　　　　　　　(Prison)

What's the **BIG** idea?
(Why are you doing that?)　　*　He's in the **BIG** leagues
　　　　　　　　　　(In the top level of competition)

It's **BIG** as life
(Actual; real)　　*　You **BIG** lug　*　It's **BIG** as a minute
　　　　　　　(You dear person)　　　　　　　(Tiny)

BIG mouth!
(A negative comment to a　　　　*　　　　A **BIG** noise
loud-talking, obnoxious person)　(A high-ranking person)

He's **BIG** on...　　　　　　*　　　　The **BIG** picture
(Enthusiastic for...)　　　　　　(The larger considerations)

A **BIG** ticket item　　　　　*　　　　**BIG** time!
(A costly item)　　　　　　　　　　([A great amount]
　　　　　　　　　　　　[Very important] [Wonderful]!)

B

I'm having a **BIG** time
(A wonderful experience)

*   He's in the **BIG** time
(Famous; a leader in his field)

That's **BIG** of you
([Generous] [Also used
mockingly to mean stingy])

*   **BILL** it as...
(Describe; explain it as...)

*   I got a clean **BILL**
of health
([I'm in good health]
[There are no charges against me])

It fills the **BILL**
(It's satisfactory)

Foot the **BILL**
(Pay the costs)

*   He'll sell you a **BILL** of goods
(Cheat; take advantage of you)

Run up a **BILL**
(Accumulate debts)

*   He'll stick you with the **BILL**
(Leave it for you to pay)

BILLS
(Money)

*   The looney **BIN**
(A mental institution)

*   I'm in a **BIND**
(I have problems)

BINGO!
([I found it!] [That's it!])

*   In the cat**BIRD** seat
(In a key position)

BIRD-dog it
(Watch; search for it)

*   A **BIRD** in the hand is
worth two in the bush
(A thing one has is more valuable
than a thing promised)

A strange **BIRD**
(An odd, unusual person)

A little **BIRD** told me * **BIRDS** of a feather flock together
(I was told a secret)   (Similar people tend to associate)

B

It's for the **BIRDS**   * In my **BIRTHDAY** suit
(Very bad; undesirable)   (Naked)

The bug **BIT** me   * I **BIT** off more than I can chew
(I became enthusiastic)   (Overestimated what I could do)

Chomping at the **BIT**   *   A two-**BIT** crook
(Anxious to begin)   (An unimportant crook)

A **BIT** much   * The **BIT** is in my teeth   * Wait a **BIT**
(Excessive)   (I have the responsibility)   (Wait briefly)

The whole **BIT**   *   I'll **BITE**   *   **BITE** the bullet!
(Everything)   (So, what's the answer?)   (Act; decide!)

BITE the dust   *   [Get] [Grab] a **BITE**
(Die)   (A quick meal)

BITE his head off   *   Put the **BITE** on him
(Criticize him)   (Ask him for funds)

BITE your tongue!   *   [Two] [four] [six] **BITS**
(Keep silent!)   ([$ 0.25] [$ 0.50] $ 0.75])

It isn't worth two-**BITS**   *   It's a **BITTER** pill
(It has little value)   (It is difficult to accept)

He'll **BLAB** [his head off]   *   **BLABBER**mouth!
(Talk too much)   (You talk too much and carelessly)

BLACK and blue   *   In the **BLACK**
(Bruised; hurt)   (Profitable)

B

I got a **BLACK** eye
(My [eye] [reputation] was hurt)

In **BLACK** and white
(In clear language)

I draw a **BLANK**
(I can't remember)

A **BLAST**
(A lot of fun)

He's **BLASTED**
(Drunk)

What the **BLAZES**!
(An expression of surprise)

BLESS your heart!
(You are wonderful,
thank you!)

A **BLIND** alley
(It goes nowhere)

Turn a **BLIND** eye to it
(Pretend it's not there)

I have a **BLIND** [side] [spot]
(I'm insensitive)

*   The **BLACK** sheep
of the family
(The family embarrassment)

*   **BLANK** him
(Don't let him score)

*   He's a wet **BLANKET**
(He's negative; unenthusiastic)

*   Going full **BLAST**
(At its greatest capacity)

*   Hotter than **BLAZES**
(Very warm)

*   I **BLEED** for you!
(I can't feel sorry for you)

* A **BLESSING** in disguise
(It has unexpected values)

*   He'll fly **BLIND**
(Proceed without a clear view)

* He'll [rob] [steal] you **BLIND**
(He's a crook)

*   **BLIND**-sided
(Surprised)

* On the **BLINK**
(It won't operate)

B

He has **BLINKERS** on
(He doesn't see what
is so visable)

* Ignorance is **BLISS**
(Sometimes it is better
not to know)

I've been around [the **BLOCK**]
(I have experience)

* He's a chip off
the old **BLOCK**
(He's just like his father)

It's on the chopping **BLOCK**
(It is being eliminated)

* **BLOCK**head!
(Stupid!)

Knock his **BLOCK** off!
(Hit him hard!)

* I have a mental **BLOCK** on...
(I never remember...)

There is bad **BLOOD**
between them
(They hate each other)

* My **BLOOD** will boil
(I'll become very angry)

...in cold **BLOOD**
(Without feeling; pity)

* It cost **BLOOD**
(It's very expensive)

He has **BLOOD** in his eye
(He looks angry)

* It's for **BLOOD**
(Deadly; very serious)

It's in his **BLOOD**
(His [ancestry] [nature])

* Too rich for my **BLOOD**
(More than I can afford)

You can't squeeze **BLOOD**
out of a turnip
(It won't yield anything)

* Sweat **BLOOD**
(Be tense; worried)

* **BLOOD** will tell
(Family [characteristics]
[loyalties] will dominate)

My **BLOOD** is up
(I'm angry; defiant)

38

The **BLOOM** is off the rose   *   **BLOTTO**
(It's old; not fresh)   (Drunk; unconscious)

BLOW!   *   **BLOW** them away!
(Leave!)   ([Kill] [Overwhelm] them!)

It will **BLOW** [you away]   *   I'll **BLOW** my cool
   [your mind]   (Get angry; excited)
(Amaze; stun you)

               *   It will **BLOW** my cover
I'll **BLOW** [a gasket]   (Reveal my secret identity)
[my lid] [my stack] [my top]
(Become very angry)   * **BLOW** your own horn
                      (Promote yourself)

He'll **BLOW** hot and cold
(His views are very changeable)   *   I'll **BLOW** it
                   ([Fail] [Waste my chance])

BLOW the joint
(Leave the place)   * A low **BLOW**   * **BLOW** it off!
            (An unfair action)   (Reject it!)

I'll **BLOW** off
(Become angry)   *   A **BLOW** out
          ([A big party] [A ruptured tire])

It will **BLOW** over
([Become calm again] [End])   *   **BLOW** smoke
                 ([Boast] [Talk uselessly])

BLOW off steam
(Ease tension by yelling)   *   I'll **BLOW** [into] town
              ([Come to] [Leave] town)

A **BLOW** up
(A big argument)   *   I'll **BLOW** my wad
              (Use all my money)

B

BLOW the whistle!   *   That's the way the wind **BLOWS**
(Reveal the facts)   (That's the situation)

BLUE   *   Black and **BLUE**
(Sad; troubled)   (Bruised; hurt)

It will [be a bolt] [come]   *   **BLUE** chip
   out of the **BLUE**   (Very high value)
(Be a surprise)

          *   Out of a clear **BLUE** sky
Once in a **BLUE** moon   (Without warning)
(Very rarely)

          *   A **BLUE**-ribbon group
He talks a **BLUE** streak   (A prestigious group)
(Very fast)

         *   True **BLUE**
In the wild **BLUE** yonder   (Very loyal)
(In the distant sky)

      * [Crying] [Singing] the **BLUES**
Call his **BLUFF**   (Depressed and telling his troubles)
(Urge him to do what
   he said he would do)   *   At first **BLUSH**
          (On first examination or hearing)

Above **BOARD**
(Correct; proper)   *   Across-the-**BOARD**
         (Applies to everything)

It will go by the **BOARD**
(Be withdrawn)   * Back to the drawing **BOARD**
        (Start from the beginning again)

He's on **BOARD**
(He [is here] [concurs])   *   I went over**BOARD**
        (Too far; to an extreme)

B

40

I'll miss the **BOAT**
(Lose a good opportunity)

We're in the same **BOAT**
(We share the same situation)

My **BOD**
(My body)

＊

It does a **BODY** good to...
(It is [helpful] [pleasing] to...)

BODY language
(Communication through
body and eye movements)

My blood will **BOIL**
(I'll become very angry)

＊

Hard-**BOILED**
(Firm; tough)

A **BOLT** out of the blue
(A surprise)

Get down to nuts and **BOLTS**
(To what is really important)

He'll **BOMB** out
(Fail)

＊ He has back**BONE**
(Courage; resolve)

＊ Don't rock the **BOAT**
(Don't [cause trouble]
[try to change things])

＊ Show**BOATING**
(Trying to attract attention
by conspicuous actions)

A busy**BODY**
(One who gets into
other people's affairs)

＊ Mind-**BOGGLING**
(Beyond understanding)

＊ **BOGUS!**
(That's awful!)

BOIL it down
(Use fewer words)

＊ **BOILER**plate
(Language full of details)

＊ I'll shoot my **BOLT**
(Use all my resources)

＊ A **BOMB**
(A failure)

＊ A **BONE** to chew on
(To think and talk about)

B

A **BONE** of contention
(A matter in dispute)

*   Cut to the **BONE**
(Make deep reductions)

Dry as a **BONE**
([No moisture at all]
[Very boring])

* I work my fingers to the **BONE**
(I work very hard)

*

A funny **BONE**
(A sense of humor)

BONEhead!
(Ignorant fool!)

*

JawBONE with them
(Talk with them)

I have a **BONE** to pick with you
(A complaint to make)

*   Throw him a **BONE**
(Make a small concession to him)

Bare **BONES**
(Plain; simple)

*

I feel it in my **BONES**
(I anticipate; predict it)

It needs flesh and **BONES**
(More details; substance)

*

In my **BONES**
(In my nature)

I make no **BONES** about it
(I say what I mean)

*

A saw **BONES**
(A surgeon)

It will go **BONK**
(Stop operating)

*

I'll go **BONKERS**
(Crazy)

Put a bee in her **BONNET**
(Give her an idea)

*

Don't say **BOO**
(Keep silent)

It's a **BOO BOO**
(A [bruise] [mistake])

*

BOOB tube
(Television)

B

BOOBY hatch
(An insane asylum)

Go by the **BOOK**
(Follow instructions)

Make **BOOK** on it
(It's certain)

It's an open **BOOK**
(No mystery about it)

Put that in your **BOOK**
(Note it)

Throw the **BOOK** at him
(Punish him to the fullest degree)

I wrote the **BOOK** on...
(I'm the expert on...)

Hit the **BOOKS**
(Start studying)

Lower the **BOOM** on him
(Punish him)

Give him the **BOOT**
(Dismiss him)

I'll bet my **BOOTS**
(I'm certain)

*   The **BOOK** is closed
(The matter is settled)

*   **BOOK** him
(Formally charge him with crimes)

*   Not in my **BOOK**!
([Not if I can prevent it]
[I don't agree] [Never]!)

* Take a page from his **BOOK**
(Imitate him)

*   I read you like a **BOOK**
(I understand you; your goals)

* I'm a **BOOK** worm
(I love to read)

* He'll cook the **BOOKS**
(Alter data to meet his needs)

*   One for the **BOOKS**
(Very unusual; a record)

* **[BOONDOCKS] [BOONIES]**
(Remote areas)

*   He's ...to **BOOT**
(Also; in addition)

B

I'm shaking in my **BOOTS**
(I'm afraid)

* **BOOT**strap yourself
(Rely upon your own resources)

BOOTY
(Money)

* **BOP** him! [one!]
(Hit him!)

I'm **BORED** [silly]
[out of my skull] [stiff]
(Life is dull for me)

* A **BORN** loser
(One who usually fails)

* He was **BORN** with a
silver spoon in his mouth
(His family is rich)

Don't **BORROW** trouble
(Don't seek problems)

BOSOM [buddy] [friend]
(Close friend)

* He's **BOSSY**
(He likes to tell people what to do)

I have the best of
BOTH worlds
(I can't lose either way)

* Hot and **BOTHERED**
(Very angry)

* I hit the **BOTTLE**
(I got drunk)

I **BOTTLE** things up
(Conceal my emotions)

* Chief cook and **BOTTLE** washer

Scrape the **BOTTOM**
of the barrel
(Use the poorest quality)

(The manager)

* I'll bet my **BOTTOM** dollar
(I'm certain)

BOTTOM fishing
(Pursuing bad options)

* Get off your **BOTTOM**!
([Move!] [Start!])

Get to the **BOTTOM** of it
(To its root or key feature)

B

44

From the **BOTTOM** of my heart
(With great sincerity)

It hit rock **BOTTOM**
(As low as it could go)

BOTTOMS up!
(Empty your glass!)

I **BOUGHT** into it
(I [invested in it]
[thought it was true])

Give it a **BOUNCE**
(Try it)

I'll lose my **BOUNCE**
(My energy)

I'm **BOUND** and determined
(I'm firm in my course)

It grew by leaps and **BOUNDS**
(Very fast)

BOW out
(Leave; resign)

It will **BOWL** you over
(Surprise you)

* The **BOTTOM** line
(The final result)

* It's a **BOTTOMLESS** pit
(Its needs are unlimited)

* He **BOUGHT** it [the farm]
(He [accepted the idea]
[is dead])

* The check will **BOUNCE**
(A bank will reject it
for lack of funds)

* It has no **BOUNCE**
(It's weak; lacks spirit)

* Tough **BOUNCE**!
(Bad luck!)

* It's **BOUND** to...
(It's certain to...)

* He's out of **BOUNDS**
([Outside the playing field]
[Behaving badly])

* It's no **BOWL** of cherries
(It's not easy)

* I'm in a **BOX**
(I don't have good options)

B

He's on his soap**BOX**
(Giving his views)

*   Atta**BOY**!
(An expression of praise;
encouragement)

Act like a big **BOY**
(Behave more like an adult)

*   **BOY**-o-**BOY**!
(I'm amazed!)

He's the fairhaired **BOY**
(He gets special   * I won't be your whipping **BOY**
treatment)   (Be blamed for your actions)

One of the big **BOYS**
(A person of high rank)

*   He [gone] **BOZO**
(Crazy)

That **BOZO**
(That [fellow] [bum])

*   My **BRAIN**child
(My idea; invention)

He's a [feather] [lame] **BRAIN**
(He's stupid)

* It's a hair**BRAIN** idea
(Silly; without merit)

Can I pick your **BRAIN**?
(Ask you for information)

*   Rack your **BRAIN**
(Think very carefully)

A **BRAIN**storm
(A brilliant idea)

* Get your **BRAIN** together
(Think carefully)

They are a **BRAIN**trust
(A source of ideas; wisdom)

*   It's a no-**BRAINER**
(Simple; requires no wisdom)

Offer the olive **BRANCH**
(Be conciliatory)

*   **BRAND** [spanking] new
(Fresh; not used before)

46

He has **BRASS**   *   Get down to **BRASS** tacks
(He is self-assured; tough)   (To fundamentals)

Top **BRASS**   *   **BREAD**   *   Break **BREAD** with me
(The bosses;   (Money)   (Eat with me)
  the leaders)
                               *
                                          The **BREAD**winner
By a hair's **BREADTH**   (The family money earner)
(By the smallest amount)
                               *
I'll **BREAK** my back   A **BREAK**
(Try very hard)   (A helpful development)

                               *
BREAK bread with me   It will **BREAK** the bank
(Eat with me)   (Make me poor)

                               *
I'll [catch] [get] a **BREAK**   **BREAK** camp!
(Be lucky)   (Pack and move)

                          *   The **BREAK**down is...
I had a **BREAK**down   (The chief elements are...)
([A mental collapse]
[My vehicle won't work])   * **BREAK** it down for me
                                (Explain it to me)
I'll **BREAK** even
(Recover my expenses)   * The [fever] [heat] will **BREAK**
                               (The temperature will drop)
Give me a **BREAK**!
([Stop that nonsense!]   *   **BREAK** new ground
[Have pity on me!])   (Innovate; pioneer)

He'll **BREAK** your heart   *   **BREAK** the ice
(Cause you much sadness)   (Get people to talk)

B

BREAK it in * A **BREAK**-in
(Make sure it works properly) (An illegal entry)

BREAK into... * **BREAK** a leg!
(Become involved in...) (Good luck!)

All hell will **BREAK** loose * It's make or **BREAK**
(It will get very exciting) (The decisive point)

I'll **BREAK** my neck * **BREAK** the news to him
([Get hurt] [Try very hard]) (Inform him)

BREAK it off * **BREAK** out * It will **BREAK** out
(End it) (Escape) (Start)

The straw that will **BREAK** * It will **BREAK** for him
the camel's back (His fortunes will improve)
(The decisive factor)

* **BREAK** it up!
It will **BREAK** him up! ([Disperse!]
(Be a blow to him) [Stop fighting!])

He'll **BREAK** me up * We'll **BREAK** up
(Make me laugh) (End our association)

He'll **BREAK** his word * It's the **BREAKS**
(Fail to keep his promise) (It's determined by luck)

Make a clean **BREAST** of it * Wait with baited **BREATH**
(Tell the truth) (Anxiously)

B

48

Don't hold your **BREATH**　　　＊ As I live and **BREATH**!
　(Don't wait; it won't　　　　　　　　　([A hello greeting]
　happen soon)　　　　　　　[An expression of amazement])

I said it under my **BREATH** ＊ Don't waste your **BREATH**
　(In a whisper)　　　　　　　　(It's useless to say more)

A **BREATHER**　　　　　　　＊　　　　**BREATHING** room
　(A pause; a rest)　　　(Time and space to think; maneuver)

That's a different　　　　＊　[It's] [I won in] a **BREEZE**
　BREED of cat　　　　　　　　([Very easy] [Easily])
　(A changed situation)

　　　　　　　　　　　＊　　　　Shoot the **BREEZE**
A **BRICK**　　　　　　　　　　　　　(Chat with people)
　(A loyal solid person)

　　　　　　　　　　＊　　He's several **BRICKS**
I'll cross the **BRIDGE**　　　　　　　short of a load
　(Made my decision)　　　　　　　　(Not very smart)

A lot of water has gone　＊ Don't burn your **BRIDGES**
　under the **BRIDGE**　　　　　(Keep a retreat route open)
　(Much has happened since...)

　　　　　　　　　　　　＊　　Oh, very **BRIGHT**!
He's **BRIGHT**-eyed and　　　　　　　(That's dumb!)
　bushy-tailed
　(Fresh and ready to go)　　＊　　It's a **BRIGHT** idea
　　　　　　　　　　(An imaginative idea/approach)

He's a **BRIGHT** light
　(An outstanding person)　　＊ Look on the **BRIGHT** side
　　　　　　　　　　　　　　(Be optimistic)

B

BRING him around
([Gain his support]
[Invite him to visit]
[Restore him to consciousness])

BRING up the rear
(Be the last in line)

I had a good up**BRINGING**
(I was taught good manners
and got a good education)

He's too big for his **BRITCHES**
(He acts more important
than his capacities justify)

Go for **BROKE**
(Make a maximum effort)

I'll get the **BROOM**
(Lose my job)

What **BROUGHT** that on?
(What caused that behavior?)

He's a [high] [low] **BROW**
(He [likes high quality]
[is dull; prefers
low quality])

It will raise eye**BROWS**
(Cause surprise)

* **BRING** down the house
(Thrill the audience)

* **BRING** it off
(Make it succeed)

* **BRING** him up
(Provide him care and education)

* **BRING** home the bacon
(Get [income] [results])

* **BR0**
(Brother)

* I'm [dead] [flat]
[stone] **BROKE**
(I have no funds)

* Everybody and his **BROTHER**
(A large crowd)

* Don't **BROW**beat me
(Don't bully me!)

* Do it up **BROWN**
(Get it done with style)

* I'll get **BROWNIE** points
(Gain credit; favor; recognition)

B

He's cruising for a **BRUISE**   *   I'll get the **BRUSH** off
(Asking for trouble)   (Be dismissed; rejected)

BRUSH up on...   *   **BUB**   *   What's the hub-**BUB**?
(Renew your   (A fellow; guy)   (Excitement; uproar)
  knowledge of...)

                                     *   He's half a **BUBBLE** off plumb
[BUCK] [SawBUCK]   (He crazy)
([$ 1.00] [$10.00])

                          *   More bang for the **BUCK**
Make a fast **BUCK**   (More cost-effective)
(A quick profit)

               *   **BUCK** for...   *   **BUCK** him [up]
                     (Seek promotion;   ([Oppose him]
Pass the **BUCK**   gain)   [Encourage him])
(Blame others)

                          *   The **BUCK** stops here
I'm tight with the **BUCK**   (I take full responsibility)
I hate to spend money)

                          *   A [drop] [spit] in the **BUCKET**
Kick the **BUCKET**   (A tiny amount)
(Die)

                     *   **BUCKLE** down to business
He'll **BUCKLE** under   ([Be serious] [Start work])
(([Quit] [Surrender])

                     *   It's [big] [major] **BUCKS**
Nip it in the **BUD**   ([A lot of money] [High cost])
(End it at the beginning)

                          *   A bosom **BUDDY**
A fuss **BUDGET**   (Close friend)
(A person who complains a lot)

In the **BUFF**
(Naked)

     *   You don't **BUFFALO** me
(You don't [fool] [intimidate] me)

The **BUG** bit me
(I became enthusiastic)

     *   It's cute as a **BUG'S** ear
(Small and adorable)

Put the **BUG** in his ear
(Give him the idea)

     *   I can't kick the **BUG**
(I'm still ill)

BUG him
(Listen secretly
to his conversations)

     *   It will **BUG** me
(Bother me)

     *   **BUG** [off] [out]!
(Leave; go away!)

A shutter **BUG**
(One who likes taking pictures)

     *   [BUGS] [BUGGY]
(Crazy)

Work out the **BUGS**
(Solve the problems)

     *   **BUILD** a better mousetrap
(Improve the product)

Jerry-**BUILT**
(Poorly constructed)

     *   Rome wasn't **BUILT** in a day
(Some things take a long time to do)

BULL!
([Lies!] [Nonsense!])

     *   **BULL**dog it through
(Push it until it's done)

It's cock and **BULL**
(False)

     *   Take the **BULL** by the horns
(Accept the challenge and act)

[Shoot the **BULL**]
[Have a **BULL** session]
(Talk; tell stories)

     *   Bite the **BULLET**
(Act; decide!)

B

It's no magic **BULLET**
(No magic solution)

* Sweat **BULLETS**
(Be really anxious)

I have a **BUM** [arm] [ticker]
(My [arm] [heart] is in
bad condition)

* A **BUM** deal
(A bad arrangement)

*

A **BUM** rap
(A false; unfair accusation)

It will **BUM** him out
(Make him very unhappy)

* Give him the **BUM'S** rush
(Throw him out)

BUM steer
(Bad advice)

* A stumble **BUM** * I'm **BUMMED**
A **BUMMER** (A clumsy; inept person) (Troubled)
(A bad thing) (In bad condition)

I'll **BUMP** into him
(Meet him by chance)

* He's like a **BUMP** on a log
(Inactive; lazy)

BUMP him off!
(Kill him)

* **BUMPING** along
(Moving slowly)

I have goose **BUMPS**
(I'm [frightened] [thrilled])

* Take your **BUMPS**
(Your disappointments)

She has a **BUN**
in the oven
(She is pregnant)

* Thanks a [**BUNCH**] [**BUNDLE**]!
([Thank you very much]
[That's not helpful!])

He'll drop a **BUNDLE**
(Lose a lot of money)

* I'm a **BUNDLE** of nerves
(I'm very tense)

B

Don't get your pants * He's worth a **BUNDLE**
  in a **BUNDLE** (A lot of money)
(Don't get agitated; excited)

* **BUNK** down
A lot of **BUNK** * **BUNS** (Go to sleep)
(Bad information) (Buttocks)
(Nonsense)

* Bust your **BUNS**
  (Work very hard!)

BURN
(Be electrocuted) * Don't **BURN** your bridges
  (Keep a retreat route open)

BURN him!
(Shoot him!) * **BURN** the midnight oil
  (Work late at night)

He has [money] [time] to **BURN**
(A lot of [money] [time]) * He has **BURN** out
  (He's exhausted)

I did a slow **BURN**
(My anger grew slowly) * I'll **BURN** [up]
  (Get angry)

I was **BURNED**
(I had a bad experience) * It's on the [back]
  [front] **BURNER**
I'm **BURNING** the candle at both ends (It has a [low]
(Exhausting myself) [high] priority)

My ears are **BURNING** * It's **BURNING** a hole
(Someone is talking about me) in my pocket
  (I feel compelled to use it)

A **BURNING** [issue] [question]
(Very relevant; sensitive) * **BURY** the hatchet
  (Make peace)

B

Don't **BURY** your head in the sand   *   Miss the **BUS**
(Don't avoid the facts)   (Lose a good opportunity)

Don't beat [about]   *   A bird in the hand is
   [around] the **BUSH**   worth two in the **BUSH**
(Say what you are thinking)   (A thing one has is worth
     more than a thing promised)

BUSHED
(Tired)   *   He hides his light under a **BUSHEL**
     (He hides his abilities; deeds)

Beat the **BUSHES** for...
(Search hard for...)   *   Bright-eyed and **BUSHY**-tailed
     (Fresh and ready to go)

BUSIER than a
   one-armed paperhanger   *   [Buckle] [Get] [Knuckle]
(Extremely busy)   down to **BUSINESS**!
     ([Be serious!] [Start work!])

Drum up **BUSINESS**
(Stimulate activity)   *   No [funny] [monkey] **BUSINESS**
     ([Don't try to deceive me!]
Give him the **BUSINESS**!   [No foolishness; tricks!])
(Attack; put
   pressure on him)   *   Do a land office **BUSINESS**
     (Be very busy)

I mean **BUSINESS**
(I'm serious; determined)   *   I can do it like
     nobody's **BUSINESS**
A **BUST**   (Very easily; without much effort)
(A failure)

     * **BUST** your [back] [buns] [butt]
I'll **BUST** my buttons   [gut] [head] [rear] [tail]
(Be excited and proud)   (Work very hard)

B

BUST him   * **BUST** him! [one]   * Don't **BUST** for it
([Arrest him]   (Hit him!)   (Don't make a big effort)
[Reduce his rank])

        * **BUST** out!   * I **BUST** out laughing
Flat **BUSTED**   (Escape!)   (Started laughing)
(Without money)

         *   In the hustle and **BUSTLE**
BUSY as [a bee] [all get out]   (In the rush of activity)
(Very active)

      *   He's a **BUSY**body   * Get **BUSY**!
No if's,   (He gets into other   (Start work!)
and's, and **BUT'S**   people's affairs)
(Without reservation)   *   **BUTT**
                         (Buttocks)

[Bust] [Work] your **BUTT** off
([Try] [Work] hard)   * [Dead] [Sitting] on his **BUTT**
                        (Inactive; lazy)

Dump his **BUTT**!
(Stop associating   *   [Get] Off your **BUTT**!
with him!)   ([Move!] [Start!])

Don't **BUTT** in!   * He's the **BUTT** of jokes
(Don't interrupt)   (The jokes are about him)

BUTT out!   * He's a pain in the **BUTT**
(Go away!)   (A pest; an obnoxious person)

My **BUTT** will be in a sling   *   **BUTTER**fingers!
(I'll be in trouble)   (You always drop things)

I have **BUTTER**flies in my stomach   * **BUTTER** him up
(I'm anxious and fearful)   (Get his interest by flattery)

                                             B

BUTTONhole him
(Find and talk to him)

* A hot **BUTTON** issue
(Very lively; sensitive)

BUTTON [your lip!] [up!]
(Be silent!)

* [Right] [On the **BUTTON**!
([Correct!] [Exactly on target; time])

Push his **BUTTON**
([Antagonize him]
[Get his attention])

* **BUTTON** it up
([Finish; complete it]
[Put it in a secure condition])

He's **BUTTONED** up
([Very disciplined; quiet]
[Conservative])

* I'll bust my **BUTTONS**
([Be very excited and proud])

*

BUY up the market
(Seek control of the supply)

BUY him off
(Bribe him)

*

BUY him out
(Acquire his share)

BUY off on it
(Accept it; concur)

*

He'll catch a **BUZZ**
(A brief exhilaration
caused by alcohol or drugs)

I'll **BUY** that
(I agree with it)

What's the **BUZZ**?
([The latest information; rumors]
[Excitement])

* **BUZZ** me
(Phone me)

* **BUZZ**word
(A word that gains
temporary popularity)

In the **BY** and **BY**
(Soon; eventually)

* Hard to come **BY**
(Rare)

* Hard **BY** the...
(Very close to...)

How did you come **BY** it?   *   Drop **BY**
(How did you get it?)   (Come to see me)

Let **BY**gones be **BY**gones   *   **BY** and large
(Forgive and forget it)   (Generally,...)

I have a little put **BY**   *   Run it **BY** him
(I saved a little money)   (Get his views)

Squeak **BY**   *   Stand **BY**!
(Barely [survive] [win])   ([Attention!] [Wait a moment!])

An old stand**BY**   *   I won't stand **BY** and...
(Something reliable used before)   (I won't tolerate...)

BY thunder!   *   **BY** the way,...
(An expression of [amazement]   (Incidentally,...)
of determination])

   *   **BYE BYE**!
Kiss it good**BYE**   (Goodbye!)
(Consider it lost)

  *   **BYEE**!
(Unfriendly way of telling
someone to leave)

B

Chapter C

C Note   * He's gone, kit and **CABOODLE**
($ 100.00 bill)   (He left with all his things)

CAGE   * Rattle his **CAGE**   * We're in **CAHOOTS**
(Jail)   (Torment him)   (We're secret allies)

Raise **CAIN**   * Have your **CAKE** and eat it too
([Act wildly] [Complain])   (Gain from an action
            and suffer no loss)

[Piece of **CAKE**!]
[It's a **CAKE**walk!]   * [Frosting] [Icing] on the **CAKE**
(A very easy task)   (An extra value added)

Selling like hot**CAKES**   *   You take the **CAKE**!
(Very popular)   ([You win the prize]
         [You're unbelievable!])

A **CALAMITY** Jane
(One who sees the worst side of things) * **CALL** his bluff
         (Urge him to do what
CALL him on the carpet   he said he would do)
(Demand that he
 explain his conduct)   *   Too close to **CALL**
         (Very hard to judge)

A close **CALL**
(Trouble was barely avoided) * **CALL** it a [day] [night]
         (Quit work now)

CALL off the dogs!
(Stop pursuit!)   *   **CALL** him down!
         ([Challenge][Criticize]him)

C

It's my **CALL**
(I'll make the decision)

* He had no **CALL** to do it
(No justification; reason)

CALL it off!
(Cancel it!)

* **CALL** them off!
(Order them to [leave] [stop])

CALL him [on it] [out]
(Challenge him [to fight])

* **CALL** it quits
([Resign] [Stop doing it])

CALL it as you see it
(Use your best judgement)

* **CALL** the [shots] [tune]!
(Be the boss!)

A wake-up **CALL**
(An alert; a warning)

* His **CALLING** is...
(His profession; work is...)

Duty **CALLS**
(I must go to the toilet)

* **CALM** down!
(Quiet yourself!)

They **CAME** out of the woodwork
(As though from hiding)

* The straw that will
break the **CAMEL'S** back
(The decisive factor)

Break **CAMP**!
(Pack and move!)

* I'm in his **CAMP**
(I support him)

* Skip **CAMP**
(Disappear; leave)

Happy **CAMPER**
(A contented person)

* **CAN**
(Toilet)

* Catch as catch **CAN**
(Unplanned)

CAN do [!][?]
([I agree!]
[Can you do it?])

* **CAN**-do fellow
(A person always
willing to try)

* No **CAN** do!
(I [can't] [won't]
do it!)

C

CAN it!   *   Out on my CAN
([Be quiet!] [Stop it!])   (Dismissed; fired)

CAN you tie that?   *   He CAN whistle for it!
(Can you [believe] [equal that?])   (He'll never get it)

A CAN of worms   *   I'm burning the
(A lot of problems)   CANDLE at both ends
          (Exhausting myself)

It doesn't hold a CANDLE to...
(It's not equal to...)   *   A loose CANNON
       (Undisciplined; unrestrained)

A feather in his CAP
(An honor)   *   My CAP is off to you!
          (I congratulate you!)

I set my CAP for her
(I'm wooing her)   *   A CARD [shark] [sharp]
       (A card player who cheats)

A drawing CARD
(A [person who] [thing that]   *   The wild CARD
  attracts interest)   (The unpredictable factor)

I hold all the CARDS   *   It's in the CARDS
(I have control)   (It's inevitable)

Play your CARDS right   * My CARDS are on the table
(Do everything correctly)   (I have revealed my situation)

[I don't give a CARE!]   *   A devil-may-CARE attitude
[A lot I CARE!] [Who CARES?]   (Free of concerns)
(I don't care)

                C

Take **CARE**! [of yourself!]
(An expression of goodbye)
([Be careful!])

* Take **CARE** of him!
([Kill] [Punish] him!)

* Call him on the **CARPET**

Roll out the red **CARPET**
(Greet with special ceremony)

(Demand that he explain
his conduct)

He was **CARRIED** off
(He died)

* He **CARRIES** water for
(He does chores for…)

It will **CARRY** you away
(You will become enthusuastic)

* **CARRY** the ball
(Assume responsibility)

CARRY the day
(Win)

* I can **CARRY** the freight
(I'm a hard worker)

CARRY her off
(Kidnap her; take her away)

* I'll **CARRY** [it off]
[out my mission]
(I'll succeed)

CARRY on!
(Continue with your duties!)

* He'll **CARRY** on
something awful
(Become very agitated)

I **CARRY** the torch for…
(I love…)

* **CARRY** it through
(Finish the job)

He's **CARRYING** on with…
(He is linked
romantically with…)

* I upset the apple**CART**
(Foiled the plan)

Don't put the **CART** before the horse
(Don't get things
out of sequence)

* Basket **CASE**
([Hopeless] [Very sick])

C

62

Crack the **CASE**
(Solve the problem)

CASE the [joint] [place]
(Examine it)

I'm on the **CASE**
(I'm working on it)

An open and shut **CASE**
(The facts are clear)

I'll **CASH** in my chips
([Die] [Quit])

It's a **CASH** cow
(It produces a lot of money)

I'm hard up for **CASH**
(I have no money)

CAST it off
(Discard it)

Bell the **CAT**
(Get someone to agree
to do something)

That's a different
breed of **CAT**
(A changed situation)

* Don't make a federal
CASE of it
(Don't make it too important)

* Get off my **CASE**!
(Don't [bother] [press] me!)

* He's on my **CASE**
(He's making trouble for me)

* Get down to **CASES**!
([Be specific]
[What do you mean?])

* [Cold **CASH**] [**CASH** money]
[**CASH** on the barrelhead]
(Actual money)

* Hit him up for **CASH**
(Ask him for money)

* Spot **CASH** * **CAST** off!
(A quick cash payment) (Start moving!)

* The **CAT** is out of the bag
(The secret is revealed)

* In the **CAT**bird seat
(In a key position)

* Look what the **CAT** dragged in!
(Look who came in!)

C

He's a fat **CAT**
(Rich donor)

* Suffering **CAT**fish!
(Expression of amazement; frustration)

He had a **CAT**fit
(He became very angry)

* It's the **CAT'S** [meow!]
[pajamas!] [whiskers!]
(It's wonderful!)

He's a scaredy **CAT**
(He's afraid; a coward)

The **CAT** has his tongue
(He won't speak)

* There is more than one
way to skin a **CAT**
(Various means may be
used to reach a goal)

Raining **CATS** and dogs
(Very hard rain)

* I must play **CATCH**-up ball
(I'm losing and must work
hard to win)

I'll **CATCH** a break
(Be lucky)

* I'll **CATCH** a buzz
(Brief exhilaration caused
by alcohol or drugs)

CATCH as **CATCH** can
(Unplanned)

* You wouldn't **CATCH** me
dead doing that
(I never would do that)

I'll **CATCH** my death of cold
(Become ill with a cold)

It will **CATCH** your eye
(Get your attention)

* I'll **CATCH** [the dickens!] [it!]
(Be severely criticized)

CATCH him [flatfooted]
([Unprepared]
[n the act of doing it])

* I'll **CATCH** flak
(Be blamed)

* **CATCH** forty winks
(Get a little rest)

C

64

It will **CATCH** [hold] [on]
(Be accepted)

CATCH you later!
(An expression of goodbye!)

CATCH him with his pants down
(When he is not ready)

I'll **CATCH** up
(I won't be behind)

It's **CATCHING**
([People imitate it]
[It's contagious])

I'm **CAUGHT** up with...
(Very involved with...)

He's a **CAUTION**
(An unusual person)

Not a red **CENT**!
(Not a penny)

Dollars and **CENTS**
(Money)

Get your two **CENTS** in
(Make your comments)

* **CATCH** [it? [on?]
(Do you understand?)

* Will he **CATCH** on?
(Discover the truth)

* It's **CATCH** 22
(I can't win either way)

* What's the **CATCH**?
([The surprise factor]
[The hidden complication])

* It's **CATCHY**
([It's lively]
[It gets one's attention])

* **CAUSE** a [rhubarb] [stir]
(Create excitement; problems)

* I hit the **CEILING**
(Became angry)

* He's off **CENTER**
(Different; strange)

* For two **CENTS**, I...
(For almost nothing, I...)

* Don't stand on **CEREMONY**
(Don't be too formal)

C

That's for **CERTAIN**
(That's true)

CHAIN smoke
(Smoke continuously)

Rise to the **CHALLENGE**
(Meet the challenge)

I don't stand a [ghost of a]
CHANCE [in hell]
(I have no hope of...)

A sporting **CHANCE**
(A reasonable risk)

CHANGE
(Money)

It will **CHANGE** hands
(Possession will shift)

CHANGE your
[mind] [tune]
(Change your views)

I know it **CHAPTER**
and verse
(I memorized it)

I'm in **CHARGE**
(I'm [the boss] [in control])

* Jerk his **CHAIN**
([Remind him of his situation]
[Bring him back to reality])

* **CHALK** it up to...
(That's the reason for it)

* [Fat] [Slim] **CHANCE**!
([It's hopeless]
[Little hope of success])

* Jump at the **CHANCE**
(Be eager to do it)

* **CHANCES** are that...
(It is likely that...)

* For a **CHANGE**, I'll...
(To be different, I'll...)

* **A CHANGE** of heart
(A change of opinion)

* He'll short**CHANGE** you
(Cheat you)

* A [shady] **CHARACTER**
([A person of bad or
doubtful reputation]
[An unusual person])

The **CHARGE** will stick
(Remain valid)

* A good-time **CHARLIE**
(A fun-loving person)

It works like a **CHARM**
(It functions very well)

* I live a **CHARMED** life
(I'm very lucky)

A **CHARMER**
(One who captivates people)

* A wild goose **CHASE**
(A useless [errand] [search])

He's **CHASING** rainbows
(He's unrealistic)

* A classy **CHASSEY**
(An outstanding figure)

Chit**CHAT**
(Unimportant talk)

* Cut the **CHATTER**!
(Be quiet!)

[Dirt] [On the] **CHEAP**
(Very low cost)

* A **CHEAP**shot
(A petty, needless insult; comment)

A **CHEAP**skate
(A stingy person)

* Talk is **CHEAP**
(It's easier to talk than to act)

CHECK!
(I concur!)

* The **CHECK** will bounce
(A bank will reject it
for lack of funds)

Double **CHECK** it
(Be certain of it) * **CHECK** in at... * **CHECK** it [out]
(Register at a hotel) (Investigate it)

The story doesn't **CHECK** out
([The facts don't support it]
[It's false])

* Take a rain **CHECK**
(A chance to do a
delayed thing at a later date)

C

A reality **CHECK**
(A fresh look at the
true situation)

* Get a **CHECK**-up
(A physical examination)

* **CHECK** up on him
(Investigate him)

I said it tongue in **CHEEK**
(I was [teasing] [not sincere])

* [He has his **CHEEK**]
[He's **CHEEKY**]
(He's impudent; rude)

CHEERS!
(A drinking toast)

CHEESY
(Cheap; shoddy)

* **CHEEZ** it!
(Attention! Be careful!)

A big **CHEEZE**
(A high ranking person)

* Say **CHEEZE**!
(Smile!)

It's no bowl of **CHERRIES**
(It not easy)

* Play it close to the **CHEST**
(Be secretive)

Get it off your **CHEST**
(Say what you want to say)

* It will put hair
on your **CHEST**
(Make you a man)

An old **CHEST**nut
(An old joke; myth)

* Pull his **CHEST**nuts
out of the fire
(Rescue him and his interests)

I bit off more than
I can **CHEW**
(I overestimated what I could do)

* A bone to **CHEW** on
(To think and talk about)

CHEW the [fat] [rag]
(Talk)

* **CHEW** him out
(Criticize him)

C

I have a lot to **CHEW** on
(To consider)

* A **CHICK**
(A girl)

CHICKEN feed
(A small amount of money)

* **CHICKEN**-[hearted] [livered]
(Cowardly; hesitant; scared)

He'll **CHICKEN** out
(Back away in fear)

* Play **CHICKEN**
(A deadly game to see
who moves first)

I'm no spring **CHICKEN**
(I'm not young)

* Don't count your
CHICKENS before they hatch
(Never assume success
before it happens)

Your **CHICKENS** will
come home to roost
(You will have to deal
with problems you cause)

* **CHIEF** cook and
bottlewasher
(The manager)

The **CHIEF** honcho
(The leader)

* My brain**CHILD**
(My idea; invention)

CHILD'S play
(Tame; easy)

* He's in his second **CHILD**hood
(He thinks he is a child)

CHILL him
([Intimidate him] [Kill him])

* **CHILL**[it!] [out!]
([Relax!] [Calm yourself!])

He's **CHILLING** at...
(Waiting impatiently at...)

* Keep your **CHIN** up!
(Have courage!)

Don't lead with your **CHIN**
(Don't seek trouble)

C

I can take it on the **CHIN**   *   An old **CHINA** hand
(I'm tough)   (A person of long experience)

He's a **CHIP** off the old block   *   Blue **CHIP**   *   **CHIP** in
(He's just like his father)   (High value)   (Contribute)

He has a **CHIP** on his shoulder   *   I'll cash in my **CHIPS**
(He is angry and belligerent)   ([Quit] [Die])

When the **CHIPS** are down   *   **CHIT** chat
(When it is really important)   (Unimportant talk)

CHOCK-full of...   *   A Hobson's **CHOICE**
(All of the space is used)   (The option chosen when
                                 no other option exists)

Don't preach to the **CHOIR**
(Don't try to convince those   *   He'll **CHOKE**
   already convinced)   (Become [silent] [unable to act])

[**CHAMPING**] [**CHOMPING**]   *   I'll get the **CHOP**
   at the bit   (Lose my job)
(Anxious to begin)

               *   I'll lick my **CHOPS**
CHOPPERS...   (Be impatient to enjoy...)
(Teeth)

        *   It's on the **CHOPPING** block
It struck a **CHORD**   (It is being eliminated)
(An emotional response)

         *   **CHOW** down!   *   **CHUCK** it in!
CHUCK him out!   (Eat!)   (Resign!)
(Remove him!)

CHUCK it out!   * They're [CHUMMY] [CHUMS]
(Throw it away!)   ([Friendly] [Friends])

He's a CHUMP   * Poor as a CHURCH mouse
(He is easily fooled; cheated)   (Very poor)

See you in CHURCH!   * A [lead pipe] CINCH
(A goodbye expression)   (Very easy)

He'll go full CIRCLE   * I'll [be] [drop out]
(Return to where he started)   of CIRCULATION
                           (Withdraw from social
In the CIRCUMSTANCES,...   or other contacts)
(In that situation,...)

           *   Don't fight CITY hall
A CITY slicker   (Don't antagonize those in power)
(An urban person)

            *   Stake a CLAIM to...
CLAM [S]   (Assert your right to...)
([$ 1.00] [Dollars])

         * CLAM up!   *   CLAPPER
A CLASS act   (Be silent!)   (Voice)
(High quality)
        * He has CLASS * A CLASSY chassey
     (He acts with great style)   (An outstanding figure)

He has CLAY feet   * I got a CLEAN bill of health
(He is false;   (['m in good health]
  hypocritical; weak)   [There are no charges against me])

[Make a CLEAN breast of it!] [Come CLEAN!]
(Tell the truth!)

C

I have **CLEAN** hands
(I'm innocent)

*   **CLEAN** house!
(Make drastic changes!)

I'm **CLEAN** as a
  [hound's tooth] [whistle]
  (There is no evidence against me)

* Keep your nose **CLEAN**
(Avoid trouble)

*

I'm **CLEAN** out
(I have none left)

CLEAN him out
(Take all his [money] [possessions])

*

A **CLEAN** slate
(A fresh beginning)

I'm [squeaky] **CLEAN**
(No one can make
  any charge against me)

* A **CLEAN** sweep
([A complete victory]
[A total removal of...])

I'll **CLEAN** up
([Make money]
[Wash and refresh myself])

* **CLEAN** up your act!
(Reform yourself!)

He'll take me to the **CLEANERS**
(Ruin me financially)

* (**CLEAR** as [a bell] [day])
[Chrystal **CLEAR**]

The coast is **CLEAR**
(No one is there)

([Very understandable]
[Unambiguous])

CLEAR the deck!
([Remove things not needed]
[Cancel all appointments])

*

CLEAR out!
([Go!] [Leave!])

* I'm [out] in the **CLEAR**

CLEAR out lock,
  stock, and barrel!
(Go and take your things)

([There is no case against me]
[I no longer can be caught])

C

CLEAR sailing
(No obstacles ahead)

* Send it in the CLEAR
(Uncoded)

Out of a CLEAR blue sky
(Without warning)

* CLEAR it up
(Resolve the problem)

It will go CLEAR [up] to...
(All the way to...)

* CLEAR it with...
(Get the concurrence of...)

We CLICK
(We relate well)

* Things are CLICKING
(Working well)

A CLIFF-hanger
(A close contest to the end)

* The CLINK
(Jail)

At a [fancy] [fast] CLIP
(Very fast)

* A CLIP joint
(A place where prices are too high)

CLIP him [one]!
(Hit him!)

* CLIP his wings
(Reduce his influence; power; role)

CLOAK and dagger
(Very secret)

* Run out the CLOCK
(Stall until all the time is gone)

His face would stop a CLOCK
(He's very ugly)

* He's a CLOCK-watcher
(Always anxious
to leave work)

It will go off like
CLOCKwork
(According to plan)

* A CLOSE [call] [shave]
(Trouble was barely avoided)

C

Too **CLOSE** to call
(Very hard to judge)

*

Cut it **CLOSE**
(Take risks)

Play it **CLOSE** to your
[chest] [vest]
(Be secretive)

* Keep a **CLOSE** eye on him
(Watch him carefully)

*

CLOSE [at hand] [to home]
(Near)

CLOSE it out
(Liquidate it)

*

CLOSE your [trap] [yap]!
(Be silent!)

The book is **CLOSED**
(The matter is settled)

*

He's a **CLOSET**...
(He hides his preferences)

I have no skeletons
in my **CLOSET**
(There are no bad things
about me kept secret)

*

Water **CLOSET**
(Toilet)

CLOSING in on...
(Reducing the distance to...)

*

On **CLOUD** nine
(Very excited; happy)

Under a **CLOUD**
(Suspected of...)

* In **CLOVER**
(Wealthy)

* Dumb **CLUCK**!
(Stupid!)

I haven't a **CLUE**
(It's a mystery to me)

*

CLUE me in
(Inform me)

A **CLUNK**
(A poorly performing machine)

* I'm always
there in a **CLUTCH**
(I help when it is needed)

CLUTCHING at straws
(Desperate)

C

Pour on the **COALS**   *   The **COAST** is clear
(Increase the effort)   (No one is there)

Sugar**COAT** it   *   **COCK** and bull
(Make it look better than it is)   (False)

COCK of the walk   * Don't go off half-**COCKED**
(Master of the situation)   (Poorly prepared)

COCKEYED   *   Knock him **COCKEYED**
(Crazy) (Wrong)   (Make him unconscious)

The last nail in the **COFFIN**   *   **COIN**
(The thing that ended it)   (Money)

...in **COLD** blood   *   **COLD** cash
(Without [feeling] [pity])   (Actual money)

I'll [catch] [my death of]   *   **COLD** comfort
 [come down with a] **COLD**   (Not very consoling)
(Become ill with a cold)
                                    *   I [have it down]
                                            [know it] **COLD**
I have **COLD** feet   (I memorized it)
(I'm [scared] [hesitant])

                                    *   I have you **COLD**
A **COLD** [fish] [potato] [turkey]   ([All evidence is
(An aloof, unfriendly person)   against you]
                                            [You can't escape])
COLD-hearted
(Brutal; cruel)

                                    *   **COLD** as hell!
                                               (Very cold)

C

It hit me **COLD**
(I was stunned; surprised)

* He'll blow hot and **COLD**
(His views are very changeable)

Knock him **COLD**
(Make him lose his senses)

* It leaves me **COLD**
(It doesn't interest me)

Out in the **COLD**
(Deserted; fired; rejected)

*

Give him the
COLD shoulder
([Ignore] [reject] him)

COLD sober
(Completely alert)

*

Quit **COLD** turkey
(Suddenly)

[Pour] [Throw] **COLD** water on it
(Discourage it)

* It will be a
COLD winter in hell
(A very rare occasion)

COLLAR him!
(Catch him!)

* I was hot under the **COLLAR**

Cool and **COLLECTED**
(Calm and confident)

(Very angry)

*

It's a horse of
a different **COLOR**
(It's a different situation)

Let's see the **COLOR**
of your money
(Show me the money)

* Off **COLOR**
(Improper; offensive)

I'll come through
with flying **COLORS**
(Succeed; meet the test)

* Show your true **COLORS**
(Reveal your real character)

Examine it with a fine-tooth **COMB**
(Thoroughly)

* **COME** across!
([Give it to me!] [Do what you promised])

C

I'll **COME** across as...
(Be perceived as...)

*   I'll **COME** across it
(I'll find it)

COME again?
(Repeat what you said)

*   **COME** up for air
(Stop work for a while)

He'll **COME** [along] [around]
([He'll finally agree]
[He'll visit])

* You all **COME** back!
(Goodbye!)

* It will **COME** out of the blue
([Without warning] [A surprise])

Hard to **COME** by
(Rare)

* How did you **COME** by it?
(How did you get it?)

COME clean!
(Tell the truth!)

* It will **COME** [a cropper] [to grief]
(It will fail)

It's a **COME** down
(A demotion)

* When you **COME** down to it,...
(Finally,...)

COME down on him
(Attack; criticize him)

* I'll **COME** down with...
(Become ill with...)

Easy **COME**, easy go
(What I get I don't keep long)

* **COME** and get it!
(You can eat now!)

He'll **COME** on like gangbusters
(In a forceful manner)

* **COME** to grips with it
(Address it directly)

It will **COME** in handy
(Be very useful)

* It will **COME** to a head
(To a crisis)

C

COME hell or high water
(Despite all obstacles,...)

A COME [hither] [on] look
(A flirting look)

How COME?
(Why?)

Where do I COME in?
(What is my [role] [share]?)

My ship will COME in
(I'll be successful)

A light bulb will COME on
(Understanding will develop)

It will COME to light
(Be found; revealed)

He'll COME loose
[at the seams]
(Become [crazy] [disorganized])

COME into money
([Get] [Inherit] money)

It will COME [in] [to] nothing
(It will fail; be useless)

What will COME of it?
(What will happen to it?)

COME off of it!
(Stop that nonsense!)

It will COME off as...
(Appear as...)

COME off as expected
(As planned)

COME on!
([Hurry!] [You're joking!]
[I don't believe it!])

[Aw, COME on!]
[C'MON!]
([Why don't you do it?]
[Do it!])

A COME on
(A possibly false incentive)

He'll COME on to you
(Pay special attention to you)

He'll COME into his own
(Gain his own identity)

It will COME out of the blue
(Be a surprise)

C

78

COME out for...
(Declare support for...)

* How will it COME out?
(What will be the outcome?)

COME to pass
(Happen)

* ...to COME down the pike
(To arrive)

COME to the point!
(To the essential thing)

* I'll COME [out] [up]
[smelling like] roses
(I'll do unexpectedly well)

COME to your senses!
(Try to think rationally)

* It will COME up short
(Be inadequate)

They'll COME thick and fast
(In great numbers and quickly)

* COME to think of it,...
(I also remember that...)

COME through with flying colors
(Succeed; meet the test)

* COME through for me!
(Help me!)

It will COME through
(It will happen; be done)

* It will COME through
in the clear
(Uncoded)

He'll COME to
(Regain consciousness)

* It has COME to this
(This is the outcome)

It will COME out in the wash
(The truth will be revealed)

* He COMES off that way
(He is perceived that way)

Do what COMES naturally
(By habit; instinct)

* If worse COMES to worse
(If there is no other choice)

My COMFIES
(My comfortable clothes)

C

He's a **COMER**
(He'll likely be very successful)

Cold **COMFORT**
(Not very consoling)

It's **COMING** along
(Progress is being made)

A long day **COMING**
(Long delayed)

It's **COMING** down [today]
(Happening [today])

It's **COMING** out
of our ears
(We have too much of it)

Where is he **COMING** from?
(What is his motive; objective?)

He doesn't know if
he's **COMING** or going
(He is confused)

You have another
[guess] [think] **COMING**!
(You have misjudged!)

I have it **COMING**
([It's owed to me]
[I deserve it])

COMING up on...
(Near to...)

COMMODE
(Toilet)

He's up and **COMING**
(Likely to succeed)

CUMMUNE with nature
(Go to the toilet)

Pillar of the **COMMUNITY**
(A respected community leader)

Bet the **COMPANY**
(Commit everything)

We've got **COMPANY**
(Someone is [coming] [watching])

Keep **COMPANY** with...
(Go socially with...)

I part **COMPANY** with him
(I disagree with him)

COMPARE notes
(Exchange information)

C

A **CON** man
(A swindler)

* As far as I'm **CONCERNED**...
(In my situation,...)

A twinge of **CONSCIENCE**
(A troubled conscience)

* In [mint] [tip-top]
CONDITION
([New] [Excellent condition])

I [am well-**CONNECTED**]
[have **CONNECTIONS**]
(I have influential friends)

* **CONK** out
(Stop functioning)

CONNED
(Fooled; swindled)

* He's **CONNING** us
(Lying)

Have a **CONNIPTION** fit
(Become very agitated)

* To your heart's **CONTENT**
(As much as you want)

A bone of **CONTENTION** is...
(A matter in dispute is...)

* Chief **COOK**
and bottlewasher
(The manager)

He'll **COOK** the books
(Alter data to meet his needs)

* **COOK** his goose
(Ruin him)

A **COOK** off
(A cooking competition)

* **COOK** up a...
(Develop; prepare a...)

That's the way the
COOKIE crumbles)
(The way things happen)

* A **COOKIE** duster
(A mustache)

He's a [smart] [tough] **COOKIE**
([A bright person]
[A strong, enduring person])

* I'll [lose] [toss]
my **COOKIES**
(Vomit)

C

COOKING with gas   *   A **COOK'S** tour
(Doing things correctly)   (Many things are seen briefly)

What [is **COOKING**] [**COOKS**]?   * He's **COOL**
(What is happening?)   (Casual; charming)

It's **COOL**   * I'll [blow] [lose] my **COOL**!
(Just ahead of   (Get angry; excited)
current style)

    *   I'm **COOL** [and collected]
I'll **COOL** my heels   [as a cucumber]
(Wait a long time)   (Calm and confident)

COOL [your jets!] [it man!]   *   Keep your **COOL**
(Relax!)   (Remain calm)

Play it **COOL**   *   It's **COOL** with us   * **COOLER**
(Keep calm)   (We're comfortable with it)   (Jail)

Fly the **COOP**!   *   **COOP** him up!
(Escape!)   (Limit his freedom)

He'a crazy **COOT**   * He'll **COP** it   * A **COP** out
(an insane person)   (Steal it)   (A [betrayal]
    [false argument])

He'll **COP** out [on us]
([Desert; fail us] [Quit])   *   **COP** a plea
    (Cooperate with the prosecution
CORK it!   to reduce charges or penalties)
(Stop talking!)

    *   That's a **CORKER**!
    (Unusually good)

C

A CORNball   *   Just around the **CORNER**
(A silly person)   (Very near)

He's around the **CORNER**   *   [**CORNER** him]
(He's crazy)   [Back him into a **CORNER**]
        (Leave him no good options)

From the **CORNER** of my eye
(The edge of my vision)   *   **CORNER** the market
        (Seek control of the supply)

He's in our **CORNER**
(He helps; supports us)   *   It will turn the **CORNER**
        (Become more successful)

Cut **CORNERS**
(Save money/time by doing   *   **CORNY**
   less than required)   (Silly; trite)

It **COST** [blood] [a pretty penny]   *   The **COST** is on me
(It's very expensive)   (I'll pay the expense)

They **COST**...a pop   *   It **COST** an arm and leg
(Each one costs...)   (Very expensive)

I'll eat the **COSTS**   *   I don't **COTTON** to him
(I won't recoup what I spent)   (I don't admire him)

In tall **COTTON**   *   A **COUCH** potato
(Prosperous)   (One who always watches television)

COUGH it up!   *   **COUGH** up...
([Show us you have it!]   ([Produce] [Pay for]...)
[Give it to us!])

COULD be!   *   Don't COUNT your
(It's possible!)   chickens before they hatch
                                                (Never assume success
He's down for the COUNT   before it happens)
([He's in serious trouble]
[A fighter down; referee counting])   *   A no-COUNT
                                                (A bad person)
COUNT [heads] [noses]
(Estimate the vote)   *   COUNT on [it!] [me!]
                                        ([It's certain] [You can rely upon me])
COUNT me out!
(I won't participate)   *   It's a free COUNTRY
                                                (Do what you wish)

Not by a COUNTRY mile
(Not even close)   *   Screw up your COURAGE
                                                (Be brave)

Par for the COURSE
(Normal; as expected)   *   The ball is in my COURT
                                                (The next move is mine)

My day in COURT
(A time to give my views)   *   Full COURT press
                                                (A maximum effort)

Kissing COUSINS
(Related, but not by blood)   *   COVER your [backside]
                                                              [rear]
COVER all bases   (Maneuver to avoid blame)
(Prepare well)
                                                It will blow my COVER
                         *   (Reveal my
A COVER [operation] [story]   true identity)
([Activity with a false identity]
[Story told to obscure the
true nature of something])

C

COVER your tracks
(Camouflage your actions)

* It's underCOVER
(A hidden; secret activity)

I COVER the waterfront
(I have many responsibilities)

* COVER [for] me!
([Protect me!]
[Draw attention away from me!])

It's a cash COW
(It produces a lot of money)

* Don't have a COW!
([Relax!] [Don't get agitated!])

Holy COW!
(An expression of amazement)

* A sacred COW
(An activity or organization
immune from criticism or harm)

Wait until the COWS
come home
(For a very long time)

* A COZY [affair] [deal]
([Intimate]
[An arrangement to
benefit only a few])

He's [always CRABBING]
[CRABBY]
(A person who is ill-tempered
and complains a lot)

* A CRACK
(A negative, hurtful comment)

I had a CRACK at it
(A chance; an opportunity)

* CRACK the case
(Solve the problem)

The CRACK of dawn
(At first light of day)

* A CRACKdown
(A tougher enforcement of rules)

CRACK jokes
(Tell funny stories)

* Take a CRACK at it
(Try to do it)

Take a CRACK at him
(Attack; criticize him)

C

A **CRACK** unit
(Well-trained, disciplined unit)

*   **CRACK** up
([Lose control; go crazy]
[Start laughing])

He'll **CRACK** me up
(Make me laugh)

*   It will **CRACK** up
(Become a wreck)

It will **CRACK** him up
(Be a major blow to him)

*   It's not what it's
CRACKED up to be
(It doesn't deserve
its reputation)

He's [**CRACKED**] [**CRACKERS**]
(He's crazy)

CRACKER jack
(Excellent)

* I look like death on a **CRACKER**
(I look sick; troubled)

Get **CRACKING**!
(Start moving!)

* What's **CRACKING**?
(What's happening?)

It will fall through   *
the **CRACKS**
(Be [neglected] [unnoticed])

CRAM it down his throat
(Force him to
[accept[[do] it)

I'll **CRAMP** his style
(Limit what he can do; say)

*   I can't **CRANK** it
(My abilities have declined)

Nooks and **CRANNIES**
(Little hidden places)

*   Cut the **CRAP**!
(Stop the lies; nonsense!)

He'll **CRAP** out * A **CRAP**shoot * **CRASH** at my place
(Fail; lose)   (A gamble)   (Live with me)

C

I **CRASHED**   *   It will stick in my **CRAW**
(I lost all energy)   (Really bother me)

I'm **CRAZY** [about] [for] her   *   A **CRAZY** coot
(I admire her very much)   (An insane person)

CRAZY like a fox   *   Don't get **CRAZY** on me
(Crafty; cunning; sly; wise)   (Don't start acting strange)

...like **CRAZY**!   *   **CRAZY** man!   *   Plumb **CRAZY**
(...Very much!)   ([Silly] [Wonderful]!)   (Very irrational)

Stir **CRAZY**   *   **CREAM** of the crop
(Troubled by confinement)   (The best)

CREAM off the...   *   **CREAM** them
(Take the best; leave the rest)   (Beat; overwhelm them)

CREASE him!   *   It does him **CREDIT**
(Shoot him)   (It gives him honor)

Give him **CREDIT**   *   I'm up a **CREEK**
(Recognition; esteem)   without a paddle
          (I have problems but no remedies)

He [is a **CREEP**]
   [gives me the **CREEPS**]   *   A **CRICK** in the neck
(He [is an undesirable person]   (A painful neck)
  [makes me feel uneasy])

           *   **CRISP** ones
CROAK   *   That's a **CROCK**!   (Dollars)
(Die)   (It's not true; nonsense!)

CROCKED * **CROCODILE** tears * By hook or **CROOK**
(Drunk)   (False sorrow)   (By any means)

A two-bit **CROOK**   * Did anything **CROP** up?
(An unimportant thief)   (Did anything happen?)

Cream of the **CROP**   * It will come a **CROPPER**
(The best)   (It will fail)

I'll **CROSS** the bridge   * He'll [double-] **CROSS** us
(Make my decision)   ([Go against our interests]
                                   [Betray us])

CROSS your fingers
(Have hope)   * **CROSS** my heart; hope to die
                          (What I said is true)

Our paths will **CROSS**
(We'll meet again)   * It would **CROSS** the line
                            (Be unacceptable behavior)

It's star-**CROSSED**
(It always has problems) * Our wires were **CROSSED**
                          (We had poor communications)

At a **CROSS**roads
(A decision is needed) * Don't **CROW** * Eat **CROW**
                          (Don't boast)   (Admit errors)

As the **CROW** flies
(Moving in a straight line)   *   The in-**CROWD**
                                        (Those in positions
Don't **CROWD** [it] [your luck]   of power and influence)
(Don't seek too much now)

                            *   Don't **CROWD** me!
Work the **CROWD**   (Don't press me!)
(Greet people; seek their support)

C

88

CROWN him
(Hit him)

A lot of **CRUD**
(Nonsense)

Don't **CRUD** it up
(Don't lower quality)

He's **CRUISING** for a bruise
(Asking for trouble)

That's the way the
cookie **CRUMBLES**
(The way things happen)

He's **CRUMMY**
(A disagreeable person)

It won't be tea and **CRUMPETS**
(It won't be easy)

In a **CRUNCH**
(A crisis; an emergency)

I have a **CRUSH** on her
(I'm attracted to her)

In the **CRUSH**,...
(During the busy time,...)

You've got your **CRUST**!
(You are impudent!)

The upper **CRUST**
(The rich; elite class)

A **CRY** baby
(One who complains a lot)

CRY all the way to the bank
(Complain about something
but profit from it)

A far **CRY** from...
([A long way from...]
[Very different from...])

A hue and **CRY**
(A clamor)

Don't **CRY** over spilled milk
(Don't grieve about
what can't be undone)

CRY uncle!
(Surrender; quit!)

A **CRY** in the wilderness
(A lonely, hopeless appeal)

Don't **CRY** wolf
(Don't give false alarms)

C

CRYING [the blues]   * A CRYING need for...
  [in his beer]   (A great need for...)
  (Depressed; telling his troubles)

                          *   A CRYING shame
CRYSTAL clear   (A sad situation)
  (Unambiguous)   * He's CUCKOO
                          ([Crazy] [Silly] [Not smart])

Cool as a CUCUMBER
  (Calm; confident)   * Off the CUFF   * On the CUFF
                          (Improvised)   (On credit)

My CUP runneth over
  (Many nice things are   *   It's not my CUP of tea
   happening to me)   (I don't prefer it)

He's down in his CUPS   * It will CURL your hair
  (Depressed and sad)   (Frighten you)

It's CURTAINS!   *   Throw him a CURVE
  (The end)   (Surprise him)

A CUSHY job   * CUSS   * A good CUSS
  (An easy, well-paid job) (Swear)   (A likable fellow)

CUSS him out!   * He's a [rough] [tough] CUSTOMER
  (Criticize him)   ([A dangerous; mean person]
                       [Someone difficult to persuade])

A CUT above
  (Better than...)   *   CUT to the bone
                                   (Make deep reductions)

CUT the [chatter] [gab]!
  (Stop talking!)   *   Fish or CUT bait!
                                    (Produce or quit!)

                                              C

CUT it close
(Take risks)

CUT the crap!
(Stop the lies; nonsense)

CUT him down [to size]
(Reduce his influence; role)

It doesn't **CUT** any
  ice with me
(It's not important to me)

CUT him in
(Give him a role; share)

Anyway you **CUT** it
(However you calculate it)

He'll make the **CUT**
(He'll survive to compete)

He can't **CUT** the mustard
(He can't do the job)

I'm not **CUT** out for this
(I'm not [suited] [trained] for this)

I was **CUT** to the quick
(Hurt; offended)

*   **CUT** corners
(Save money/time by doing
    less than required)

*   **CUT** a deal!
(Make an agreement)

*   It's **CUT** and dry
([Clear and unambiguous]
[As expected; no surprises])

*   **CUT** in
(Ask to dance with
someone's partner)

*   I can **CUT** it
(I can do the job)

*   I'll **CUT** loose
([I'll leave]
[Lose self-control])

*   **CUT** it out!
(Stop doing it!)

* My work is **CUT**
out for me
(I know what I must do)

*   **CUT** him short
(Interrupt him)

C

Take a short **CUT**
([Do less than required]
[A route of less
distance/time])

CUT to...
(Move to...)

A **CUT** up
(A funny person)

CUTE as a bug's ear
(Small and adorable)

On all **CYLINDERS**
(Very active; busy)

* **CUT** me some slack!
([Give me more [room] [time]
[Let me rest!])

* I **CUT** my teeth on...
(I got my first training;
experience on...)

* Oh, that's **CUTE**!
(That's awful!)

* On the **CUTTING** edge
(On the frontier of thinking)

C

Chapter D

Smack **DAB** on...
(On the exact spot)

Do-**DADS**
(Useless attachments)

Upsy **DAISY**!
(Get up!)

Water over the **DAM**
(Old history; not relevant now)

A **DAME**
(A woman)

He's a [fancy **DAN**] [**DANDY**]
(An overdressed person)

Don't give me that
  song and **DANCE**
(Don't try to charm or fool me)

That's [Jim] [just] **DANDY**!
(That's awful!)

[**DANG** it all!] [I'll be **DANGED**!]
(Alternatives to swear words)

I'm in the **DARK**
(I'm not informed)

* Cloak and **DAGGER**
(Very secret)

* He'll push up **DAISIES**
(Be dead)

* Not worth a tinker's **DAM**
(It has no value)

* What's the **DAMAGE**?
(The cost)

* **DAMN** him with faint praise
(Praise him in meager ways)

* **DANCE** on air
(Be very happy)

* My **DANDER** is up
(I'm angry)

* Fine and **DANDY**!
([I agree!] [Wonderful!])

* I don't give a **DANG**!
(I don't care!)

* Full of **DARING** do
(Adventurous)

D

93

A **DARK** horse
(A possible candidate of
unknown appeal)

* A shot in the **DARK**
(A guess; a gamble)

* A voice in the **DARK**
(A voice heard but not heeded)

Whistling in the **DARK**
(Acting naively, hoping
things will be all right)

* Don't **DARKEN** my door!
(You are not welcome here!)

It's not worth a **DARN**
(It has no value)

* **DARN** [right!] [tooting!]
(That's the truth!)

Do your **DARNDEST!**
(Make your best effort!)

* **DARNED** if I do and
DARNED if I don't
(I can't win either way)

Slap **DASH**
(Fast but careless)

* I **DATE** her
(I accompany her socially)

* Up-to-**DATE**
(Current; fresh)

DATED
(Obsolete)

* The crack of **DAWN**
(At first light of day)

Another **DAY** another dollar
(A routine work day)

* Call it a **DAY**
(Stop work for the day)

Carry the **DAY**
(Win)

* My **DAY** in court
(A time to give my views)

I had a field **DAY**
(I had many successes)

* It's a [bad] [good] hair **DAY**
([I have many problems]
[All is going well])

I had my **DAY**
(My time is passed)

D

94

In my hay**DAY**
(My best years)

It's going to be a long **DAY**
(A day full of problems)

A long **DAY** coming
(Long delayed)

Make my **DAY**!
(Do it, but you will regret it!)

It's not my **DAY**!
(I'm having troubles)

The other **DAY**
(Recently)

Save it for a rainy **DAY**
(For emergency needs)

My **DAY** in the sun
(My brief time of publicity)

He won't give us
the time of **DAY**
(He won't help or
even see us)

It's an up **DAY**
(A good day)

*   [Knock] [Scare] the living
    DAYlights out of him!
    ([Make him unconscious!]
    [Frighten him!])

*   **DAY** in and **DAY** out
    (For many days)

*   It's a red letter **DAY**
    (A day to celebrate)

*   It will make my **DAY**!
    (Make me happy)

*   From **DAY** one
    (The first day)

*   Plain as **DAY**
    (Clearly evident)

*   The **DAY** is shot
    (The day is ending)

*   That will be the **DAY**!
    ([It will never happen!]
    [That would be worth celebrating!])

*   Tomorrow is another **DAY**
    (Resume work tomorrow)

*   It's one of those **DAYS**
    (It has been a bad day)

D

All in a **DAY**'s work
(Normal; routine)

Razzle-**DAZZLE**
(Colorful action; display)

A **DEAD** beat
(One who doesn't pay debts)

I'm **DEAD** broke
(I have no funds)

You wouldn't catch me
  DEAD doing that!
(I never would do it)

It's drop **DEAD**... * The drop
([The best]   **DEAD** date
[Certain...]) (The final date)

A **DEAD** end
(It goes nowhere)

We're [**DEAD** even]
  [in a **DEAD** heat]
(No one is winning yet)

It's a **DEAD** givaway
(It reveals what is hidden)

Don't beat a **DEAD** horse
(It's useless; don't waste time)

My salad **DAYS**
(My [better] [youthful]
[inexperienced] years)

* It's **DEAD** [on arrival]
       [in the water]
    ([It has no future]
     [It's stalled])

* **DEAD** on his [butt]
       [kiester] [rear]
(Inactive; lazy; unmotivated)

* Drop **DEAD**!
  (An unfriendly way of
   saying goodbye)

* I'm a **DEAD**
  [duck] [pigeon]!
  ([I have no chance]
   [I'll be killed!])

* He's a **DEAD** eye
  (He has keen vision)

* **DEAD** [on his feet]
       [to the world]
([Exhausted] [In deep sleep])

* Knock them **DEAD**!
  (Captivate; thrill them!)

D

Knock yourself **DEAD**!
(Make an extra effort)

It's a **DEAD** letter
(It's Useless)

It's a **DEAD** loss
(Worthless)

In the **DEAD** of the night
(Middle of the night)

DEAD [right] [wrong]!
(Clearly [right] [wrong])

A **DEAD** ringer for...
(Nearly a twin of...)

DEAD set on...
(Determined)

I'm **DEAD** sure
(I'm certain)

DEADER that a
  door nail
(Very dead)

[Ace] [cut] [reach]
  [strike] [swing] a **DEAL**
(Make an agreement)

* **DEAD** last
(The final one)

* Do your **DEAD** level best
(Do the best as you can)

* I'm [**DEAD** meat!]
[a **DEAD** pigeon!]
(I'll be killed!)

* You're **DEAD** on!
(Correct!)

* I have him **DEAD** to rights
(My case against him is firm)

* At a **DEAD** run
(Very fast)

* Come to a **DEAD** stop
(To a complete stop)

* **DEAD** in the water   * **DEAD** wrong
(Stalled)   (Completely wrong)

* Turn a **DEAF** ear   * **DEAL**!
(Pretend not to hear)   (I agree!)

* [It's a] Big **DEAL**!
(It's [exciting!]
[nothing to
get excited about])

D

97

A [bum] [raw] **DEAL**
(A bad; unfair arrangement)

A cozy **DEAL**
(An arrangement
benefiting only a few)

It's a done **DEAL**!
(It's all arranged)

Done **DEAL**!
([We agree!]
[It's all arranged!])

DEAL from the top of the deck
(Be honest)

I'll get the short
end of the **DEAL**
(Be treated unfairly)

DEAL me in!
(I'll join the activity)

DEAL me in!
(I'll join the activity)

No **DEAL**!
(I won't do it!)

A square **DEAL**
(An honest arrangement)

What's the **DEAL**?
(What is proposed?)

[He'll wheel and **DEAL**]
[A wheeler **DEALER**]
(One who likes to manipulate;
make arrangements)

I'll catch my
DEATH of cold
(Become ill
with a cold)

I look like **DEATH**
on a cracker
(I look sick; troubled)

The kiss of **DEATH**
(An act that dooms something)

It will be the **DEATH** of me
(It will ruin me)

Put him to **DEATH**
(Kill him)

I'm tickled to **DEATH**
(Very pleased)

A snap **DECISION**
(Quick; without much thought)

D

Use it to **DEATH**
(To the fullest extent)

Deal from the top of the **DECK**
(Be honest)

DECK him!
(Knock him down!)

Stack the **DECK**
(Prearrange the result)

What's on **DECK**?
(What is next?)

DEEP
(Profound)

He's off the **DEEP** end
([Beyond his capacities]
[He's going to extremes])

Skin **DEEP**
(Shallow)

Give him the third **DEGREE**
(Question him thoroughly)

Make a **DENT** on it
(Have an impact on it)

* Clear the **DECK**!
([Remove things not needed]
[Cancel all appointments])

* He doesn't play
with a full **DECK**]
(He's not very smart)

* Hit the **DECK**! [running!]
(Lay down flat!)
([Begin action at once!])

* **DECKED** out with...
(Outfitted; dressed with...)

* In **DEEP** do-do
(In real trouble)

* **DEEP** six it!
([Get rid of it!]
[Sink it!])

* I'm in **DEEP** water
([In trouble] [Beyond
my capacities])

* **DELIVER** [the goods]
(Do what you promised)

* He'll get his just **DESERTS**
(What he deserves)

D

I'm bound and **DETERMINED**
(I'm firm in my course)

* What the **DEUCE**?
(Expression of amazement)

A real **DEUSER**
(Very special)

* Between the **DEVIL**
and the deep blue sea
(Danger on all sides)

The **DEVIL** is in the **DETAILS**
(Real problems are often
found in obscure details)

* He's **DEVIL**-may-care
(Free of cares; concerns)

Give the **DEVIL** his due
(Note the abilities of
an evil person)

* There's the **DEVIL** to pay
(The result will be awful)

A **DIAMOND** in the rough
(An unpolished but very
special person)

* Speak of the **DEVIL**
(We talk about you,
and you appear)

No **DICE**!
(I won't do it!)

* **DIBS** on it!
([I want a share of it]
[It's mine and mine only])

A **DICK**
([A detective]
[A fool])

* [Like] The **DICKENS** I will!
(I won't do it!)

Full of the **DICKENS**
(He's [very lively]
[gets into trouble])

* Catch the **DICKENS**
(Be severely criticized)

* Don't **DIDDLE** [with it]
(Don't waste time on it)

He does **DIDDLY** squat
(He does nothing)

* I'll **DIE**   * It's do or **DIE**
(Be embarrassed)   (The decisive time)

D

DIE down   * Cross my heart, hope to **DIE**
(Recede; subside)   (What I said is true)

He'll **DIE** in...   * You'll **DIE** laughing
(His audiences will be small in...)   (Be very amused)

Never say **DIE**!   * It will **DIE** on the vine
(Don't quit!)   (Be neglected)

Split the **DIFFERENCE**   * Sing a **DIFFERENT** tune
(Compromise halfway)   (Change what you are saying)

DIG in your heels!   * **DIG** in!   * I **DIG** you [man]!
(Resist stubbornly)   (Start [eating]   ([I understand you!]
            [working]!)   [I like you!])

DIG up...
(Find)   * You **DIG**?   * Our [**DIGS**] [**DIGGINGS**]
       (Do you understand?)   (Our home)

Hot **DIGGITY** dog!   * I take a **DIM** view of it
(Wonderful!)   (I'm dubious; skeptical)

A **DIME** a dozen   * Get off the **DIME**!
(Very common)   (Get moving!)

Don't nickel and **DIME** us   * On my own **DIME**
(Don't be so frugal)   (At my own expense)

I don't have thin **DIME**   * It can turn on a **DIME**
(I have no money)   (Change directions quickly
                                in a small space)

D

A **DING**-a-ling   * Don't **DING** me   * A wing **DING**
(A fool)   (Don't pester me)   (A big party)

Rinky-**DINK**   *   A **DIP**   * It's a hum**DINGER**
(Small and   (Stupid person)   (It's remarkable)
  unprofessional)

          *   **DIPPY**   *   **DIRT** cheap
Don't do me **DIRT**   (Foolish)   (Very low cost)
(Don't cause me trouble)

         *   I have **DIRT** on him
Hit the **DIRT**!   (Embarrassing information)
(Lay down flat!)

        *   I hit pay **DIRT**
Don't wash our **DIRTY**   ([Found valuable [information]
  linen in public   [treasure])
(Don't discuss our
  problems in public)   *   A **DIRTY** look
                  (An angry look)

He'll play **DIRTY** pool
(He's treacherous; dishonest)   *   Quick and **DIRTY**
                 (Improvised; rushed)

DIRTY tricks
(Actions to confuse; deceive)   *   **DIRTY** work
           ([Work none want to do]
He was **DISAPPEARED**   [Dishonest activity])
(He was [hidden] [killed])

       * **DISCOMBOBULATED**
A blessing in **DISGUISE**   (Disoriented)
(It has unexpected values)

        *   **DISH** it [out] [up]!
DISH it out   ([Talk] [Serve it!])
(Give heavy punishment)

D

She's quite a **DISH**
(Very attractive)

DISH up a...
(Create; develop; produce)

Dull as **[DISH] [DITCH]** water
(Very plain; uninteresting)

They'll **DISS** me
(Show me no respect)

DITCH it!   * **DITSY**
(Get rid of it!)   (Silly)

DO away with it!
(Destroy; get rid of it!)

DO [away with him!] [him in!]
(Hurt; kill him!)

A big **DO**
(A big [argument] [party])

Make a big **DO** about it
(Cause a lot of excitement)

DO it up brown
(Get it done with style)

Can **DO** [!] [?] [No can **DO**!]
([Agreed!] [Can you do it?])
(I [can't] [won't] do it!)

A can-**DO** fellow
(He's always willing to try)

DO-dads
(Useless attachments)

Full of daring **DO**
(Adventurous)

DO your darndest
(Make your best effort)

It's **DO** or die
(The decisive time)

I'm dying to **DO** it
(Anxious to do it)

I don't **DO**...
(That activity doesn't interest me)

DO good
(Try to help others)

A **DO**-gooder
(One who tries to help others)

He'll **DO**
(Be satisfactory)

D

DO him   *   DO the honors
(Play his role)   (The tasks to be done)

It's a fine how DO you DO   *   Make DO
(A bad development)   ([Improvise]
                              [Be satisfied with what you have])

Don't DO me! [dirt!]
(Don't take advantage of me)   *   It will [not] DO
                                    (It's [not] satisfactory)

DO a number on...
(Punish...)   *   DO your number
                                     (Perform your act)

DO it by the numbers
(According to plan)   *   I'm out to DO it
                              (I'm [planning] [trying] to DO it)

DO him [out of it]
([Take advantage of] [cheat] him)   *   DO your part
                                     (Carry out your role)

DO the [place] [scene]
(See what there is to see)   *   DO them proud
                                     (Make them proud)

DO right by him
(Treat him fairly)   *   I'll DO you a solid
                                     (Something good for you)

DO what it takes
(What is necessary) * DO tell! *   DO your thing
                     (Is that so?) (Your special thing)

DO time
(Be in jail)   *   It will DO the trick
                                     (Produce the desired outcome)

It will unDO him
(Confuse; disorient him)

                                                    D

I [am well-to-**DO**]   *   Will **DO**!
  [**DO** right well]   ([I agree!]
(I'm [successful] [wealthy])   [I'll do it!])
(I have a good income)

                 *   That will **DO**!
That will **DO** it   ([Enough!] [Silence!])
(It is satisfactory)

                *   What will it **DO**?
What's to **DO**?   (How fast will it go?)
(How can we [amuse] [busy] ourselves?

             * That doesn't **DO** it for me
It will **DO** me a world of good   (I'm not satisfied)
(Be good for me)

             *   The **DO**'s and don't's
DOCK his pay   (What to do; not do)
(Reduce his wages as a penalty)

            * Just what the **DOCTOR** ordered
A **DODGE**   (Exactly what is needed)
([An excuse] [A false thing])

            *   It **DOES** me [credit] [good]
Easy **DOES** it!   ([It gives me honor]
(Be [calm] [gentle])   [It is helpful to me])

That **DOES** it!   *   That **DOES** it for me
(My patience is exhausted)   (That convinced me)

[It's] A **DOG**   * Bird-**DOG** it   * Bull**DOG** it through
(An undesirable   (Search for it)   (Push it until it is done)
thing)

         * Hot [diggity] **DOG**!   * **DOG**-eat-**DOG**
Hot **DOG**   (Wonderful!)   (A grim struggle)
(A roasted wiener)

D

I don't have a **DOG**
in this fight
(I'm not [interested]
[involved])

*

DOGgone!
(An alternative to
a swear word)

*

It will **DOG** him
(Remain troublesome to him)

In the **DOG**house
(In trouble)

*

Hot **DOG** it
(Seek attention by
conspicuous actions)

[It's] [I lead] a **DOG'S** life
(A miserable existence)

*

He's a **DOG** in the manger
(He won't share with others)

A **DOG** and pony show
(An elaborate presentation)

*

Put on the **DOG**
(Entertain lavishly)

Shaggy **DOG** stories
(Humorous but long, boring stories)

*

He'll **DOG** my steps
(Pursue me closely)

DOG tired   *   The top **DOG**
(Exhausted)   (The boss)

*

The tail will wag the **DOG**
(A small factor will
control the larger outcome)

Work like a **DOG**
(Very hard)

He's **DOGGING** it
(Not making a real effort)

*

Call off the **DOGS**!
(Stop pursuit!)

Rain cats and **DOGS**
(Rain very hard)

*

He's gone to the **DOGS**
(His condition is bad)

My **DOGS** are killing me
(My feet hurt)

*

Let sleeping **DOGS** lie
(Don't stir up old problems)

D

106

He's **DOING** backflips * **DOING** what comes naturally
(He's very excited)   (By habit or instinct)

Nothing **DOING**!   *   There is [nothing]
(No!)   [something] **DOING**
    ([It is very quiet]
It will take some **DOING**   [Something is happening])
(A big effort will be needed)

    *   How are you **DOING**?
It's your **DOING**   (How are you?)
(You are responsible)

    *   What's **DOING**?
Those are my **DOINGS**   ([What is happening?]
(My activities)   [A hello greeting])

That's where the **DOINGS** are   *   She's a **DOLL**
(Where things are happening)   (She's beautiful)

DOLL it up   * Another day, another **DOLLAR**
(Make it look better)   (A routine work day)

Pay top **DOLLAR**   *   Turn a **DOLLAR**
(The highest price)   (Earn; get money)

Hotter than a   *   **DOLLARS** and cents
 two-**DOLLAR** pistol   (Money)
(Very popular)

    *   **DOLLARS** to doughnuts,...
DOLLED up   (The probability is that...)
(Made more attractive)

    *   **DONE**!
    (I agree!)

D

[Be] [Have] **DONE** with it!　＊ Been there; **DONE** that!
([Stop] [End] it!)　　　　　　(I had that experience)

DONE deal!　　　　　　＊ I'm **DONE** [for] [in]!
([It's all arranged]　　　　　　(I'm beaten)
[We agree!])

　　　　　　＊ It isn't **DONE**　＊ A who-**DONE**-it
DONE to a turn　(It's not our custom)　(A mystery story)
(Prepared perfectly)

　　　　　　　　＊　　　Do's and **DON'T'S**
In deep **DOO DOO**　　(What to do and not to do)
(In real trouble)

　　　　　　　＊　　By the back **DOOR**
Don't darken my **DOOR**!　(Indirectly; secretly)
(You are not welcome here!)

　　　　　　　＊　Get your foot in the **DOOR**
Deader than a **DOOR**nail　(Take the first step
(Very dead)　　　　　　to gain an objective)

Show him the **DOOR**!　＊ You make a better **DOOR**
(Dismiss him; tell him to leave)　　than a window!
　　　　　　　(You're blocking my view!)
The wolf is at the **DOOR**
(We have many debts; no money)　＊ It's a **DOOZY**!
　　　　　　　(It's extraordinary!)

A DOPE　＊ The latest **DOPE**
(A fool)　(Latest information)　＊　**DOPE** it out
　　　　　　(Try to understand it)

Get a **DOSE** of your own medicine
(The treatment you give others)　＊ On the **DOT**
　　　　　　(Exactly on time)

D

A **DORK**   * **DORKY**!   * It's hunky **DORY**
(A fool)   (Disgusting!)   (Very satisfactory)

Sign on the **DOTTED** line   *   **DOUBLE**check it!
(Indicate your approval)   (Be certain of it!)

He'll **DOUBLE**-cross us   *   On the **DOUBLE**!
(Betray us)   (Hurry!)

I did a **DOUBLE**take   * I got a **DOUBLE** whammy
(Surprised, I looked   (I was hit from two sides)
twice to be sure)

                          * Give him the benefit of the **DOUBT**
A **DOUBTING** Thomas   (Doubt him but don't argue)
(A skeptical person)

                              *   A lot of **DOUGH** [re me]
Dollars to **DOUGH**nuts,...   (Money)
(The probability is...)

                   * Back **DOWN**!   * Bear **DOWN**!
[Bed] [Bunk] **DOWN**!   (Concede; withdraw!)   (Try hard)
(Go to sleep!)

                              *   Boil it **DOWN**
The break**DOWN** is...   (Use fewer words)
(The chief elements are...)

                              *   Break it **DOWN** for me
I had a break**DOWN**   (Explain it to me)
([A mental collapse]
[My vehicle won't work])   * Bring **DOWN** the house
                                     (Thrill the audience)

[Buckle] [Get] [Knuckle]
  DOWN to business   * [Call] [Dress] him **DOWN**!
([Be serious!] [Start work!]) ([Challenge] [Criticize] him!)

D

[Calm] [Settle] [Simmer] **DOWN**! * Come **DOWN** with...
([Quiet yourself!] [Relax!])   (Become ill with...)

Catch him with   * When the chips are **DOWN**
his pants **DOWN**   (When it is really important)
(When he is unprepared)

            * Chow **DOWN**!   * **DOWN** cold
Come **DOWN** on him!   (Eat!)   (Memorized)
([Attack] [Criticize] him!])

            * When you come **DOWN** to it
A [come] [let] **DOWN**   (Finally,...)
(A [demotion] [disappointment])

            * It's [coming] [going]
He's **DOWN** for the count   **DOWN** [today]
([He's in serious trouble]   (Happening [today])
[A fighter down; referee counting])

            * A crack**DOWN**
DOWN in [his cups]   (Tougher rule enforcement)
[the dumps] [the mouth]
(Depressed; sad; dejected) * Cut him **DOWN** [to size]
               (Reduce his influence)

It will die **DOWN**
(Recede; subside)   * Dress him **DOWN**!
               (Criticize him severely!)

Dumb **DOWN**
(Act less smart than you are!) *   **DOWN** to earth
                  (Sensible)
Ease **DOWN**!   * Face him **DOWN**!
([Back away!] [Relax!])   (Meet his challenge)

He'll [fall] [lie] **DOWN** on the job * Don't get **DOWN**
(He won't perform his duties)   (Don't get depressed)

D

110

Get **DOWN** to [brass tacks] [cases]   *   I won't go
([To fundamental issues]   **DOWN** for you!
  [Be specific])   (Accept blame for your actions)

How will it go **DOWN**   *   It will go **DOWN** [hard]
  (What will the reaction be?)   (It will be [accepted]
              [difficult to accept])

DOWN to a gnat's eyelash
  (To the last detail)   *   Let your hair **DOWN**
                 (Confide)

A hand-me-**DOWN**
  (Used before; not new)   *   He beat me hands **DOWN**
                  (Easily)

DOWN the hatch!   * Keep your head **DOWN**
  ([A drinking toast]   (Don't [take chances] [be seen])
  [Swallow your drink!])

              *   **DOWN** [hearted]
DOWN [at the heels]   (Sad; depressed)
  [on my luck] [and out]
  (Poor; without job)   *   Hold [**DOWN** the fort]
                 [things **DOWN**]

DOWN home   (Take care of things
  (My family's home area)   while I'm away)

Hoot him **DOWN**!   *   Hunker **DOWN**!   * Keep it **DOWN**!
  (Ridicule him)   (Stay low!)   (Be less noisy!)

A knock-**DOWN**, drag-out...   *   Lay **DOWN** the law!
  (A furious argument; fight)   (Make clear what
                 the rules are)

They will lay **DOWN** their lives
  (Sacrifice themselves)

D

A let **DOWN**
(A disappointment)

           * He let us **DOWN**
           (He disappointed us)

Let him **DOWN** gently
(Don't be harsh with him)

           * **DOWN** the [line] [pike]
           (In the future)

Go **DOWN** the line with it
(Support it all the way)

           * I'll live it **DOWN**
           (Overcome my embarrassment)

He'll look **DOWN**
  [his nose at] on us
(Act like he is superior to us)

           * Things are looking **DOWN**
           (Prospects are poor)

The low **DOWN** is...
(The facts are...)

           * He's low **DOWN**
           (A bad person)

He's **DOWN** on me
(He disapproves of me)

           * Nail it **DOWN**
           (Get a firm agreement)

...to come **DOWN** the pike
(To arrive)

           * I have it **DOWN** pat
           (I memorized it)

      * Pipe **DOWN!**   * Play it **DOWN**
A put **DOWN**   (Quiet!) (Give it little attention)
(An action intended
  to humiliate someone)

           * Put your foot **DOWN**
           (Insist firmly)

Run him **DOWN**
([Try to find him]
[Criticize him])

           * Get the run**DOWN** on...
           (Get the facts about...)

I'm run **DOWN**
(In poor health)

           * He was run **DOWN**
           (Hit by a vehicle)

D

112

Scarf it **DOWN**
(Eat it quickly)

He'll sell us **DOWN** the river
(Betray us)

When things settle **DOWN**
(Become more stable)

A shake **DOWN**
([Tests to find and solve problems]
[Gain of resources
by extortion/deception])

It's a [show] [stare] **DOWN**
(A confrontation)

That's the **DOWN**side of...
(The bad part of...)

Slow **DOWN**!
([Go slowly!] [Relax!])

Slug it **DOWN**!
(Drink it!)

Stand **DOWN**!
(Leave your post; duties)

Play it straight **DOWN** the middle
(Don't take risks)

He has it **DOWN** to a T
(He knows all the details)

Take him **DOWN**!
([Remove] [Kill] him!)

Take him **DOWN** a peg [or two]
(Reduce his [overconfidence] [status])

Don't talk **DOWN**
[your nose] to me!
(Don't [lecture] [patronize] me)

Throw **DOWN** the glove
(Give a challenge)

Thumbs **DOWN**!
(It is rejected!)

DOWN the tube
(Fail; go bankrupt)

A **DOWN**turn
(Decline in activity)

Turn it **DOWN** [flat]
(Reject it [without reservation])

It was a turn **DOWN**
(A rejection)

Turn it upside **DOWN**!
(Search it thoroughly!)

D

Water it **DOWN**
(Dilute; weaken it)

* It went **DOWN** the wrong hatch
(I swallowed wrong and choked)

DOWN to the wire
(Uncertain to the end)

* A **DOWNER**
(A discouraging experience)

It's **DOWN**right...
(Clearly...)

* Ups and **DOWNS**
(Good and bad times)

A dime a **DOZEN**
(Very common)

* Six of one and half
a **DOZEN** of the other
(It makes very little difference)

In dribs and **DRABS**
(In small amounts)

* He has **DRAG**
(Influence and power)

DRAG your feet!
(Delay!)

* He's in **DRAG**
(A man dressed as a woman)

It's a **DRAG**
(Boring and disagreeable)

* The main **DRAG**
(The principal street)

A knock-down **DRAG** out...
(A furious fight)

* He's a **DRAG** on...
(He's negative; causes delays)

Look what the cat
DRAGGED in!
(Look who came in!)

* **DRAGGING** my [fanny] [tail]
(Very tired)

DRAT it!
([An expression of
dismay/disappointment]
[An alternative to a swear word])

* **DRAW** a bead on...
(Aim at...)

D

I **DRAW** a blank
(I can't remember)

* The luck of the **DRAW**
(Random chance)

DRAW him out
(Get him to talk;
reveal information)

* **DRAW** a line [in the sand]
(Establish a firm limit)

Top **DRAWER**
(High quality)

* He's slow on the **DRAW**
(He reacts slowly)

He's a **DRAWING** card
(He attracts interest)

* Back to the **DRAWING** board
(Start from the beginning again)

A **DREAMBOAT**
(A very attractive fellow)

* A pipe **DREAM**
(An unrealistic idea; goal)

He is **DRESSED**
to [kill] [the nines]
(Very well dressed)

* **DRESS** him down!
(Criticize him!)

* It's window **DRESSING**
(A display designed to make
something look better than it is)

In **DRIBS** and drabs
(In small amounts)

* When the ink **DRIES**
(When the details are settled)

Get my **DRIFT**?
(Do you understand
what I am saying?)

* **DRILL** him!
(Shoot him!)

What's the **DRILL**?
([What is supposed to happen?]
[What process is to be used?])

* ...into the **DRINK**
(Into the water)

D

He has taken to **DRINK**
(He is an alcoholic)

* A **DRIP**
(An obnoxious person)

He has no **DRIVE**
(No energy; motivation)

* He'll **DRIVE** you [nuts!]
[up the wall!]
(Aggravate; bother you)

A pile **DRIVER**
(A hard worker;
a forceful leader)

* In the **DRIVER'S** seat
(In control)

What is he **DRIVING** at?
(What is his objective?)

* Don't **DROP** the ball
(Don't lose the opportunity)

A **DROP** in the bucket
(A very small amount)

* He'll **DROP** a bundle
(Lose a lot of money)

DROP [by] [in]
(Come to see me)

* **DROP** dead!
(Unfriendly goodbye expression)

It's the **DROP** dead...
(The best; perfect...)

* **DROP** dead [date] [time]
(Final [date] [time])

What did he **DROP** for it?
(Pay for it)

* At the **DROP** of a hat
(Very quickly)

DROP me a line
(Write to me)

* It will **DROP** off
(Become quiet; slack)

He has the **DROP** on us
(He holds the advantage)

* A **DROP** out
(One who left school
without graduating)

D

DROP out [of circulation]
(Withdraw from social contacts)

Waiting for the other
shoe to **DROP**
(Something else bad to happen)

I almost **DROPPED** my socks
(I was very surprised)

DROWNING his sorrows
(Dealing with grief by drinking)

It's a **DRUG** on the market
(There is too much of it)

DRUM up business
(Stimulate activity)

DRUM it into him
(Make sure he understands)

Tighter than a **DRUM**
(Very tense)

DRUNK as a lord
(Very drunk)

Punch **DRUNK**
([Confused]
[Dazed])

If I had my **DRUTHERS**
(My preference)

He's **DRY**
(Sober; humorless)

DRY as a bone
([No moisture]
[Very boring])

Cut and **DRY**
([Clear; unambiguous]
[No surprises])

He's not **DRY** behind the ears
(Young and inexperienced)

Hung out to **DRY**
(Left defenseless to suffer)

High and **DRY**
(Isolated)

A **DRY** run
([A training exercise; rehearsal]
[A fruitless effort])

DRY up!
(Be quiet!)

DUB [him] [it]...
(Call [him] [it]...)

Like water off
a **DUCK'S** back
(It has little impact)

D

I'm a dead **DUCK!**
(I have no chance!)

        *   A queer **DUCK**
(A strange person)

DUCK the question
(Try to evade answering)

      *   It's a sitting **DUCK**
(Exposed; undefended)

It's **DUCK** soup
(Very easy; simple)

    * Our **DUCKS** are in a row
(We are ready)

That's [just] **DUCKY!**
(It's awful!)

    * A fuddy **DUDDY**
(A cautious; unfashionable person)

[Fancy] **DUDE**
(An over-dressed person)

    *   Hi **DUDE!**
(A hello greeting)

A smart **DUDE**
(A bright person)

 * Nice **DUDS**
(Clothes)

 * Give the devil
his **DUE**
(Note the abilities of
an evil person)

Pay your **DUES**
(Do enough to qualify)

         * [Get] Off your **DUFF!**
([Move!] [Start!])

DUKE it out!
(Settle it by fighting)

        * Put up your **DUKES!**
(Use your fists!)

He's **DULL** as [dish] [ditch] water
(Plain; uninteresting)

        * **DUMB** cluck!
(Stupid)

DUMB down!
(Act less smart than you are)

        * **DUMB** like a fox
(Cunning; sly, wise)

DUMB luck
(Entirely by chance)

D

118

He's no **DUMMY**   *   **DUMP** his butt!
(He's smart; shrewd)   (Stop associating with him!)

DUMP him!   * **DUMP** on him   * They'll **DUMP** us
(Fire him!)   ([Put the blame on]   (Abandon us)
                 [Criticize] him)
He's [down] in the
  DUMPS   * A slam **DUNK** situation
(Depressed; sad)   (The outcome is certain)

DUST him!   * He'll [bite] [kiss] the **DUST**
(Kill him!)   (Die)

He'll eat my **DUST**   * Wait until the **DUST** settles
(I'll stay ahead of him)   (Until conditions are stable)

A **DUST** up   *   A cookie **DUSTER**
(An argument; fight)   (A mustache)

We're going **DUTCH**   *   In **DUTCH**
(Each will pay his/her bill)   (In trouble)

Talk to him   * **DUTY** calls   *   **A DWEEB**
  like a **DUTCH** uncle   (I need a toilet)   (An obnoxious
(Advise him sternly)   person)

DYED in the wool   * I'm **DYING** to do it
([Genuine] [A loyal believer])   (Anxious to do it)

It's **DYNAMITE**!   * Play with **DYNAMITE**
([Very risky!]   (Take great risks)
[Exceptional!] [Great!])

D

Chapter E

An **EAGER** beaver
(Energetically ambitious person)

* He has an **EAGLE** eye
(Keen vision)

He'll bend my **EAR** [off]
(He'll talk and talk)

* Cute as a bug's **EAR**
(Small and adorable)

Put the bug in his **EAR**
(Give him the idea)

* Turn a deaf **EAR**
(Pretend not to hear)

Give me your **EAR**
(Listen to me)

* He has his **EAR** to the ground
(He keeps himself informed)

Knock him on his **EAR**
(Hit; overwhelm him)

* He's on his **EAR**
(He's angry; upset)

In one **EAR** and out the other
(A message not listened to carefully)

* Out on my **EAR**
(Dismissed; fired)

Play it by **EAR**
(Flexibly, without a plan)

* I'm standing on my **EAR**
(Extremely busy)

Stick it in your **EAR**
(I completely disagree
with what you say!)

* He has a tin **EAR**
([He doesn't listen carefully]
[He isn't sensitive to...])

I got an **EARFUL**
(I heard a lot)

* In the **EARLY** going
(In the beginning)

EARLY on
([In the beginning] [Soon])

* I **EARN** my [keep] [salt]
(Support myself)

E

120

I'm all **EARS**   *   My **EARS** are burning
(I'm listening carefully)   (Someone is talking about me)

It's coming out of our **EARS**   *   He's [not dry] [green]
(We have too much of it)   behind the **EARS**
                                                    (He's young; inexperienced)

Keep it between your **EARS**
(Don't tell it to anyone)   *   I have long **EARS**
                                                              (I have ways of
Get your **EARS** lowered   getting information)
(Get a haircut)
                                            *   It's music to my **EARS**
Keep your eyes and **EARS** open!   (It makes me happy)
(Be alert!)
                                    *   My **EARS** will perk up
Pin his **EARS** back   (I'll listen carefully)
(Beat; humiliate him)
                                    *   Up to my **EARS** in...
Down to **EARTH**   (Very involved in...)
(Sensible; realistic)
                                    *   The salt of the **EARTH**
What on **EARTH**?   (A fine person)
(An exclamation of amazement)
                                    *   Why on **EARTH**?
EASE [down] [it] [up]   (For what reason?)
([Relax!] [Back away!])
                                    *   Ill at **EASE**
EASY come; **EASY** go   (Awkward; uncomfortable)
(What I get I don't keep long)
                                    *   **EASY** does it!
EASY on the eye   (Be [calm] [gentle])
(Attractive)

E

Go **EASY** [on him]   *   It's an **EASY** go
(Treat him gently)   (It's simple)

EASY going   *   Let him up **EASY**
(Gentle; relaxed; unhurried)   (Don't be harsh with him)

An **EASY** mark   *   **EASY** money
(A gullible person)   (Simple to obtain)

Nice and **EASY**!   *   **EASY** pickings
(Be [careful] [gentle])   (Easy to get)

       *   **EASY** as pie   * [Rest] [Stand] **EASY**!
            (Very simple)   (Relax!)
On **EASY** street
(Rich)   *   Take it **EASY**!
                              ([Goodbye!] [Relax!]
Take it **EASY** on him   [Go slow] [Be calm]
(Be gentle with him)   [Get some rest!])

He'll **EAT** you alive   * Have your cake and **EAT** it too
(Overwhelm you)   (Gain from an action
                             and suffer no loss)

I'll **EAT** the costs
(I won't recoup what I spent)   *   **EAT** crow
                        (Admit your error)

It's dog-**EAT**-dog
(A grim struggle)   *   He'll **EAT** my dust
                   (I'll stay ahead of him)

I have to **EAT**
(I need income)   *   He'll **EAT** it up
                   (Greatly enjoy it)

E

He'll **EAT** out of my hands
(I'll control him)

He'll **EAT** my head off
(Severely criticize me)

EAT humble pie
(Be contrite)

EAT three squares a day
(Eat well)

What's **EATING** him?
(What's bothering him?)

The cutting **EDGE**
(The frontier of thinking)

He has a hard **EDGE**
(He is ruthless; tough)

On the ragged **EDGE**
(Exhausted; at the limit)

An **EDGE** in his voice
(A tension)

It had a bandwagon **EFFECT**
(It caused many people
to change their thinking)

* He'll **EAT** [his head off]
[us out of house and home]
(Consume a lot of food)

* **EAT** your heart out!
([Be jealous of me!] [Suffer!])

* He'll **EAT** my lunch
(Get credit for my ideas; work)

* I'll **EAT** my words
(Regret what I said)

* The proof of the pudding
is in the **EATING**
(Quality is uncertain until tested)

* I have the **EDGE**
(An extra advantage)

* He's over the **EDGE**
(Crazy)

* [I'm] [My teeth are] on **EDGE**
(I'm very anxious; nervous)

* I can't get in a word **EDGE**wise
(It's difficult to
get into the discussion)

* Spare no **EFFORT**!
(Do everything possible)

E

Here's **EGG** in your beer!   * I got **EGG** on my face
(A drinking toast)   (I was embarrassed)

A good **EGG**   * He'll lay an **EGG** * My nest **EGG**
(A likable person)   (Fail)   (My saved money)

He'll lay an **EGG** * It's my nest **EGG** * **EGG** him on
(Fail)   (My saved money)   (Urge him to act)

Don't put all your   *   I walk on **EGGS**
  EGGS in one basket   (I have to be very careful)
(Don't rely too much
  on one factor/option)   *   Behind the **EIGHT** ball
                                  (In a difficult position)

He did a one-**EIGHTY**
(A complete reversal of position)   *   My **ELBOW!**
                                  ([Nonsense!] [I disagree!])

Give him **ELBOW** room
(Space to maneuver)   *   I rub **ELBOWS** with...
                                  (I'm [near to...]
He has sharp **ELBOWS**   [Associate with...])
(He is very aggressive)

                            *   **ELECTED** at-large
A white **ELEPHANT**   (By a vote of the
(An unwanted; unprofitable thing)   whole electorate)

The **ELEPHANT'S** share * At the **ELEVENTH** hour
(The biggest amount)   (The last moment)

ELIMINATE the fat   * So what **ELSE** is new?
(Remove what isn't needed)   (It's not new or surprising)

E

He is something **ELSE**
  (Very different; special)

    * He is somewhere **ELSE**
  (Thinking about other things)

The be-all and **END**-all
  (The best version of something)

    *   A dead **END**
  (It leads nowhere)

He's off the deep **END**
  ([Beyond his capacities]
  [He's going to extremes])

    *   My **END**game
  (My final objective)

    * The **END** of the [line] [road]
  ([The final point]

That's the living **END**!
  (I can't tolerate more!)

    [Death])

It's the living **END**!
  (The [ultimate]
  [greatest] thing!)

    * Get your rear **END** in gear!
  (Start moving!)

    *

Your hair will stand on **END**
  (You will be scared)

    I'm at the **END** of
  my [rope] [tether]
  ([I have no more strength]
  [All of my options are poor])

I'll get the short **END**
  of the [deal] [stick] *
  (I'll be treated unfairly)

  At the [tag] [tail] **END** of...
  (The last section of...)

I'll **END** up a...   *
  (I'll finally become a...)

  [Hold up your **END**]
  [Keep your **END** up]
  (Carry your share)

He doesn't know which **END** is up
  (He is ignorant; inexperienced)

    * I'm at wits **END**!
  ([I'm frantic!]

Rear-**ENDED**
  (Hit from the rear)

  [I don't know what to do!])

E

At loose **ENDS**
(Unemployed; drifting)

*

Tie up loose **ENDS**
(Settle all details)

I make **ENDS** meet
(I support myself)

*

Odds and **ENDS**
(Miscellaneous things)

It's **ENDS**ville
([It has no future]
[A remote place])

*

The king's **ENGLISH**
(Proper English)

*

Let well **ENOUGH** alone
(Don't disturb things)

ENOUGH [already!]
[is **ENOUGH**!]
([Stop it!]
[An expression of impatience])

*

Fair **ENOUGH** [!] [?]
([That's equitable]
([Do you agree?])

Good **ENOUGH**!
([Yes] [I agree])

*

Sure **ENOUGH**,...
(And then, as expected...)

Sure **ENOUGH** [!] [?]
([I agree!] [Is that a fact?])

*

It's a sure **ENOUGH**...
(A genuine...)

[Expand] [Push] the **ENVELOPE**
(Go beyond the limits of current
accepted behavior/practice)

*

Green with **ENVY**
(Jealous)

I had a narrow **ESCAPE**
([I barely survived]
[I was almost caught])

*

It was a ballpark **ESTIMATE**
(A quick judgment, without
careful analysis)

I'll [bet] [lay] **EVEN** money
(Wager dollar for dollar)

*

I'll break **EVEN**
(Recover my expenses)

E

Get **EVEN**   * **EVEN** handed   * On an **EVEN** keel
(Retaliate)   (Fair)   (In a steady way)

We're **EVEN** [Steven]   *   In any **EVENT**,...
(We [have the same score]   ([Anyhow,...]
 [are equal])   [Whatever happens,...])

In the **EVENT** that,...   *   In all **EVENTS**,...
(If this happens,...)   ([Anyway,...] [However,...])

That's a ...turn of **EVENTS**   * **EVERY** so often,...
(A change in circumstances)   (Occasionally)

EVERYbody and his brother   *   He has a finger
(A large crowd)   in **EVERYTHING**
                                         (He is very [busy] [involved])

Hold **EVERY**thing!
(Wait!)   *   Much in **EVIDENCE**
                                             (Easily seen; prominent)

EXAMINE it with
 a fine-tooth comb   *   A poor **EXCUSE** for...
(Very thoroughly)   (A bad substitute for...)

EXPAND the envelope   * Come off as **EXPECTED**
(Go beyond the limits of   (As planned)
 currently accepted behavior/practice)

                                    * They're **EXPECTING**
A fishing **EXPEDITION**   (Awaiting birth of a baby)
(A search for information)

                            *   A hairy **EXPERIENCE**
A lot of **EXPERIENCE** under my belt   (Frightening)
(I've learned a lot)

E

A mountain-top **EXPERIENCE**
(A remarkable experience)

* The apple of my **EYE**
(My favorite person)

EYEball it
(Go look at it)

* It's **EYE**ball to **EYE**ball
(A tense confrontation)

In hock up to my **EYE**balls
(I have large debts)

* I'm up to my **EYE**balls in...
(I have much more than I need)

I didn't bat an [**EYE**] [**EYE**lash]
(I [showed no surprise]
[was very casual])

* I got a black **EYE**
(My [reputation]
[eye] was hurt)

Turn a blind **EYE** to it
(Pretend you don't see it)

* He has blood in his **EYE**
(He looks angry)

It will raise **EYE**brows
(Cause surprise)

* It will catch your **EYE**
(Get your attention)

Keep a close **EYE** on him
(Watch him carefully)

* From the corner of my **EYE**
(The edge of my vision)

He [is a dead]
[has an eagle] **EYE**
(He has keen vision)

* Easy on the **EYE**
(Attractive)

He has a fat **EYE**
(He was hit in the eye)

* We see **EYE** to **EYE**
(We agree)

Give her the **EYE**
(Flirt with her)

* He gave me a fishy **EYE**
(Examined me suspiciously)

E

Down to a gnat's **EYE**lash * Keep you **EYE** out for him
(To the last detail) (Look for him)

More than meets the **EYE** * Here's mud in your **EYE**!
(Part is hidden) (A drinking toast)

It's an **EYE** opener * [My] [In a pig's] **EYE**
([Revealing] [Surprising]) (Nonsense!)

A private **EYE** * Shut **EYE**
(A private detective) (Sleep)

I would give my **EYE**teeth for... * Have an **EYE** toward...
(Make great sacrifice for...) (Show concern for...)

Keep a weather **EYE** out for... * In the wink of an **EYE**
(Watch carefully for...) (Very quickly)

A worm's **EYE** view * He **EYE**'D me
(A low level perspective) (He [saw] [focused on] me)

Bright-**EYED** and bushy-tailed * Pie-**EYED**
(Fresh and ready to go) ([Drunk] [Very tired])

Keep you **EYES** [and ears] open! * Four **EYES**
(Be alert!) (One who wears glasses)

[Hawk-] [Sharp-] **EYES** * It hit me between the **EYES**
(Keen vision) (I saw it at once)

It will knock your **EYES** out * Lay [Set] **EYES** on...
(You will be amazed!) (See; observe)

E

I made **EYES** at...
(Flirted with...)

My **EYES** were bigger
than my stomach
(I took too much to eat)

* A sight for sore **EYES**
(A pleasure to see)

* He'll show his
teeth in his **EYES**
([His anger] [His resolve])

E

Chapter F

Put the best **FACE** on it
  (The best appearance possible)

* His **FACE** would stop
a clock
  (He is very ugly)

FACE him down!
  (Meet his challenge)

* I've got egg on my **FACE**
  (I was embarrassed)

FACE [facts] [the music]
  [up to it]
  (Confront realities)

* It will fall flat on its **FACE**
  (Fail)

It flies in the **FACE** of...
  (It contradicts...)

* In your **FACE**!
  (I challenge you!)

He has a long **FACE**
  (He looks sad)

* I'll lose **FACE**
  (Be embarrassed; humiliated)

A **FACE** to **FACE** meeting
  (A direct encounter)

* A **FACE** off
  (A confrontation)

Plain as the nose on his **FACE**
  (Clearly evident)

* Out of my **FACE**!
  ([Back] [Go] away!)

A poker **FACE**
  (Unrevealing)

* Keep a straight **FACE**
  ([Don't smile] [Remain serious])

He'll throw it in my **FACE**
  (He'll remind me of it)

* It's **FACE** value is...
  (Its evident value is...)

A bald-**FACED**... * Two-**FACED** * The **FACILITIES**
(A totally false...)   (Treacherous)   (The toilet)

A **FACT** of life
(A reality)

* The **FACT** of the matter is...
(The truth is...)

I tell it to you for a **FACT**
(It's the truth)

* That's a **FACT**!
(I agree!) (I'm certain of it!)

My fudge **FACTOR**
(An amount included to
cover possible errors)

* The X **FACTOR**
(The unknown factor)

* Tell him the **FACTS** of life
(About sex)

Face **FACTS**!
(Confront realities!)

* It doesn't square with the **FACTS**
(It is contrary to realities)

Do a **FADE**
(Disappear; hide)

* Damn him with **FAINT** praise
(Praise him in meager ways)

FAIR enough!
([agree!]
[It's equitable])

* **FAIR** enough?
(Do you agree!)

* **FAIR** game
(A legitimate target)

He's the **FAIR**haired boy
(He gets special treatment)

* **FAIR** to middling
(Just satisfactory)

No **FAIR**!
(It violates the rules)

* It's a **FAIR** [far] piece
(A long distance)

[A **FAIR** shake]
[**FAIR** and square]
(Honest; equitable)

* **FAKE** it
(Pretend)

* **FAKE** him out!
(Bluff; trick him)

A **FALL** back position
(A position to retreat to if needed)

* I'll **FALL** behind
(Lag)

F

It will **FALL** [through the cracks]
[between the stools]
(Be unnoticed; neglected)

He'll **FALL**
down on the job
(He won't perform well)

It will **FALL** flat on its face
(Fail; not happen as expected)

He'll **FALL** for her
(Fall in love)

Don't **FALL** for it
(Don't be fooled; misled)

The **FALL** guy
(The one blamed; punished)

FALL in with...
(Become associated with ...)

FALL out from...
(The results of...)

He's riding for a **FALL**
(Careless; asking for trouble)

It will **FALL** [short] [through]
(It won't [be enough]
[happen as expected])

Take the **FALL**
(Take the blame
for someone else)

Like **FALLING** off a log
(Very easy to do)

We had a **FALLING** out
(We became estranged)

He has high**FALUTIN** ways
(He tries to act very important)

She wears the pants
in the **FAMILY**
(She is the boss)

It runs in the **FAMILY**
(Others in the family
[act] [look] the same)

The **FAMILY** black sheep
(The family embarrassment)

It's going **FAMOUSLY**
(Very well)

It hit the **FAN**
(Caused great excitement/trouble)

A **FAN** of...
(An admirer)

F

He's traveling at a **FANCY** clip * He's a **FANCY**
(Very fast)   [Dan] [dude] [pants]
                                         (An overdressed person)

Footloose and **FANCY** free
([Unattached romantically]   *   **FANCY** footwork
[Without cares/troubles])   (Careful preparation)

He'll **FANCY** himself a...   *   I don't **FANCY** it
(Consider himself a...)   (I don't like it)

FANCY that!   * My **FANNY** * Dragging my **FANNY**
(Imagine that!)   (Buttocks)   (Very tired)

Trip the light **FANTASTIC**   *   I went **FAR** afield
(Dance)   (I wasn't focused)

FAR be it from me   *   Few and **FAR** between
(I wouldn't think of it)   (Rare)

He's in the **FAR** beyond   * As **FAR** as I'm concerned,...
(He's dead)   (With respect to my interest,...)

A **FAR** cry from...   *   It's a **FAR** fetch
([A long way from...)   (It's far from here)
[Very different from...])
                                     *   It's **FAR**-fetched
Too **FAR** gone   (Hard to believe)
(Hopeless)   * So **FAR** so good
                                     (It's all right, up to now)

FAR out!
(Wonderful!)   * A **FAR** piece * From **FAR** and wide
                  (A long distance)   (From many places)

F

134

...to a **FARE**-thee-well   *   He [bet] [bought] the **FARM**
(To an extreme)   ([He commited everything]
                                                   ([He's dead])

FAST asleep   *   A **FAST** buck
(In deep sleep)   (A quick profit)   *   At a **FAST** clip
                                                          (Very fast)

A **FAST** friend   *   Hard and **FAST** rules
(Close friend)   (Fixed; rigid rules)   *   Hold **FAST**!
                                                          (Stay [steady!][where
He travels in the **FAST** lane   you are!])
([He's aggressive and has advanced quickly]
 [He parties; spends a lot])

He'll play **FAST** and loose   *   Don't try to pull
(Act without authority)   a **FAST** one
                                          (To cheat or deceive me)

Don't **FAST** talk me!
(Try to persuade me   *   They'll come thick and **FAST**
 with deceptive talk)   (In great numbers and quickly)

He's **FAST** on the uptake   *   **FASTER** than quick
(He learns fast)   (Very quick)

A **FAT** cat   *   **FAT** chance!   *   Chew the **FAT**
(A rich donor)   (It's hopeless)   (Talk)

Eliminate the **FAT**   *   He has a **FAT** eye
(Remove what is not needed)   (He was hit in the eye)

The **FAT** is in the fire   *   A **FAT** head
([The decision is made]   (A stupid person)
 [Action has begun])

F

Living off the **FAT** of the land
(Very expensively)

FAT and sassy
(Rich; satisfied with himself)

Grand**FATHER** him in
(Qualify him because
of his prior status)

He's an odds on **FAVORITE**
(He has the best chance to win)

A **FEATHER** in his cap
(An honor)

Birds of a **FEATHER**
flock together
(Similar people tend to associate)

I'll **FEATHER** my nest
(Act for my own profit)

Horse**FEATHERS**!
(Nonsense!)

I'm **FED** up! [to my teeth!]
([Angry and impatient]
[I can't tolerate more!])

Don't make it a **FEDERAL** case
(Don't make it too important)

* He has a **FAT** lip
(He was hit in the mouth)

* Fickle finger of **FATE**
(Pure chance)

* Your **FATHER'S** mustache!
(Nonsense)

* Whom does he **FAVOR**?
(Resemble; look like)

* Swallow your **FEARS**!
(Be brave)

* A **FEATHER** [brain] [head]
(A stupid person)

* In fine **FEATHER**
(Dressed very well)

* **FEATHERS** will fly
(There will be a fight)

* Don't ruffle his **FEATHERS**
(Don't make him angry)

* I was spoon-**FED**
(Given [wonderful service]
[only limited information])

136

Put on the **FEED** bag
(Let's eat)

Chicken **FEED**
(A small amount of money)

Don't **FEED** me that line!
(I don't believe that)

I **FEEL** it in my bones
I [anticipate] [predict] it)

FEEL the heat
(The pressure; tension)

FEEL at home
([Relax] [Be comfortable])

I don't have a **FEEL** for it
(I don't understand it)

FEEL him out
(Determine his attitude)

I **FEEL** for you!
([I understand your needs]
[I have no sympathy for you!])

I **FEEL** no pain
(I'm drunk)

I **FEEL** the pinch
(I'm aware of shortages)

I **FEEL** punk
(Not well)

I have a funny **FEELING** about...
(My intuition warns me that...)

My gut **FEELING** is...
(My instinct is...)

No hard **FEELINGS**
(No lasting anger)

I'm **FEELING** my oats
(I'm very confident)

He **FEELS** sorry for himself
(His situation discourages him)

I'm back on my **FEET**
(I [am well]
[have resources] again)

He has clay **FEET**
(He is false, hypocritical, weak)

I have cold **FEET**
(I'm scared)

He's dead on his **FEET**
(Exhausted)

F

Drag your **FEET**!
(Delay!)

*

Hold his **FEET** to the fire
(Make sure he does
what is required)

He's good on his **FEET**
(He's a quick thinker)

*

His **FEET** are on the ground
(He is solid; sound)

I have itchy **FEET**
(I'm restless)

*

Jump in with both **FEET**
(Make a full commitment)

Kick up your **FEET**
(Have a good time)

*

He has two left **FEET**
(He is awkward; clumsy)

Stand on your own two **FEET**
(Be self-reliant)

*

Sweep her off her **FEET**
(Charm; overwhelm her)

My **FEET** are talking to me
(They ache; are tired)

*

His **FEET** aren't wet yet
(He's inexperienced; untested)

It **FELL** through the cracks
(It was neglected; unnoticed)

*

It **FELL** into my lap
(I got it without effort)

A [A-1] [game] **FELLOW**
([An excellent person]
[Very courageous])

*

A [regular] [stout] **FELLOW**
(A good, loyal person)

A **FELLOW** traveler
(A sympathizer)

*

He's over the **FENCE**
(He's gone; escaped; deserted)

Which side of the
FENCE is he on?
(What position
does he support?)

*

He's sitting on the **FENCE**
(He's neutral; indecisive)

F

FESS up!   * A far **FETCH**   * **FETCH** it
(Tell the truth!)   (Far from here)   (Go get it)

Far-**FETCHED**   * It won't **FETCH** much
(Hard to believe)   (It's of little value)

In fine **FETTLE**   * The **FEVER** will break
(In excellent condition)   (The temperature will drop)

I had a **FEW**   *   **FEW** and far between
(I've been drinking)   (Rare)

A **FIB**   * **FIBBING**   * **FICKLE** finger of fate
(A lie)   (Lying)   (Pure chance)

Don't **FIDDLE**   *   Fit as a **FIDDLE**
(Don't waste time)   (In good health)

Don't play second **FIDDLE** to... *   **FIDDLE**sticks!
(Be first, not subordinate to...)   (Nonsense!)

Don't **FIDDLE** with it   * Don't **FIDDLE** with me!
(Don't touch it)   (Don't get involved with me!)

A **FIDDLER**   * A **FIDIDILER**   * I had a **FIELD** day
(Violin player) (A time waster)   (I had many successes)

Out in left **FIELD**   *   Play the **FIELD**
(Remote; isolated)   (Keep your options open)

...something **FIERCE**   *   A **FIFTH** wheel
(With great intensity)   (A useless role)

F

Go **FIFTY-FIFTY** with me
(Share equally with me)

* I don't give a **FIG**!
(I don't care!)

Don't **FIGHT** city hall *
(Don't antagonize the powerful)

I don't have a dog
in this **FIGHT**
(I'm not involved)

FIGHT to the finish!
(Struggle to the end) *

FIGHT [it out!]
[tooth and nail!]
(Fight fiercely!)

Put up a **FIGHT**
(Struggle hard)

*
FIGHTING [language] [words]
(Provocative)

Throw the **FIGHT**
(Act defeated and quit)

*
FIGHTING mad
(Very angry)

Go **FIGURE**!
(Too hard to predict)

* How do you **FIGURE** it?
(What is your judgment?)

FIGURE on it
(You can be certain of it)

*
FIGURE it out!
([Solve the problem]
[Try to explain it])

I can't **FIGURE** you [out]
(I don't understand your thinking)

FIGURE it up
(Calculate its total)

* It **FIGURES**
(It makes sense; seems true)

I've had my **FILL**
(I can't tolerate more)

* **FILL** me in
(Tell me what happened)

No one can **FILL** his shoes
(Can replace him adequately)

* **FILLED** to the gills
(Drunk)

F

A smoke-**FILLED** room
(A place where a
small group is negotiating)

FILTHY rich
(Very wealthy)

In the **FINAL** analysis
(Considering everything...)

FINE and dandy!
([All right!] [Wonderful!]
[It's awful!])

It's **FINE** how-do-you-do
(A bad development)

Walk a **FINE** line
(Be very careful) (impartial)

He's **FINE**-lining it
(Making careful distinctions)

He has a **FINGER** in everything
He is very involved)

FINGER him
(Identify him)

He has a light **FINGER**
(He's a thief)

* Backing and **FILLING**
(Making excuses; evasive)

*

It **FILLS** the bill
(It is satisfactory)

* **FILTHY** lucre
(Money)

* A **FIN**
(A $ 5.00 bill)

*

Examined it with a
FINE-toothed comb
(Very thoroughly)

* In **FINE** [feather] [fettle]
([Dressed very well]
[In excellent condition])

* It's mighty **FINE**
(Excellent)

* The **FINE** print
(The obscure but
critical details)

* Fickle **FINGER** of fate
(Pure chance)

* He didn't lift a **FINGER**
(Gave no help)

* I put my **FINGER** on...
(I found; identified...)

F

At my **FINGER** tips   *   I work my **FINGERS** to the bone
(Easily available)   (I work very hard)

Butter**FINGERS**!   *   Cross your **FINGERS**!
(You always drop things!)   (Have hope!)

Too many **FINGERS** in the pie   *   Fight to the **FINISH**!
(Too many people involved)   (Struggle to the end)

FINISH him off!   *   **FINISH** it! [off!]
(Kill him!)   ([Eat] [Use] it all!]) ([Kill it!])

I'm **FINISHED**!   *   He's a **FINK**
(I [am beaten] [have no hope])   (An informer)

Don't **FINK** out on us   *   He's a ball of **FIRE**
(Betray; desert us)   (He has great energy)

[Great] Balls of **FIRE**!   *   Pull his chesnuts
(An expression of amazement)   out of the **FIRE**
                         (Rescue him and his interests)

The fat is in the **FIRE**
([The decision is made]   *   Hold his feet to the **FIRE**
[Action has begun])   (Make sure he does
                     what is required)

He's [on **FIRE**!]
[all **FIRED** up!]   *   **FIRE** him!
([Angry] [Successful]   (Dismiss him!)
[Enthusiastic])

          *   Strike while the **FIRE** is hot
...like a house a**FIRE**   (Act when it is most timely)
(Very fast)

F

142

Many irons in the **FIRE**
(Many projects underway)

Where there is smoke
there is **FIRE**
(A hint of trouble may
indicate real trouble)

What's on the **FIRE**?
(What's the agenda?)

Set the world on **FIRE**
(Do great things)

A visiting **FIRE**man
(An important guest
treated with honor)

At **FIRST** blush,...
(On first examination/hearing)

At **FIRST** light
(At dawn)

FIRST runner-up
(The second winner)

Like shooting **FISH** in a barrel
(Very easy to do)

Suffering cat**FISH**!
(An expression of amazement)

* Out of the frying pan
into the **FIRE**
(From one trouble to another)

* It's sure-**FIRE**
(Certain)

* I'm under **FIRE**
(Being criticized)

* Where is the **FIRE**?
(Don't go so fast!)

* What's so all-**FIRED** important?
(What is so critical?)

* I won't get to **FIRST** base
(I will fail)

* Learn it **FIRST** hand
(From your own experience)

* [**FIRST** off,...]   * **FIRST** rate!
[In the **FIRST** place,...]   (Excellent!)
(To start,....)

* **FISH** or cut bait!
(Produce or quit!)

* Big **FISH** [in a little pond]
(A high ranking person in a
small place/organization)

F

He's a cold **FISH**
(An aloof, unfriendly person)

* Neither **FISH** nor fowl
(Not clearly defined)

He has other **FISH** to fry
(Other interests to promote)

* A different kettle of **FISH**
(A very different situation)

Some kettle of **FISH**
(A troubled situation)

*

I smoke like a **FISH**
(Smoke continuously)

It's a **FISH** [story] [tale]
(An exaggerated story)

* He's a **FISH** out of water
(Not right for the job)

Bottom **FISHING**
(Pursuing bad options)

* A **FISHING** expedition
(A search for information)

He gave me a **FISHY** eye
(Examined me suspiciously)

*

It's **FISHY** to me
(It seems false)

I made money hand over **FIST**
(Easily and in large amounts)

* I'm tight-**FISTED**
(I hate to give up money)

A [cat] [conniption]
[holy] **FIT**
(Outburst of anger; agitation)

*

FIT as a fiddle
(In very good health)

I **FIT** [right] in
(I adapted; adjusted well)

* He'll [throw a] [have a]
[hissy] **FIT**
(Become very angry)

FIT to be tied
(Very angry)

*

It **FITS** like a glove
(Perfectly)

F

144

If the shoe **FITS**, wear it
(If that describes you,   *   It **FITS** me to a "T"
  acknowledge it)   (It's perfect for me)

Examine it **FIVE** ways to Sunday   *   Give me **FIVE**!
(Very thoroughly)   (Shake hands!)

Take **FIVE**!   *   **A FIVER**   *   I'm in a **FIX**
(Relax!)   (A $ 5.00 bill)   (I have a problem)

Get a **FIX** on him   *   The **FIX** is [in] [on]
(Get data about him)   (The result is pre-arranged)

A quick **FIX**   *   **FIX** him up
(An temporary remedy)   ([Take care of his injuries]
                   [Get him a social companion])

FIX [him] [his wagon]
([Harm; punish him])   *   It's **FIXED**
([Make problems for him])   (The result is pre-arranged)

I'm well-**FIXED**   *   I'm **FIXING** to...
(I [am rich] [have a good job])   (Preparing to...)

I'm having trouble   *   A red **FLAG**
FIXING my mouth   (A danger signal)
(Trying to decide what to say)

                  *   Catch **FLAK**
He's [a **FLAKE**] [**FLAKY**]   (I'll be blamed; criticized)
([Odd] [Undependable])

                *   Keeper of the **FLAME**
I'm her old **FLAME**   (Someone who keeps
(Her former lover)   a cause alive)

F

I was **FLAMED**
(Very angry)

A **FLAP** is on
(A crisis; an emergency)

A **FLASH** in the pan
(A quick but useless effort)

I'm **FLAT** [broke] [busted]
(I have no funds)

A **FLAT**foot
(A policeman)

In [nothing] [no time] **FLAT**
(At once)

        * **FLAT** out
(Asleep; exhausted)

A **FLAT** turn-down
(Total rejection)

It needs **FLESH** and bones
(More details; substance)

FLESH it out
(Provide the details)

Press the **FLESH**
(Shake hands;
  interact with a crowd)

        *   A **FLAP** jaw
(One who talks too much)

* He's **FLAPPING** his trap
(Talking too much)

        *   **FLAT** on my back
(Ill and in bed)

        *   It will fall **FLAT**
[on its face]
(Not happen as expected)

     * Catch him **FLAT**-footed
([In the act of doing it]
[Unprepared])

   * Go **FLAT** out for...
(Without reservation)

     * Thick as [**FLEAS**] [**FLIES**]
(Very numerous)

     * It's him in the **FLESH**
(It's actually him)

     * He got his pound of **FLESH**
(Full payment)

     * **FLICK**   * **FLICK** off!
(A movie)   (An unfriendly
goodbye)

F

146

I have butter**FLIES**
  in my stomach
  (I'm anxious; fearful)

*

As the crow **FLIES**
(Moving in a straight line)

*

It **FLIES** in the face of...
(Contradicts)

Time **FLIES**
  (Goes by quickly)

*

Top **FLIGHT**
(Excellent)

*

A skin**FLINT**
(A stingy person)

A **FLIP** answer
  (Casual; unthoughtful)

*

A **FLIP** flop
  (A reversal of position)

Don't be **FLIP**!
(Impertinent)

*

FLIP for it
(Decide the matter
  by a coin toss)

Don't **FLIP** your [lid] [wig]
  (Don't get angry; excited)

FLIP out
  (Become crazy; very excited)

*

FLIP the switch
(Turn the switch)

He's doing back**FLIPS**
  (He's very excited; happy)

*

FLOAT on air
(Be very happy)

It will not **FLOAT**
  (Not be accepted)

*

FLOAT the idea
(See how people react to it)

Birds of a feather
  FLOCK together
  (Similar people tend to associate)

*

FLOG it
(Heavily promote it)

*

It will **FLOOR** him
(Overwhelm; stun him)

On the ground **FLOOR**
  (At the beginning)

F

FLOOR it!   *   Take the **FLOOR**   *   A **FLOP**
(Drive away fast!)   (Rise to speak)   (A failure)

A flip **FLOP**   *   Go with the **FLOW**
(A reversal of position)   (Do what others are doing)

Don't [**FLUB**] [**FLUFF**] it!   *   It's **FLUFF**
(Don't [fail] [make errors])   (It lacks meaning; substance)

FLUNK out   *   He's **FLUSH**   *   He's a bar **FLY**
(Fail)   (Has a lot of money)   (He drinks a lot in bars)

FLY blind   *   **FLY** the coop
(Proceed without a clear view)   (Escape)

[Feathers] [Fur] will **FLY**   *   **FLY** off the handle
(There will be a fight)   (Get very angry)

FLY high   *   Go **FLY** a kite!
(Be very stimulated; successful)   ([Go away!]
   [I don't care
I let **FLY** with...   what you say!])
(I said...)

   *   A **FLY**-by-night organization
The **FLY** in the ointment   (A temporary organization
(The main problem/weakness)   of poor reputation)

On the **FLY**   *   I'll **FLY** by the
(Moving very fast)   seat of my pants
   (Without experience or a plan)

F

Straighten [out] [up]
and **FLY** right!
(Control yourself and act properly)

*

It won't **FLY**
(It's not acceptable)

*

Take a **FLYER**
([Gamble] [Try it])

Come through with
with **FLYING** colors
(Succeed; meet the test)

*

Off to a **FLYING** start
(A [fast] [good] beginning)

In like **FLYNN**
(Accepted)

*

He's out of **FOCUS**
(He's not fully aware)

An old **FOGEY**
(An out-of-date person)

*

I haven't the
FOGGIEST notion
(I know nothing)

He's in the **FOLD**
(He has joined; is a member)

*

It will **FOLD** [up]
(Go out of business)

FOOD that will stick
to your ribs
(A substantial meal)

*

FOOD for thought
(Something to consider)

I wear my **FOOD** well
(I drop food on my clothes)

*

Don't **FOOL** around!
(Don't [waste time] [flirt]
[have sex])

Don't **FOOL** with it!
(Don't touch it!)

*

Don't **FOOL** with me!
(Don't bother me!)

He's nobody's **FOOL**
(He's smart)

*

It's **FOOL** proof
(Simple; easy to use)

A **FOOL** thing to do
(Stupid; unwise)

F

No **FOOLING** [?][!]
([Is it] [It's] true [?] [!])

* Pennywise; pound **FOOLISH**
(Wise in small matters;
unwise in large matters)

He's living in
a **FOOL'S** paradise
(He's [misleading himself]
[acting naively])

* He'll play us for **FOOLS**
(Treat us as if we are stupid)

* Off on a bad **FOOT**
(A poor beginning)

It's a political **FOOT**ball
(It's entangled in
political maneuvering)

* Put your best **FOOT** forward)
(Show yourself to your
greatest advantage)

FOOT the bill
(Pay the costs)

* Get your **FOOT** in the door
([Take the first step
to gain an objective]
[Be accepted])

A flat**FOOT**
(A policeman)

Hot **FOOT** it! [over!]
(Get here quickly!)

* **FOOT**loose and fancy free
([Unattached romantically]
[Without cares])

He has a loose **FOOT**
and no roof
(He's a wanderer) * My **FOOT**! * Put your **FOOT** down
(Nonsense!) (Insist firmly)

I put my **FOOT** into it
(I blundered)

* I put my **FOOT** in my mouth
(Said the wrong thing)

Off on the [right]
[wrong] **FOOT**
(A [good] [wrong] start)

* The shoe is on the other **FOOT**
(The matter is now seen
from another perspective)

F

He'll shoot himself in the **FOOT**
(Blunder)

* A tender**FOOT**
(An untested beginner)

Don't be under **FOOT**!
(I don't want to
stumble over you)

* Fancy **FOOT** work
(Careful preparation)

* Catch him flat**FOOTED**
([In the act of doing it]
[Unprepared])

Pussy**FOOTING** around
([Being very cautious]
[Stealthy])

* Play **FOOTSIE** with...
(Collaborate with...)

I'm all **FOR** it
(I favor it)

* I'm done **FOR**! * Give me a **FOR** instance
(I'm beaten) (An example)

He's out **FOR** me
(Trying to find and hurt me)

* It's **FOR** real
(It's genuine)

I'll give you what **FOR**!
(Punish you)

* **FORGET** it!
(Give it no more attention)

You **FORGET** yourself!
(You have lost your
proper sense of conduct)

* **FORK** it over!
(Give it to me!)

Hold [down] the **FORT**
(Take care of things
while I'm away)

* He'll hold **FORTH**
(Give people his views)

* Put **FORTH** a...
([Propose] [Exert] a...)

...and so **FORTH**
(...and more follows)

F

Catch **FORTY** winks * Put your best foot **FORWARD**
(Get a little rest) (Show yourself to
your best advantage)

FOUL play
(Violent, harmful action) * Don't **FOUL** up
(Don't make mistakes)

Don't **FOUL** it up
(Don't make a mess of it) * He's a **FOUL** up
(A failure)

I'll be **FOUND** out * **FOUR** bits
(The truth about me ($ .50) * **FOUR** eyes
will be revealed) (One who wears glasses)

He's **FOUR** square * A two-by-**FOUR**
(Honest; impartial) (A very small place)

Scatter to the **FOUR** winds * On all **FOURS** with...
(In all directions) (In complete agreement with...)

Neither fish nor **FOWL** * [Crazy] [Dumb] like a **FOX**
(Not clearly defined) (Crafty; cunning; wise)

He'll [out]**FOX** you * A **FOXY** lady
(Be more clever than; fool you) (Attractive; desirable)

He'll **FRAME** me * Worn to a **FRAZZLE**
(Arrange for me to be (Very tired)
unjustly accused)
* **FREAK** out
A **FREE**-for-all ([Go crazy]
(Everyone is fighting) [Become very agitated])

F

152

It's a **FREE** country
(Do what you wish!)

It's for **FREE**
(At no cost)

I'm home **FREE**
(There are no more obstacles)

There's no **FREE** [lunch] [ride]
(Everything has a cost)

Scot **FREE**
(Completely free)

FREE on up
(Make one available)

FREE-wheeling
(Operating without
[restraint] [a plan])

* Footloose and fancy **FREE**
([Unattached romantically]
[Without cares])

* I have a **FREE** hand
(Full authority to act)

* A **FREE**loader
(One who survives on charity/
gifts rather than work)

* It's a **FREE** ride
(It costs nothing)

* He's a **FREE** [spirit] [thinker]
([He doesn't think in ordinary ways]
[An unrestrained person])

* It's a **FREEBIE**
(It costs nothing)

* **FREEZE!** * The **FREEZER**
(Don't move!) (Stop!)   (Jail)

Not until hell
FREEZES over
(It will never happen)

* I can carry the **FREIGHT**
(I'm a hard worker)

Pay the **FREIGHT**
(Pay the costs)

* I'm **FRESH** out of...
(My supply is now gone)

A **FRIEND** in need
(One who helps when
help is needed)

* [Bosom] [Fast] **FRIENDS**
(Close friends)

F

I [am][look] a **FRIGHT**! * **FRISK** him! * On the **FRITZ**
(I look horrible)   (Search him!)   (Not functioning)

I have a **FROG** in my throat * It's on the **FRONT** burner
(My voice is hoarse)   (It has a high priority)

It's a **FRONT** for...   *   Put up a good **FRONT**
(An entity used to hide   (Behave confidently)
  the identity of another entity)

                              *   He's up **FRONT**
I cover the water**FRONT**   (Candid)
(I have many responsibilities)

                              *   It **FROSTED** me
FROSTING on the cake   (It made me angry)
(A extra value added)

                      *   He has other fish to **FRY**
Hi, small **FRY**!   (Other interests to promote)
(Greeting to small child)

                      *   They're small **FRY**
Out of the **FRYING** pan   (Unimportant people)
  into the fire
(From one trouble to another)   *   A **FUDDY**-duddy
                          (A cautious; unfashionable person)

FUDGE
(Deliberately alter facts; cheat) * It's my **FUDGE** factor
                               (An amount included to
He's **FULL** of [baloney]   cover possible error)
[beans] [prunes]!
(He's wrong!)   *   I have a belly **FULL**
                                (I can't tolerate more)

Going **FULL** blast
(At its greatest capacity)

F

[Chock] [Plum] [Plumb] **FULL**   * He'll go **FULL** circle
(All the space is used)   (Return to where he started)

It's a **FULL** court press   *   He's not playing with
(A maximum effort)   a **FULL** deck
                                                (He's not very smart)

He's **FULL** of the dickens
(Very lively; gets into trouble)   *   My hands are **FULL**
                                                      (I'm very busy)

He's **FULL** of himself
(He has a large ego)   *   He has a snoot **FULL**
                                              (He's drunk)

FULL steam ahead!
(Move vigorously!)   *   It's in **FULL** swing
                                        (Very active)

He's **FULL** of vinegar
(Energy; spirit)   *   He's a barrel of **FUN**
                                        (Humorous)

[Make **FUN** of] [Poke **FUN** at] him
(Ridicule him)   *   Lay out **FUNDS**
                                  (Provide money)

It's your **FUNERAL**
(You will have to accept   *   Where is the **FUNERAL**?
the consequences)   (Why are you so sad?)

They were **FUNNING**   *   You're **FUNNING** me!
(Joking; having fun)   (Trying to deceive me)

He acts **FUNNY**   *   He has a **FUNNY** bone
(He behaves strangely)   (A sense of humor)

F

No **FUNNY** business!
(Don't try to deceive me)

* I have a **FUNNY**
feeling about...
(My intuition warns me that...)

See you in the **FUNNY** papers!
(Goodbye!)

* That's **FUNNY** [?] [!]
(Something odd; strange is
happening!)

FUR will fly
(There will be a fight)

* Don't make a big
FUSS about it
(Don't get agitated; it's
not important)

A **FUSS** [budget] [pot]
(A complainer)

Kick up a **FUSS**
(Create a disturbance)

* He's **FUSSING**
(Complaining)

F

156

Chapter G

G's   *   Cut the **GAB**!   *   He has a gift of **GAB**
($ 1,000 bills)   (Stop talking!)   (He is very articulate)

I **GAD** about with...   *   A **GAG**
(Associate; travel with)   ([A funny story] [A prank])

Don't lolley**GAG** [around]   *   I'm ahead of the **GAME**
(Don't waste time)   ([I have an early advantage]
                            [I'm well prepared])

I'm back on [my] **GAME**
(Playing well again)   *   A new ball **GAME**
                            (A new [situation] [start])

Beat him at his own **GAME**
(Beat him at what he does best)   *   Cat and mouse **GAME**
                            (A contest of pursuit vs. escape)

My end **GAME**
(My final goal)   *   Fair **GAME**   *   I'm **GAME** to do it
              (A legitimate target)   (Willing)

A **GAME** fellow
(Very courageous)   *   The name of the **GAME** is...
                            (Its character; main purpose)

He's playing a shell **GAME**
(Operating fraudulently)   *   The only **GAME** in town
                            (Where the main activity is)

The **GAME** is up
(You are [beaten] [discovered])   *   What's his **GAME**?
                            (His objective; purpose)

Don't play **GAMES**!
(No tricky maneuvers!)   *   **GAMS**   *   Take a **GANDER**!
                    (Legs)   (Look at that!)

He'll come on
like **GANG**busters
(In a forceful manner)

* They'll **GANG** up on us
(Combine and overwhelm us)

* **GARBAGE** in; **GARBAGE** out
(Use of poor data
leads to a bad result)

The **GARDEN** variety
(Common; ordinary)

It's a **GAS**! * Cooking with **GAS** * Step on the **GAS**!
(A lot of fun!) (Doing things correctly) (Hurry!)

He'll run out of **GAS**
(Have no energy; be exhausted)

* Blow a **GASKET**
(Become very angry)

Give him the **GATE**
(End the relationship)

* I **GATHER** that...
(I judge that...)

It **GAVE** me a turn * In high **GEAR** * Get your rear
(It startled me) (Very active) end in **GEAR**!
(Start moving!)

GEAR up!
(Prepare to act!)

* [Shift] [Switch] **GEARS**
(Change pace; strategy)

A stroke of **GENIUS**
(A brilliant idea)

* A **GENTLEMAN** and a scholar
(A fine person)

The **GENUINE** article
(Authentic)

* **GET** [about] [to] it!
(Start!)

GET it across that...
(Make it understood that...)

* **GET** your act together!
(Organize yourself better)

G

158

GET [after] [with] it!   * I'll GET up in [age] [life]
([Do it!] [Pay attention!])   ([Become older]
[Be more up-to-date])   [To higher rank; income])

We GET along   * When you GET along
([We relate well]   (Become older)
[Our resources are adequate])

     * GET along with you! [now!]
A GETaway   ([Leave!] [Stop that nonsense!])
(A vacation place)

     * I'll GET away [with it]
I'll GET the [axe] [broom] [chop]   (I [will escape]
((Lose my job)   [won't be caught])

GET back at him   * GET off my back!
(Gain revenge against him)   (Don't nag me!)

I GET bang out of it   * GET in bed with them
(I enjoy it)   (Join with them)

GET it behind you   * GET the better of...
(Move on with your life)   (Dominate...)

Let's GET a bite   * GET to the bottom of it
(Have a quick meal)   (To its root; core)

GET off your [bottom]   * GET your brain together
[butt] [duff]!   (Think carefully)
([Move!] [Start!])

     * I'll GET a break   * GET [busy!]
I'll GET by   (Be lucky)   [to work!]
(I'll be all right)   (Start work!)

G

GET off my case!
(Don't [bother] [press] me!)

GET your two cents in
(Make your comments)

GET it off your chest!
(Say what you want to say!)

Come and **GET** it!
(You can eat now!)

GET [cracking] [off the dime]!
(Start moving!)

GET a dose of
your own medicine
(Suffer the treatment
you give others)

Don't **GET** down
(Become depressed)

GET my drift?
(Do you understand
what I'm saying?)

GET even!
(Retaliate!)

GET a fix on...
(Get data about...)

GET [your foot] in the door
(Take a first step to
gain an objective)

A lot of **GET** up and go
(Energy and initiative)

It has **GET**-go
(Energy; power)

GET while the getting is good
([Leave while you can!]
[Get what you can, quickly!])

From the **GET**-go
(The beginning)

He'll **GET** [your goat]
[on your nerves] [to you]
(Bother; irritate you)

GET going!
([Leave now!]
[An unfriendly
goodbye])

GET him going
(Prod him into action)

Let's **GET** going!
(Let's start!)

GET something going
(Start [an activity]
[a relationship])

GET in good with him
(Get him to accept you)

G

160

It will never **GET**
  off the ground
  (It will never start)

GET a handle on it
  ([Control] [Understand] it)

GET it [into] [through]
  your [head] [skull] that...
  (Try to understand that...)

He'll **GET** his
  (Be killed)

GET your hooks on him
  (Catch him)

GET off your high horse!
  ([Stop being aloof!]
  [You overvalue yourself])

GET in on it
  (Participate)

GET in with...
  (Develop good
   relations with...)

I don't **GET** it!
  (I am puzzled)

     * I let it **GET** to me
     ([Bother] [Overwhelm me])

* He'll **GET** in your hair
  (Annoy you)

* **GET** the upper hand
  (Gain control)

* **GET** the hang of it
  (Understand how it functions)

* **GET** him!
  ([Find and punish him!]
  [Look at him!])

* **GET** hold of yourself!
  (Control yourself!)

* **GET** [on your horse!] [humming!]
  ([Move!] [Start!])

* He'll **GET** into it
  (Get into an argument; fight)

* **GET** in some...
  (Find time for...)

* I'll **GET** [it!] [the works!]
  ([Be killed!] [Gain it all]
  [Be given the finest treatment])

* **GET** the lard out!
  (Move!)

G

GET in your licks * **GET** a life!
([Your punishing blows] ([Do something useful!]
[Help shape the results]) [Start living!] [Be realistic!])

GET lost! * **GET** the message * **GET** mileage from...
(Go away!) (Do you understand?) (Benefit from...)

GET a move on! * I'll **GET** off
([Hurry!] [Start!]) ([Escape punishment]
[Charges will be dropped])

GET off it!
(Stop that nonsense!) * **GET** it off him
(From him)

How does he **GET**
off acting that way? * Here is where I **GET** off
(Why does he behave that way?) ([Die] [Where I leave])

Tell him where to **GET** off * It will **GET** old with me
(Tell him what you think of him) (I'll [lose patience]
[become bored] with it)

I'll **GET** on
(Cope; manage) * **GET** on him! * **GET** on it!
(Criticize him!) (Deal with it!)

GET [on with] [to] it!
(Start doing it!) * We **GET** on
(We relate well)

GET [on with you!]
[out of here!]) * **GET** out!
(You are joking!) (Leave! Go away!)

...as all **GET** out! * I'm out to **GET** him
(Very energetically) (Find and punish him)

G

I'll **GET** over it
([I'll recover]
[My mood will change])

* I can't **GET** over it!
(I'm still amazed!)

GET up a party
(Plan a party)

* **GET** it over with!
(Do it now!)

I'll **GET** it on a silver platter
(Without effort)

* **GET** the picture?
(Do you understand?)

GET to the point!
(To the essential thing)

* **GET** my point?
(Is my message clear?)

GET with the program!
(Be alert!)

* **GET** real!
(Be realistic!)

GET a rise out of him
(Seek a response; a reaction)

* I'll **GET** the sack
(Lose my job)

GET [this show on the road]
[on the stick!]
(Start moving!)

* **GET** this! [straight!]
(Listen carefully!)

GET down to brass tacks
(To fundamentals)

* **GET** into the swim
(Into the routine of activities)

GET your teeth into it
(Become actively involved)

* **GET** on his tail
([Follow him!]
[See that he does his job])

A **GET**-together
(A meeting; gathering)

* **GET** in touch with…
(Communicate with…)

G

GET out of town!   *   GET through to him
(You're joking!)   (Make him understand)

GET out from under   * He'll GET under your skin
(Free yourself from debt)   ([Annoy] [Interest] you)

My GET up   * GET up for it * GET up and go
(My clothes; costume) (Prepare yourself)   (Energy)

GET the upper hand   *   I'll GET used to it
(Gain control)   (Become accustomed to it)

GET a wiggle on * I'll GET wind of it * GET wise!
([Hurry!]   (Learn about it) (Don't be stupid!)
[Be realistic!])

               *   GET with it!
GET the word out   ([Be alert!]
(Tell everyone about it)   [Be more stylish])

The word will GET out   *   GET off work
(The information   ([Be excused from work]
will become known)   [Finish work for the day])

Don't GET me wrong * He GETS away with murder
(Don't misunderstand me) (He escapes punishment
              for his misdeeds)

What GETS into him?
(What causes that behavior?) * If he GETS it into
               his head,...
I'm a go-GETTER   (If he develops a firm idea,...)
(I take advantage
of opportunities)

G

164

What are you **GETTING** at?   *   Get while the
(What do you seek?)   **GETTING** is good!
                        ([Get what you can quickly]
Not a **GHOST** of a chance   [Leave while you can!])
(No hope at all)

            *   I'll give up the **GHOST**
From **GIDDYAP** to whoa   ([Die]) [Abandon hope])
(From beginning to end)

              *   He has a **GIFT** of gab
Don't look a **GIFT**   (He is very articulate)
   horse in the mouth
(Don't examine a gift too carefully)   *   **A GIG**
                                 (A temporary job)
GIG him!
(Fault him for poor   *   Filled to the **GILLS**
   performance/appearance)   (Drunk)

Green around the **GILLS**   * **GIN** mill   * **GIN** up a...
(Nauseated)   (A bar)   (Quickly prepare a...)

A **GISMO**   * **GIT**!   * **GIVE** him the air
(Device; gadget)   (Leave!)   (Jilt him)

GIVE it your all!   *   A **GIVE**away
(Make a maximum effort!)   (Something of value
                    given/sold without payment)
It's a dead **GIVE**away
(It reveals what is hidden)   *   **GIVE** him the [axe]
                          [boot][broom]
GIVE him both barrels!   (Fire; remove him)
(Make a strong attack on him)

G

GIVE him wide berth!
(Avoid him!)

GIVE me a break!
([Stop that nonsense!]
[Help me!])

GIVE him the business!
([Attack] [Pressure] him!])

GIVE him the cold shoulder
(Avoid; stay far from him)

GIVE the devil his due
(Note the abilities
of an evil person)

GIVE me your ear
(Listen to me)

GIVE her the eye
(Flirt with her)

GIVE me five!
(Shake hands)

GIVE up the ghost
([Die] ([Abandon hope])

GIVE ground
(Compromise;
retreat)

*

GIVE it a [bounce]
[go] [try] [whirl]
(Try it)

* **GIVE** him the bum's rush!
(Throw him out!)

* I don't **GIVE** a [care] [dang]
[fig] [hang] [hoot] [rip]!
(I don't care!)

* **GIVE** him credit
(Esteem; recognition)

* **GIVE** him the benefit of the doubt
(Doubt him, but don't argue)

* **GIVE** him elbow room
(Space to maneuver)

* I would **GIVE** my eyeteeth for...
(Make a great sacrifice for...)

* **GIVE** him the gate
(Spurn him; end the relationship)

* **GIVE** him a [good] going over
([Examine him carefully])
[Punish him heavily])

* Don't **GIVE** me
that [guff!] [jazz] [line] [stuff]!
(Nonsense; I don't believe it!)

G

GIVE it the gun!
(Start moving fast!)

GIVE him a big hand
(A lot of applause)

GIVE it to him
(I'm impressed with him)

Don't **GIVE** any of your lip!
(Silence!)

GIVE it the once over
(Examine it)

GIVE it [a rest] [up]!
([Stop it!])
(Don't [do] [say] it again!)

GIVE it your best shot!
(Perform as well as you can)

GIVE him the slip
(Escape from him)

GIVE it to him! [straight]
([Punish] [Shoot] him!])
([Be honest with him])

..., **GIVE** or take
(Approximately)

 ❋   **GIVE** me a hand!
(Help me!)

 ❋   **GIVE** him his head!
([Punish him!])
([Allow him more authority])

 ❋   I **GIVE** in!
(I[agree!][quit!])

 ❋   It will **GIVE** [out] [way]
(Collapse)

 ❋   **GIVE** it a plug
(Promote it)

 ❋   It will **GIVE** rise to...
(Cause; lead to...)

 ❋ **GIVE** him the high sign
(Send him a signal)

 ❋ Something has to **GIVE**
(Adjust; change; move)

 ❋   **GIVE** me some sugar!
(I want a hug!)

 ❋   The **GIVE**-and-take
(Lively debate)

G

GIVE him the third degree! * GIVE him a hard time!
(Question him thoroughly) (Make trouble for him)

GIVE me a tumble * GIVE up [!] [?]
(Let me court you) ([Surrender!] [Do you surrender?])

GIVE way! * GIVE it great weight
(Abandon your effort!) (Consider it very important)

GIVE him what [for!] [have you!] * GIVE us the word
([Criticize] [Punish] him!) (Tell us)

What GIVES! * He GIVES me the
(A greeting) [creeps] [shivers] [willies]!
(He makes me uneasy; frightens me)

He's a GLAD-hander
(His friendliness * GLAD rags
is not genuine) (One's best clothes)

He has a GLASS jaw * Knock back a GLASS
(He's vulnerable; easily hurt) (Have a drink)

GLITZY * A GLOOMY gus * He's in his GLORY
(Extravagant) (A pessimist) (Getting honor; pleasure)

It fits like a GLOVE * We work hand and GLOVE
(Perfectly) (We are a team)

Throw down the GLOVE * Handle him with
(Give a challenge) kid GLOVES
(Very carefully; tactfully)

G

168

Take the **GLOVES** off
(Stop being gentle)

* It will un**GLUE** him
(Confuse; disorient him)

A **GLUTTON**
 for punishment
(One who asks for trouble)

* Down to a **GNAT'S** eyelash
(To the last detail)

* Straining at a **GNAT**
(Using much energy for
an unimportant purpose)

GO [after] [for] [to] it!
(Try to do it!)

GO ahead!
([Do it] [Proceed])

* I'll **GO** it alone
(Do it myself)

GO along with it
(Concur; support it)

* We **GO** around and around
(We argue)

I **GO** [around] [out] with her
(I accompany her socially)

* I'm back to **GO**
(I must start again)

Don't **GO** back on me
(Don't break your promise)

* **GO** to bat for him
(Help him)

I'll **GO** you one better
(I have an even better story)

* I'm the **GO**-between
(I help the parties
relate to each other)

It will **GO** by the board
(Be [abandoned] [delayed])

* It will **GO** bonk
(Stop operating)

GO bonkers * **GO** by the book
(Crazy)   (Carefully follow
    instructions)

* **GO** for broke!
(Make a maximum effort!)

G

Don't **GO** off half-cocked   *   It will it **GO** down [hard]
(Poorly prepared)   (It will be accepted)
                                         ([It will be difficult to accept])

I won't **GO** down for you
(Accept blame for your actions)   *   Easy come, easy **GO**
                                        (What I get I don't keep long)

GO easy!
(Relax!)   *   **GO** easy on him   *   It's an easy **GO**
                   (Treat him gently)   (It's simple)

GO fifty-fifty with me   *   **GO** figure!
(Share equally the cost)   (It's too hard to predict)

I'm [fixing] [good] to **GO**   *   **GO** flat out for...
(Getting ready to leave)   (Without reservations)

GO with the flow   *   **GO** [for it] [with] it!
(Do what others are doing)   ([Attempt] [Try] it!)

I **GO** for her   *   It has get-**GO**   *   From the get-**GO**
(I'm attracted to her)   (Power)   (The beginning)

I'm a **GO**-getter   *   A lot of get up and **GO**
(I actively use opportunities)   (Energy and initiative)

Give it a **GO**!   *   It's [a **GO**] [no **GO**]
(Try it!)   ([It's all right to start]
                                              [The answer is "No"])

GO-GO   *   **GO** for the gold!
(Very active)   (Be the champion!)
                                  *   He's got to **GO**!
                                       (Remove him!)

G

Got to **GO**!
(I must leave!)

They **GO** hand in hand
(They belong together)

Have a **GO** at it!
(Try it!)

A happy-**GO**-lucky person
(Carefree)

How do we **GO** on ...?
(What's our position on...?)

GO in for...
(Show great interest in...)

Let **GO**!
(Relax!)   * Let it **GO**!
(Forget it!)

I let myself **GO**
([Became shabby] [Gained weight]
[Lost control of myself])

GO out on a limb for...
(Take risks for...)

Make it a **GO**
(Make it function)

* They **GO** hand in hand
(They belong together)

* You can **GO** hang!
(I don't care about you
or what you think!)

* I have to **GO**
([Find a rest room] [Leave])

* It will **GO** off without a hitch
(Without problems)

* **GO** like a house afire!
(Very fast)

* It will **GO** over
like a lead balloon
(The response will be bad)

* I was let **GO**
(My job was ended)

* **GO** light on him
(Be gentle with him)

* I have little to **GO** on
(I lack information)

* He'll make a **GO** of it
(Succeed)

G

GO to the mat with him   *   It's no GO!
([Argue] [Fight] with him)   (I [can't] [won't] do it!)

GO on!   *   GO on!   *   He's on the GO
([Really?]   ([Try it!] [Move!])   (Very active)
[Your joking!])   (Continue speaking)

                                *   GO out for...
GO all out!   (Compete for...)
(Make a full effort!)

                        *   How did it GO over?
It will GO over big   (What was the reaction to it?)
(People will [like]
[not like] it)   *   He'll GO places
                                        (Be successful)

GO along for the ride
(Share the experience; risks)   *   This GO-round,...
                                        (This time; cycle)

They'll GO smack
(Become worthless)   *   We GO steady
                                (We go out only with each other)

GO straight
(Operate honestly)   *   Stuck on GO
                                        (Unable to proceed)

Don't GO there!
(Don't [talk] [think] about that) * There you GO! [again!]
                                (You see, I was right!)
GO through with it   (You are [doing] [saying]
(Do [the job] [what was planned])   it again!)

It's touch and GO   *   Tough GO!   *   It's a tough GO
(The outcome is   (It's sad;   (A difficult challenge)
uncertain)   unfortunate)

G

172

GO [under] [to the wall]   *   GO underground
([Fail] [Become bankrupt])   (Hide)

Way to GO!   *   GO by the wayside
([Wonderful!] [Perfect!])   (Be discarded)

From the word GO,...   *   It's worth a GO
(From the beginning)   (It should be tried)

He'll get your GOAT   *   GOBBLEdegook
(Bother; irritate you)   (Complicated; useless words)

GOD speed!   *   Anything GOES!   *   Here GOES!
(Goodbye) (Good luck!)   (No rules apply)   (It's moving!)

How GOES it?   *   That's how it GOES   *   It GOES to
(A greeting)   (That's fate)   show you that...
(It confirms that...)

It GOES with the territory
(It's part of the job)   *   What GOES?   *   I won
([A greeting]   GOING away
I'm GOING bananas   [What's happening?])   (Easily)
(Crazy)

*   GOING like a bat out of hell
I don't know if I'm   (Very fast)
coming or GOING
(I'm confused)   *   It's GOING down [today]
(It's happening [today])

We're GOING Dutch
(Each will pay his/her bill)   *   In the early GOING
(In the beginning)

G

Easy **GOING**
(Gentle; relaxed; unhurried)

* It's **GOING** famously)
(Proceeding very well)

Get **GOING**!
([Leave!]
[An unfriendly
goodbye])

* Let's get **GOING**!
(Let's start!)

* Get him **GOING**
(Prod him into action]
[Get him moving])

* I'm **GOING** to get him
(Find and punish him)

How is it **GOING**?
([A greeting)
[How is your progress?])

* It's **GOING** [good] [great guns]
(The situation is very good)

I have a lot **GOING** for me
(I have many advantages)

* He's **GOING** on...
(He's nearly...years of age)

What's **GOING** on?
(What is happening?)
(Also, a greeting)

* What is he **GOING** on?
([What information does he have?]
[Where does he get his energy?])

The **GOINGS** on
(The activities)

* It's been **GOING** on for years
(It has a long history)

Give him a **GOING** over
([Examine him carefully]
[Punish him])

* Get something **GOING**
(Start an activity)

* They [have something **GOING**]
GOING [strong][swimmingly]
(Operating very well)
[are **GOING** together]
(Are romantically linked)

Go for the **GOLD**!
(Be the champion)

* Good as **GOLD**
(Safe; reliable)

G

174

He has a heart of **GOLD**   * It's a **GOLD** mine
(He is very generous)   (A very profitable activity)

By guess and by **GOLLY**   * He's **GONE** to the dogs
(In an unplanned way)   (His condition is bad)

GONE for good * He's a **GONE** goose * **GONE** to grass
(Permanently)   (He has no future)   (Retired)

[Half] [Too far] **GONE**   * To hell and **GONE** again
(In [very bad]   (Far away; a long distance)
[a hopeless] condition)

                *   He's **GONE** down hill
I've **GONE** in for...   (Declined in [health] [status])
(Developed interest in...)

                * He's **GONE**, kit and caboodle
He's **GONE** loco   (He left with his things)
(Crazy)

          * He's **GONE** on her   * **GONE** to pot
I'm a **GONER**   (Infatuated with her) (In bad condition)
(I'm doomed)

        * Let by**GONES** be by**GONES** * It's a **GOOD**...
            (Forgive and forget)   (Approximately...)

It's all for
  the **GOOD**   *   It's **GOOD** for another...
(It is helpful)   (It will function for another...)

He's a **GOOD** [apple] [egg] [Joe] * It does [a body] [me]
(A likeable. fine person)   [my heart] **GOOD**
                  (It [helps] [pleases] me)
It doesn't make for **GOOD** business
(It doesn't promote good business)

G

A **GOOD**-time Charlie
(A fun-loving person)

* He's a **GOOD** cuss
(A likeable fellow)

Do **GOOD**
([Succeed]
[Help others])

* **GOOD** enough!
([Agreed!] [Yes!])

* So far so **GOOD**
(It's all right up to now)

*

Put on a **GOOD** front
(Behave confidently)

He's **GOOD** on his feet
(He is a quick thinker)

*

Get while the getting is **GOOD**!
([Leave while you can!]
[Get what you can, quickly!])

Get in **GOOD** with him
(Get him to accept you)

* We're **GOOD** to go
(Ready to move)

It's going **GOOD**
(The situation is very good)

* Give him a **GOOD**
going over
([Examine him carefully]
[Punish him heavily])

GOOD as gold
(Safe; reliable)

It's a **GOOD** hair day
(Things are going well)

* He's in **GOOD** hands
(He is cared for effectively)

He has a **GOOD** head for it
(He is smart)

* Kiss it **GOOD**bye
(Consider it lost)

Make **GOOD** the loss
(Restore the loss)

* Make **GOOD**
(Succeed)

For **GOOD** measure
(In addition)

* Mighty **GOOD**!
(Very good!)

G

I make **GOOD** money   *   He has **GOOD** moves
(I'm well paid)   (He manages himself well)

My **GOOD** name   * **GOOD** as new   * **GOOD** night!
(My reputation)   (Almost new)   (Expression of dismay)

No **GOOD**   *   He's up to no **GOOD**
(Not satisfactory)   (Doing bad things)

Use his **GOOD** offices   *   Pretty **GOOD**
(Get his help; support)   (Very good, but not
                                 necessarily excellent)

It's **GOOD** and proper
(Done correctly)   *   A **GOOD** scout
           (An honorable; helpful person)

Get on his **GOOD** side
(Seek his approval)   *   He's a **GOOD** sport
         (He behaves well even if he loses)

[All] In **GOOD** time
(Eventually)   *   **GOOD** for you!
                    (You did well!)

I'm as **GOOD** as my word
(Honest and dependable)   * What's the **GOOD** word?
                       (A greeting)

It will do me a world of **GOOD**
(It will be beneficial)   *   A do-**GOODER**
         (One who tries to help others)

GOODIES
(Things of value)   *   Honest to **GOODNESS** [?][!]
           (Is it really [so?] [true?])

Deliver the **GOODS**   (It's really [so!] [true!])
(Do what you promised)

G

I have the **GOODS** on him   *   He'll sell you
(The evidence against him)   a bill of **GOODS**
                               (Cheat; take advantage of you)

He's a **GOODY** two-shoes
(He's too correct and proper)   *   He'll **GOOF**
                                     (Fail)

Don't **GOOF** around! * He's a **GOOF**[-ball] [-off]
(Don't [be funny!]   (A [useless fool] [silly person])
[waste time!])

            * **GOOF** off   * **GOOFY**
It's a **GOOF**-up   (Stop working and have fun)   (Crazy)
(A mistake)

                         *   Gobblede**GOOK**
I have **GOOSE** bumps   (Complicated; useless words)
(I'm [frightened] [thrilled])

                       *   A wild **GOOSE**chase
Cook his **GOOSE**   (A useless [errand] [search])
(Ruin him)

                   *   He's a gone **GOOSE**
I'm loose as a **GOOSE**   (He has no future)
([Free; unrestricted]
[Very supple]   * Whose ox is being **GORED**
[I have diarrhea])   (Who suffers the pain; the loss?)

I **GOT** it bad!   *   I **GOT** a break
(It controls me)   (I was lucky)

We've **GOT** company!   *   You've **GOT** crust!
(Someone is [coming] [watching])   (You are impudent!)

I **GOT** an earful   *   **GOT** to [go] [scoot]!
(I heard a lot)   (I must leave!)

G

178

He's **GOT** to go!   *   You've **GOT** your guts
(Get rid of him!)   (Your are impertinent)

I've **GOT** to hand it to you!   You've **GOT** to have heart!
([I congratulate you!]   (Courage; strength)
[You impress me!])

            *   He **GOT** it
You **GOT** it [!] [?]   (He was [killed] [wounded])
([You're correct!] [It's yours!]
[Do you understand?])   *   You **GOT** me!
            (I [am discovered!] [surrender!]
I **GOT** it [licked] [made]!   [don't know the answer])
(I [solved the problem]
[am successful])   *   **GOTCHA!**
            (I [beat] [captured] you!]
He's out of his **GOURD**   [understand what you are saying]
(He's crazy)   [found you are wrong])

HooseGOW   * It's a **GRAB** bag   * **GRAB** a bite
(Jail)   (It contains many things)   (A quick meal)

How does that **GRAB** you?   *   It's up for **GRABS**
(How do you react to that?)   (Anyone can [take] [win] it)

His saving **GRACE** is...   *   Make the **GRADE**
(His redeeming quality) is...)   (Succeed; qualify)

Take it with a **GRAIN** of salt * It goes against my **GRAIN**
(Be skeptical)   (It violates my nature)

GRAND   *   **GRAND**father him in
($ 1,000)   (Exempt him because of his prior status)

G

I **GRANT** that...　　　*　　　**GRAND**standing
(I concede that...)　　　　　(Trying hard to get attention)

Take it for **GRANTED**　　*　　I heard it through
(Assume it's true)　　　　　　the **GRAPEVINE**
　　　　　　　　　　　　　　(From rumors)

His comments were sour **GRAPES**
(He disparaged what　　*　**GRASPING** at straws
he couldn't have or do)　　(Desperate)

No **GRASS** grows under his feet　*　Gone to **GRASS**
(He keeps very busy)　　　　　　　　(Retired)

Knee high to a **GRASS**hopper　*　A **GRASS**-roots reaction
(Young and very small)　　　　(A local popular reaction)

A snake in the **GRASS**　*　It's **GRAVY**　*　A **GRAVY** train
(A treacherous person)　　(All profit)　(A source of profit)

My hair will turn **GRAY**　　　　*　　　**GREASE** him!
(It will distress me greatly)　　　　(Kill him!)

A [**GREASE** joint]　　　　　*　A **GREASE** monkey
　[**GREASY**] spoon　　　　　　　(A mechanic)
(Cheap restaurant with poor food)

　　　　　　　　　　　　*　**GREASE** his palms
GREASE the skids　　　　　　(Bribe him)
(Reduce the obstacles)

　　　　　　　　　　*　　　　　**GREASED**
...like **GREASED** lightning　　　(Drunk)
(Very fast)

G

180

He's slicker than
  a **GREASED** pig
(Slippery; too clever
  to be trusted)

* Going **GREAT** guns
(Progress is excellent)

* That's [just] **GREAT**!
(That's [awful!] [wonderful!])

No **GREAT** shakes
(Not exciting)

* **GREEN**[backs]
(Money)

He's [**GREEN** behind the ears]
  [a **GREEN**horn]
(Inexperienced)

* **GREEN**
  with envy
  (Jealous)

GREEN around the gills
(Nauseated)

* A **GREEN** light
(A sign to proceed)

It **GREW** legs
(It disappeared)

* On the **GRIDDLE**
([In trouble] [The focus of attention])

It will come to **GRIEF**
(It will fail)

* **GRILL** him
(Interrogate him)

He has an axe to **GRIND**
(He has his own agenda)

* Back to the [old] **GRIND**
(My regular work)

It's a **GRIND**
(Boring; tiresome)

* Keep your nose to the **GRIND**stone
(Stay busy)

Get a **GRIP** on yourself
(Gain control of yourself)

* I'll lose my **GRIP**
(My skill; talent)

Come to **GRIPS** with it
(Address it directly)

* **GROOVY**!
(Wonderful!)

* **GROSS**!
(Vulger!)

G

I'll **GROSS** out
(Eat to much)

*

Break new **GROUND**
(Innovate; pioneer)

He has his ear
 to the **GROUND**
(He keeps himself informed)

*

His feet are on the **GROUND**
(He is solid; sound)

It will never get off the **GROUND**
(It will never start)

*

On the **GROUND** floor
(At the beginning)

Hit the **GROUND**! [running!]
(Lie flat!] [Begin action at once!])

*

Give **GROUND**
(Compromise; retreat)

He mopped up the
 GROUND with me
(He beat me badly)

*

I don't know him from
a hole in the **GROUND**
(He's a stranger to me)

The **GROUND** rules
(Rules of conduct
 for a contest)

*

Don't plow old **GROUND**
(Don't repeat what has
been said or done before)

Hit the **GROUND** running!
(Begin action at once!)

*

Run it into the **GROUND**
(Destroy; ruin; weaken it)

Stand your **GROUND**!
(Stay firm; resolute!)

*

My old [stamping]
[stomping] **GROUND**
(My old neighborhood)

Go under**GROUND**
(Hide)

*

Do the **GROUND** work
(Prepare well)

You're **GROUNDED**!
(Your freedom is restricted)

*

We'll **GROW** the...
(Expand the...)

G

182

He'll **GROW** on you * No grass **GROWS** under his feet
(You will be attracted   (He keeps very busy)
to him over time)

* **GRUB** * **GRUB**stake
GRUBBIES (Food) (An investment
(Old clothes) to start an activity)

He's [a **GRUMP**] [**GRUMPY**] * **GRUNGY**
(A person of poor temper) (Dirty; filthy)

I was off [my] **GUARD** * You have another
(I wasn't alert) **GUESS** coming!
(You misjudged)

By **GUESS** and by golly
(In an unplanned way) * Be my **GUEST** * **GUFF**
(Take what you want) (Nonsense)

He's on a **GUILT** trip
(He blames himself * **GUILTY** as sin
for everything) (Very guilty)

Beating his **GUMS** * **GUM**shoe * Don't **GUM** it up!
(Talking uselessly) (A detective) (Don't ruin it!)

[Give it the **GUN!**] [**GUN** it!] * **GUN** for him!
(Start moving fast!) (Hunt for and attack him)

A hired **GUN** * He'll jump the **GUN**
(A mercenary) (Start too soon!)

A shot**GUN** marriage * **GUN**-shy
(A marriage by coercion) (Afraid; distrustful)

G

Ride shot**GUN** with...
(Accompany; protect...)

A smoking **GUN**
(Evidence directly linked
to a crime)

A son of a **GUN**
(A very unpleasant person)

Under the **GUN**
(Under great pressure)

He's **GUNNING** for you
(He wants to hurt you)

Going great **GUNS**
(Progress is excellent)

Stick to your **GUNS**
(Maintain your position)

A gloomy **GUS**
(A pessimist)

All **GUSSIED** up
(Dressed very elaborately)

Bust your **GUT**!
(Work very hard)

My **GUT** feeling is...
(My instinct is...)

GUT it out!
(Persevere!)

No **GUTS**
(No courage)

You've got your **GUTS**!
(You are impertinent)

Spill your **GUTS**!
(Reveal what you know!)

He'll split a **GUT**
(Become angry)

He's **GUTSY**
(Courageous)

The fall **GUY**
(The one blamed
punished)

One heck of a **GUY**
(A fine, likeable person)

An okay **GUY**
(A good, decent person)

A stand-up **GUY**
(A courageous; loyal person)

A wise **GUY**
(A sarcastic; bothersome person)

G

Chapter H

Kick the **HABIT**   *   **A HACK**
(Break your dependence on...)   (A person of modest skills
                                                      hired to do routine tasks)

I can't **HACK** it
(I can't do the job)   *   It will **HACK** him off
                                                            (Make him angry)

My **HACKLES** are up
(I'm angry)   * I **HAD** at him   * I've been **HAD**
                                 (Attacked him)   (Taken advantage of)

We **HAD** it out
(We has an argument)   *   I've **HAD** it [up to here!]
                                              ([I quit!] [I've lost all patience!])

I **HAIL** from...
(My home was in...   * It's a [bad] [good] **HAIR** day
                                      ([I have many problems today]
A **HAIR**brain idea   [Things are going well])
(Silly; without merit)

                                      *   By a **HAIR'S** breath
It will put **HAIR** on your chest   (By the smallest amount)
(Make you a man)

                                        *   It will curl your **HAIR**
I let my **HAIR** down   (Frighten you)
(I confided)

                              * Your **HAIR** will stand on end
He'll get into your **HAIR**   (You will be scared)
([You will be attracted to him]
[Annoy you])   * My **HAIR** will turn gray
                                            (It will distress me greatly)
I can't find hide nor **HAIR** of him
(He has disappeared)

                                                            H

I missed by a **HAIR**　　　　*　　It's a **HAIR**-raiser
(By a tiny amount)　　　　　　(It's [scary] [thrilling])

He'll tear his **HAIR**　　　　*　　He didn't turn a **HAIR**
(React with grief)　　　　(He showed no [concern] [interest])

Within a **HAIR**　　　　　*　　The fair-**HAIRED** boy
(Very close)　　　(The one who gets special treatment)

Don't split **HAIRS**　　　　*　　A **HAIRY** experience
(Argue over little details)　　(Thrilling but frightening)

HALE and hearty　　　　*　　It's not **HALF** bad
(Very healthy)　　　　　　(It's really good)

HALF-baked　　　　　*　　My better **HALF**
(Silly; unsound)　　　　　　(My wife)

Don't go off **HALF**-cocked　　*　　It's **HALF** gone
(Poorly prepared)　　　　(In very bad condition)

A **HALF**-hearted effort)　　*　　**HALF** in jest
(Done without enthusiasm)　　(Partly for fun)

I don't know the **HALF** of it　*　I have **HALF**-a-mind to...
(I don't have the full story)　　(I'm inclined to...)

What's the hoo-**HAH**?　　*　Don't fight city **HALL**
(The excitement)　　(Don't antagonize the powerful)

I don't do things by **HALVES**　　*　**HAM**-handed
(I do things with enthusiasm)　　(Clumsy)

H

186

We went at it   *   **HAMMING** it up
  HAMMER and tongs   (Being theatrical in
(We fought fiercely)   exaggerated ways)

My John **HANCOCK**   *   The back of my **HAND** to you
(Signature)   (I'm angry with you)

I know it like the   *   He's going to hell
  like the back of my **HAND**   in a **HAND**basket
(I'm completely familiar with it) (Going to ruin and fast)

Give him a big **HAND**   *   A bird in the **HAND**
(A lot of applause)   is worth two in the bush
               (A thing one has is more
[Close] At **HAND**   valuable than a thing promised)
(Near)

        *   A **HAND**-me-down
Learn [first] [second] **HAND**   (Something used before;
(From [your own]   not new)
  [other's] experience)

      *   I have a free **HAND**
[Give] [Lend] me a **HAND**   (Full authority to act)
(Help me)

      *   We work **HAND** in glove
They go **HAND** in **HAND**   (We are a team)
(Together)

      *   Go hat in **HAND**
I've got to **HAND** it to you!   (Beg; plead)
([I congratulate you!]
  [You impress me!])   *   I have it in **HAND**
                (Under control)

H

187

I [have] [keep] a **HAND** in
(I [am involved]
 [stay involved] in...)

*   **HAND** him his head
(Beat; overwhelm him)

*

A hired **HAND**
(A paid employee)

Don't lay a **HAND** on him!
(Don't touch him!)

*

Don't **HAND** me that line!
(I don't believe it!)

I live from **HAND** to mouth
(I'm very poor)

* Off **HAND**, I...
(My guess is that...)

* It was off-**HAND**
(Casual; unplanned)

It was off-**HAND**
(Casual; unplanned)

*

HAND it [off] to him
(Give him responsibility for it)

An old [China] **HAND**
(A person of long experience)

*

A **HAND**out
([Given without charge]
[Materials given as a
part of a briefing])

Out of **HAND**
(Beyond control)

*

Reject it out of **HAND**
(Totally and completely)

HAND it over!
(Surrender it!)

* I made money **HAND** over fist
(I made a lot of money easily)

He's a real **HAND**
(He's very experienced)

*

My right **HAND**
(A close helper)

It's second **HAND**
(It's already used)

* Don't [show] [tip] your **HAND**
(Reveal your intentions)

Sleight of **HAND**
(Deception; tricks)

H

Take a **HAND**
(Join; participate)

* Take him in **HAND**
(Control him)

Try your **HAND**
(Attempt to do it)

* He won't turn a **HAND**
(He won't [help] [work])

A **HAND** up
(Help given in a way
that promotes self-reliance)

* **HAND** him up!
(Surrender him!)

* Get the upper **HAND**
(Gain control)

I had the whip **HAND** over...
(I had control over...)

* Win her **HAND**
(Get her to marry you)

The **HAND**writing is on the wall
(The [situation is]
[facts are] clear)

* Even-**HANDED**
(Fair; impartial)

It was a left-**HANDED** way of...
(Indirect way of...)

* [Ham] [heavy]-**HANDED**
(Clumsy; insensitive)

High-**HANDED**
(Arbitrary)

* Catch him red-**HANDED**
(In the act of doing it)

I'm short-**HANDED**
(My staff is too small)

* It's under-**HANDED**
(Dishonest)

He's a glad **HANDER**
(His friendliness is not genuine)

* He's a **HANDFUL**
(He requires a lot of attention)

Fly off the **HANDLE**
(Get very angry)

* Get a **HANDLE** on it
([Control] [Understand] it)

H

HANDLE him with kid gloves
(Very [carefully] [tactfully])

It will change **HANDS**
(Possession will shift)

He'll eat out of my **HANDS**
(I'll control him)

He's in good **HANDS**
(He is cared for effectively)

If I lay **HANDS** on him,...
(If I [catch] [find] him,...)

I get **HANDS**-on
[experience] [training]
(I learn by actually
[doing] [using]...)

Sit on your **HANDS**
(Do nothing)

Take it into   *
your own **HANDS**
(Move to control it)

He'll throw up his **HANDS**
(Quit in frustration)

I wash my **HANDS** of it
(I'm through with it)

*   He beat
us **HANDS** down
(Easily)

*   I have clean **HANDS**
(I'm innocent)

*   My **HANDS** are full
(I'm very busy)

* Keep your **HANDS** off!
(Don't interfere!)

*   **HANDS**-off policy
(Don't get involved)

*   He's on my **HANDS**
(I'm responsible for him)

* He'll play into our **HANDS**
(Act in ways that
give us advantages)

Take it off my **HANDS**
(Take responsibility for it)

*   My **HANDS** are tied
(I have no choice)

* I have time on my **HANDS**
(I'm not busy)

H

He'll wring his **HANDS**
(Be very anxious; worried)

*

I'm **HANDY**
(I have useful skills)

It will come in **HANDY**
(Be very useful)

*

HANG around
(Don't go away)

HANG [around] [out] with...
(Associate with...)

*

HANG him out to dry
(Leave him defenseless, to suffer)

Get the **HANG** of it
(Understand how it works)

*

I don't give a **HANG**!
(I don't care!)

You can go **HANG**!
(I don't care about you
or what you think)

*

I'll **HANG** my hat on it
(Use it as a justification...)

*

I'll **HANG** my hat on it
(You can be certain of it)

HANG onto your hat!
(Careful, we're moving!)

*

Where I **HANG** my hat
(Where I [live] [work])

HANG here
(Stay here)

*

HANG a [left] [right]
(Turn [left] [right])

Let it **HANG**
(Delay action)

* **HANG** loose!
HANG the story on... (Relax; be patient!)
(Base the story on...)

* **HANG** on!
([Persevere!]
[Wait a minute!])

HANG one on
(Get drunk)

*

HANG out there
(Be there)

H

It's our **HANG**out   *   Let it all **HANG** out
(Our gathering place)   (Tell the whole truth)

He'll **HANG** you out   *   Give him more rope
([Severely criticize you]   and he'll **HANG** himself
[Leave you open to attack])   (Give him more discretion
and he will make mistakes)

HANG out your shingle
(Advertise your   * **HANG** [in there] [tough]!
skills/services)   (Persevere!)

We'll **HANG** together   *   **HANG** it up!
(Collaborate)   ([Stop it!] [Quit!])

A **HANG**-up   * He has a **HANG**-up about...
(A delay)   (A problem; special concerns about...)

Where do you **HANG**?   *   I'll be **HANGED**!
(Live)   (I'm amazed!)

I'll be **HANGED** if I will...!   *   A cliff**HANGER**
(I won't even consider it!)   (A close contest to the end)

Busier than a   *   **HANGING** by a whisker
one-armed paper**HANGER**   (Barely surviving)
(Extremely busy)

*   It will leave us **HANGING**
There **HANGS** the tale   (Without a decision)
(That's the key to the story)

*   I **HANKER** to...
I **HAPPENED** upon...   (I desire to...)
(Unexpectedly [came to...] [met...])

H

That's where it's **HAPPENING**
(Where the action; excitement is)

* **A HAPPY** camper
(A contented person)

HAPPY landing!
([A drinking toast]
[Have a good trip!])

* **HAPPY**-go-lucky fellow
(Carefree)

* Slap **HAPPY**
([Weary] [Reckless])

* Play **HARD**ball
(Be ruthless)

HARD by the...
(Very close to...)

*

HARD-[boiled] [nosed]
(Firm; tough)

HARD up for cash
(Without funds)

*

HARD to come by
(Rare)

It will go down **HARD**
(It will be difficult to accept)

* He has a **HARD** edge
(He is ruthless; tough)

HARD and fast rules
(Fixed; rigid rules)

* No **HARD** feelings
(No lasting anger)

A **HARD**-headed person
([A careful thinker]
[Stubborn person])

* He has a **HARD** heart
(He is cruel)

The school of **HARD** knocks
(Where one learns from
hard experience)

* I'm between a rock
and a **HARD** place
(I face hard choices)

I'm **HARD**-[pressed] [put] to...
(I find it difficult to...)

*

It's a **HARD** sell
(It's difficult to sell)

It's **HARD** to swallow
(Difficult to accept)

H

HARD to take!   *   Give him a **HARD** time
([Such a sacrifice!]   (Make trouble for him)
[It's wonderful!])

              *   He'll do **HARD** time
He **HARPS** about...   (Be jailed for a long time)
(Talks continuously about...)

            *   He's a **HAS**-been
He **HAS** it together   (He is no longer famous)
(He is well-organized; confident)

           *   I made a **HASH** of it
It's old **HASH**   (I ruined it)
(Out-of-date)

        * **HASH** it out   *   Settle his **HASH**
A **HASSLE**   (Talk to see if the   (Punish him)
(A lot of   problem can be resolved)
trouble)   *   **HASSLE** him
                     (Annoy; pester him)

Move post**HASTE**!
(Fast)   * At the drop of a **HAT** * Go **HAT** in hand
           (Very quickly)   (Beg; plead)
Go **HAT** in hand
(I'll beg; plead)   *   I'll hang my **HAT** on it
                  (I'm certain of it)
I'll hang my **HAT** on it
(Use it as a justification for...) * Where I hang my **HAT**
                 (Where I [live] [work])
[Hang] [Hold] onto your **HAT**!
([Careful!] [Calm yourself!]) * Keep it under your **HAT**
                (Don't tell anyone)
My **HAT** is off to you!
(I congratulate you)   *   Old **HAT**   * Pass the **HAT**
            (Out of fashion)   (Ask for funds)

H

Pull it out of your **HAT**   *   Put that in your **HAT**
(Do it magically)   (Note it)

He's talking through his **HAT**   *   Booby **HATCH**
(He is confused; wrong)   (An insane asylum)

Don't count your chickens   *   Down the **HATCH**!
  before they **HATCH**   ([A drinking toast]
(Never assume success   [Swallow your drink!])
  before it happens)

                     *   **HATCH** up a...
It went down the wrong **HATCH**   (Plan a...)
(I swallowed wrong and choked)

                    *   Bury the **HATCHET**
Over the long **HAUL**   (Make peace)
(Over a long period of time)

               *   **HAUL** out of here!
He's **HAULING**!   *   **HAVE** at it!   (Leave here!)
(Speeding)   ([Do it!] [Try it!])

                   *   I **HAVE** it bad
HAVE done with it   (It controls me)
([Stop] [End] it!)   * I **HAVE** a hand in...
         (I'm involved in...)   * **HAVE** a heart!
I **HAVE** him!   (Be kind!)
([Beaten] [Found] him!)

                *   Let's **HAVE** it!
Let him **HAVE** it!   ([Make your report!] [Speak!]
([Hurt] [Kill] him!)   [Say what you are thinking!])
(Allow him to keep it)

              *   I won't **HAVE** it!
I **HAVE** an out   (I won't tolerate it!)
([An alibi; excuse] [A way to escape])

                                        H

HAVE it out with him   *   HAVE a seat
(Confront him and try   (Sit down)
to resolve things)

                   *   I HAVE what it takes
..., or what HAVE you   (Spirit; stamina to
(Or, whatever else may be involved)   [survive] [win])

Give him what HAVE you!   *   HAWK it
([Criticize] [Punish] him!])   (Promote it)

He has HAWK eyes   *   A night HAWK
(Keen vision)   (A person often active
                         late at night)

It ain't HAY   *   In my HAY day
(Don't undervalue it)   (My best years)   * HIT the HAY!
                                  (Go to sleep)

Make HAY while the sun shines)
(Act when conditions   * It was a HAYmaker
are favorable)   (A blow that made him unconscious)

He'll go HAYwire   *   He'll hem and HAW
([Crazy] [Out of control])   (Speak slowly and pause)

The HEAD   *   In the back of my HEAD
(Toilet)   (In my deep memory)

He has [a big] [swell] HEAD   *   Bite his HEAD off!
[It will go to his HEAD]   (Severely criticize him!)
(He's conceited;
impressed with himself)   * He'll blab his HEAD off
                          (Talk too much)

H

[Air] [Block] [Bone] [Feather]
[Thick] **HEAD**
(Ignorant fool!)

*   A bull**HEAD**
(A stubborn person)

* Don't bury your **HEAD** in the sand
(Don't avoid the facts)

I'll bust my **HEAD**
(Work very hard)

*   It will come to a **HEAD**
(To a crisis)

Keep your **HEAD** down
(Don't [take chances] [be seen])

*   He'll eat [his] [my]
HEAD off
([Consume a lot of food]
[Severely criticize me])

Get it through your **HEAD**!
(Try to understand it)

He'll gets it into his **HEAD**
(Develop a firm idea/resolve)   * Give him his **HEAD**
(Allow him more authority)

He has [a good] [the] **HEAD** for it
([He is smart] [Well qualified])   * Hand him his **HEAD**!
(Beat; overwhelm him!)

A hard **HEAD**
([A careful thinker]
[A stubborn person])

* Go **HEAD** to [**HEAD**] [toe]
(Fight bitterly)

HEAD over heels
(Without reservation)

*   **HEAD** [for the hills!]
[on out!] [out!]
([Escape!] [Leave!])

Hold your **HEAD** [high!] [up!]
(Be proud)

*   Hold it over his **HEAD**
(Use it to intimidate him)

A hot **HEAD**
(A person with
a quick temper)

*   Where do I **HEAD** in?
(How do I approach the subject?)

H

Tell him where to   *   [Keep] [Don't lose]
HEAD [in] [off]   your **HEAD**!
(Tell him what you   ([Control yourself!]
think of him)   [Think carefully!])

[Knuckle] [Meat] [Pin] **HEAD**!   *   He has a level **HEAD**
(Dumb fool!)   (He is a calm; balanced thinker)

Don't mess with my **HEAD**! * It hits the nail on the **HEAD**
(Don't confuse me!)   (It's exactly right)

Off his **HEAD**   *   **HEAD** him off!   *   Meet it **HEAD** on
(Crazy)   (Intercept him!)   (Confront it)

It's on his **HEAD**   *   It's on its **HEAD**
(He is responsible)   (Disorganized; turned over)

[Out of his]   *   I'm over my **HEAD**
   [soft in the] **HEAD**   (Beyond my capacities/experience)
(Insane)

                             *   He has rocks in his **HEAD**
HEAD and shoulders above...   (He's crazy)
(Clearly superior)

                             *   Go soak your **HEAD**!
A sore**HEAD**   (I don't care what you say/do!)
(An angry; mean person)

                             *   I'll stand on my **HEAD**
He has a swell **HEAD**   (Make a great effort)
(He is conceited;
   impressed with himself)   *   I can't make **HEAD**
                                            nor tail of it
                                         (It's very confusing to me)

H

198

Tell him where   *   He's [tetched] [touched]
   to **HEAD** in!   in the **HEAD**
(Tell him what you think of him!)   (Insane)

Off the top of my **HEAD**   *   It will turn his **HEAD**
(My guess is that...)   (He'll be influenced by
                                   [flattery] [success])

Use your **HEAD**!
(Think carefully)   *   I know where my **HEAD** is
                           (I'm clear on what I am doing)

That's where my **HEAD** is
(That's what I am thinking)   *   Work your **HEAD** off
                                        (Very hard)

Play **HEADS** up ball!
(Be an alert; effective player)   *   Count **HEADS**
                                      (Estimate the vote)

We're at logger**HEADS**
(Unable to agree)   *   Let's put our **HEADS** together
                                      (Collaborate)

HEADS up!
(Be alert; careful)   *   A **HEADS**-up person
                             (An able, confident person)

I got a clean bill of **HEALTH**
([There are no charges against me]   *   Thanks a **HEAP**!
 [I'm in good condition])   ([I appreciate your help!]
                                      [That's not very helpful!])

A **HEAP** of trouble
(A lot of problems) * You **HEAR**? * I won't **HEAR** of it!
                    (Understand?)   (I won't consider it)

HEAR me out!
(Listen to me!)   *   I **HEAR** tell that...
                                     (I understand that...)

H

HEARD through the grapevine
(From rumors)

It's un**HEARD** of
(There are no precedents)

He's all **HEART**!
(He's very [stingy] [generous])

Bless your **HEART**!
([You are wonderful!]
[Thank you!])

He'll break your **HEART**
(Cause you much sadness)

To your **HEART'S** content
(As much as you want)

Eat your **HEART** out!
([Suffer!] [Be jealous of me!])

It does my **HEART** good
(It pleases me)

Have a **HEART**!
(Be kind)

My **HEART** is not in it
(I'm not enthusiastic)

* I **HEARD** it from
the horse's mouth
(From the person who
actually said it)

* The **HEART** of it is...
(Its central feature is...)

* He's a...at **HEART**
(In reality, he is a...)

* From [the bottom of] my **HEART**
(With great sincerity)

* A change of **HEART**
(A change of opinion; position)

* Cross my **HEART**,
hope to die
(What I said is true)

* He has a **HEART** of gold
(He is very generous)

* He has a [hard] [soft] **HEART**
(He is [cruel] [gentle/forgiving])

* You've got to have **HEART**
(Courage; strength)

* I know it by **HEART**
(I have memorized it)

H

A light **HEART**
(Free of concerns)

*

Don't lose **HEART**!
(Don't dispair!)

The **HEART** of the matter
(The central feature)

* My **HEART** is in my mouth
(I'm frightened)

He's a person after
my own **HEART**
(We share interests; values)

*

His **HEART** is in
the right place
(His motives are good)

A soft place in
my **HEART** for...
(A special affection for...)

* My **HEART** is set on it
(I want it very much)

*

Pull his **HEART** strings
(Appeal to his emotions)

Take **HEART**!
(Be encouraged; have hope)

*

Take it to **HEART**
(Consider it seriously)

Take the **HEART** out of it
(Remove its key feature)

* Take the **HEART** out of him
(Demoralize him)

A **HEART** to **HEART** talk
(A serious, confidential talk)

*

My **HEART** throb
(The one I love)

It warms my **HEART**
(Makes me feel good)

* I wear my **HEART** on my sleeve
(I don't hide my feelings)

Big-**HEARTED**
(Generous)

* Chicken-**HEARTED**   * Cold-**HEARTED**

Down-**HEARTED**
(Depressed; sad)

(Cowardly)

(Brutal; cruel)

H

A half-**HEARTED** effort
(Done without enthusiasm)

* Tender-**HEARTED**
(Caring; compassionate)

Hale and **HEARTY**
(Very healthy)

* The **HEAT**
(Police)

* The **HEAT** will break
(The temperature will drop)

A dead **HEAT**
(No one is winning yet)

*

Feel the **HEAT**
(The tension; pressure)

In the **HEAT** of...
(In the middle of...)

*

The **HEAT** is on
(The police are actively
hunting for...)

Pack **HEAT**
(Carry a gun)

*

Take the **HEAT**
(Accept responsibility and
its consequences)

Turn up the **HEAT**
(Apply more pressure)

* Get the **HEAVE**-ho
(Be fired)

I'm in [hog] [seventh] **HEAVEN**
(Things are wonderful for me)

* **HEAVEN** knows that...
(God knows that...)

No way in **HEAVEN**
(No chance at all)

* **HEAVY**!
(Profound)

* **HEAVY**-handed
(Clumsy; insensitive)

HEAVY lifting
(Hard work)

* One **HECK** of a guy
(A fine; likeable person)

Hot and **HEAVY**
(Vigorous)

* It gives me the **HEEBIE** jeebies
(Makes me uneasy)

Pay no **HEED**
(Don't be concerned)

H

202

Take **HEED!**   * **A HEEL**   * Well-**HEELED**
(Be careful!)   (An unprincipled person)   (Wealthy)

Cool my **HEELS**   * Dig in your **HEELS!**
(Wait a long time)   (Resist stubbornly)

Down at the **HEELS**   * Head over **HEELS**
(Destitute; poor)   (Without reservation)

Kick up your **HEELS!**   * On the **HEELS** of...
(Have a good time)   (Immediately after...)

[Show him] [Take to] your **HEELS!**   * **A HEIST**
([Get ahead of him] [Retreat!])   (A robbery)

The **HELL** of it is...   * All over **HELL'S** half acre
(The difficult truth is...)   (Everywhere)

Going like a [bat]   *   **HELL'S** bells!
 [shot] out of **HELL**   (An expression of
(Very fast)   amazement or frustration)

HELL-bent for leather   * All **HELL** will break loose
(Moving fast)   (It will become very exciting)

Not a chance in **HELL**   *   Cold as **HELL**
(No hope at all)   (Very cold)

A cold winter in **HELL**   * Come **HELL** or high water,...
(A very rare occasion)   (Despite many problems,...)

H

Not until **HELL** freezes over
(It will never happen)

To **HELL** and gone again
(Far away; a long distance)

Going to **HELL**
in a handbasket
(Going to ruin and fast)

It isn't worth a
hoot in **HELL**
(It has no value)

A **HELL** of an idea!
(A wonderful concept)

Like **HELL** I will!
(I won't do it!)

It's **HELL** on him
(He's suffering a lot)

It will be **HELL** to pay
(The result will be awful)

The **HELL** you say!
(Is that true?)

Scarce as **HELL**
(Very rare)

Scare the **HELL** out of him
(Frighten him)

I gave him unshirted **HELL**
(Severely criticized him)

It went to **HELL**
(It deteriorated badly)

That's a **HELLOVA** note!
(That's an awful development!)

HELLO?
(Are you listening?)

HELP out
(Give assistance)

HELP yourself
([Serve yourself]
[Take what you want])

HEM and haw
(Speak slowly and pause)

Madder than a wet **HEN**
(Very Angry)

Scarce as **HEN'S** teeth
(Rare)

My John **HENRY**
(My signature)

H

Ride **HERD** on...
(Check carefully...)

*   **HERE** [it] goes!
(It's moving; we're starting!)

Get out of **HERE**!
([I don't believe it!] [Go away!])

*   Hang **HERE**!
(Stay here!)

HERE'S [how] [looking at you]
(Drinking toasts)

* From **HERE** on out
(After now)

I'm out of **HERE**!
(Goodbye!)

* Neither **HERE** nor there
([Not clearly determined] [Irrelevant])

See **HERE**!
([Not so fast!] [How dare you!])

* A red **HERRING**
(A distraction to divert
attention from the real issue)

HET up
(Agitated; angry)

*   **HI** dude!
(A hello greeting)

I can't find **HIDE** nor hair of him
(He has disappeared)

* No skin off my **HIDE**
(It means nothing to me)

Tan his **HIDE**!
(Punish him!)

*   He **HIDES** his light
under a bushel
(He hides his abilities; deeds)

HIGH
([Drunk] [Excited by drugs])

* He's a **HIGH** brow
(He likes high quality)

HIGN and dry
(Isolated)

* His **HIGH** [falutin] [and mighty] ways
(He tries to act very important)

[Fly] [Ride] **HIGH**
(Very [stimulated] [successful])

H

In **HIGH** gear   *   **HIGH**handed
(Very active)   (Arbitrary)

Hold your head [**HIGH**!][up!]   *   Live **HIGH** off the hog
(Be proud!)   (Very luxuriously)

Get off your **HIGH** horse!   *   **HIGH** jinks
([Stop being aloof!]   (Pranks!)
[You overvalue yourself])
         *   Knee **HIGH** to a grasshopper
Search **HIGH** and low   (Young and very small)
(Everywhere)

Get off your **HIGH** and mighty!   *   **HIGH**-minded
(Your buttocks and act!)   (Guided by fine principles)

HIGH noon   * On a **HIGH**   * I'm **HIGH** on...
(The decisive time)   (Successful)   (I strongly favor...)

Keep a **HIGH** profile   *
(Stay active and visable)   A **HIGH** roller
          (One who gambles; spends
               a lot of money)
Give him the **HIGH** sign
(Send him a signal)   *
           HIGHtail it out!
           ([Escape!] [Run!])
It's **HIGH** time
(It's overdue] [it finally happened])   *   Come hell or
                 HIGH water
A **HIGH** wire act   (Despite many problems,...)
(Very risky)

     *   He's **HIGHER** than a kite
        (He's [on drugs] [drunk])

H

A **HIGHER**-up
(Of higher rank)

Not worth a **HILL** of beans!
(Worthless)

He's over the **HILL**
([An inactive older person]
[He's past his prime period])

Old as the **HILLS**
(Very old)

He's full of **HIMSELF**
(He has a large ego)

HIP hop
(An inner city youth culture)

He'll shoot from the **HIP**
(Act without thinking)

He'll have a **HISSY** fit
([Become very angry]
[Petulant])

He **HIT** below the belt
(He acted unfairly)

I **HIT** the bottle
(I got drunk)

* Take a **HIKE**!
([Go away!] [Leave!])

* He's gone down **HILL**
(Declined in [health] [status])

* Up **HILL** [all the way]
(Very difficult)

* Head for the **HILLS**!
(Escape!)

* Live life to the **HILT**
(To the fullest degree)

* **HIP**
([Stylish] [The latest fashion]
[Deliberately casual])

* He's a **HIRED** [gun] [hand]
(A [mercenary] [paid employee])

* He's **HISTORY**
(He [is dead] [has no future])

* A [smash] **HIT**
(A great success)

* **HIT** the books
(Start studying)

H

I **HIT** the [ceiling] [roof]   *   It **HIT** me cold
(Became angry)   (I was stunned; surprised)

HIT the [deck] [dirt]!   * **HIT** the [deck] [ground] running!
(Lay down flat)   (Begin action at once)

It **HIT** me between the eyes   *   It **HIT** the fan
(I saw it at once)   (Caused great excitement/trouble)

HIT the [hay] [sack]!   *   It **HIT** home with me
(Go to sleep!)   (It greatly impressed me)

HIT him where he lives   *   I **HIT** the jackpot
(Give him pain he feels)   ([I had great success]
[I won the prize])

A **HIT** list
(A group of [people] [things]   *   A **HIT** man
to be [destroyed] [removed])   (An executioner)

HIT me!   *   **HIT** or miss
(Deal me a card)   (Carelessly done)

It **HIT** the nail on the head   *   They **HIT** it off
(It was perfect)   (They related well)

He'll **HIT** on you   *   **HIT** on him!
([Try to charm; seduce you]   ([Attack him!]
[Give you special attention])   [Focus on him!])

I **HIT** on the idea   *   I **HIT** pay dirt
(I developed the idea)   (I found valuable
[information] [treasure])

H

Pinch **HIT** for...   * **HIT** the road!   * He **HIT** the skids
(Substitute for...)   (Leave!)   (He's on his way to ruin)

It will **HIT** the spot   * It **HIT** the street   * I **HIT** town at...
(It will be perfect)   (Became public)   (I arrived at...)

HIT him up for...   * I **HIT** the wrong note
(Ask him for...)   (I didn't communicate well)

It will go off without a **HITCH**   *   Get **HITCHED**
(Without problems)   (Married)

HITHER and yon   * A come **HITHER** look
(This way and that)   (A flirting look)

Get the heave-**HO**   *   **HOBNOB** with...
(Be fired)   (Associate with...)

A **HOBSON'S** choice   * I'm in **HOCK** up to my
(The option chosen when   [elbows] [eyeballs] [eyebrows]
no other option exists)   (I have large debts)

I'm in **HOG** heaven   * Live high off the **HOG**
(Things are wonderful for me)   (Very luxuriously)

He'll **HOG** it   *   **HOG**-tied
(He'll [not share] [keep control of] it)   (Helpless)
([Stay in front of the camera] [Eat a lot])
                                *   **HOG** wild
He'll go [at] [for] it whole **HOG**   (Crazy; out of control)
([Without reservation] [greedily])
(He'll be completely fooled)

H

209

HOGwash!   * HOKEY   * HOLD it against him
(Nonsense!)   (Crazy)   (Blame him)

HOLD back   *   Don't HOLD your breath
([Don't reveal what you know]   (It won't happen soon)
[Don't make a full effort])

                          * It doesn't HOLD a candle to...
I HOLD all the cards   (It's not equal to...)
(I have control)

                          * It will [catch] [take] HOLD
HOLD down a job   (Be accepted)
(Be employed)

                          *   HOLD [fast!] [the line!]
HOLD his feet to the fire   (Stay [steady!] [where you are!]
(Make sure he does   [Make no change])
  what is required)

                          * HOLD [things down] [the fort]
He'll HOLD forth   (Take care of things
(Give people his views)   while I am gone)

Get HOLD of yourself!   * HOLD onto your hat!
(Control yourself!)   ([Get ready for action!]
                                  [Be careful!])

HOLD your head [high!] [up!]
(Be proud!)   *   HOLD him to it
                             (Make him keep his promise)

HOLD your [horses!] [shirt!]
([Wait!] [I don't agree!])   * HOLD [it!] [everything!]
                                        (Wait!)

HOLD [the line!] [off!]
  [on!] [the phone!] [up!]   *   HOLD [them] off
([Wait!] [Stop!] [No retreat!]) (Delay [their advance])

H

It's on **HOLD**
(Action on it is suspended)

HOLD on to it
(Keep it)

I'll **HOLD** my own
([I'll compete effectively]
[Maintain my position])

He's a **HOLD** out
(He has not agreed yet)

He'll **HOLD** out on you
([Fail to support you]
[Not inform you fully])

HOLD out that...
(Promise that...)

HOLD it over his head
(Use it to intimidate him)

HOLD it over
([Continue it longer]
[Delay it])

HOLD the phone!
([Wait!] [Stop!])

HOLD your [peace!] [tongue!]
(Keep silent!)

I won't **HOLD** still for that!
(I won't [tolerate it!]
[remain quiet!])

Put a **HOLD** on it
(Stop action on it)

A toe **HOLD**
(A first step)

It doesn't **HOLD**
[true] [up] [water]
([It isn't supported by the facts]
[It's false])

What's the **HOLD** up?
(The delay)

A **HOLD** up
(A robbery)

Can he **HOLD** up?
(Endure)

HOLD up your end
(Meet your responsibilities)

I **HOLD** with you
(I agree with you)

I'm **HOLDING** the bag
(I'm blamed; held responsible)

H

No **HOLDS** barred
(No restrictions apply)

* My ace in the **HOLE**
(My secret advantage)

It's burning a **HOLE** in my pocket
(I feel compelled to use it)

* Button**HOLE** him
(Find and talk to him)

I don't know him from
a **HOLE** in the ground
(He's a stranger to me)

* I'm in the **HOLE**
(I'm losing money)

HOLE up there
(Hide; stay there)

* It's in the **HOLE**
(It's successful)

I don't give two
hoops and a **HOLLAR**
(It's not important to me)

* A **HOLE** in the wall
(A very small place)

* **HOLY** cow!
(An expression of amazement)

Have a **HOLY** fit
(Become very angry)

* I'm at **HOME** with it
(Comfortable with it)

Bring **HOME** the bacon
(Get [income] [results])

* Your chickens will
come **HOME** to roost
(You will have to deal
with problems you cause)

It's was close to **HOME**
(Near)

Wait until the cows come **HOME**
(For a very long time)

* Down **HOME**
(My family's home area)

Feel at **HOME**!
([Relax!] [Be comfortable!])

* I'm **HOME** free
(I face no more obstacles)

H

212

It hit **HOME** with me
(It greatly impressed me)

The take-**HOME** message is...
(The key point to remember)

On the **HOME** stretch
(Near the end)

The chief **HONCHO**
(The leader)

An **HONEST** John
(An honest man)

HONKER
(Nose)

* Do the **HONORS**
(The tasks to be done)

The [**HOO**-hah] [**HOOP**teedo]
(The agitation; excitement)

Around Robin **HOOD'S** barn
(A lengthy process)

He'll **HOOD**wink you
(Fool; mislead; take advantage of you)

HOOF it!
(Walk!)

By **HOOK** or crook
(By any means)

* He'll eat you out of
house and **HOME**
(Consume a lot of food)

* No one's **HOME**
(He's unresponsive)

* It's nothing to write
HOME about
(It's not very good)

* **HONEST** to goodness[!][?]
HONESTLY [!][?]
([It's really true!]
[Is it true?])

* **HOOCH**
(Liquor)

* A **HOOD**
(A crook)

* He's in his
second child**HOOD**
(He thinks he is a child)

* **HOOEY!**
(Nonsense!)

* There they were, on the **HOOF**
(Alive; in real life)

H

I'm [off] [on] the **HOOK**
([No longer responsible for...]
[liable] for...])

* It's on the **HOOK**
(It's status is indefinite)

* I did it on my own **HOOK**
(On my own initiative)

I went for it **HOOK**,
line, and sinker
(Without reservation)

* We'll **HOOK** up
(Meet)

It will **HOOK** you
(It will control you; become a habit)

* A **HOOKER**
(A prostitute)

Play **HOOKY**
([Be absent without permission]
[Take time off the job])

* **HOOKS**
(Hands)

Get your **HOOKS** on him
(Catch him)

* A lot of **HOOP**lah
(Noise; celebration)

I don't give two **HOOPS** and a hollar
(It's not important to me)

* **HOOSE**gow
(Courtroom; jail)

It's a **HOOT** * **HOOT** him down
(It's funny) (Ridicule him)

* I don't give a **HOOT**
(I don't care)

It isn't worth a **HOOT** [in hell]
(It has no value)

* Hip **HOP**
(An inner city culture)

HOP in! * **HOP** to it! * A **HOP**, skip, and a jump
(Get inside) (Start doing it!) (Very near)

I'm **HOPING** against **HOPE**
(The chances are small, but I hope)

* **HOPPED** up
(Excited [by a drug])

H

214

The place is **HOPPING**
(Busy; very active)

＊ **HOPPING** mad
(Very angry)

[Blow] [Toot] your own **HORN**
(Promote yourself)

＊ A green**HORN**
(An inexperienced person)

HORN in
(Intervene; meddle)

＊ I'm on the **HORN**
(Making a phone call)

I'll be **HORN**swaggled!
(An expression of amazement)

＊ He's a tin **HORN**
(False; not genuine)

Take the bull by the **HORNS**
(Accept the challenge and act)

＊ **HORNY**
(Sexually deprived)

Don't **HORSE** around!
(Don't be funny!)

＊ Don't put the cart
before the **HORSE**
(Don't get things out
of sequence)

A **HORSE** of another color
(A different situation)

Don't beat a dead **HORSE**
(It's useless; don't waste time)

＊ He's a dark **HORSE**
(A possible candidate of
unknown popular appeal)

HORSEfeathers!
(Nonsense!)

Get off your high **HORSE**!
([Stop being aloof!]
[You overvalue yourself])

＊ Don't look a gift
HORSE in the mouth
(Don't examine a
gift too closely)

＊ I heard it from the
HORSE'S mouth
(From the person who actually said it)

H

[Get] On your **HORSE**!　　　*　　　A **HORSE** race
([Leave!] [Move!] [Start!])　　　　(A close competition)

A war **HORSE**　　　*　　Hold your **HORSES**!
(A long time [fighter] [worker])　　([Wait!] [I don't agree!])

He'll **HOSE** you　　　*　　　　　　It's **HOT**
(Exploit; trick you)　　　([Popular] [Illegal; stolen])

HOT air　　　　　*　He'll blow **HOT** and cold
(Exaggerated talk)　　(His views are very changeable)

HOT [and bothered]　　　*　A **HOT** [button issue]
　[under the collar]　　　　　　　　　[ticket item]
(Very angry)　　(Very [lively] [sensitive] [popular])

Selling like **HOT** cakes　　*　**HOT** [diggity] dog!
(Very popular)　　　　　　　　　(Wonderful!)

HOT dog it　　　　*　　　**HOT** foot it [over]!
(Seek attention by　　　　　　(Get here quickly)
conspicuous actions)

　　　　　　　　　　*　　　He's **HOT** for...
A **HOT** head　　　(He wants very much to...)
(A person with a quick temper)

　　　　　　　　　　　*　　　**HOT** and heavy
A **HOT** line　　　　　　　　　(Vigorous)
(A special communication
system for quick messages)　*　In a **HOT** minute
　　　　　　　　　　　　　　　(Immediately)

A **HOT** potato
(Something very controversial)

H

HOT off the press
(Newly printed)

* A **HOT** prospect
(A probable buying customer)

In **HOT** pursuit
(Following closely behind)

* He's [red] **HOT**
([Angry]
[Performing superbly])

A **HOT** rod
(An auto altered for
higher speed or power)

* On the **HOT** seat
(Under great pressure)

A **HOT** shot
([An important person] [A star]
[A very talented person])

* Not so **HOT**
(Not very good)

* Strike while the iron is **HOT**
(Act when it is timely)

It's **HOT** stuff
([Stolen goods] [Very popular])

* I'm **HOT** to trot
(Ready to go; move)

I'm in **HOT** water
(In trouble)

* I have the **HOTS** for...
(I'm very attracted to...)

It's not so **HOTSY** totsy
(There are problems)

* It's **HOTTER** than blazes
(Very warm)

HOTTER than a
[two-dollar] pistol
(Very popular)

* I'm clean as a
HOUND'S tooth
(There is no
evidence against me)

At the eleventh **HOUR**
(The last moment)

In the small **HOURS**
(The first hours after midnight)

* ...like a **HOUSE** afire
(Very fast)

H

Bet the **HOUSE**　　*　The big **HOUSE**　*　Clean **HOUSE**
(Commit everthing)　　　(Prison)　　　(Make drastic changes)

Bring down the **HOUSE**　　　　　*　　In the dog**HOUSE**
(Thrill the audience)　　　　　　　　(In trouble)

He'll eat you out of **HOUSE** and home　*　On the **HOUSE**
(Consume a lot of food)　　　　　　　　(Free; no charge)

An out**HOUSE**　　　　　　　*　　A **HOUSE** warming
(Outdoor toilet)　　　　　　　(Celebration at new home)

No rough**HOUSING**　　　　　　*　I allowed as **HOW**…
(No [fighting] [vigorous play])　　(I admitted that…)

And **HOW**!　*　**HOW** be you?　*　**HOW** come?
([Yes!] [I agree!])　(How are you?)　　(Why?)

A fine **HOW**-do-you-do　*　**HOW** [goes it?] [is it going?]
(A bad development)　　　　([A form of greeting]
　　　　　　　　　　　　[What progress is being made?])

Here's **HOW**!
(A drinking toast)　　　　　　*　　　Know **HOW**
　　　　　　　　　　　　　　　(Experience)

HOW'S that?　*　A night to **HOWL**
(What did you say?)　　(To have a good time)

According to **HOYLE**　　*　What's the **HUB**-bub?
(According to the rules)　(Excitement; noise; uproar)

A **HUE** and cry　　　　　*　　　　**HUH**!
(A clamor)　　　([I'm puzzled] [What did you say?])

H

218

Uh **HUH**
([Yes] [I'm listening])

The **HULLA**baloo
(Excitement; noise; uproar)

Eat **HUMBLE** pie
(Be contrite; sorry)

It's a **HUM**dinger
(It's remarkable)

It's **HUMMING**
(Working smoothly)

Get **HUMMING**!
(Start moving!)

He can **HUMP** it!
(I don't care what he thinks)

I'm over the **HUMP**
(I have successfully
passed a critical point)

HUMPING along
(Moving but slowly)

I'm not one **HUNDRED** percent
(Not feeling well)

He's **HUNG** over
(He had too much liquor)

A **HUNG** jury
(Hopelessly divided)

He's [all] **HUNG** up [on it]
([He's stopped; delayed]
[It troubles him a lot])

HUNG out to dry
(Left defenseless to suffer)

He has a lean **HUNGRY** look
(He seems very ambitious)

A **HUNK**
(A male with a fine figure)

It's **HUNKY** dory
(Very satisfactory)

HUNKER down!
(Stay low!)

HURRY up!
(Move faster!)

Put a **HURT** on him!
(Make him suffer!)

H

I'm **HURTING**
(Suffering)

* I'm **HURTING** for...
(I want...very much)

It's **HUSH, HUSH**
(Secret)

* **HUSH** money
(Money paid to assure
someone's silence)

HUSH it up
(Keep it from becoming known)

* In the **HUSTLE**
and bustle of...
(In the rush of activity)

You are **HUSTLING** me
(Trying to [take adantage of me]
[sell me something])

* **HYPER**
(Very excited)

H

Chapter I

Break the **ICE**
(Get people to talk)

* It doesn't cut any **ICE** with me
(It has no importance to me)

ICE him!
(Kill him!)

* He's on **ICE**
(In jail)

* It's on **ICE**
(Delayed; suspended)

He's on thin **ICE**
(He doesn't have good
preparation or support)

* He has **ICE** in his veins
(He has no compassion)

* He gives away **ICE** in winter
(He gives worthless gifts)

It's the tip of the **ICEBERG**
([Much more of it is hidden]
[It's just the beginning])

* It's **ICING** on the cake
(A further value added)

It's **ICKY**!
(It's a mess; repulsive)

* **I.D.**
(Identification)

What's the [big] **IDEA**?
(Why are you doing that?)

* It's a [bright]
[hell of an] **IDEA**

Float the **IDEA** (An [imaginative] [wonderful] idea)
(See how people react to it)

* I have no **IDEA**
(I know nothing about it)

I hit on the **IDEA**
(Developed the idea)

* I was taken with the **IDEA**
(Impressed with it)

No **IF's**, and's, or but's
(Without reservations)

* **IGNORANCE** is bliss
(Sometimes it's better not to know)

I

ILL at ease   * He's the spitting **IMAGE** of...
(Awkward; uncomfortable)   (He closely resembles...)

By any stretch of **IMAGINATION**   * What is so all-fired
(No matter how you imagine it)   **IMPORTANT**?
                         (What is so critical?)

It's **IN**   * I'm all **IN**
(Very popular; stylish)   (Exhausted)   * We're **IN**!
                         (We did it; we succeeded)

Get your two cents **IN**!
(Make your comments)   *   Where do I come **IN**?
                    (What's my [role] [share]?)

The **IN**-crowd
(Those in positions of influence/power)   *   Do him **IN**
                   ([Foil] [Kill] him]!)

I'm done **IN**!
(I'm beaten!)   *   I'm **IN** [like Flynn]
                   (I'm well accepted)

I have it **IN** for him
(I plan to hurt; punish him)   *   What is **IN** it for him?
                (What will he gain from it?)

You are **IN** for...
(You can expect...)   *   I'm **IN** for it
                   (I'll be punished)

What are you **IN** for?
(What offense got you in jail?)   *   Get **IN** with...
              (Develop good relations with...)

Get **IN** on it
(Join; participate in it)   *   Go **IN** for...
               (Show interest in...)

IN the know about...
(Informed about...)

I

I let myself **IN** for it
(I didn't protect myself)

*

Let him **IN** on it
(Inform him about it)

I'm **IN** on it
(Involved with it)

*

I'm really **INTO** it
(Heavily involved with it)

INCHING along
(Going very slowly)

* It will add **INSULT** to **INJURY**
(Make things even worse)

When the **INK** dries
(When the details are settled)

* The **INS** and outs
(The details; the facts)

I know it **INSIDE** and out
(I know it very well)

* The **INSIDE** scoop
(The real story)

Give me a for **INSTANCE**
(An example)

* For all **INTENTS**
and purposes
(In every sense,...)

What gets **INTO** him?
(Why does he behave that way?)

*

I'm **INTO** it
(Concerned; involved)

Strike while the **IRON** is hot
(Act when it is most timely)

*

IRON it out!
(Resolve the issues)

Many **IRONS** in the fire
(Many projects underway)

*

As **IS**
(In its present condition)

What **IS** [it] with you [anyway]?
(What is your problem?)

* A [burning] [hot] **ISSUE**
(Very sensitive)

He doesn't have **IT**
(He lacks leadership, strength; personality)

I

So be **IT**!
([That's the way it will be!]
[All right!])

That's **IT**!
([That's final!] [I withdraw!])

I had an **ITCH** to do it
(A strong urge)

May you **ITCH** where you can't scratch!
(May you be in misery!)

I have **ITCHY** feet
(I'm restless)

*

Stay on **IT**!
(Keep dealing with it!)

*

Step on **IT**!
(Hurry!)

*

That's **IT** for us
([Our relationship is ended]
[That satisfies our concerns])

* I'm **ITCHING**
to do it
(I desire very much to do it)

*

A hot ticket **ITEM**
(Very popular)

I

Chapter J

JACK　＊　He's cracker **JACK**　＊　I hit the **JACK**pot
(Money)　　(Excellent)　　　　　(Won the prize)

JACK up prices　　　　＊　　　**JACK** of all trades
(Sharply increase prices)　　(One who has many skills)

I'm in a **JAM**　　　　＊　　　A calamity **JANE**
(In trouble)　　(One who sees the worst side of things)

JAWbone with them　　　＊　　　A flap **JAW**
(Talk; negotiate)　　(One who talks too much)

He has a glass **JAW**　　＊　　He likes to **JAW**
(He's vulnerable; easily hurt)　　(He talks a lot)

Don't give me that **JAZZ!**　　＊　　**JAZZY**
([Don't try to fool; mislead me]　([Wonderful] [Flashy])
[Don't give me false compliments])

　　　　　　　　　　　　＊　　It gives me the
A JERK　　　　　　　heebie **JEEBIES**
(A stupid; undesirable person)　　(Makes me uneasy)

Don't **JERK** me around!　　＊　　**JERK** his chain
(Don't tell me one　　　([Remind him of his situation]
　thing and mean another)　　[Bring him back to reality])

A knee-jerk **REACTION**　　＊　A **JERK**water town
(Automatic; predictable)　　(A small, remote place)

It's a tear**JERKER**   *   **JERRY**-built
(A very sad story)   (Poorly constructed)

Half in **JEST**   *   Cool your **JETS**!   *   **JIFFY**
(Partly in fun)   (Relax!)   (Toilet)

I'll be there in a **JIFFY**   *   The **JIG** is up
(Very soon)   ([I've been caught; discovered]
                           [It's over; finished])

That's [just] **JIM** dandy!
(That's [awful!] [wonderful!])   *   High **JINKS**
                                  (Pranks)

Don't **JIVE** me!
(Don't [lie to me!]   *   A bang-up **JOB**
[exaggerate!])   (Excellently done)

A cushy **JOB**   *   He'll [fall] [lie] down on the **JOB**
(An easy, well-paid job)   (He won't perform his duties)

Knock off the **JOB**   *   Nice **JOB**!   *   A put-up **JOB**
(Stop working)   (Well done!)   (The outcome is
                                arranged in advance)

Do a [royal] **JOB** on him
(Give him a lot of trouble)   *   A snow **JOB**
                          (A deceptive sales effort)

He'll stick you with the **JOB**
(Leave you to do it)   *   [An average] [A good] **JOE**
                       ([An ordinary] [likeable] person])

A smart **JOE**
(A bright person)   *   **JOHN**   *   My **JOHN** [Hancock]
                 (Toilet)   [Henry]
                             (My signature)

J

226

An honest **JOHN**
(An honest man)

＊ It's who struck **JOHN**
(A useless debate about
who hit first)

He's a **JOHNNY** come lately
(He has not been here long) ＊ He's **JOHNNY** on the spot
(Always there when necessary)

The **JOINT**
(Jail)

＊ [Blow] [Case] the **JOINT**!
([Leave the place!]
[Carefully examine the place])

It's a clip **JOINT**
(A place where prices
are too high)

＊ A grease **JOINT**
(A cheap restaurant with poor food)

The **JOINT** is jumping
(The place is very busy)

＊ His nose is out of **JOINT**
(He is alienated)

A **JOKER**
(A funny person)

＊ He is the butt of **JOKES**
(The jokes are about him)

He cracks **JOKES**
(Tells funny stories)

＊ My **JOLLIES**
(My pleasures)

Keep up with the **JONES**
(Maintain a similar living standard)

＊ A kill**JOY**
(A person who
suppresses enthusiasm)

A snap **JUDGMENT**
(Quick decision without much thought)

＊ The **JUG**
(Jail)

Let him stew in his own **JUICE**
(Suffer trouble he caused)

＊ Mumbo **JUMBO**
(Confused; garbled words)

J

I'll **JUMP** at the chance   * **JUMP** in with both feet
(Be eager to do it)   (Make a full commitment)

He'll **JUMP** the gun   *   **JUMP** him!
(Start too soon)   (Attack; surprise him)

I had the **JUMP** on him   * A hop, skip, and a **JUMP**
(I was ahead of him)   (Very near)

JUMP in the lake!   *   **JUMP** ship!
(I don't care what you [do] [say]!)   ([Desert!] [Quit!])

JUMP start it   * **JUMP** down his throat
(Apply special energy to start it)   (Criticize him!)

A puddle **JUMPER**   * The [joint] [place] is **JUMPING**
(A small airplane)   (It is very busy)

JUMPY   * A hung **JURY**   * A rigged **JURY**
(Nervous)   (Badly divided)   (It's decision is arranged
                               in advance)

The **JURY** is still out
(No decision yet)   *
                  JURY-rigged
       (A quick, temporary arrangement)

JUST around the corner
(Near)   * He'll get his **JUST** deserts
                   (What he deserves)

JUST a second!
(Wait, I want to think about it!)   *   **JUST** like that!
                   (Easily; quickly)

It doesn't do it **JUSTICE**
(It's not adequate; suitable)

J

Chapter K

KALE　　　　　*
(Money)

KAYO'D　　　　*
(Knocked unconscious)

KEEL over　　　*
(Collapse)

KEEP　　　　*
(Jail)

KEEP the ball rolling
(Keep things active; moving)

KEEP company with...
(Go socially with...)

KEEP it down!
(Be less noisy!)

KEEP it between your ears
(Don't tell it to anyone)

KEEP your end up
(Carry your share)

KEEP [an eye out]
　[your eyes peeled] for...
　([Look for] [Try to find]...)

He'll go **KA**-plooey
(Lose control of himself)

On an even **KEEL**
(In a steady way)

[Peachy] **KEEN!**
(Excellent; wonderful)

KEEP back!
(Keep your distance!)

*　**KEEP** your chin up!
(Have courage)

*　**KEEP** [your] cool!
(Stay calm!)

*　I'll earn my **KEEP**
(Support myself)

*　**KEEP** your ears
and eyes open
(Be alert)

*　**KEEP** [a close] [an]
eye on him
(Watch him carefully)

K

KEEP a straight face
(Remain serious; don't smile)

* **KEEP** your hand in
(Stay involved)

KEEP your hands off!
(Don't interfere!)

* **KEEP** it under your hat
(Don't tell anyone)

KEEP your [head]
[wits] [about you]
(Think carefully)

* **KEEP** your head down
(Don't [take chances] [be seen])

KEEP the lid on
(Keep things quiet;
under control)

* **KEEP** up with the Jones
(Maintain a similar living standard)

* **KEEP** your lid on!
(Wait; be patient!)

KEEP it under your lid
(Don't tell anyone)

* **KEEP** him in line
(Control him)

KEEP a stiff upper lip
(Be brave; resolute)

* **KEEP** mum
(Silent)

KEEP your nose clean
(Avoid trouble)

* **KEEP** you nose to grindstone
(Stay busy)

KEEP your nose out of it!
(Don't interfere)

* **KEEP** on! * **KEEP** him on
(Persevere!) (Continue his job)

KEEP plugging
(Keep trying)

* **KEEP** your shirt on!
(Be patient!)

KEEP tabs on him
(Watch him closely)

* It will **KEEP**
(It won't spoil)

K

230

KEEPER of the flame   *   For **KEEPS**
(Someone who keeps a cause alive)   (Forever)

Some **KETTLE** of fish   * A different **KETTLE** of fish
(A troubled situation)   (A very different situation)

Low **KEY**   *   Put the **KIBOSH** on it
(Calm; restrained)   (Reject; veto it)

It's [a **KICK**] [my **KICK**]   *   **KICK** it around
([A lot of fun]   (Consider it)
[An activity I enjoy])

I can't **KICK** the bug   *   **KICK** the bucket
(I'm still ill)   (Die)

KICK up your [feet] [heels]   *   I can't **KICK**
(Have a good time)   (I have no complaint)

*   **KICK** up a [fuss] [storm]
KICK the habit   (Create a disturbance)
(Break your dependence on...)

*   We'll all **KICK** in
It will **KICK** [in] [over]   (Jointly fund)
(Start functioning; working)

*   I'll lose my **KICK**
The **KICK**-off is...   (My energy; strength)
(The beginning is...)

* He's off on another **KICK**
My back will **KICK** out   (A new adventure; enterprise)
(Become painful)

* Get a **KICK** out of it * **KICK** him out!
(Enjoy it)   (Eject him!)

K

It [has quite] [packs] a **KICK**
(It is very strong; potent)

* Who is your side**KICK**?
(Your associate)

A **KICK** in the rear
(A major disappointment)

* **KICK** over the traces
([Escape; break loose]
[Radically change your life style])

It will **KICK** up
(Become troublesome)

* **KICK** him upstairs
(Promote him to possibly unwanted duties)

What's the **KICK**?
(The complaint)

* The **KICKER**
(The special factor)

I'm still **KICKING**
(I'm alive and well)

* It's been **KICKING** around for...
(It has a long history)

My **KICKS**...
(My fun; rewards)

* Handle him with **KID** gloves
(Very carefully; tactfully)

Don't **KID** me!
(Don't mislead me!)

* A **KID** thing
(It has special meaning
to young people)

No **KIDDING**?
([Are you joking?] [Is that so?])

* Just **KIDDING**
(Having fun; teasing)

He's [dead] on his **KIESTER**
(He's lazy; inactive; unmotivated)

* Dressed to **KILL**
(Very well dressed)

KILL him with kindness
(Treat him especially well)

* If looks could **KILL**,...
(His face showed his anger)

He's a **KILL**joy
(He suppresses enthusiasm)

He'll **KILL** me   *   You **KILL** me!
(Criticize me)   (You amaze me!)

It will **KILL** my numbers   *   Over**KILL**
(Ruin me competitively)   (More than needed)

We'll **KILL** them   *   **KILL** time
(Outplay; overwhelm them)   (Stall; wait)

He's a lady-**KILLER**   *   My dogs are **KILLING** me
(He attracts women)   (My feet hurt)

Make a **KILLING**   * Out of **KILTER**   * **KIND** of like…
(Gain much money) (Not functioning) (Somewhat like…)

Thank you **KINDLY**   * Kill him with **KINDNESS**
(Thank you very much)   (Treat him especially well)

KING'S English   * The **KING**pin   *   **KINKY**
(Proper English)   (The chief)   (Deviant)

KISS of death   *   **KISS** the dust
(An act that dooms something)   (Die)

KISS it [goodbye] [off]   *   **KISS** up to him
([Forget it] [Reject it]   (Falsely praise him)
[Consider it lost])

     *   **KISSER**   *   **KISSING** cousins
He's gone, **KIT**   (Face)   (Related but not by blood)
and caboodle
(He left with all   * Everything but the **KITCHEN** sink
his things)   (Nearly everything is included)

K

Go fly a **KITE**!
([Go away!]
[I don't what you say])

* He's higher than a **KITE**
(On drugs; drunk)

* **KLINK**
(Jail)

It's a **KLUNK**
(A poorly performing machine)

* It's on the **KLINK**
(It's broken)

*

A **KLUTZ**
(He's clumsy)

I have a **KNACK** for it
(I know how to do it)

* **KNEE** high to a grasshopper
(Young and very small)

KNEEjerk reaction
(Automatic; predictable)

*

It's the bee's **KNEES**!
(It's wonderful!)

He's weak in the **KNEES**
(He lacks courage; firmness)

*

My **KNIGHT** in
shining armor
(My hero)

[Back] [Tend] to your **KNITTING**
(Focus on your own affairs)

I **KNOCK** [about] [around] with...]
(Associate with...)

*

KNOCK back a glass
(Have a drink)

KNOCK his [block] [pants]
[socks] off!
([Hit him hard!] [Overwhelm him!])

* **KNOCK** him
[cockeyed] [cold] [for a loop]
[off his pins]
[sideways] [unconscious]
([Stun] [Surprise him]
[Make him lose all sensation])

KNOCK the daylights
out of him
(Make him lose all sensation)

KNOCK them dead!
(Captivate; thrill them)

K

KNOCK yourself [dead] [out]   *   Don't **KNOCK** it
(Make an extra effort)   (Don't criticize it)

A **KNOCK** down, drag out… * **KNOCK** him on his ear
(A furious argument; fight)   ([it] [Overwhelm him])

It will **KNOCK** [your eyes] [you] out! * **KNOCK** it off!
(You will be amazed!)   (Quit doing it!)

KNOCK [off] [out]…   *   It's a **KNOCK**-off
(Make; produce…)   (An unethical copy of something)

KNOCK [off the bank]   *   **KNOCK** off the…
  [over the place]   (Eat; use all of it)
  (Rob it)

                  *   **KNOCK** him off!
KNOCK off [the job] [work]   ([Defeat] [Kill] him!)
([Stop working] [Quit early])

                 *   It's a **KNOCKOUT**!
She's a **KNOCKOUT**!   (It's supurb!)
(A very beautiful lady)   (A fighter is unconscious)

KNOCK on wood!   * Opportunity **KNOCKS**
(A superstitious saying,   (Circumstances present
  to ward off evil or encourage   opportunities)
  good things to happen)

             * The school of hard **KNOCKS**
Take your **KNOCKS**   (Where one learns
(Your disappointments)   from hard experience)

Tie the **KNOT**   *   Tied up in **KNOTS**
(Get married)   (Stymied; unable to act)

K

I **KNOW** what I am about
(I have experience; skills)
(My purpose is clear)

*　　　　What do you
　　KNOW about that?
(An expression of amazement)

In the **KNOW** about...
(Informed about...)

* I don't **KNOW** him from
[Adam] [a hole in the ground]
(He is a stranger to me)

For all I **KNOW**,...
(I'm not sure, but it is possible)

* I **KNOW** it like the
back of my hand
(I'm completely
familiar with it)

He doesn't **KNOW** beans
(He knows nothing)

I **KNOW** it [cold]
[chapter and verse]
[by heart]
(I have memorized it)

* He doesn't **KNOW** whether
he's coming or going
(He is confused)

* I **KNOW** where you live
He doesn't **KNOW** which end is up　　(I understand
(Inexperienced; ignorant)　　　　your situation)

I don't **KNOW** the half of it
(I don't have the full story)

*　　I **KNOW** where
my head is at
(I'm clear on what I'm doing)

I **KNOW** [it] in my heart
(I feel it to be so)

*　　　　**KNOW**-how
(Experience; skills)

I'm in the **KNOW**
(I'm informed)

* I **KNOW** from nothing
(I'm uninformed)

I **KNOW** [my onions] [the ropes] [my stuff]
(I'm well-qualified)

K

236

I don't rightly **KNOW**
(I'm not sure)

* I **KNOW** [the score]
  [a thing or two]
  ([I know how things work]
  [I have experience])

What do you **KNOW**[!][?]
(An expression of surprise)

* I **KNOW** what's what
  (I'm informed)

Wouldn't you **KNOW**?
(It was predictable)

* Heaven **KNOWS** that...
  (God knows that...)

KNUCKLE down to business!
(Start work!)

* **KNUCKLE**head!
  (Fool!)

He'll **KNUCKLE** under
(Quit; surrender)

* I have white **KNUCKLES**
  (I'm scared)

It will **KONK** out
(Stop functioning)

* I'm **KONKED** out
  (Exhausted; not feeling well)

He's [a **KOOK**] [**KOOKY**]
(A strange; crazy person)

* **KOW**tow to...
  (Bow; defer to...)

The old **KROCK**
(An unpleasant older person)

K

Chapter L

Straight-**LACED**   *   He's a **[LADIES'** man]
(Very proper; conservative)   **[LADY**-killer]
        (He attracts women)

A foxy **LADY**
(Attractive; desirable)   *   **LAID** back
        (Reserved; relaxed)

What has been **LAID** on?
(What is [the agenda] [planned]?)   *   **LAID** up
        (Ill; incapacitated)

Jump in the **LAKE**!
(I don't care what you [do] [say]!)   *   I'm on the **LAM**
        (I fled; escaped)

In two shakes of a **LAMB'S** tail
(Very quickly)   *   A **LAME** brain
        (A stupid person)

It's between you, me, and the **LAMP** post
(It's a secret)   *   **LAMPS**
        (Eyes)

Living off the fat of the **LAND**
(Very rich)   *   That's the lay of the **LAND**
        (That describes the [place] [situation])

See how the **LAND** lies
(Investigate the situation)   *   Do a **LAND** office business
        (Be very busy)

LAND running
(Ready to act at once)   *   Happy **LANDING**!
        ([A drinking toast]

He travels in the fast **LANE**   [Have a good trip!])
([Aggressive, he has advanced quickly]
[He parties and spends a lot])

L

238

Body **LANGUAGE**
(Communication through
body and eye movement)

On the back of his **LAP**
(On his buttocks)

Living in the **LAP** of luxury
(Very expensively)

Get the **LARD** out!
(Move!)

By and **LARGE**,...
(Generally,...)

Down to a gnat's eye**LASH**
(To the last detail)

A tongue **LASHING**
(Severe criticism)

Dead **LAST**
(The final one)

On my **LAST** leg
(Near the end of my
[resources] [strength])

LAST minute
(Done quickly, late
in the process)

* Fighting **LANGUAGE**
(Provocative)

* You talk my **LANGUAGE**
(We think the same)

* It fell into my **LAP**
(I got it without effort)

* It's in my **LAP**
(I must decide)

* He'a at **LARGE**
(He hasn't been caught)

* Elected at **LARGE**
(By a vote of the
whole electorate)

* Thirty **LASHES**
with a wet noodle
(A meaningless punishment)

* I had the **LAST** laugh
(Finally, I had the advantage)

* At [long] **LAST**!
(Finally!)

* The **LAST** of the Mohicans
(The last of its kind)

L

Our **LAST** resort   * You have seen the **LAST** of me
(Our final option)   (You won't see me again)

It's the **LAST** straw   *   The **LAST** word in...
(No more will be tolerated) (Most advanced version of...)

LATCH onto it   *   The **LATCH** string is out
(Acquire it)   (Guests are welcome)

...of **LATE**   * He's a Johnny come **LATELY**
(Recently)   (He has not been here long)

[Catch] [See] you **LATER**!   *   The **LATEST** dope
(Goodbye!)   (Latest information)

In a **LATHER** * **LATRINE** * The **LAUGH** is on him
(Angry)   (Toilet)   (He fooled himself)

I had the last **LAUGH**   * I'll **LAUGH** up my sleeve
(Finally, I had the advantage) (Be privately amused)

I bust out **LAUGHING**   * You'll die **LAUGHING**
(Started laughing)   (Be very amused)

LAUNDRY list   * We take in each other's **LAUNDRY**
(Agenda)   (We [keep each other busy] [help each other])

LAY an egg   * **LAY** eyes on...   *   **LAY** out funds
(Fail)   (See; observe)   (Provide money)

Don't **LAY** a hand on him!   * If I **LAY** hands on him,...
(Don't touch him!)   (If I [catch] [find] him,...)

L

240

That's the **LAY** of the land   *   **LAY** down the law!
(That describes the   (Make clear what the rules are!)
  [place] [situation])

                          *   He'll **LAY** down his life
LAY you even money   (Sacrifice his life)
(Let's wager dollar for dollar)

                    *   **LAY** for him!
I'll **LAY** you odds that...   (Try to [catch] [surprise] him)
(Give you a betting advantage)

                          *   **LAY** off!
LAY it [off] on him   ([Back away!]
(Put the [blame]   [Stop your criticism!])
  [responsibility] on him)

                    *   **LAY** it on!
LAY it on him   ([Assign the work!]
(Tell him the story; the facts)   [Put pressure on ...])

LAY it on the line!   *   **LAY** him out
(Be very candid)   (Criticize; punish him)

LAY out for a while   *   **LAY** it to rest
(Be absent; away for a while)   ([Bury] [End] it)

LAY it on his shoulders   *   **LAY** it on thick
([Give him the responsibility]   (Exaggerate)
  [Blame him])

                    *   Don't **LAY** that trip on me!
It will go over   (Don't blame me!)
  like a **LEAD** balloon
(The response will be bad) * Don't **LEAD** with your chin
                               (Don't ask for trouble)

L

LEAD a dog's life
(A miserable existence)

* He'll **LEAD** him
around by the nose
(Control him)

He'll **LEAD** us on
([Lie to] [Deceive] us)

* Get the **LEAD** out!
(Hurry!)

It's a **LEAD** pipe cinch
(Very easy)

* He's one of our
LEADING lights
(One of our outstanding people)

A fig **LEAF**
(A thing used to conceal)

* Turn over a new **LEAF**
(Start fresh)

He's in the big **LEAGUES**
(In the top level of competition)

* **LEAK** the story
(Deliberately give
information prematurely)

He has a **LEAN** and hungry look
(He seems very ambitious)

LEAN on him!
([Coerce; put pressure on him]
[Depend upon his strength/help])

* I'm **LEANING** toward...
(I'm attracted to...)

* It grew by **LEAPS**
and bounds
(Very fast)

LEARN the [ABC's] [ropes]
(The fundamentals)

I'll **LEARN** [first] [second] hand
(From my [own] [others] experience)

* **LEARN** it by heart
(Memorize it)

At [the] **LEAST**,...
(The minimum)

* To say the **LEAST**,...
(The mimimum I could say)

L

242

Hell-bent for **LEATHER** * **LEAVE** it alone!
(Moving very fast) ([Say no more!] [Don't touch it!])

I have **LEAVE** to do it * It will **LEAVE** us hanging
(I have permission) (Without a decision)

LEAVE no stone unturned * It **LEAVES** me cold
(Do everything possible) (It does not interest me)

He has two left **FEET** * Out in **LEFT** field
(He is awkward; clumsy) (Remote; isolated)

It was a **LEFT**-handed way * Hang a **LEFT**!
(Indirect) (Turn left)

I look **LEFT**-legged * I'm **LEFT** out
(Awkward) (Rejected)

I'll get **LEFT**overs * It happens **LEFT** and right
(Things not needed by others) (Everywhere)

It cost and arm and **LEG** * Break a **LEG**!
(Very expensive) (Good luck!)

Get a **LEG** on! * I'm on my last **LEG**
(Hurry!) (Near the end of my resources; strength)

Pull his **LEG** * Shake a **LEG**! * I don't have a **LEG**
(Tease him) (Hurry!) to stand on
(My arguments
He'll talk an arm and **LEG** off you   are not supported)
(He won't stop talking)

L

He has a **LEG** up on us
(He is ahead of us)

* I look left-**LEGGED**
(Awkward)

It's **LEGIT** * It grew **LEGS** * I have my sea **LEGS**
(Genuine) (It disappeared) (I'm moving steadily again)

Stretch your **LEGS**
(Take a walk)

* I'm on **LEISURE** street
(I'm wealthy)

It's a **LEMON**
(It's faulty; worthless)

* **LEND** me a hand
(Help me)

I'll go to [any **LENGTH**]
[great **LENGTHS**]
(As far as necessary)

* We're on the same
wave **LENGTH**
(We think the same way)

LET me [alone] [be]!
(Don't bother me!)

* **LET** it alone!
([Don't get involved!]
[Don't say another word!])

LET well enough alone
(Don't disturb things)

* **LET** it be!
([Say nothing more about it!]
[Don't touch it!])

He **LET** us down
(He disappointed us)

* It was a **LET** down
(A disappointment)

LET him [down gently] [up easily]
([Spare him embarrassment]
[Don't be harsh with him])

* I **LET** [fly] [loose] with...
(I said...)

I **LET** it [get to] [throw] me
([Really bother] [Overwhelm] me)

* **LET** go!
(Relax!)

L

244

LET it go   *   I was **LET** go   *   I **LET** myself go
(Forget it)   (My job was ended)   ([Became shabby; fat]
                                        [Lost control of myself])

LET your hair down
(Confide)   *   **LET** it [hang] [ride]
                                     (Delay action)

LET it all hang out
(Tell the whole truth)   *   **LET** him have it!
                               ([Allow him to keep it]
LET'S have it!   [Hurt] [kill] him!])
([Make your report!] [Speak!]
[Say what you are thinking!])   *   **LET** him in on it
                              (Inform him about it)

I **LET** myself in for it
(I didn't protect myself)   *   **LET** him off
                  (Drop all charges against him)

Don't **LET** on that...
(Don't reveal that...)   *   **LET** her rip!
                  ([Start moving!] [Release it!])

LET off steam
(Yell to ease tension)   *   **LET** him stew [in his own juice]
                            ([Remain angry]
LET up!   *   No **LET** up   [Suffer troubles
(Relax!)   (No pause or slowing)   he made for himself])

That **LETS** me out   *   It's a dead **LETTER**
([I have lost]   (It's useless)
[I'll no longer be involved])
                          *   ,...to the **LETTER**
                              (In full detail)
It's a red-**LETTER** day
(A day to celebrate)   *   **LETTUCE**
                  (Money)

                                               L

Do your [dead] **LEVEL** best
(The best you can)

* He has a **LEVEL**-head
(He is a calm; balanced thinker)

On the **LEVEL**?
(Is it true?)

* He's on the **LEVEL**
(He can be trusted)

LEVEL with us!
(Tell the truth!)

* I'll **LICK** my chops
(Be impatient to enjoy...)

LICK [him!] [it!]
([Beat] [defeat] him!]
[Solve the problem])

* Not a **LICK**
(None at all)

* A **LICK** and a promise
(A quick; incomplete effort)

It's not worth a **LICK**
(It's useless)

LICKETY split
(Very quickly)

* I got it **LICKED**
(I solved the problem)

* Get in your **LICKS**
Take your **LICKS**
(Your defeats; disappoinments)
([Your punishing blows]
[Help shape the results])

I'll blow my **LID**
(Become very angry)

* Don't flip your **LID**!
(Don't get angry; excited!)

Keep the **LID** on
(Keep things quiet; under control)

* Keep your **LID** on!
(Wait; be patient!)

Keep it under your **LID**
(Tell no one)

* Put a **LID** on it
([Limit it!] [Keep it quiet!])

L

LET sleeping dogs lie
(Don't stir up old problems)

* He'll **LIE** down on the job
(He won't perform his duties)

LIE low!
(Hide!)

* You **LIE** like a rug
(You always tell lies)

I told a little white **LIE**
(A lie told to shield
someone from the truth)

* See how the land **LIES**
(Investigate the situation

It's big as **LIFE**
(Actual; real)

* You bet your **LIFE**!
(You can be sure of it)

I live a charmed **LIFE**
(I'm very lucky)

* My **LIFE** is an open book
(No mystery about it)

A fact of **LIFE**
(A reality)

* [It's] [I lead] a dog's **LIFE**
(A miserable existence)

For the **LIFE** of me,...
(I can't explain it)

* Tell him the facts of **LIFE**
(About sex)

Get up in **LIFE**
(Achieve higher rank;
more income)

* Get a **LIFE**!
([Do something meaningful!]
[Start living!] [Be realistic!])

Live **LIFE** to the hilt
(To the fullest degree)

* My **LIFE** is on the line
(I'm risking my life)

A low **LIFE**
(An undesirable person)

* He'll lay down his **LIFE**
(Sacrifice his life)

L

Not on your **LIFE**!
(Never!)

* He's the **LIFE** of the party
(He brings interest; excitement)

In the prime of **LIFE**
(In full vigor)

* I live the **LIFE** of Riley
(I live comfortably)

It has a short shelf **LIFE**
(It won't last long)

* He's the **LIFE** and soul of...
(The key person)

The time of my **LIFE**
(A wonderful experience)

* He didn't **LIFT** a finger
(He gave no help)

He gave me a **LIFT**
(He [raised my morale]
[gave me a ride])

* **LIFT** it
([Plagiarize] [Steal] it)

* The heavy **LIFTING**
(The hard work)

A bright **LIGHT**
(An outstanding person)

* A **LIGHT** will come on
(Understanding will develop)

It will come to **LIGHT**
(Be found; revealed)

* Trip the **LIGHT** fantastic
(Dance)

He has a **LIGHT** finger
(He is a thief)

* At first **LIGHT**   * Go **LIGHT** on him
A green **LIGHT**   (At dawn)   (Be gentle with him)
(A sign to proceed)

*.   A **LIGHT** heart
(Free of concerns)

He hides his **LIGHT**
under a bushel
(He hides his deeds;
abilities)

* A little **LIGHT** went on
(Suddenly, I [had an idea] [understood])

L

Make **LIGHT** of it   *   MoonLIGHT
(Give it no importance)   (Work on more than one job)

LIGHT out!   *   Out like a **LIGHT**
([Leave!] [Go quickly!])   ([Unconscious] [In deep sleep])

I see the **LIGHT**   *   Shed **LIGHT** on it
(I understand better now)   (Investigate; reveal it)

The spot**LIGHT** is on...   *   He's a **LIGHT**weight
(The attention is on...)   (He has little [brains] [influence])

There's **LIGHT** at the end of the tunnel * **LIGHTEN** up!
(We may have success soon)   (Relax!)

Like greased **LIGHTNING**   * He's a **LIGHTNING** rod
(Very fast)   (He attracts criticism)

The candidate hopes that   * He's one of our [bright]
  LIGHTNING will strike him   [leading] **LIGHTS**
(That he'll be the surprise choice) (An outstanding person)

[Knock] [Scare] the [living]   *   It's **LIGHTS** out
  day**LIGHTS** out of him!   ([Death]
([Overwhelm] [Scare] him!)   [Loss of consciousness])

[Punch] [Put] out his **LIGHTS**   *   How do you **LIKE**
(Make him unconscious)   them apples?
                                   (What is your reaction to...?)

...**LIKE** crazy
(...very much)   * **LIKE** [the dickens] [hell] I will!
                                         (I won't do it)

L

That's **LIKE** him
(That's his normal behavior)

Kind of **LIKE**...
(Somewhat like...)

That's more **LIKE** it!
(That's a better result)

He **LIKES** to jaw
(He talks a lot)

Go out on a **LIMB** for...
(Take risks for...)

That's the **LIMIT**!
(I can tolerate no more)

It's off **LIMITS**
([Access is prohibited]
[It's prohibited conduct])

The bottom **LINE** is...
(The final result is...)

Sign on the dotted **LINE**
(Indicate your approval)

Down the **LINE**
(In the future)

* Just **LIKE** that!
([Easily] [Quickly])

* Work **LIKE** mad!
(Very hard)

* In all **LIKELIHOOD**,...
(Probably,...)

* The **LIKES** of which I
have never seen
(I've seen nothing like it before)

* The sky is the **LIMIT**
(No restrictions)

* You are the **LIMIT**!
(You [are unusual!]
[test my patience!])

* Make a bee**LINE** for...
(Move straight to...)

* It would cross the **LINE**
(Be unacceptable behavior)

* Go down the **LINE** with it
(Support it all the way)

* Draw the **LINE** [in the sand]
(Establish a firm limit)

L

250

Drop me a **LINE**
(Write to me)

Don't [feed] [give] [hand]
   me that **LINE**!
(I don't believe it!)

I went for it hook, **LINE**,
   and sinker
(Without reservation)

A hot **LINE**
(A special communication
   line for quick messages)

Keep him in **LINE**
(Control him)

My life is on the **LINE**
(I'm risking my life)

I'm on the **LINE**
(Using the phone)

He's out of **LINE**
(Behaving badly)

The party **LINE**
(An agreed-upon position
   of a group/organization)

*   The end of the **LINE**
([The final point] [Death])

*   Walk a fine **LINE**
(Be [careful] [impartial])

*   Hold the **LINE**!
([Wait!] [Stop!]
[Make no change!] [Endure!]
[No retreat!])

*   In **LINE** for...
([In a position to receive...]
[Eligible for...])

*   Lay it on the **LINE**!
(Be very candid)

*   It's on **LINE**
(In active service)

*   It's on the **LINE**
(It's future will be decided)

*   **LINE** it out for him
(Make it clear to him)

*   The punch **LINE**
(The key point made)

*   Put yourself on the **LINE**
(Make a clear commitment)

L

SideLINE him
(Take him out of action)

* Toe the LINE!
(Obey the rules!)

Top of the LINE
(Highest cost and quality)

* What's his LINE?
([His type of work; profession]
[His agenda; objective])

What's the LINE?
(The theme; strategy)

Read between the LINES
(Look for hidden meanings)

* Don't wash our dirty
LINEN in public
(Don't discuss our
problems in public)

A ding-a-LING
(A fool)

* He's fine-LINING it
(Making careful distinctions)

It has a silver LINING
(An unexpected value)

* The LION'S share
(The biggest amount)

[Button] [Zip] your LIP!
[Don't give me LIP!]
[None of your LIP!]
([Silence!] [Say nothing!])

* He has a fat LIP
(He was hit in the mouth)

* Pay LIP service to it
(Note a problem but do
nothing about it)

Keep a stiff upper LIP
(Be brave and resolute)

* A hit LIST
(A group of [people] [things]
to be [killed] [removed])

My laundry LIST
(My agenda)

You are on my LIST!
(I'm very angry with you)

* LISTEN up!
(Listen carefully)

L

I **LIT** into him   * I **LIT** out   *   **LIT** up
(I attacked him)   (Left quickly)   (Drunk)

Pick of the **LITTER**   * A **LITTLE** bird told me
(First choice)   (I was told a secret)

I have **LITTLE** to go on   * A **LITTLE** light went on
(I lack information)   (Suddenly, I [had an idea] [understood])

I told a **LITTLE** white lie   * As I **LIVE** and breath!
(A lie told to shield someone from the truth)   (An expression of amazement)

I can **LIVE** with it   * I **LIVE** a charmed life
(I can accept it)   (I'm very lucky)

I **LIVE** a dog's life   * I'll **LIVE** it down
(A miserable existence)   (Overcome my embarrassment)

I **LIVE** hand-to-mouth   * I **LIVE** high off the hog
(I'm very poor)   (Very luxuriously)

I have a **LIVE** one   * **LIVE** it up!
(A probable customer)   (Enjoy it!)

LIVE up to it   * That's where I **LIVE**!
(Do what is required)   ([That affects me!] [I've had experience with that!])

I know where you **LIVE**   * A **LIVE** wire
(I understand your situation)   (A very active person)

L

Chicken-**LIVERED**
(Cowardly)

* Hit him where he **LIVES**
(Give him pain he feels)

They'll lay down their **LIVES**
(Sacrifice their lives)

* It's the **LIVING** end!
([I can't tolerate more!])
(The [greatest] [ultimate] thing!)

LIVING [in the lap of luxury]
[off the fat of the land]
(Rich and living expensively)

* He's **LIVING** in a
fool's paradise
(He's fooling himself;
acting naively)

Pardon me for **LIVING**!
(Excuse me for being alive!)

* He's several bricks
short of a **LOAD**
(He's not very smart)

Get a **LOAD** of that!
(Look at that!)

Take a **LOAD** off
(Sit down!)

* He's **LOADED** [for bear]
([Drunk] [Rich] [Carrying a great burden])

It's a **LOADED** question
(Designed to produce a
particular answer)

* I un**LOADED** on him
(I told him what I thought
[of him])

A free **LOADER**
(One who survives on gifts/
charity rather than work)

* Clear out, **LOCK**
stock, and barrel!
(Go and take your things!)

LOCK-up
(Jail)

* He'll **LOCK** up
(Refuse to cooperate)

* It's [all] **LOCKED** up
([Arranged] [Certain])

Gone **LOCO**
(Crazy)

*

He's like a bump on a **LOG**
(He is inactive; lazy)

L

Like falling off a **LOG**
(It's very easy to do)

I sleep like a **LOG**
(Very deeply)

We're at **LOGGER**heads
(We're unable to agree)

A **LOLLAPALUZZA!**
(Something remarkable)

Don't **LOLLEY**gag
(Don't waste time)

All by my **LONE**some
(It's me, alone)

A **LONE** wolf
(One who prefers to
act alone)

A **LONG** day coming
(Long delayed)

It's going to be a **LONG** day
(A day full of troubles)

I have **LONG** ears
(I have ways of
getting information)

He has a **LONG** face
(He looks sad)

[In] [Over] the **LONG**
[haul] [pull] [run]
(Over a long period of time)

At **LONG** last!
(Finally!)

It's **LONG** on...
(It has a lot of...)

The **LONG** and short of it is...
(In summary,...)

That's the **LONG** and short of it
(That tells the whole story)

It's a **LONG** shot
(It has only a small chance)

So **LONG!**
(Goodbye!)

Not by a **LONG** stretch
(Hardly any chance at all)

Over the **LONG** stretch
(For a long time)

My **LONG** suit is...
(My special strength is...)

L

LONG time no see!   * He's **LONG** in the tooth
(A greeting)   (He is very old)

LOOK after him   * **LOOK** alive!   * I **LOOK** bad
(Care for him)   (Be alert!)   (I have a poor image)

I **LOOK** like death on a cracker   * A dirty **LOOK**
(I look sick; troubled)   (An angry look)

He'll **LOOK** down   * Things will **LOOK**
[his nose at] [on] us   [down] [rosy] [up]
(Act superior to us)   (Conditions will [deteriorate]
                                       [improve])

I **LOOK** a fright
(I look horrible)   * Don't **LOOK** a gift
                                  horse in the mouth
LOOK for him to...   (Don't examine a gift
(Expect that he will...)   too carefully)

LOOK to him for...   * A come [hither] [on] **LOOK**
(He is responsible for...)   (A flirting look)

He has a lean hungry **LOOK**   * I don't have a **LOOK**-in
(He seems very ambitious)   (I have no chance)

LOOK into it   * **LOOK** out! [for...]
(Examine it)   ([Beware!] [Watch for...])

LOOK out for him   * I **LOOK** [poorly] [tough]
([Protect him]   (I'm in bad condition)
[Try to find him])

L

256

Take a **LOOK**-see
(Examine the situation)

LOOK sharp!
(Be alert!)

You **LOOK** [smart] [smashing]!
(You are [dressed very well]
[very attractive] [beautiful])

Don't **LOOK** for
for trouble
(Don't seek problems)

LOOK him up
(Try to find him)

LOOK up to him
(Respect him)

She's a **LOOKER**
(Very attractive)

Here's **LOOKING** at you!
(A drinking toast)

I'm on the outside
LOOKING in
(Unable to participate)

He's ratty **LOOKING**
(He appears shabby)

If **LOOKS** could kill
(His face showed his anger)

I'm **LOOKING** to...
(Planning to...)

[Knock] [Throw] him
for a **LOOP**
(Stun; surprise him)

The **LOONEY** bin
(A mental institution)

Out of the **LOOP**
(Not involved in the information
flow or decision process)

He's **LOOPED**
(Drunk)

LOOPY
(Crazy)

All hell will break **LOOSE**
(It will become exciting)

A **LOOSE** cannon
(An undisciplined;
unrestrained person)

LOOSE change
(A small amount of money)

L

He'll come **LOOSE** [at the seams]
(Become crazy)

* I'll cut **LOOSE**
([Leave] [Lose self-control])

At **LOOSE** ends
(Unemployed; drifting)

* Tie up **LOOSE** ends
(Settle all details)

Foot **LOOSE** and fancy free
([Without cares; troubles]
[Unattached romantically])

* He has a **LOOSE**
foot and no roof
(He is a wanderer)

I'm **LOOSE** as a goose
([I'm free] [Very supple]
[I have diarrhea])

* [Hang] [Stay] **LOOSE**!
([Be more patient; relax!]
[Goodbye!])

I let **LOOSE** with...
(I said...)

* He's on the **LOOSE**
(He's free; escaped)

Play fast and **LOOSE**
(Act without authority)

* He has a screw **LOOSE**
(He's crazy)

He has a **LOOSE** tongue
(He talks too much
and indiscreetly)

* **LOOSEN** up!   * **LOOT**
(Relax!)   (Money)

* Drunk as a **LORD**
(Very drunk)

I'll **LOSE** my [bounce]
[kick] [punch] [zip]
(My energy; strength)

* I'll **LOSE** my cookies
(Vomit)

Don't **LOSE** your [cool] [head]
(Keep control of yourself)

* I'll **LOSE** face
(Be embarrassed; humiliated)

L

I'll **LOSE** my grip
(My skills; talents)

*

Don't **LOSE** heart
(Don't despair)

He'll **LOSE** his [marbles] [mind]
(Become insane)

* You'll **LOSE** me
(I won't support you)

I'll **LOSE** out
([Be defeated] [Miss my chance])

* I'll **LOSE** my shirt
(Lose a lot of money)

Don't **LOSE** sight of...
(Don't neglect to consider...)

* Don't **LOSE** the thread
(Stay focused)

He'll **LOSE** his tongue
(He won't talk)

* **LOSE** by a whisker
(By a small amount)

A born **LOSER**
(One who usually fails)

* I'm **LOSING** it!
(Becoming [angry] [sluggish])

You're **LOSING** me!
(I no longer understand you)

* A **LOSING** streak
(A series of losses)

I'm **LOSING** my touch
(My skill)

* I'm at a **LOSS** to...
(I can't explain...)

A dead **LOSS**   * Make good the **LOSS**   * Get **LOST**!
(Worthless)   (Restore the loss)   (Go away!)

No love **LOST** between them
(They hate each other)

* **LOST** in the shuffle
(Forgotten; neglected)

LOST [in thought] [to the world]
([Preoccupied] [In deep sleep])

* A **LOT** on the ball
(Ability)

L

A **LOT** I care!
(I don't care!)

A **LOT** of [crud] [malarkey]!
(Lies; exaggerated talk)

It's all over the **LOT**
(It's not focused)

A **LOT** rides on it
(It's critical)

Don't **LOUSE** [it] up!
(Don't spoil it!)

For the **LOVE** of me,...
(I don't understand it)

LOWball it
(Show it with
a deceptively low cost)

A **LOW** down...
(A bad...)

A **LOW**life
(A bad person)

LOWER the boom on him
(Punish him)

* I have a **LOT** to chew on
(To consider)

* I have a **LOT** going for me
(I have many advantages)

* I have a **LOT** on my plate
(I'm very busy)

* Thanks a [whole] **LOT**!
([I appreciate your help]
[That's not very helpful!])

* Fall in **LOVE**
(Become infatuated with)

* No **LOVE** lost between them
(They hate each other)

* A **LOW** blow
(Unfair act)

* A **LOW** brow
(One who [is dull]
[prefers low quality])

* Search high and **LOW**
(Everywhere)

* **LOW** key
(Calm; restrained)

* Keep a **LOW** profile
(Avoid attention)

* I'm running **LOW**
(My stocks are down)

* Get your ears **LOWERED**
(Get a haircut)

Don't [crowd] [press] [push]
your **LUCK**
(Don't seek too much)

* Down on my **LUCK**
(Poor; without a job)

* The **LUCK** of the draw
(Random chance)

Dumb **LUCK**
(Entirely by chance)

I'm in **LUCK**
(By chance, things are
favorable to me)

* I'll **LUCK** out
(Things will develop
to my advantage)

My **LUCK** has run out
(My good fortune is gone)

* A stroke of **LUCK**
(An unexpected
favorable development)

Tough **LUCK**! * Try your **LUCK**
([Sorry!]   (Try to do it)
[I don't care!])

* Happy-go-**LUCKY**
(Carefree)

LUCKY stiff
(A fortunate person)

* [Filthy] **LUCRE**
(Money)

You big **LUG**!
(You dear person!)

* It's a **LULU**!
(It's extraordinary)

He can **LUMP** it
(I don't care what he thinks)

* Take your **LUMPS**
(Your disappointments)

He'll [eat] [steal] my **LUNCH**   * There's no free **LUNCH**
(Get credit for my ideas; work)   (Everything has a cost)

He's out to **LUNCH**
(He is not alert)

* Living in the lap of **LUXURY**
(Very expensively)

L

Chapter M

[Fighting] [Hopping]
[Whopping] **MAD**
(Very angry)

* [Raving] [Stark] [Staring] **MAD**
([Crazy] [Very unrealistic])

MADDER than a wet hen
(Very angry)

* Work like **MAD**
(Very hard)

* You **MADE** your bed, now lie in it
(Suffer the result
of your decision)

We've been **MADE**
([Betrayed] [Discovered])

I **MADE** [eyes] [a pass] at...
([Flirted with...]
[Tried to seduce...])

* I've got it **MADE**
(I'm successful)

* I **MADE** a hash of it
(I ruined it)

I **MADE** it to...
([Arrived at...] [Reached...])

* It **MADE** it with me
(It convinced me)

Show what you are **MADE** of
(Show your capacities;
courage; strengths)

* He's **MADE** up to...
(Disguised to look like...)

There's a method to his **MADNESS**
(He has a strategy)

* It's no **MAGIC** bullet
(No magic solution)

The **MAIN** drag
(The principal street)

* The **MAIN** man
(The boss)

My **MAIN** man
(My [boyfriend] [husband])

* **MAJOR** bucks
(A lot of money; high cost)

M

MAKE [away] [off] with it
(Steal; take it)

MAKE book on it
(It's certain)

MAKE my day!
(Do it, but you'll regret it!)

MAKE a dent on it
(Have an impact on it)

Don't **MAKE** a big [do]
[fuss] [production] about it
([Don't get agitated; excited]
[It's not important])

I **MAKE** ends meet
(I support myself)

MAKE it go
(Get it to function)

MAKE good the loss
(Restore the loss)

MAKE hay while the sun shines
(Act when conditions
are most favorable)

MAKE a [hit] [move] on him!
(Attack him!)

＊ I **MAKE** no bones about it
(I say what I mean)

＊ It's **MAKE** or break
(The decisive point)

＊ It will **MAKE** my day!
(Make me happy)

＊ **MAKE** do
([Be satisfied with
what you have] [Improvise])

＊ You **MAKE** a better
door than a window
(You're blocking my view)

＊ He'll **MAKE** [it]
[a go of it]
(He'll succeed)

＊ **MAKE** good
(Succeed)

＊ **MAKE** the grade
([Qualify] [Succeed])

＊ I can't **MAKE** head
or tail of it
(It is confusing to me)

M

MAKE it with them
(Gain their acceptance)

MAKE a [killing] [mint]
(Gain a lot of money)

MAKE a monkey out of him
(Make him look silly)

MAKE a move on him!
(Attack; threaten him!)

Don't **MAKE** too much of it
(Give it no importance)

MAKE nice to him
(Treat him with kindness)

MAKE off with it
(Steal; take it)

On the **MAKE**
([Very ambitious]
[Looking for a sexual conquest])

I can **MAKE** it out
(Judge its shape)

MAKE out with her
(Seduce her)

＊ He didn't **MAKE** it
(He didn't [arrive] [survive])

＊ **MAKE** light of it
(Give it no importance)

＊ **MAKE** the most of it
(Gain the most from it)

＊ **MAKE** a move on her
(Try to charm her)

＊ **MAKE** a name for...
(Gain a reputation for...)

＊ What do you **MAKE** of it?
(How do you assess it?)

＊ What do you **MAKE** on it?
(What is your profit?)

＊ **MAKE** [out] like you...
(Pretend that you...)

＊ **MAKE** out like a bandit
(Profit greatly)

＊ How did he **MAKE** out?
(What was the result for him?)

＊ I can't **MAKE** you out
(I don't understand you)

M

MAKE it out
([Prepare; complete it]
[Succeed in escaping])

* **MAKE** him out to be...
(Portray him to be...)

*

MAKE a [pass at] [play for] her
([Court] [Flirt with] her)

MAKE it on your own
(Succeed by your
own efforts)

Put the **MAKE** on him
([Ask] [Force] him to do it)

* **MAKE** it rain
(Bring in business)

MAKE it right * **MAKE** it so * **MAKE** yourself scarce
(Fix it)   (Do it)   ([Hide] [Don't be seen])

MAKE short work of it
(Do it quickly)

* **MAKE** [it snappy] [tracks]!
(Hurry!)

MAKE a splash * **MAKE** it tick * **MAKE** time for me
(Get attention)   (To function)   (Reserve time for me)

MAKE time with her
(Court her)

*

MAKE it up
([Invent a story]
[Recover the lost time])

MAKE it up to me
(Repay what you owe me)

* We'll **MAKE** up
(Be reconciled)

Don't **MAKE** waves
(Don't [try to change things]
[cause trouble!])

* A hay**MAKER**
(A blow that makes
one unconscious)

What **MAKES** him tick?
(What [is his essence?]
[explains his behavior?])

* It **MAKES** my mouth water
(I want it very much)

M

265

A lot of **MALARKEY**
([Exaggerated talk]
[Nonsense] [Lies])

*   A bag **MAN**
(One who carries money to
others for illegal purposes)

The [big] [main] [top] **MAN**
(The boss)

*   A con **MAN**
(A swindler)

Cool it **MAN**! * It's crazy **MAN**!
(Relax!)   (It's [silly] [wonderful]!)

*   I dig you **MAN**
(I [like]
[understand] you)

My [main] [old] **MAN**
(My [boyfriend] [husband])

*   He's Odd **MAN** out
(He different from the rest)

I'm my own **MAN**
(I'm [my own boss] [independent])

*   The point **MAN**
(The person who arrives first
to scout or prepare things)

The **MAN** on the street
(An ordinary person)

*   It's a **MAN'S** thing
(It has special meaning to men)

A yes-**MAN**
(One who agrees without
giving his real views)

* He's a dog in the **MANGER**
(He won't share with others)

Mind your **MANNERS**
(Use good manners)

*   In so **MANY** words,...
(In summary,...)

All over the **MAP**
([Everywhere] [Without focus])

* Put us on the **MAP**
(Make us well known)

He'll lose his **MARBLES**
(Become insane)

*   Tell it to the **MARINES**!
([I don't believe it!] [Nonsense!])

M

An easy **MARK**
(A gullible person)

* He's [off] [on] the **MARK**
(He is [wrong] [right])

[Buy up] [Corner] the **MARKET**
(Seek control of the supply)

* It's a drug on
the **MARKET**
(There is too much of it)

The **MARKET** fell off
(Prices went down)

* A shotgun **MARRIAGE**
(A marriage by coercion)

Go to the **MAT** with him
(Fight him fiercely)

* The whole shooting **MATCH**
([All of it] [Everything])

Fact of the **MATTER** is...
(The truth is...)

* The [heart] [root] of the **MATTER**
(Its central feature)

Take **MATTERS** into
your own hands
(Take control)

* **MAX**
(Maximum)

* I'll **MAX** out
(Reach my peak effort)

Be that as it **MAY**,...
([Anyway,...] [However,...])

*

The real **McCOY**
(It's genuine)

Out in **McGUILLICUDY'S** pasture
(Far away; remote)

* As for **ME**,...
(With regard to me,...)

That's **ME**!
(That's my
style; nature)

* A square **MEAL**
(A substantial meal)

* Our **MEAL** ticket
(Our financial
supporter)

I **MEAN** business!
(I'm serious; determined)

* He throws a **MEAN** punch
(He hits hard)

M

He has a **MEAN** streak
(At times he is very mean)

* By all **MEANS!**
([Yes!] [I agree!])

For good **MEASURE**
(In addition,...)

* Take his **MEASURE**
(Judge what he can do)

MEASURE up!
(Meet requirements)

* I'm dead **MEAT**
(I'm doomed)

* **MEAT**head!
(Dumb fool!)

The **MEAT** of it
(The core of it)

* It's my **MEAT**
(It's perfect for me)

Get a dose of
your own **MEDICINE**
(The treatment
you give others)

* Take your **MEDICINE**
(Your earned punishment)

* **MEET** it head on!
(Confront it!)

A face-to-face **MEETING**
(A direct encounter)

* There's more than
MEETS the eye
(Part is hidden)

Where the rubber **MEETS** the road
(Where the real test occurs)

* **MELLOW** out!
(Calm yourself!)

It's a **MEN'S** thing
(It has special meaning to men)

* I have a **MENTAL** block on
(I can never remember...)

It's the cat's **MEOW!**
(It's wonderful!)

* Don't **MESS** [around] with...
(Don't [get involved...]
[touch it]!)

Don't **MESS** around!
(Act quickly!)

M

Don't **MESS** with [me] [my head]!   * It's a **MESS** of...
(Don't annoy; bother me!)   (A lot of...)

Don't **MESS** up!   *   Get the **MESSAGE**?
(Don't make errors!)   (Do you understand?)

The take-home **MESSAGE** is...   * It's **MESSING** [you]
(The key point to remember is...)   [your mind]
                          (It's really bothering you)

There's **METHOD** to his madness
(He has a strategy)   * Slip him a **MICKEY** [Finn]
                          (A drugged drink)

That's my **MIDDLE** name
(That's what I do best)   * In the **MIDDLE** of nowhere
                          (An isolated; remote place)

A **MIDDLE** of the roader
(One who avoids extremes)   *   Play it straight
                                 down the **MIDDLE**
Fair to **MIDDLING**   (Don't take risks)
(Just satisfactory)

                     *   Burn the **MID**night oil
It's **MIGHTY** [fine] [good] [strong]   (Work late at night)
(It's excellent)

                  *   Get off your high
His high and **MIGHTY** ways   and **MIGHTY**!
(He tries to seem very important)   (Get off your
                          buttocks and act!)

Not by a country **MILE**
(Not even close)   * Go the second **MILE**
                          (Do more than expected)

Get **MILEAGE** from...
(Benefit from...)

M

MILK it
(Exploit it)

* Don't cry over spilled **MILK**
(Don't grieve about what can't be undone)

A gin **MILL**
(A saloon)

* Run of the **MILL**
(Very common)

I've been through the **MILL**
(I have a lot of experience)

* Thanks a **MILLION**!
([I appreciate your help!]
[That's not very helpful!])

A **MILL**stone around his neck
(A troublesome burden)

* It will blow your **MIND**
(Amaze; stun you)

MIND-boggling
(Beyond understanding)

* He'll change his **MIND**
(Change his views)

I have [half-a-**MIND**
(I'm inclined to...)

* [In] [To] my **MIND**
(The way I view it...)

He'll lose his **MIND**
(Become insane)

* It's messing your **MIND**
(It's really bothering you)

He has a narrow **MIND**
(He is biased; prejudiced)

* Never **MIND**
(Forget it)

If your of a **MIND**,...
(If you wish,...)

* It's on my **MIND**
(I'm thinking about it)

He's [out of his]
[not in his right] **MIND**
(He's insane)

* **MIND** your P's and Q's
(Use good manners)

M

Don't [pay him much **MIND**] [**MIND** him]   * I gave him
(Give him little attention)   a piece of my **MIND**
                                                 (I told him what I thought)

Put your **MIND** to it
(Focus on it)   *   Speak your **MIND**
                                        (Say what you are thinking)

He has a steel trap **MIND**
(He is rigid)   *   Take it to **MIND**
                                             (Note; remember it)

If I take a **MIND** to...
(If I decide to...)   *   Turn it over in your **MIND**
                                             (Consider it)

He has a one-track **MIND**
(He thinks of only one thing)   *   **MIND** you,...
                                                  (I emphasize,...)

What's on your **MIND**?
(What are you thinking?)   *   High-**MINDED**
                                        (Guided by fine principles)

Simple-**MINDED**
([Foolish] [Unsophisticated])   * I'm **MINDING** the store
                                                 (I'm in charge?)

I'm of two **MINDS**
(I see two alternatives)   *   It's a gold **MINE**
                                        (A very profitable activity)

Back to the salt **MINE**
(Back to the job)   *   It's in **MINT** condition
                                                  (It's new)

Make a **MINT**   * Big as a **MINUTE**
(A lot of money)   (Tiny)   * In a hot **MINUTE**
                                            (Immediately)

Last **MINUTE**
(Done quickly; late in the process)

M

Up to the **MINUTE**
(Current; fresh)

* Wait a **MINUTE**!
(Wait [, I'm not sure!]
[briefly!])

Smoke and **MIRRORS**
(False display to
disguise something)

* He didn't **MISS** a beat
(He never hesitated or paused)

He doesn't **MISS** a [bet] [trick]
(He's alert to opportunities

* I'll **MISS** [the bet;
boat; bus] [out on it]
(Lose a good opportunity)

Hit or **MISS**
(Carelessly done)

* A near **MISS**
(Very close)

I **MISSED** it by a hair
(By a tiny amount)

* I'm from **MISSOURI**
(I'm skeptical)

A **MITE**...
(A bit...; a little...)

* It's a **MIX** up
(Things are confused)

MIX it up
(Argue; fight)

* It's a **MIXED** bag
(It's good and bad)

I'm **MIXED** up [with...]
([Involved with...]
[Confused] [Troubled])

* Last of the **MOHICANS**
(The last of its kind)

* **MOM**
(Mother)

* **MOM** and pop store
(Small, family-owned)

Spur of the **MOMENT**
(Suddenly)

* My **MOMENT** in the sun
(My brief time of publicity)

He's a **MONDAY**
morning quarterback
(He gives advice <u>after</u> decisions are made)

M

272

It's **MONEY** in the bank
(It's success is certain)

* [Bet] [Lay] you even **MONEY**
(Let's wager dollar for dollar)

He has **MONEY** to burn
(He's wealthy)

* Cash **MONEY**
(Actual money)

Let's see the color of your **MONEY**
(Show me the money)

* Come into **MONEY**
([Get] [Inherit] money)

Easy **MONEY**
(Simple to obtain)

* For my **MONEY**,...
(As I see it,...)

I make good **MONEY**
(I'm well paid)

* I make **MONEY** hand
over fist
(Easily and in large amounts)

Hush **MONEY**
(Money paid to ensure
someone's silence)

* He's [in] [out of] the **MONEY**
(He [won a leading position] [is rich])
(He lost)

My **MONEY** is on...
(My choice is...)

* It's on the **MONEY**
(It's correct; on target)

Pin **MONEY**
(A small amount of money)

* Put your **MONEY** where
your mouth is
(Prove you mean what you say)

Give him a run for his **MONEY**
(Compete vigorously with him)

* **MONEY** talks
(Money gives one power)

Don't **MONKEY** around!
(Don't [be funny] [waste time])

* The **MONKEY** is
on my back
(It's my responsibility)

No **MONKEY** [business] [shines]   * A grease **MONKEY**
(No foolishness; tricks)   (A mechanic)

Make a **MONKEY** out of him   *   It's a **MONKEY**
(Make him look silly)   wrench in our affairs
                                                (It complicates; spoils things)
Not in a **MONTH** of Sundays!
(It will never be!)   * A **MOOCHER**   * **MOOLA**
                                     (A beggar)   (Money)

Once in a blue **MOON**
(Very rare)   *   **MOONING**
                           (Deliberately exposing one's buttocks)
He's **MOONING** over...
(In a reverie about...)   *   Moon**LIGHT**
                                  (Work on more than one job)

MOP up
(Get it all done)   * He **MOPPED** up the ground with me
                                    (He beat me badly)

That's **MORE** like it
(It's much better)   *   What's **MORE**,...
                                                    (In addition,...)

A Monday **MORNING** quarterback
(He gives advice <u>after</u>   *   **MOSEY** [on] down
decisions are made)   (Go to...)

Make the **MOST** of it   * For the **MOST** part,...
(Gain the greatest   (Generally,...)
advantage from it)

                                      * He's tied to his **MOTHER'S**
The **MOTOR** kicked in   apron strings
(Started functioning)   (Dependent upon his mother)

M

A **MOTOR** mouth   * A **MOUNTAIN**-top experience
 (A person who keeps talking)   (A remarkable experience)

Cat and **MOUSE** game   * Poor as a church **MOUSE**
 (A contest of pursuit vs. escape)   (Very poor)

Build a better **MOUSE**trap   * Bad**MOUTH** him
 (Improve the product)   (Say bad things about him)

[Big] [Smart] **MOUTH**!   * Blabber**MOUTH**!
 (A negative comment to a   (You talk too much
  loud-talking, obnoxious person)   and carelessly)

Down in the **MOUTH**   * I'm having trouble
 (Dejected; sad)   fixing my **MOUTH**
    (Trying to decide what to say)

I put my foot in my **MOUTH**
 (I said the wrong thing)   * I live hand to **MOUTH**
    (I'm very poor)

My heart is in my **MOUTH**
 (I'm frightened)   * I heard it from the horse's **MOUTH**
    (From the person who actually said it)

Don't look a gift horse
 in the **MOUTH**   * Put your money where
 (Don't examine a gift too closely)   your **MOUTH** is
    (Prove you mean what you say)

A motor **MOUTH**
 (A person who keeps talking)   * Don't **MOUTH** off!
    (Keep silent!)

He will [run off at the]
 [run his] **MOUTH**   * He was born with a silver
 [shoot his **MOUTH** off]   spoon in his **MOUTH**
 (Talk too much)   (His family is rich)

M

275

It leaves a bad taste   *   It makes my **MOUTH** water
   in my **MOUTH**   (I want it very much)
(It bothers; troubles me)

Spread by word of **MOUTH**   *   You took the words
(By each person telling others)   out of my **MOUTH**
           (You said what I intended to say)
You said a **MOUTHFUL**
([I agree] [You spoke wisely])   *   **MOVE** in on him
           ([Compete with him]
MOVE on!   *   Get a **MOVE** on!   [Attack; threaten him!])
(Don't stay here!)   (Hurry!)
          * [Make] [Put] a **MOVE** on him!
Make a **MOVE** on her   (Attack; threaten him)
(Try to charm her)

         *   **MOVE** your tail!
A **MOVER** and shaker   (Hurry!)
(One who has power and uses it)

      *   He has good **MOVES**
He has **MOXIE**   (He manages himself well)
(A lot of nerve)

    * It's a bit **MUCH**   * **MUCH** in evidence
MUCH obliged!   (Excessive)   (Prominent)
(Thanks!)

    * You're too **MUCH**!   * A **MUCKETYMUCK**
   (You are really unusual!)   (A very important person)

Here's **MUD** in your eye!   *   His name is **MUD**
(A drinking toast)   (He is very unpopular)

He's a stick in the **MUD**   *   He'll **MUFF** it
(He [destroys enthusiasm]   (Lose his opportunity)
[opposes change])

M

MUG   *   He's a MUG   *   They will MUG him
(A face)   (An evil person)   (Beat and rob him)

MUG him   *   A MUG shot
(Photograph him   (A police picture of
for criminal files)   a jailed person)

He's MUGGING it   *   Keep MUM
(Making funny faces)   (Silent)

MUM'S the word   *   MUMBO jumbo
(Stay silent)   (Confused; garbled words)

It's MURDER   * He gets away with MURDER
(It's very bad; difficult)   (He escapes punishment
                         for his misdeeds)

It's MUSIC to my ears
(It makes me happy)   *   Face the MUSIC!
                     (Confront realities)

He has no MUSCLE
(He has no influence;   * Your father's MUSTACHE!
lacks power; is weak)   (Nonsense!)

He can't cut the MUSTARD   * It won't pass MUSTER
(He can't do the job)   (It's not acceptable)

I'm beside MYSELF   * I'm pinching MYSELF
(Very anxious)   (Making sure my
                   experience is real)

M

Chapter N

NAH!
(No!)

*

The last **NAIL** in the coffin
(The thing that ended it)

Deader than a door**NAIL**
(Very dead)

*

NAIL him down
(Get a firm agreement)

It hit the **NAIL** on the head!
(It's perfect!)

*

NAIL it!
(Get it done!)

A thumb**NAIL** sketch
(A brief description)

*

Fight tooth and **NAIL**
(Fiercely)

He's tough as **NAILS**
([Very strong] [Enduring])

*

He's a **NAMBY**pamby
(He is weak; indecisive)

The **NAME** of the game is...
(It's character; purpose is...)

*

My good **NAME**
(My reputation)

You **NAME** it
(..., and everything else)

*

Make a **NAME** for yourself
(Gain a reputation)

That's my middle **NAME**
(That [is what I do best]
[describes me exactly])

*

His **NAME** is mud
(He is very unpopular)

*

NAME your poison
(Choose your drink)

I had a **NARROW** escape
(I [was almost caught]
[barely survived])

*

He has a **NARROW** mind
(He is biased; prejudiced)

On the straight and **NARROW**
(Operating honestly)

278

NARY a...   * He's a **NASTY** piece of work
(Not even one...)   (He's a bad person)

NATCH!   * He's a **NATURAL** for... * Do what comes
(Naturally!)   (He is perfect for...)   **NATURALLY**
                                        (By habit; instinct)

I need to commune with **NATURE**
(Go to the toilet)   * It's second **NATURE** with me
                               (I act by habit; instinct)

In the **NATURE** of things
(The way things are)   *   A **NEAR** miss
                                            (Very close)

It's nowhere **NEAR**
(Not even close)   * **NEAT** as a pin *   **NEAT!**
                      (Very tidy)   (Very good!)

The **NECESSARY** room
(The toilet)   *   It's [an abatross] [a millstone]
                              around my **NECK**
                         (A troublesome burden)

I'll break my **NECK**
(Try very hard)
                      *   A crick in the **NECK**
                             (A painful neck)

I'll [get] [take] it in the **NECK**
(Be the one blamed)
                          *   **NECK** and **NECK**
                             (A very close contest)

A pain in the **NECK**
(A pest; an obnoxious person)
                          *   Stick your **NECK** out
                             (Take chances; risks)

I'm up to my **NECK** in...
(Deeply involved in...)
                          * My **NECK** of the woods
                             (My home area)

Rubber **NECKING**
(Examining things)

N

They are **NECKING**
(Passionately kissing)

*   It's all I **NEED**!
(I don't need more trouble!)

A crying **NEED** for...
(A great need for...)

*   A friend in **NEED**
(Someone who helps
when help is needed)

NEEDLE him!
(Annoy; pester him)

* On pins and **NEEDLES**
(Anxious; uneasy)

NEGATIVE!
(No!)

*   **NEITHER** fish nor fowl
(Not clearly defined)

NEITHER here nor there
([Not clearly defined] [Irrelevant])

* A **NERVOUS NELLY**
(A very nervous person)

A **NERD**
([A socially awkward person]
[An overly intellectual person])

*   You've got [some]
[your] **NERVE**!
(You are impudent; rude!)

I'm a bundle of **NERVES**
(I'm very tense)

*   He'll get on your **NERVES**
(Bother; irritate you)

NERVOUS in the service
(In doubt; fearful)

* **NERVY**   *   My **NEST** egg
(Impertinent)   (My saved money)

I'll feather my **NEST**
(Act for my own profit)

*   **NEVER** say die!
(Don't quit!)

NEVER mind!   * **NEVER** in the world!
(Forget it!)   (I'll never agree!)   *   It's [brand]
[spanking] **NEW**

So what else is **NEW**?
(It's not new or surprising)

(Fresh; not used before)

N

Good as **NEW**
(Almost new)

That's **NEW** [on] [to] me
(I did not know that before)

A **NEW** [twist] [wrinkle]
([Something different]
[A new problem])

[So] What's **NEW**?
(A greeting)
(What's the latest information?)

He's bad **NEWS**
(He causes trouble)

What's the bad **NEWS**?
(How much do I owe?)

Break the **NEWS** to him
(Inform him)

The **NEWS** peg
(The theme or central point of the story)

For **NEXT** to nothing
(At very little cost)

I'm **NEXT** to nowhere
(I made little progress)

It's **NEXT** to nowhere
(Isolated; remote)

NICE [duds] [threads]
(Clothes)

NICE and easy!
(Be [careful] [gentle]!)
(Go slow!)

NICE job!
(You performed well!)

In the **NICK** of time
(At the right moment)

Make **NICE** to him
(Treat him with kindness)

Don't **NICKEL** and dime us
(Don't be so frugal)

It's not worth a plugged **NICKEL**
(It's worthless)

It's [on] your **NICKEL**
([You speak first; then I'll talk]
[You pay the cost])

Don't take any
wooden **NICKELS**
(Don't get cheated)

N

NIFTY! * Call it a **NIGHT** * In the dead of the **NIGHT**
(Excellent!)   (Quit for the night)   (Middle of the night)

Good **NIGHT!**   * A fly-by-**NIGHT** organization
(An expression of dismay)   (A temporary organization
                            of poor reputation)

A **NIGHT** [hawk] [owl]
(A person active late at night)   * A **NIGHT** to howl
                                         (To have a good time)

It's a one-**NIGHT** stand
(A single [appearance]   * I'll do it willy **NILLY**
[sexual experience])   (I have no other choice)

I'm on cloud **NINE**   * A stitch in time saves **NINE**
(Very excited; happy)   (Act to avoid
                           trouble later)

The whole **NINE** yards
([A clear victory]   *   Dressed to the **NINES**
[Everything])   (Very well dressed)

He's a **NINNY** * I had a **NIP** * **NIP** it in the bud
(A fool)   (A drink)   (End it at the beginning)

It's **NIP** and tuck * It's **NIPPY** * **NIX!** * He's **NO**-account
(A close contest)   (Cold)   (No!)   (Bad)

It's a **NO**-brainer * **NO** [can do] [dice] [go] [sale] [soap]!
(It's simple;   ([I won't do it!]
requires little wisdom) [I'm unable to do it])

He's **NO** show   * **NO** way! * **NO** two ways about it
(He didn't   (I won't do it!)   (It's certain)
arrive as expected)

N

282

Like **NOBODY'S** business! * He's **NOBODY'S** fool
(Very easily; not difficult)   (He's smart)

He's a **NOBODY** * He'll get the **NOD** * **NOGGIN**
(He's not important) (Be the one chosen)   (Head)

He's a big **NOISE**   *   Nuts to that **NOISE**!
(A high ranking person)   ([I don't agree!] [Nonsense!])

What's the **NOISE**? * ....bar **NONE** * **NONE** of your lip!
(News; rumors)   (With no exceptions)   (Silence!)

A lot of stuff and **NONSENSE**   *   I'm **NON**-plussed
([Lies] [Foolishness])   (Puzzled)

It's a **NON**-starter   * Get it through your **NOODLE**
(It has no future)   (Try to understand)

He's off his **NOODLE** * Thirty lashes with a wet **NOODLE**
(He's crazy)   (A meaningless punishment)

Use your **NOODLE**!   *   **NOOKS** and crannies
(Think carefully!)   (Little hidden places)

It's high **NOON**   * **NOPE**! * [Put] [Tie] on the **NOSE**bag
(The decisive time) (No!)   (Eat)

Keep your **NOSE** clean   * Plain as the **NOSE** on his face
(Avoid trouble)   (Clearly evident)

He has a **NOSE** for it * Keep your **NOSE** to the grindstone
(A special ability; skill)   (Stay busy)

He's a hard**NOSE** guy
(Very firm; tough)

He leads him around
by the **NOSE**
(He controls him)

NOSE to **NOSE**
(Very close)

Keep your **NOSE** out of it
(Don't interfere)

He has a sharp **NOSE**
([He is good at finding things]
[He has a keen smell])

He'll [snub] [thumb] his
NOSE at me
(Scorn; not respect me)

I can take it on the **NOSE**
(I'm tough)

It's [right] under your **NOSE**
(Very near you)

He's **NOSEY** [**NOSYING** around]
(Examining;
questioning)

NOT in my book!
(Not if I can prevent it!)

*

* His **NOSE** is out of joint
(He is alienated)

He'll [look] [talk]
down his **NOSE**
(Act superior to us)

* On the **NOSE**   * I'll **NOSE** him out
(Exactly on target)   (Barely defeat him)

* I pay through the **NOSE**
(It costs me a lot)

* Show your **NOSE** at...
([Appear at...] [Come to...])

* No skin off my **NOSE**
(It means nothing to me)

* Stick your **NOSE** out and...
(Go outside and...)

* Don't turn up your **NOSE** at it
(Don't reject it)

* I won by a **NOSE**
(By a small amount)

* Count **NOSES**   * **NOT**
(Estimate the vote)   ([No!] [I won't!])

* **NOT** on your life!
(Never!)

N

Often as **NOT**,...   *   ...and what **NOT**   * What**NOTS**
(Usually)   (..., and other things too)   (Various things)

Top **NOTCH**   *   That's a [hell of a] [hellova] **NOTE**
(High quality)   (That's an awful development)

I hit the wrong **NOTE**   *   Bank**NOTES**
(I didn't communicate well)   (Money)

Compare **NOTES**   * It will come [in] [to] **NOTHING**
(Exchange information)   (It will fail; be useless)

NOTHING doing!   *   There is **NOTHING** doing
(No!)   (It is very quiet)

In **NOTHING** flat   *   I know from **NOTHING**
(At once)   (I have no information)

For next to **NOTHING**   * Wear next to **NOTHING**
(At very little cost)   (Almost naked)

I have **NOTHING** on him   *   **NOTHING** to it!
(I have no evidence against him)   (It's easy!)

It's **NOTHING** to [sneeze]   * It's **NOTHING** to speak of
  [sniff] at   (Not worth mentioning)
(It has real value)

                              *   He has **NOTHING** upstairs
It's **NOTHING** to write home about   (He is dumb)
(It's not very good)

                         * I haven't the foggiest **NOTION**
I'll take a **NOTION** to...   (I know nothing)
(Have a sudden urge to...)

[Every] **NOW** and [again] [then]
(Occasionally)

* From **NOW** on,...
(After this time,...)

It's [in the middle of] [next to]
[miles from] **NOWHERE**
(A remote; isolated place)

* It's **NOWHERE** near...
(Not even close to...)

* I'm next to **NOWHERE**
(I made little progress)

Do a **NUMBER** on...
([Kill...] [Punish...])

* Do your **NUMBER**
(Perform your act)

I have his **NUMBER**
(I know his [agenda] [plans]
[strengths/weaknesses])

* My opposite **NUMBER**
(The person whose opposing
role matches mine)

My **NUMBER** is up
(I'll [be caught] [die])

* We're a **NUMBER**
(We go together socially)

Do it by the **NUMBERS**
(According to plan)

* It will kill my **NUMBERS**
(Ruin me competively)

He's [a **NUT**] [**NUTS**] [**NUTTY**]
[off his **NUT**]
(Crazy; foolish; odd)

* An old chest**NUT**
(An old joke; myth)

Pull his chest**NUTS** out of the fire
(Rescue him)

* Get down to **NUTS** and bolts
(To what is really important)

He'll drive you **NUTS**
(Aggravate; bother you)

* **NUTS** to [you] [that noise]!
([Nonsense!] [I don't agree!])

From soup to **NUTS**
(It includes everything)

* That's it in a **NUT**shell
(In brief, that's the story)

N

Chapter O

I'm feeling my **OATS**
(I'm very confident)

* He's sewing his wild **OATS**
(Spending his time/energy
seeking pleasures)

Much **OBLIGED**!
(Thank you!)

* Rise to the **OCCASION**
(Meet the challenge)

He's [**ODD**] [an **ODD** ball]
(Strange; different; unique)

* He's **ODD** man out
(He's different from the rest)

Against all **ODDS**
(Despite many obstacles)

* They are at **ODDS**
(They differ)

By all **ODDS**
(In all ways,...) * **ODDS** and ends
(Miscellaneous things) * He's an **ODDS**-
on favorite
The **ODDS** are that
(The probability is that...) (He has the best chance to win)

What are the **ODDS** that...? * I'll lay you **ODDS** that...
(The chances that...?) (I'll give you a betting advantage)

I'm **OFF**
(I'm leaving)

* It's an on and **OFF** affair
([Occasional] [Uncertain])

Blow **OFF** * I'm **OFF** by... * It's **OFF**
(Be very angry) (My error is...much) (Cancelled)

I'm **OFF** and running
(I'm on my way)

* I won't take that **OFF** you!
(I won't tolerate that from you!)

OFF with you!   *   **OFFER** the olive branch
([Go!] [Leave!])   (Be conciliatory)

Do a land **OFFICE** business   *   [Stand] [Stump] for **OFFICE**
(Be very busy)   (Be a candidate)

Use his good **OFFICES**   *   Stand-**OFFISH**
(Get his help; support)   (Aloof; distant)

Every so **OFTEN**   * **OFTEN** as not,...   *   Uh-**OH**!
(Occasionally)   (Usually,...)   (There could be trouble!)

OH boy!   *   **OH** yeah[!] [?]
(An expression of [concern]   ([I don't agree!] [Is that so?])
[dismay] [surprise])

             *   Burn the midnight **OIL**
It's snake **OIL**   (Work late at night)
(It's worthless)

           *   He's selling snake **OIL**
The fly in the **OINTMENT**   (He's a cheat; a swindler)
(The main problem; weakness)

             *   **O.K.** [**OKAY**!]
It's A-**O.K.**   ([All right!] [Yes!] [I agree!])
(It's all right)

      * An **OKAY** guy   *   An **OLD** bat
I'm her **OLD** flame   (A good, decent man)   (An unpleasant
(Her former lover)   older person)

An **OLD** fogey   *   It will get **OLD** with me
(An out-of-date person)   (I'll [lose patience] [be bored])

An **OLD** hand   *   It's **OLD** [hash] [hat]
(A person of long experience)   (Out-of-date; fashion)

O

288

OLD as the hills   *   Her OLD man
(Very old)   (Her [boyfriend] [father] [husband])

He's OLD shoe   * Offer the OLIVE branch * ON the cheap
(Easy to be with)   (Be conciliatory)   (Very low cost)

A come-ON look   * Get ON him!   *   Get ON with it!
(A flirting look)   (Criticize him!)   ([Do] [Start] it!)

Get ON with you!   * It's ON the house   * I'm ON it
(You're joking!)   (Free; no charge)   (I'm dealing with it)

I'm in ON it   *   It's [still] ON
(I'm involved with it)   (It [is scheduled] [will still happen])

It's a off and ON affair   *   He's ON [and ON] about...
(Occasional; uncertain)   (He keeps talking about...)

He [goes] [runs] ON and ON   *   I'm ON my own
(He talks continuously)   (I [live by] [support] myself)

From now ON,...   * ... and so ON   * Take him ON
(After this time,...) (..., and more follows) (Challenge him)
                                                 (Hire him)

I'm ON to you
(I know your agenda; thinking)   *   You're ON!
                                                (All right, I'll do it!)

All at ONCE   * ONCE and for all
(Suddenly)   (For the last time)   * ONCE in a blue moon
                                                        (Rarely)

Give it the ONCE-over
(Examine it quickly)   * [Belt] [bop] [bust] him ONE!
                                                   (Hit him!)

O

ONE for the books!   *   From day ONE,...
([Very unusual] [A record])   (The first day)

It's ONE of those days   * He did a ONE-eighty
(It has been bad today)   (A complete reversal of position)

He'll pull a fast ONE * Free ONE up * Hang ONE on
(Cheat; deceive; mislead) (Make one available) (Get drunk)

I have a live ONE   *   That's ONE on me
(A probable customer)   (I was fooled; misled)

Put ONE over on him   * Here's ONE for the road!
(Fool; trick him)   (A drinking toast on saying goodbye)

Back to square ONE * I'm ONE up on... * Crisp ONES
(To the beginning)   (I'm ahead him)   (Dollars)

I know my ONIONS   * No OOMPH   * OOPS!
(I'm well-qualified) (No glamor; vitality)   ([I'm sorry!]
                                                      [I made a mistake])

An OPEN bar   *   OPEN and above board
(The drinks are free)   (Proper; correct)

It's an OPEN book   * An OPEN and shut case
(No mystery about it)   (The facts are clear)

He's an OPEN person   * It's an eye-OPENER
([Easy to talk with] [Frank])   ([Revealing] [Surprising])

For OPENERS   * A cover OPERATION
(To begin; start,...)   (An activity with a false identity)

O

OPPORTUNITY knocks   * Take the **OPPORTUNITY** to...
(Opportunities arise)   (Use the opportunity to...)

Window of **OPPORTUNITY**   * My **OPPOSITE** number
(A limited time;   (The person whose opposing
chance to do something)   role matches mine)

He went into **ORBIT**   *   In apple pie **ORDER**
(Became very angry)   (In fine condition)

The pecking **ORDER**   *   In short **ORDER**
(A system for ranking things)   (Soon)

A tall **ORDER**   *   Just what the doctor **ORDERED**
(A difficult challenge)   (Exactly what is needed)

A fly-by-night **ORGANIZATION**   * The **OTHER** day,...
(A temporary organization   (Recently,...)
of poor reputation)

                    *   I'm **OUT** and about
He's **OUT** [after] [for] [to get] me   (I'm active)
(He's trying to find and hurt me)

                        *   Bail **OUT**!
He's **OUT** of bounds   (Escape; go; leave!)
([Behaving badly]
[Outside the playing field])   *   I'm **OUT** on my
                            [can] [ear] [rear]
I'm **OUT** in the cold   (Fired; rejected; dismissed)
(Dismissed) (Isolated)

                        *   I'm **OUT** to do it
He'll do you **OUT** of it   ([Planning] [Trying] to do it)
(Cheat; take advantage of you)

O

I'm **OUT**...[dollars]
(I have lost...(dollars)

     *

       Down and **OUT**
    (Poor and without a job)

OUT of my face!
[Back] [Go] away!)

     *

    A crack **OUT**fit
(Well-drilled, disciplined unit)

OUTfox him
([Fool him]
[Be more clever than he is])

     *

    Get **OUT** of here!
    (You are joking!)

     *

    Go all **OUT**!

I have an **OUT**
(A way to escape the problem)

    (Make a maximum effort!)

    * I'm **OUT** of here! * **OUT**house

I know it inside **OUT**
(I'm very familiar with it)

    (Goodbye!) (Outdoor toilet)

     *

    It's **OUT**

The jury is still **OUT**
(No decision yet)

    ([No longer in style] [Rejected])

    * He's **OUT** of it * Odd man **OUT**

An **OUT** and **OUT**...
(Clearly a...)

  ([Not involved] (He's different
  [Unconscious]) from the rest)

He's **OUT** of the money
(He lost)

    * I put myself **OUT** for you
    (I tried hard to help you)

OUT of sight!
(Remarkable; wonderful!)

     *

    Skip **OUT**
(Leave quickly; disappear!)

I'm **OUT** from under
([No longer subject to...]
[My debts are paid])

     *

    Way **OUT**!
([Just right!] [Wonderful!])

    * **OUT** of whack * It's **OUT** the window
    (Not functioning) (No longer considered)

O

Work it **OUT**!
(Solve it!)

Year in and year **OUT**
(Every year)

The ins and **OUTS**
(The details; the facts)

I'm on the **OUTS** with...
(I'm alienated from...)

On the **OUT**side looking in
(Not allowed to participate)

She has a bun in the **OVEN**
(She is pregnant)

It's all **OVER**
(Completed; ended; finished)

He was all **OVER** me
(He overwhelmed me)

He has it all **OVER** us
(He is superior to us)

It will blow **OVER**
([Become calm again] [End])

I went **OVER**board
(Too far; to an extreme)

It will bowl you **OVER**
(Surprise you)

He's **OVER** the fence
(He [deserted] [escaped] [is gone])

Hot foot it **OVER**!
(Get here quickly!)

I can't get **OVER** it
(I'm still amazed)

Get it **OVER** with!
(Do it now!)

How did it go **OVER**?
(What was the reaction to it)

I'm **OVER** my head
(Beyond my capacities)

Hold it **OVER**
([Continue it longer] [Delay it])

I'm **OVER** the hump
(I have successfully
passed a critical point)

Hung **OVER**
(Suffering from too much liquor)

OVERkill
(More than necessary)

O

Give it the onceOVER
(Examine it quickly)

     *   All OVER the place
(Everywhere)

Pop OVER to...
(Make a quick trip to...)

     *   A pushOVER
(Easy [to beat] [manipulate])

Put one OVER on...
(Fool; deceive...)

     *   He'll screw you OVER
(Cheat; exploit you)

...several times OVER
(Many times)

     *   TurnOVER is high
([Personnel] [Stock]
is replaced quickly)

I'll get leftOVERS
(Things not taken by others)

     *   I OWE him
(I'll punish him for what he did)

I OWE you one
(I'll repay you for your help)

     *   A night OWL
(A person active late in the night)

He'll come into his OWN
(Gain a separate identity)

     *   I'll hold my OWN
(I'll [compete effectively]
[maintain my position])

[Do] [Make] it on your OWN
(Succeed by your own efforts)

     *   I'm [on my OWN]
[my OWN person]
(I [am independent]
[support myself])

OWN up!
([Tell the truth!] [Admit it!])

Whose OX is being gored?
(Who suffers the loss; the pain?)

O

Chapter P

Pj's * Mind your P's and Q's * I don't have a pot to **P** in
(Pajamas)   (Use good manners)   (I am very poor)

Put it through its **PACES**   *   It's a **PACK** of...
(Test how it performs)   (A lot of...)

PACK heat   * **PACK** it in   *   A **PACK** rat
(Carry a gun)   (Quit)   (One who loves to save things)

Send him **PACKING** * He **PACKS** a [kick] [punch] [wallop]
(Tell him to leave)   (He hits hard)

PAD around   * My **PAD**   *   I'm up a creek
(Take a walk)   ([Bed] [Home])   without a **PADDLE**
                                          (I have problems
We're not on the same **PAGE**   but no remedies)
(Not communicating well)

                        * Take a **PAGE** out of his book
Turn the **PAGE**   (Imitate him)
(Move on; start fresh)

                   *   It's a real **PAGE** turner
A **PAIN** in the [butt] [neck] [rear]   (A very interesting book)
(A pest; an obnoxious person)

                            *   I feel no **PAIN**
Take **PAINS** to...   (I'm drunk)
(Make a special effort to...)

                        * **PAINT** the town red
It's the cat's **PAJAMAS**   (Celebrate and get drunk)
(It's wonderful!)

                        *   Beyond the **PALE**
                        (Outside of normal society)

Grease his **PALMS**   *   He's a namby**PAMBY**
(Bribe him)   (Weak; indecisive)

It's a flash in the **PAN**   *   Out of the frying **PAN**
(A quick but useless effort)   into the fire
                 (From one trouble to another)

He's on the **PAN**
(He has to defend his actions)   * **PAN** it   * It will **PAN** out
             (Criticize it)   ([Perform]
He's a **PANIC**   [Work] as expected)
(Funny; unusual)

           * He has ants in his **PANTS**
[Beat] [Knock] his **PANTS** off!   (He is agitated; impatient)
(Overwhelm him!)

        * Don't get your **PANTS** in a bundle!
Catch him with his   (Don't get so agitated; excited!)
   PANTS down
(When he is not ready)   *   A fancy **PANTS**
                 (An overdressed person)

I'm flying by the seat
of my **PANTS**   *   A smarty **PANTS**
(Without experience or plan) (Someone annoyingly clever)

She wears the **PANTS** in the family   * Busier than a one-
(She is the boss)   armed **PAPER**hanger
                 (Extremely busy)

He's a **PAPER** tiger
(All bluster; little action)   * See you in the funny **PAPERS**
                 (Goodbye!)

I got my walking **PAPERS**
(I was fired; lost my job)   *   **PAR** for the course
                 (As expected; normal)

P

It's not up to **PAR**   *   Don't rain on my **PARADE**
(It's below standard)   (Don't spoil on my time of joy)

He's living in a fool's **PARADISE**   * **PARDON** me for living!
(Misleading himself;   (Excuse me for being alive!)
  acting naively)

             *   A ball-**PARK** estimate
The better **PART** of it is...   (A quick judgment,
(Most of it is...)   without careful analysis)

The better **PART** of valor is to...   * **PART** company with him
(It would be wiser to...)   (Disagree with him)

Do your **PART**   *   For the most **PART**,...
(Perform your role)   (Generally,...)

PART and **PARCEL** of...   *   Take **PART** in...
(An integral portion of...)   (Participate in...)

Take his **PART**   *   In these **PARTS**   *   [Get up] [Throw]
(Defend him)   (In this area)   a **PARTY**
                                       (Plan a party)

He's the life of the **PARTY**
(He brings interest; excitement)   *   The **PARTY** line
             (An agreed-upon position
The **PARTY** is over   of a group)
(The good times are past)

        *   He's a **PARTY** pooper
He could **PASS** as a...   ([He doesn't join in the fun]
(Be mistaken for a...)   [He says discouraging things])

He'll **PASS** [away] [on]   *   **PASS** the buck
(Die)   (Shift the blame to others)

P

It will come to PASS * PASS the hat
(Happen) (Ask for funds)

Make a PASS at... * I PASS * It won't PASS muster
(Flirt with...) (I won't participate) (It is not acceptable)

Did he PASS out? I'll PASS on that * PASS the word
(Become unconscious) (Make the decision) (Tell others)

PASSING strange * Run it PAST him * I wouldn't put
(Mysterious) (Get his views) it PAST him
(He's capable of
They talk PAST each other behaving that way)
(Neither is responding to
what the other is saying) *
They'll PASTE us
(Overwhelm us)

Out in McGillicuddy's PASTURE
(Far away; remote) * Put out to PASTURE
(Retired)

A PAT on the back
(A compliment) * I have it down PAT
(I memorized it)

Stand PAT! * It's too PAT
(Stay firm; (Too neat; unreal) * A rough PATCH
resolute) (A difficult time)

It's off the beaten PATH * He led us down the
([Not easily found] [Remote]) primrose PATH
(He misled us)

I'm on the warPATH
(I'm very angry) * Our PATHS will cross
(We'll meet again)

P

298

Don't be a **PATSY**
(Someone always victimized)

South**PAW**
(A left-handed person)

[There's the devil]
[It will be hell] to **PAY**
(The result will be awful)

Dock his **PAY**
(Reduce his wages as a penalty)

PAY your dues!
(Do enough to qualify)

PAY no heed
(Do not be concerned)

I'll **PAY** through the nose
(It will cost me a lot)

A **PAY**-off
(A payment for doing
or not doing something)

It will **PAY** off
([Succeed] [Provide a good
return on investment])

PAY him under the table
(Secretly)

* Pounding the **PAVEMENT** [for]
([On street duty]
[Out working hard for...])

*   **PAY** attention!
(Listen carefully!)

*   I hit **PAY**dirt
(I found critical
[Information][treasure])

*   It doesn't **PAY**
(It's not profitable)

*   **PAY** the freight
(Pay the costs)

* Don't **PAY** him [any] [much] mind
(Give him litttle attention)

*   **PAY** them off
([Pay what you owe them]
[Bribe them])

*   The **PAY**-off
(The results of success)

*   **PAY** the piper!
(Pay [what you owe]
[for what you did])!

* Hold your **PEACE**!   * **A PEACH**
(Keep silent!)   (A wonderful person)

P

That's [just] **PEACHY**!   * **PEACHY** [keen]! * It's **PEANUTS**
(That's awful)   (Wonderful!)   (A small amount)

Work for **PEANUTS**   *   The **PECKING** order
(For very low wages)   (A system for ranking things)

Soft **PEDAL** it   *   Don't **PEDDLE** that here!
(Deal with it quietly)   (Don't tell us that!)

Keep your [eyes **PEELED**]   *   Don't say **PEEP**!
[**PEEPERS** open]   (Be silent!)
(Be alert!)

              * **PEEPERS**   *   The news **PEG**
They'll **PEG** you as...   (Eyes)   (The central point
(Identify you as...)   of the story)

Take him down a **PEG** [or two]   * He's a **PENNY**-ante...
(Reduce his overconfidence [status]) (An unimportant...)

[It cost] [he's worth]   *   A **PENNY** pincher
a pretty **PENNY**   (One who dislikes
([It's very expensive]   spending money)
[He's rich])

              *   A **PENNY** for your thoughts)
PENNYwise and pound foolish   (What are you thinking?)
(Wise in small matters;
unwise in large matters)   * I'm not 100 **PERCENT**
                                      (I'm not well)

No **PERCENTAGE** in it
(It offers no prospect for   *   **PERISH** the thought!
[gain] [profit])   (Don't even think of it!)

P

My ears will **PERK** up
(I'll listen carefully)

* **PERSNICKETY**
(Overly concerned with small details)

It will **PETER** out
(Slowly decline)

* Hold the **PHONE**!
([Stop!] [Wait!])

He can turn a **PHRASE**
(He's creative in using words)

* I have a bone to **PICK** with you
(A complaint to make)

Can I **PICK** your brain?
(Ask you for information)

* **PICK** of the litter
(First choice)

PICK him off
(Shoot him)

* **PICK** on him
(Attack; bully him)

* **PICK** a quarrel
(Start a controversy)

It's a **PICK**-up...
(Informal; not arranged earlier)

* A **PICK**-me-up
(Something to provide quick energy)

I didn't **PICK** up on it
(I didn't detect it)

* **PICK** up a ride
(Get someone to take you)

It will **PICK** up steam
(Gain energy; speed)

* **PICK** up the tab
(Pay the cost)

Things will **PICK** up
(Become active)

* **PICK** up the trail
(Discover it)

A **PICK**-up
(A stranger met and socialized with)

* A **PICK**-up vehicle
(A small, cargo vehicle)

A **PIKER**
(A person who risks only a small amounts)

* Ripe for the **PICKING**
([Mature; ready] [An easy target])

P

It's [easy] [slim] **PICKINGS**
([Easy to get] [Little of any worth])

* I'm in a **PICKLE**
(In trouble)

He's **PICKLED** * **PICKY PICKY!** * No [Sunday] **PICNIC**
(Drunk)   (You're never satisfied!)   (Very difficult)

The big **PICTURE**
(The larger considerations)

* Get the **PICTURE?**
(Do you understand?)

He's in the **PICTURE**
(He has a role)

* He's **PIDDLING** with it
(Stalling; wasting time)

In apple-**PIE** [order] [shape] * Easy as **PIE** * **PIE**-eyed
(In fine condition)   (Very simple) ([Drunk] [Tired])

Too many fingers in the **PIE**
(Too many people involved)

* Eat humble **PIE**
(Be contrite; sorry)

PIE in the sky
(Unrealistic)

* A **PIECE** of the action
(A share in the activity)

PIECE of cake!
(Very easy!)

* A [fair] [far] **PIECE**
(A long distance)

I gave him a **PIECE** of my mind
(I told him what I thought)

* Speak your **PIECE!**
(Say what you think!)

Yonder a **PIECE**
(Over there some distance)

* He's a [nasty] [real]
PIECE of work
(A [very bad] [unusual] person)

He'll go to **PIECES**
([Have a nervous collapse]
[Lose composure])

* I...you to **PIECES**
(Very much)

P

302

He's **PIFLICATED**   * In a **PIG'S** eye!   * Slicker than a
(Drunk)   (Nonsense!)   greased **PIG**
                                                             (Too clever to be trusted)

PIG out   * It's **PIG** in a poke
(Gorge yourself)   (It's uncertain)   * I'm a dead **PIGEON**
                                                             (I'll be killed!)

Down the **PIKE**
(In the future)   *   ...to come down the **PIKE**
                                                             (Arrive; come)

A **PILE** driver
(A [hard worker] [forceful leader])   *   **PILE** in
                                                             (Get in the vehicle)

Don't **PILE** on
(Don't [overload unfairly]   *   **A PILL**
       [be excessive])   (A disagreeable person)

It's a bitter **PILL**   *   It has a poison **PILL** in it
(It's difficult to accept)   (A component that will ruin it)

A **PILLAR** in the community   * **PIN** his ears back!
(A leading community leader)   (Beat; humiliate him!)

PINhead!   * **PIN** it on him   * The king**PIN**
(Dumb fool!)   (Accuse him)   (The chief)

PIN money   * Neat as a **PIN**   * **PINS**
(A small amount of money)   (Very tidy)   (Legs)

Knock him off his **PINS**   *   On **PINS** and needles
(Knock him down)   (Anxious; uneasy)

PINCH the...   * ...in a **PINCH**   * I feel the **PINCH**
(Steal the...)   (If necessary)   (The [pressure] [shortages])

P

PINCH hit for...   * PINCH pennies   *   PINCHED
(Substitute for...)   (Be thrifty)   (Arrested)

A penny PINCHER   * I'm PINCHING myself
(One who dislikes   (Making sure my experience is real)
spending money)

                 * In the PINK   *   PINK slip
Strike me PINK!   (In good health) (Job termination notice)
(I'm amazed!)

                 * Tickled PINK   *   PINKIES
He's a PIP   (Very happy)   (Fingers)
([A character]
[A special person])   * It's a PIP   * A lead-PIPE cinch
                     (Very unusual)   (Very easy)
A PIPE dream
(An unrealistic goal; idea)   *   PIPE [down!] [up!]
                              ([Be quiet!] [Give your views!])

Put that in your PIPE
  and smoke it!   *   Pay the PIPER
(I said it, and I'm not sorry!)   (Pay [what you owe]
                                    [for what you did])

PIPES   * Hotter than a [$ 2] PISTOL
(Voice)   (Very popular)   * A bottomless PIT
                              (A need that is unlimited)
PITCH in!   * What's the PITCH?
(Give help!)   (What's [happening?] [the strategy?])

PIT stop   *   It's the PITS   *   Pj's
(Toilet)   (A very bad [place] [situation])   (Pajamas)

No PIZZAZZ   * Case the PLACE * Crash at my PLACE
(Not exciting)   (Examine it)   (Live with me)

304

Do the **PLACE**
(See enjoy it)

* In the first **PLACE**,...
(To begin,...)

I'm between a rock
and a hard **PLACE**
(I face hard choices)

* The **PLACE** is [hopping] [jumping]
(Very active; busy)

All over the **PLACE**
(Everywhere)

* It's not my **PLACE** to...
(It's not my function to...)

I have a soft **PLACE**
in my heart for...
(A special affection for...)

* His heart is in the right **PLACE**
(His motives are good)

* He'll go **PLACES**
(Be successful)

It's **PLAIN** as [day]
[the nose on his face]
(Clearly evident)

* He's **PLAIN**spoken
(Candid; frank; simple)

He'll walk the **PLANK**
(Die) (Be [punished] [sacrificed])

* **PLASTERED**
(Drunk)

PLASTIC * He seems **PLASTIC** * Boiler**PLATE**
(Credit card)   (Unreal)   (Language full of details)

I have a lot on my
[PLATE] [PLATTER]
(I'm very busy)

* I'll get it on a silver **PLATTER**
(Without effort)

* **PLAY** [along] [ball] with...
([Appear to] Cooperate with...)

Don't **PLAY** around with...
(Don't [be funny!]
[flirt] [waste time])

* I must **PLAY** catch-up ball
(I'm losing and must work
hard to win)

P

PLAY hard ball   *   PLAY your cards right
(Be ruthless)   (Do everything correctly)

They'll PLAY chicken   *   Child's PLAY   *   PLAY it cool
(A deadly game to   (Easy; tame)   (Keep calm)
see who moves first)

         *   He doesn't PLAY with a full deck
He'll PLAY dirty pool   (He's not very smart)
(He's dishonest; treacherous)

        *   PLAY it [down] [up]
You PLAY with dynamite   (Give it [little]
(Take great chances)   [great] attention)

PLAY it by ear   *   He'll PLAY fast and loose
(Flexibly, without a plan)   (Act without authority)

PLAY the field   *   He'll PLAY us for [fools] [saps]
(Keep your options open)   (Consider us as if we are stupid)

PLAY footsie with...   *   Foul PLAY   *   Don't PLAY games
(Collaborate with...)   (Violent action)   (No tricky maneuvers)

He'll PLAY into our hands   *   PLAY hard ball
(Act in ways that give   (Be ruthless)
us an advantage)

        *   PLAY heads-up ball
PLAY hookey   (Be an alert, effective player)
([Be absent without permission]
[Take time off the job])   *   How will this PLAY in...?
           (How will people react to it in...?)

Make a PLAY for...
(Court; flirt with...)   *   There is no PLAY in it
            (It lacks flexibility)

P

306

It will **PLAY** out that...
(The final outcome will be...)

*   Put it into **PLAY**
(Get it into action)

Don't **PLAY** second fiddle to...
(Be first, not subordinate to...)

* It's a squeeze **PLAY**
(Great pressure is being
used to gain an objective)

PLAY it straight [down the middle]
(Be truthful) ([Don't take risks])   * **PLAY** it close to the vest
(Be secretive)

It's all **PLAYED** out
(Depleted; finished)

*   He's **PLAYING** a shell game
(Operating fraudulently)

Cop a **PLEA**
(Cooperate with the prosecution
to reduce charges or penalties)

*   **PLEASED** as punch
(Very happy)

He'll go ka**PLOOEY**
(Lose control of himself)

*   The **PLOT** thickens
(Things are becoming
more complicated)

Don't **PLOW** old ground
(Don't repeat what has
been done or said before)

*   Give it a **PLUG**
(Promote it)

PLUG him!
(Shoot him!)

*   **PLUG** him in
([Inform] [Involve] him)

Pull the **PLUG**!
(Terminate it!)

* Not worth a **PLUGGED** nickel
(Without value)

Keep **PLUGGING**!
(Keep trying!)

* He's half a bubble off **PLUMB**
(He's crazy)

*   He's **PLUMB** crazy
(Very irrational)

P

PLUMB full of...   *   **PLUMB** tuckered out
(All the space is used)   (Very tired)

Take the **PLUNGE!**   *   It's a **PLUS** * I'm non-**PLUSSED**
([Begin] [Try it]!)   (An asset)   (Puzzled)

POCKET it   *   He's in my back **POCKET**   * It's burning
(Take it   (I control him)   a hole in my **POCKET**
for yourself)   (I feel compelled to use it)

It's in my **POCKET**   *   I'm out of **POCKET**
(I have gained my goal)   (My costs are not recovered)

It's beside the **POINT**   *   It was **POINT**-blank
(It's irrelevant)   (Direct; straight to the target)

[Come] [Get] to the **POINT**   *   The end **POINT** is...
(To the essentials)   (The final; essential thing is...)

In **POINT** of fact,...   *   Get my **POINT**?
(Actually,...)   (Is my meaning clear?)

The **POINT** man   *   Stretch a **POINT**
(The person sent ahead   (Go beyond what is justified)
to scout or prepare for...)

        *   A **POINT** of view
I'll get brownie **POINTS**   (An opinion)
(Gain favor; credit; recognition)

        *   Name your **POISON**!
It has a **POISON** pill in it   (Choose your drink!)
(A component that will ruin it)

        *   **POKE** fun at him
           (Ridicule him)

P

308

It's a pig in a **POKE**   * A **POKER** face   *   The **POKEY**
(It's uncertain)   (Unrevealing)   (A jail)

A bean **POLE**   * Low man on the totem **POLE**
(A tall; thin person)   (The lowest ranking person)

POLISH off the... * **POLISH** him off!   *   Spit and
(Use all of it)   (Kill him!)   **POLISH**
                                               (Well drilled and trim)

It's a **POLITICAL** football
(It's entangled in   * He's a big fish in a little **POND**
political maneuvering)   (He is more important in
                            a small [place] [organization])

A dog and **PONY** show
(An elaborate presentation)   * **POOCH**   * **PONY** up
                                   (Dog)   (Contribute)

He'll play dirty **POOL**
(He's dishonest; treacherous)   *   An old **POOP**
                                              (An unpleasant person)

What's the **POOP**?   * **POOPED**
(Latest information)   (Very tired) * He's a party **POOPER**
                                      ([He doesn't join in fun]
[**POOR** as a church mouse]   [He says discouraging things])
[Dirt **POOR**]
(Very poor)   *   A **POOR** excuse for...
                                         (A bad substitute for...)

A **POOR** sport
(One who reacts badly to losing)   *   I look **POORLY**
                                           (I'm in bad condition)

They cost...a **POP**
(Each one costs...)   * Hi **POP**!   *   **POP** it in
                       ("Hello" to one's father   (Swallow it)
                       or to an older man)

P

POP [in] [over]   * I'll **POP** for it   * **POP** him [one]!
(Make a surprise visit)   (Pay for it)   (Hit him!)

POP the question   * Mom and **POP** store   * It will **POP** up
(Propose marriage) (Small/family-owned) (Appear suddenly)

He always **POPPING** off   * **POSH**   * A fall-back
(Talking; giving his views)   (Luxurious)   **POSITION**
                                              (A position to retreat
That's between me   * **POT**   to, if necessary)
   and the lamp**POST**   ([Toilet]
I have a secret)   [Marijuana])   * He has a **POT**
                                         (A big stomach)

A fuss**POT**   * He's gone to **POT**
(A complainer) (He's in bad condition)   * I hit the jack**POT**
                                       (Won the prize)

I don't have a **POT** to P in
(I'm very poor)   * He's a cold **POTATO**
                         (An aloof, unfriendly person)

A couch **POTATO**   * A hot **POTATO**
(A person always   (Something very controversial)
   watching television)
         * A small **POTATO**   * **POTATOES**
He got his   (An unimportant person)   (Money)
POUND of flesh
(Full payment)   * Pennywise and **POUND** foolish
                       (Wise in small matters;
POUNDING the pavement [for…]   unwise in large matters)
([On street duty]
   [Out working hard for…])   *   **POUR** on the coals
                               (Increase the effort)

POUR it on!
(Increase the pressure)

310

POUR cold water on it
(Discourage it)

He'll take a run-out POWDER
([Desert] [Leave suddenly])

I'm POWERFUL [glad]
[hungry] [tired]   * Sharp PRACTICE   * Damn him with
(I'm very...)   (Dishonest methods)   faint PRAISE
                                        (Praise him in meager ways)

Not a PRAYER!
(No chance at all!)

Full court PRESS
(A maximum effort)

Hot off the PRESS
(Newly printed)

Don't PRESS your luck
(Don't seek too much)

PRETTY good!
(Very good!) [but not
necessarily excellent])

A PRETTY profit
(A good gain)

Jack up PRICES
(Sharply increases prices)

* When it rains it POURS
  (Troubles tend to come
  come at the same time)

* Take a POWDER!
  (Leave fast!)

* Don't PREACH to the choir
  (Don't try to convince
  those already convinced)

* PRESS the flesh
  (Shake hands; interact
  with the crowd)

* I'm hard-PRESSED to...
  (I find it difficult to...)

* [It cost] [He's worth]
  a PRETTY penny
  ([It's very expensive] [He's rich])

* I'm sitting PRETTY * PRETTY sure
  (My situation is good)   (Almost certain)

* Swallow your PRIDE
  (Do the right thing even if
  it lowers your self-esteem)

P

In the **PRIME** of life
(In full vigor)

*   He led us down
the **PRIMSOSE** path
(He misled us)

The [fine] [small] **PRINT**
(Obscure but critical details)

* Take no **PRISONERS**!
(Be ruthless!)

A **PRIVATE** eye
(A private detective)

* Belly up to the **PROBLEM**
(Confront the matter)

Don't make a big
PRODUCTION [of it]
(It's not so important)

* Keep a [high] [low] **PROFILE**
([Stay active; visable]
[Avoid attention])

A pretty **PROFIT**   * Turn a **PROFIT**
(A good gain)   (Have more income than expenses)

Get with the **PROGRAM**!
(Be alert!)

* I don't have the **PROGRAM**
(I'm confused)

A lick and a **PROMISE**
(A quick, incomplete effort)

* Fool **PROOF**
(Simple; easy to use)

The **PROOF** of the pudding
is in the eating
(Quality is uncertain until tested)

* Good and **PROPER**
(Done correctly)

* A sporting **PROPOSITION**
A hot **PROSPECT**   (A risky but reasonable gamble)
(A probable customer)

*   Do them **PROUD**
He's full of **PRUNES**   (Make them proud)
(He's wrong)   * **PSYCH** him out
(Use psychological methods to intimidate him)

P

Don't wash our dirty   * The proof of the **PUDDING**
   linen in **PUBLIC**   is in the eating
(Don't discuss our problems in public)   (Quality is in doubt
                              until tested)

A **PUDDLE**jumper   * Don't **PULL** [a fast one!]
(A small airplane)   [that on me!]
          (Don't try to cheat; deceive me!)

PULL it out of your hat
(Do it magically)   * He has **PULL**   * **PULL** his leg
           (Influence)   (Tease him)

[For] [over] the long **PULL**
(Over a long time)   *   **PULL** it [off] [out]
                ([Get it done] [Rescue it])

PULL out
(Withdraw)   * **PULL** the plug! * Don't **PULL** your punches
         (Terminate it!)   ([Don't hold back] [Be frank])

PULL the rug out from under him   *   **PULL** up stakes!
(Undermine his position)   (Leave!)

PULL strings   * **PULL** his heart strings   * **PULL** a rabbit
(Use influence   (Appeal to his emotions)   out of your hat
                               (Do it magically)

PULL out all the stops!   * **PULL** through
(Make a maximum effort!)   (Survive)
                          * What are you
                        trying to **PULL**?
PULL yourself together!   (To do by possibly
(Get control of yourself!)   dishonest tactics)

PULL up!   * **PULL** your weight!   * **PULL** the wool
([Stop!] [Wait!]   (Carry your part   over his eyes
[Climb up!])   of the load)   (Confuse; deceive him)

P

Like **PULLING** teeth   *   **PUMP** him!   *   **PUMPED** up
(Very difficult)   (Question him!)   ([Angry; excited]
                                      [Highly motivated])

Beat him to the **PUNCH**   *   **PUNCH**-drunk
(Act before he does)   ([Confused] [Dazed])

PUNCH [out his lights] [him out]   *   The **PUNCH** line
(Make him unconscious)   (The key point made)

I'll lose my **PUNCH**   *   He [packs] [throws] a mean **PUNCH**
(My energy; strength)   (He hits hard)

Pleased as **PUNCH**   *   A Sunday **PUNCH**   * **PUNCH** up a...
(Very happy)   (A devastating blow)   (Produce a...)

PUNCH it up   *   Don't pull your **PUNCHES**
(Make it stronger)   ([Be frank] [Don't hold back])

Roll with the **PUNCHES**   *   A glutton for **PUNISHMENT**
(Take punishment   (One who asks for trouble)
but keep moving)
                  *   I feel **PUNK**   *   **PUNKS**
PURE and simple   (Not well)   (Inexperienced youth)
(That's it; nothing else)
                    * I saw **PURPLE**   * On **PURPOSE**
Control the **PURSE** strings   (I was angry)   (Deliberately)
(Control the money
                 * [For] [To] all intents and **PURPOSES**
In hot **PURSUIT**   (In every sense)
(Following closely behind)
                  *   **PUSH** his button
He'll **PUSH** up daisies   ([Get his attention]
(Be dead)   [Antagonize him])

P

PUSH the envelope   *   Don't PUSH it
  (Go beyond the limits of current   (Don't [overreact]
   accepted behavior/practice)   [Go too far])

Don't PUSH your luck   *   PUSH off! *   A PUSHover
  (Don't seek too much)   ([Go!] [Leave!])   (Easy to beat;
                                             manipulate)

When PUSH comes to shove   * I'm PUSHING...
  (If absolutely necessary)   (Almost; near to...)

PUSSYfooting around   *   A sourPUSS
  (Being [very cautious] [stealthy])   (A scowling person)

PUT on airs   *   PUT the [arm] [bite] on him
  (Act overly important)   (Pressure him to [do] [not do])
                               (Ask him for funds)

PUT him away!   *
  (Knock him unconscious!)   I can PUT it away
  ([Defeat] [Jail] [Kill] him!)   (Eat a lot)

PUT your back into it!   *   PUT it to bed
  (Use your strength)   ([Settle the matter]
                         [Complete; finish it])

PUT that in your [book] [hat]!
  (Note it!)   *   PUT the bug in his ear
                       (Give him the idea)

I have a little PUT by
  (I save a little money)   *   PUT him to death
                              (Kill him)

PUT on the [dog] [ritz]
  ([Entertain lavishly]   *   A PUT-down
  [Seek high style])   (An act intended to
                           humiliate someone)

P

PUT up your dukes!
(Use your fists!)

PUT on the feed bag!
(Let's eat!)

I PUT my finger on...
(I found; identified...)

PUT your best foot forward
(Show yourself to best advantage)

PUT forth a...
([Propose a...] [Exert a...])

It will PUT hair on your chest
(Test your manhood)

PUT a hold on it
(Stop action on it)

PUT [into] [in at]...
(Enter...)

How did he PUT it?
(How did he [phrase] [say] it?

PUT the kibosh on it
(Reject; veto it)

PUT a lid on it
([Limit it] [Keep it quiet])

* PUT the best face on it
(Give it the best
appearance possible)

* PUT up a [fight] [scrap]
(Struggle hard)

* PUT your foot down
(Insist firmly)

* I PUT my foot [in it]
[in my mouth]
(I blundered)

* PUT up a [good] front
(Behave confidently)

* I'm hard PUT to...
(I find it difficult to...)

* PUT a hurt on him   * PUT in for...
(Make him suffer)   (Apply for...)

* PUT it to him
([Ask] [Attack] him)

* A PUT-up job
(The outcome is arranged
in advance)

* PUT out his lights
(Knock him unconscious)

P

PUT yourself on the line
  (Make a clear commitment)

                    *   **PUT** the make on him
                        ([Ask] [Force] him to do it)

PUT us on the map
  (Make us well known)

                *   **PUT** your mind to it
                        (Focus on it)

PUT your money
  where your mouth is
  (Prove you mean what you say)

               *   **PUT** a move on him
                        (Attack; threaten him)

                         PUT on the nosebag
                *   (Eat)

PUT it off   * He was **PUT** off
  (Delay it)   ([Offended] [Ejected])

                    *   It's a **PUT**-on
                         (An act)

Don't **PUT** me on!
  (Don't try to fool me!)

                      *   I won't **PUT** you out
                (I will [be no bother to you])
He is **PUT** out with me   [not eject you])
  ([Angry] [Disappointed])

He'll **PUT** himself out for you * [He] [She] won't **PUT** out
  (Really try to help you)   (Won't [perform] [be seduced])

PUT one over on him
  (Deceive; fool him)

                    * **PUT** it through its paces
                    (Test how it performs)

I wouldn't **PUT** it past him
  (He is capable of behaving that way)

                  *   **PUT** out to pasture
                      (Retired)

PUT that in your pipe and smoke it!)
  (I said it, and I'm not sorry!)

                  *   **PUT** it into play
                  (Get it into action)

A **PUT PUT**   * **PUT** the [screws] [squeeze] on...
  (A small car)   (Put pressure on...)

                              P

He **PUT** me to shame
(He [behaved] [performed]
better than I did)

PUT it to sleep
(End; kill it)

PUT stock in...
([Give value to...]
[Rely upon...])

PUT her there!
(Shake hands!)

PUT them up!
(Hold your hands up!)

PUT him up to it
(Encourage him to do it)

I feel **PUT** upon
(Exploited; overburdened)

PUT in a good word for me
(Say something that helps me)

It's off-**PUTTING**
(It offends)

* **PUT** your shoulder to the wheel
(Assist; help)

* **PUT** my [slant] [spin] on it
(Present it in ways that help me)

* Stay **PUT**!
(Stay where you are!)

* **PUT** up or shut up!
(Do what you should
do or be silent!)

* **PUT** him up
(Provide him lodging)

* I **PUT** two and two together
(The facts led me to a conclusion)

* I **PUT** up with you
(Tolerate you)

* Well **PUT**
(Stated very well)

* **PUT** a wrap on it
(End it)

* **PUZZLE** it out
(Try to understand it)

P

Chapter Q

Mind your P's and Q's   *   On the **Q T**
(Use good manners)   (Secretly)

He's an unkown **QUANTITY**   * Pick a **QUARREL**
(Little is know about him)   (Start a controversy)

A Monday morning   *   A burning **QUESTION**
  QUARTERBACK   (Very relevant; sensitive)
(One who gives advice
  <u>after</u> decisions are made)   *   Duck the **QUESTION**
                              (Try to avoid answering)

It's a loaded **QUESTION**
(Designed to produce   *   Out of the **QUESTION**
  a particular answer)   ([Not to be considered] [Impossible])

Pop the **QUESTION**   * It's not a sporting **QUESTION**
(Propose marriage)   (It is not fair)

I was cut to the **QUICK**   *   **QUICK** and dirty
(Hurt; offended)   (Improvised; rushed)

Faster than **QUICK**   *   A **QUICK** fix
(Very fast)   (A temporary remedy)

A **QUICKIE**   *   A **QUICK** study
(Something done very fast)   (A fast learner)

I did it on the **QUIET**   *   Call it **QUITS**
(Secretly)   ([Resign] [Stop doing it])

Chapter R

Pull a **RABBIT** out of your hat
(Do it magically)

* A horse **RACE**
(A close competition)

A rat **RACE**
(A tiring, ongoing activity)

* I'm off to the **RACES**
(I'm on my way)

RACK your brain * **RACK** up a... * Chew the **RAG**
(Think carefully) (Achieve a score; record) (Talk)

All the **RAGE**
(Very stylish; popular)

* On the **RAGGED** edge
(Exhausted; at the limit)

He's **RAGGING** me * Glad **RAGS** * He'll **RAILROAD**
(Tormenting me) (Best clothes) it through
(Get it done quickly)

They'll **RAILROAD** me
(Convict me without
real evidence)

* He's chasing **RAIN**bows
(He is unrealistic)

RAIN cats and dogs
(Rain very hard)

* Take a **RAIN**check
(A chance to do a delayed
thing at a later time)

Make it **RAIN** * A **RAIN**maker
(Bring in business) (One who gets business) * Don't **RAIN**
on my parade

Right as **RAIN** * **RAIN** or shine
(Very appropriate) (In all weather)
(Don't spoil my
time of joy)

When it **RAINS** it pours
(Troubles tend to come at
the same time)

* Save it for a **RAINY** day
(For emergency needs)

R

RAISE a [beef] [fuss]   *   **RAISE** [Cain] [the roof]
(Complain)   ([Act wildly] [Complain] [Become angry])

It will **RAISE** eyebrows   *   I'll **RAISE** him
(Cause surprise)   (Provide for his care/education)

It's a hair-**RAISER**   *   **RAKE** it in
(It's scary; thrilling)   (Make a lot of money)

RAM it down his throat   *   I **RAN** [into] [onto]...
(Force him to [accept] [do] it)   (I met...)

A bum **RAP**   *   I don't give a **RAP**   *   **RAP** sheet
(A unfair accusation)   (I don't care)   (Criminal record)

Take the **RAP**   *   **RAP** with them   *   What's the **RAP**?
(The blame)   ([Talk] [Debate])   (The charges against...)

RARING to go   *   A **RASH** of...   *   He's a **RAT**
(Eager)   (A lot of...)   (He betrays people)

A pack-**RAT**   *   A **RAT** race   *   I smell a **RAT**
(One who loves   (A tiring, ongoing activity)   (I'm suspicious)
to save things)

     *   He'll **RAT** on you   *   At any **RATE**,...
It doesn't **RATE**   (Betray you)   (Anyhow,...)
(Not highly regarded)

     * [First] [Second] [third]-**RATE**
RATTLE his cage   ([Excellent] [Not first] [Poor] quality)
(Torment him)

     *   He's **RATTY** looking
He's stark **RAVING** mad   (He appears shabby)
([Crazy] [Unrealistic])

R

A **RAW** deal   *   **RAZZ** him   *   **RAZZLE**-dazzle
(An unfair scheme)   (Heckle him)   (Colorful action; display)

REACH a deal   *   **REACH**! [for the sky!]
(Make an agreement)   (Put your hands up!)

REACHING for the sky   * A grass roots **REACTION**
(Seeking a possibly   (A local popular reaction)
unrealistic goal)

              *   A knee-jerk **REACTION**
READ between the lines   (An automatic;
(Look for hidden meanings)   predictable reaction)

I **READ** you [like a book]   * How do you **READ** it?
(I understand you [and your goals] (How do you judge it?)

READ up on... * A **REAL** deuser * It's [for **REAL**]
(Brief yourself on...) (Very special) [the **REAL** McCoy]
                            (It's genuine)

Get **REAL**!   * He's a **REAL** hand
(Be realistic!)   (He's is very experienced)

He's **REAL** shoe   * The **REAL** side   * [It's] [He's] a
(A fine person;   (The truth)   **REAL** trip
gentleman)   ([A wild experience]
                           [An unusual person])

A **REALITY** check
(A fresh look at the   *   He's **REALLY** something
true situation)   (Very special; unusual)

Bring up the **REAR**   *   Bust your **REAR**!
(Be the last in line)   (Work very hard!)

Cover your **REAR**   *   He's dead on his **REAR**
  (Maneuver to escape blame)   (Lazy; unmotivated)

Get your **REAR** end in gear!   *   My **REAR** end will
(Start moving!)   be in a sling
                    (I'll be in trouble, and it will hurt)

REAR-ended
  (Hit from the rear)   *   A kick in the **REAR**
                    (A major disappointment)

Out on my **REAR**
  (Dismissed; fired)   *   He's a pain in the **REAR**
                    (A pest; an obnoxious person)

It has neither rhyme nor **REASON**
  (It makes no sense)   *   It will stand to **REASON**
                    (Be logical)

I RECKON
  (I believe; think)   *   Stand on your **RECORD**
                    (Be judged by your deeds)

His track **RECORD** is...
  (His performance over time is...)   *   Roll out the **RED** carpet
                    (Greet with special ceremony)

Not a **RED** cent!
  (Not a penny!)   *   A **RED** flag   *   Catch him **RED**-handed
                    (A danger signal)   (In the act of doing it)

It's a **RED** herring
  (A distraction to divert   *   He's **RED** hot
  attention from the real issue)   (He is performing superbly)

In the **RED**   *   A **RED**-letter day   *   Paint the town **RED**
  (In debt)   (A day to celebrate)   (Celebrate and get drunk)

I'll see **RED**   *   **RED** tape   *   **A REGULAR**
  (Be angry)   (Official requirements)   (A veteran participant)

R

A **REGULAR** fellow * **REJECT** it out of hand
(A good, loyal person) (Totally and completely)

A shirt-tail **RELATIVE** * I got **RELIGION**
(A distant relative) (Became a believer)

It **REMAINS** to be seen * Our last **RESORT**
(The outcome is not known) (Our last option)

REST assured * **REST** easy! * Give it a **REST**!
(It's certain) (Relax!) (Stop [doing] [saying] it!)

Lay it to **REST** * **REST** room * Take a **REST**
[Bury] [End] it) (Toilet) (Sit down)

REV it up! * It will cause a **RHUBARB** * It has neither
(More speed; (A lot of trouble) **RHYME** nor reason
power!) (It makes no sense)

RIB him * **RIB** tickler * A blue-**RIBBON** group
(Tease him) (A funny story) (A prestigious group)

Food that will stick to your **RIBS** * That's **RICH**!
(A substantial; satisfactory meal) ([Wonderful!] [Ironic!])

Too **RICH** for my blood * Filthy **RICH**
(More than I can afford) (Very wealthy)

Soak the **RICH** * There's no free **RIDE**
(More taxes on the wealthy) (Everything has a cost)

It's a free **RIDE** * Go along for the **RIDE**
(It costs nothing) (Share the experience; risks)

R

RIDE herd on...　　　* Let it RIDE　* Don't RIDE me!
(Check carefully on...)　(Delay action)　(Don't nag me!)

RIDE it out　* Pick up a RIDE　* RIDE shotgun with...
(Endure!)　(Try to get a ride)　(Go with and protect...)

Take him for a RIDE　　　　　*　Thumb a RIDE
([Cheat] [Take advantage　　(Try to get a ride from
of] [kill] him!)　　　　　　a passing vehicle)

He's RIDING for a fall　　　*　I'm RIDING high
(He's careless; asking for trouble)　(Very [stimulated]
　　　　　　　　　　　　　　[successful])

A lot RIDES on it　* Jury-RIGGED
(It is very important)　(A quick; temporary arrangement)

It's a RIGGED jury　* RIGHT! [O!]　* All RIGHT!
(Its decision is　(Correct!)　([Yes!] [I agree!])
arranged in advance)

　　　　　　　　　　* It's RIGHT [down] [up] my alley!
All RIGHT already!　　　　　([It's perfect for me!]
([Stop it!] [An expression　[I'm very qualified for it!])
of impatience])

　　　　　　　　　　　* RIGHT [you are!] [on!]
RIGHT [away] [off the bat] [off]　([You are correct!]
(Immediately)　　　　　　[That's it exactly!])

RIGHT on the [button] [money]　* Play your cards RIGHT
(Very accurate; correct)　(Do everything correctly)

Darn RIGHT!　* Dead RIGHT　* Do RIGHT by him
(That's the truth!)　(Clearly right)　(Treat him fairly)

R

325

It's down**RIGHT**...   *   I fit **RIGHT** in
(Clearly,...)   (I adapted; adjusted well)

Straighten [out] [up] and fly **RIGHT**!   *   I'm off on the
([Act properly] [Control yourself])   **RIGHT** foot
                                                (I made a good start)

My **RIGHT** hand   * Hang a **RIGHT**
(A close helper)   (Turn to the right)   *   His heart is in
                                                    the **RIGHT** place
It will happen left and **RIGHT**   (His motives are good)
(Everywhere)

                                        *   Make it **RIGHT**!
He's not [**RIGHT**] [in his **RIGHT** mind]   (Fix it)
(He's crazy)

                                    * It's **RIGHT** under your nose
RIGHT now!   (Very near to you)
(At once)

                                        *   **RIGHT** as rain
Serves you **RIGHT**!   (Very appropriate)
(You deserve the
  treatment you are getting)   *   It won't sit **RIGHT**
                                            (It won't be accepted)

Do it **RIGHT** smart!
(Immediately)   *   It doesn't strike me [**RIGHT**]
                                          [the **RIGHT** way]
The **RIGHT** stuff   (It doesn't seem sound)
(Ability; courage; firmness)

                                *   I'm doing **RIGHT** well
I have him dead to **RIGHTS**   (Very successful)
(My case against him is firm)

                                *   I don't **RIGHTLY** know
RIGHTLY so!   (I'm not sure)
([I agree] [That's correct!])

                                                                    R

Don't **RILE** him [up]
(Don't make him angry)

* I live the life of **RILEY**
(I live very comfortably)

It doesn't **RING** any bells
(I know nothing about it)

* **RING** his bell
([Get his attention; interest]
[Hit him in the head])

It doesn't **RING** true
(It doesn't seem correct) * **RING** him up * A **RINGER**
(Call him) ([A fake] [A substitute])

A dead **RINGER** for...
(Nearly a twin of...) * **RINKY**-dink * He's a **RIOT**
(Small, unprofessional) (A funny person)

Read him the **RIOT** act!
(Give him a strong warning)

* I don't give a **RIP**!
(I don't care!)

Let her **RIP**! * A **RIP**-off
([Start moving!] (A bad bargain)
[Release it!])

* He'll **RIP** off the...
(Cheat; rob; steal the...)

A **RIP**-[roaring] [snorter]
(A powerful; wild...)

* **RIPE** for the picking
([Mature] [An easy target]
[Vulnerable])

The time is **RIPE**
(It's ready now; timely)

* Get a **RISE** out of him
(Seek a reaction; response)

It will give **RISE** to...
(Cause; lead to...)

* **RISE** to the [challenge]
[occasion]
(Meet the challenge)

Put on the **RITZ**
([Spend a lot] [Seek high style])

* **RITZY**
(Very [extravagant]
[expensive])

He'll sell you down the **RIVER**
(Betray you)

R

Up the **RIVER**   *   The end of the **ROAD**   *   [Hit] [Take to]
(In jail)   ([The final point] [Death])   the **ROAD**
                                                         (Leave!)

Here's one for the **ROAD**
(A drinking toast on   *   Where the rubber meets the **ROAD**
   saying goodbye)   (Where the real test occurs)

Get this show on the **ROAD**!   *   A middle-of-the-**ROADER**
(Start moving!)   (One who avoids extremes)

At a cross**ROADS**   *   A rip**ROARING**...
(A critical decision is needed)   (A wild...)

He'll **ROB** you blind   *   Around **ROBIN** Hood's barn
(He's a crook)   (A lengthy process)

Don't **ROCK** the boat   *   It's **ROCK** bottom
(Don't [cause trouble]   (As low as it can go)
  [try to change things])

                   *   I'm between a **ROCK**
He [is off his **ROCKER**]   and a hard place
[has **ROCKS** in his head]   (I face hard choices)
(He's crazy)

         * On the **ROCKS** * It's on the **ROCKS**
It's **ROCKY**   (A drink with ice cubes)   (It failed)
(Unsteady)

       * A hot **ROD**   * He's a lightning **ROD**
ROGER!   (An auto altered for   (He attracts criticism)
([All right!]   higher speed or power)
 [I acknowledge   *   I'll bank**ROLL** him
  your message])   (Finance his activities)
       * Let's **ROLL**!
        (Let's move!)

R

ROLL out the red carpet
(Greet with special ceremony)

*

I'm on a ROLL
(I continue to win)

He'll ROLL over
(Acquiesce; comply)

*

ROLL out!
(Start moving!)

ROLL with the punches
([Take punishment, but
keep moving] [Be flexible])

*

ROLL up your sleeves
([Start working!]
[Do your share!])

I was ROLLED
(Robbed; victimized)

*

A high ROLLER
(One who gambles; spends
a lot of money)

Keep the ball ROLLING
(Keep things active)

*

Until that day ROLLS around
(Until that time,...)

ROME wasn't built in a day
(Some things take a long time to do)

*

[Hit] [Raise]
the ROOF
(Become very angry)

He has a loose foot and no ROOF
(He is a wanderer)

*

He'll ROOK you
(Rob; swindle you)

[Breathing] [Elbow] [Wiggle] ROOM
([Space] [Time] to maneuver)

*

The [necessary] [rest]
[throne] [wash] ROOM
(Toilet)

Your chickens will
come home to ROOST
(You will have to deal
with the problems you create)

*

Rule the ROOST
(Be the boss)

The ROOT of the matter
(The central feature)

*

ROOT for him
(Support him)

A grass-**ROOTS** reaction
(A local popular reaction)

* I'm at the end of my **ROPE**
([I have no more strength]
[All my options are poor])

Give him enough **ROPE**
and he'll hang himself
(Give him more discretion
and he'll make mistakes)

* **ROPE** him in
(Get him involved)

Learn the **ROPES**
(The fundamentals)

* I know the **ROPES**
(I'm well-qualified)

The bloom is off the **ROSE**
(It's old; not fresh)

* It's no bed of **ROSES**
(It's difficult; not easy)

* [Coming up] [Smelling like] **ROSES**
(Developing surprisingly well)

Things are looking **ROSY**
(Prospects appear good)

* Spoil him **ROTTEN**
(Pamper him)

A **ROUGH** customer
(A dangerous; mean person)

* A diamond in the **ROUGH**
(An unpolished but
special person)

No **ROUGH**housing
(No [fighting] [vigorous play])

ROUGH it
(Live without
comforts)

* A **ROUGH** patch
(A difficult time)

* **ROUGH** sledding
(Things are difficult)

* **ROUGH** and tumble
([Wild] [Very competitive])

* This go-**ROUND**
(This time; cycle)

A **ROW**
(A fight;
argument)

* Our ducks are in a **ROW**
(We are ready)

* A battle **ROYAL**
(A big fight)

Do it up **ROYAL**
(In great style)

R

Do a **ROYAL** job on...
(Give a lot of
[attention] [trouble] to...)

* **RUB** [elbows] [shoulders] with...
(Associate with...)

* Don't **RUB** [it in] [the salt in]
(Don't aggravate things)

It will **RUB** off on him
(He'll learn from it)

* **RUB** him out!   *   That's the **RUB**
(Kill him!)   (The critical problem)

It will **RUB** you
the wrong way
(Really bother you)

*

RUBBERnecking
(Examining things)

Where the **RUBBER** meets the road
(Where the real test occurs)

*   **RUBBER** stamp it
(Give it routine approval)

Don't **RUFFLE** his feathers
(Don't make him angry)

*   You lie like a **RUG**
(You always tell lies)

Pull the **RUG** out from under him
(Undermine his position)

* Snug as a bug in a **RUG**
(Very comfortable)

Sweep it under the **RUG**
(Hide the problem)

*

RULE the roost
(Be the boss)

A **RULE** of the thumb
(A useful guideline)

*

Bend the **RULES**
(Be less strict)

The ground **RULES**
(Rules of conduct for a contest)

* Hard and fast **RULES**
(Fixed; rigid rules)

Work to the **RULES**
(Do no more than the
rules require)

*   **A RUMBLE**
(A disturbance; fight)

* I'll **RUN**
(Be a candidate
for office)

R

I'll **RUN** across...   *   **RUN** that by me again
(Meet...)   (Repeat what you just said)

RUN along!   * I must **RUN** [along]   *   Have another
(Leave now!)   (I have to leave)   **RUN** at it
                                                              (Try again)

It's a **RUN** around   * Don't **RUN** up a bill
(Deceptive tactics   (Accumulate a debt)
   that waste time)

                                        *   **RUN** it [by] [past] him
RUN out the clock   (Get his views)
(Stall until all time is gone)

                                        *   At a dead **RUN**
RUN down   * **RUN** him down   (Very fast)
(In poor condition)   ([Try to find him]
                        [Criticize him])   * I was **RUN** down
Get a **RUN** down on...   (Hit by a...and
(Get the facts about...)   knocked down)

It's a dry **RUN**   *   **RUN** for it!
([A training exercise/rehearsal])   (Escape!)
 [A fruitless effort])

                                   *   He'll **RUN** out of gas
RUN it into the ground   (Have no energy; be exhausted)
(Destroy; ruin; weaken it)

                        * **RUN** him in * A **RUN** in with...
[For] [In] [Over]   (Arrest him)   (An argument with...)
   the long **RUN**
(Over a long period of time)   *   My [luck] [string]
                                                has **RUN** out
RUN of the mill   (My good fortune is gone)
(Very common)

                                                              R

Give him a **RUN** for his money   *   **RUN** him off!
  (Compete vigorously with him)   (Chase him away!)

RUN off with her   * He'll **RUN** [off at the mouth]
  (Go away with her)   [on and on]
                                              (Talk too much)

On the **RUN**   * It's a **RUN** on...
  ([Very busy]   (A heavy demand for...) * We have them
  [Trying to escape])   on the **RUN**
                                              (We defeated them)

What does it **RUN** on?   * **RUN** out of gas
  (What fuels it?)   (Have no energy; be exhausted)

He'll **RUN** out on us   * He'll take a **RUN**-out powder
  (Desert us)   (Desert; leave suddenly)

I'll **RUN** rings around him   *   **RUN** scared
  (Outperform him)   (Don't be overconfident)

I have the **RUN** of things   * I **RUN** a tight ship
  ([I have full access to everything]   (I direct my operation
  [I am in control])   firmly and effectively)

The first **RUNNER** up   * My cup **RUNNETH** over
  (The second winner)   (Many nice things are
                                              happening to me)

Hit the [deck] [ground] **RUNNING**!
  (Begin action at once!)   *   He's [in] [out of]
                                              the **RUNNING**
Land **RUNNING**!   (He [is] [is no longer]
  (Ready to act at once)   a strong competitor)

R

I'm **RUNNING** low
(My supplies
are down)

It's up and **RUNNING**
(It's functioning)

Give him the bum's **RUSH**!
(Throw him out!)

It gave me a **RUSH**
(A feeling of exhilaration)

I'm in a **RUT**
(I'm drifting; getting nowhere)

* He's **RUNNING** his mouth
(Talking too much)

* I'm off and **RUNNING**
(I'm on my way)

* It **RUNS** in the family
(Others in the family
[act] [look] the same)

* What's your **RUSH**?
(Why are you hurrying?)

R

Chapter S

I'll get the **SACK**   *   [Hit the **SACK**!] [**SACK** out!]
(Lose my job)   (Go to bed; sleep!)

It's a **SACRED** cow   *   A **SAD** [apple] **SACK**
(An activity or institution   (A person who always loses)
   immune from criticism or harm)

                * I'm [back] in the **SADDLE**
Don't **SADDLE** me with that   (I'm [at work]
(Don't burden me)   [in control] again)

SADDLE up!   * **SAFE** and sound   * I **SAID** it under
(Prepare to move!)   (All right)   my breath
                                  (In a whisper)

You **SAID** [it!]
   [a mouthful!]   * Clear **SAILING**   * Trim your **SAILS**
   ([I agree!]   (No obstacles ahead)   (Reduce your
   [You spoke wisely])   expectations)

Take the wind out   * My **SALAD** days   * No **SALE**!
   of his **SAILS**   (My [better] [youthful]   (No, I disagree!)
   (Discourage and   [inexperienced] years)
   and slow him)   * He's [above] [below]
           * **SALT** it away   the **SALT**
I must earn   (Save it)   ([An important person]
   my **SALT**   [A less important person])
(Support myself)

          * The **SALT** of the earth   * Take it with
Back to the **SALT**   (A fine person)   a grain of **SALT**
   mine   (Be skeptical)
   (Back to the job)   * Don't rub in the **SALT**
                 (Don't aggravate things)

He's not worth his **SALT**   *   All the **SAME**,...
(A worthless person)   (Nevertheless,...)

If it's all the **SAME** to you   * We're in the **SAME** boat
(If you don't object,...)   (We share the same situation)

We're not on the **SAME** page   * By the **SAME** token,...
(Not communicating well)   (Equally; similarly,...)

Don't bury your   *   Draw a line in the **SAND**
  head in the **SAND**   (Establish a firm limit)
(Don't avoid the facts)

                              *   He'll **SAND**bag us
He'll play us for **SAPS**   (Try to [coerce] [trick] us)
(Consider us stupid)

            * Don't **SASS** me! * Fat and **SASSY**
SAVE his bacon   (Don't be impudent!) (Rich; satisfied
(Rescue him)   with himself)

SAVE it!   * ..., to **SAVE** me!   * **SAVE** your skin!
(Don't say it!)   (...if my life   ([Escape]
              depended upon it!)   [Protect yourself!])
SAVE it for a rainy day
(For emergency needs)   *   **SAVE** up for...
                            (Accumulate funds for...)

SAVED by the bell
(Rescued at the last moment) * A stitch in time **SAVES** nine
                            (Act now to avoid trouble later)
His **SAVING** grace is...
(His redeeming quality is...) * **SAVVY** * A **SAW**bones
                          (Smart)   (A surgeon)
SAWbuck   * **SAW** wood
($ 10.00 bill) (Keep working)

SAWING wood
(Sleeping; snoring)

You can **SAY** that again!
([That's true!] [I agree!])

Don't **SAY** [boo!] [peep!]
(Be silent!)

SAY cheeze!)
(Smile!)

Never **SAY** die!
(Don't quit!)

You don't **SAY**!
(Is that so?)

The hell you **SAY**!
(Is that true?)

I'll **SAY**!
(I agree!)

To **SAY** the least
(It's the minimum I could say)

How do I **SAY** myself?
(How do I describe myself?)

I have the **SAY** [so]
(I make the decision)

SAY uncle!
(Surrender!)

SAY what?
(Repeat what you said)

SAY when!
(Tell me when to stop
filling your glass)

SAYS you!
(I disagree!)

It's up**SCALE**
([High price] [Stylish])

It will tip the **SCALES**
(Be the decisive factor)

A **SCAM**
(A fraud)

He's **SCAMMING** us
(Cheating us)

SCARE the [living]
[daylights] [hell] out of him
(Frighten him)

SCARE up some...
(Find some...)

SCARCE as [all get out] [hell]
[hen's teeth]
(Very rare)

Make yourself **SCARCE**
(Hide; don't be seen)

I'm **SCARED**
[out of my skin] [stiff]
(Very frightened)

Run **SCARED**
(Don't be overconfident)

He's a **SCAREDY** cat
(He's afraid; a coward)

S

SCARF it down!   * **SCAT!**   *   **SCATTER** to
(Eat it quickly!)   (Go away!)   the four winds
           (In all directions)

Behind the **SCENE**   *   Do the **SCENE**
(Out of public view)   (See what there is to see)

That's not my **SCENE**   *   A gentleman and a **SCHOLAR**
(It doesn't interest me)   (A fine person)

SCHOOL of hard knocks   *   Don't tell tales out of **SCHOOL**
(Where one learns   (Don't reveal our secrets)
from hard experience)

         * The inside **SCOOP** * It's my **SCOOP**
The straight **SCOOP**   (The real story)   (I got the story
(The facts)   before anyone else)

[Got to] **SCOOT!**   *   I know the **SCORE**
([I must leave!]   (I understand how things work)
[Leave!])

     * Settle an old **SCORE** * What's the **SCORE**?
SCOT free   (Have revenge)   (What's happening?)
(Completely free)

     * **SCOTCH** it   *   A good **SCOUT**
SCRAM!   (Veto; stop it)   (A helpful; worthy person)
(Leave!)

     * Put up a good **SCRAP** * I'll **SCRAPE** by
SCRAPE the   (Fight hard)   (I'll manage to survive)
bottom of the barrel
(Use the poorest quality)   *   I'll **SCRAPE** out a...
           (Barely gain a...)

A **SCRAPPER**   * **SCRATCH**
(A real fighter)   (Money)

S

338

We'll **SCRATCH** each
other's back
(Help each other)

Start from **SCRATCH**
(From the beginning)

It's not up to **SCRATCH**
(It doesn't meet standards)

I'm always **SCRATCHING**
(I'm very poor)

A smoke **SCREEN**
(A thing used to deceive)

[He's a **SCREW**ball]
[He has a **SCREW** loose]
(He's [crazy] [strange])

He'll **SCREW** you over
(Cheat exploit you)

[A **SCREW**] [It's **SCREWED**] up
(A confused mess)

Put the **SCREWS** to him
(Put pressure on him)

SCUTTLEbutt
(Gossip; rumors)

*   May you itch where you
can't **SCRATCH**
(May you be in misery)

* It doesn't **SCRATCH** the surface
(It hardly touches the subject)

*   I'm **SCRATCHED**
(Out of the competition)

*   He's a **SCREAM**
(Very funny)

*   Don't **SCREW** around!
(Don't waste time)

*   **SCREW** up your courage
(Be brave)

*   He's a **SCREW**-[off] [up]
(He [is lazy] [makes errors])

*   He'll **SCREW** up [the works]
([Make errors]
[Ruin things])

*   **SCRUB** it!
(Cancel it!)

* **SCUT** work
(Low level; routine work)

* A **SCUZZ**   * **SCUZZY**   * At **SEA**
(A terrible person) (Dirty; filthy) (Confused; lost)

S

Between the devil   *   I have my **SEA** legs
   and the deep blue **SEA**   (I can move steadily again)
(There is danger on all sides)

        * He'll come loose at the **SEAMS**
SEARCH high and low   (Become disorganized; crazy)
(Look everywhere)

     * **SEARCH** me!   * Take a back **SEAT**
In the driver's **SEAT**   (I know nothing)   (A lesser position)
(In control)

     * [Have] [Take] a **SEAT**   * I'll fly by the
On the hot **SEAT**   (Sit down)   **SEAT** of my pants
(Under great pressure)   (Without experience
                              or plan)

He's in his **SECOND** childhood
(He thinks he is a child)   * Don't play **SECOND** fiddle to...
                     (Be first; not subordinate to...)

It's **SECOND** hand
(It is already used)   *   Learn **SECOND** hand
                         (Indirectly, from the
Just a **SECOND**!   experience of others)
([Stop a moment!]
  [Wait, I want to think about that!])   * Go the **SECOND** mile
                     (Do more than expected)

It's **SECOND** nature
(By habit)   * **SECOND** rate   * A split **SECOND**
          (Not first quality)   (Very quickly)

Don't give it a
  SECOND thought   * I'm having **SECOND** thoughts
(It's not important)   (I'm reconsidering)

SECOND wind * [Have] [Take] **SECONDS**   * We'll **SEE**
(Renewed   (Take more food)   about that!
  energy)   (I won't let it happen)

S

SEE you [around] [in church]   * Call it as you SEE it
  (An expression of goodbye)   (Use your best judgment)

We SEE eye to eye   * What does he SEE in her?
  (We agree)   (Why is he attracted to her?)

SEE here! [now!]   * I SEE   * I SEE the light
  ([Not so fast!]   (I understand)   (I understand better now)
  [Wait, I object!])

        * Long time no SEE * Take a look-SEE
SEE him off   (A friendly greeting)   (Investigate it)
  (Say goodbye to him)

        * I'll SEE red   * He'll SEE stars
SEE it through   (Be angry)   (Be stunned)
  (Finish the job)

        * I SEE through you * SEE to it!
I'll SEE you!   (I understand your motives) (Get it done!)
  ([Goodbye!]
  [I'll meet your challenge!])   * SEEING is believing
        (If I see it, I may believe it)

I'm SEEING her
  (We have a relationship)   * It SEEMS sideways
        (Odd; strange)

You've SEEN the last of me
  (You won't see me again)   * The likes of which
        I have never SEEN
It remains to be SEEN   (It is totally strange to me)
  (The outcome is not known)

      * He'll SELL you a bill of goods
It's a [hard] [soft] SELL (Cheat; take advantage of you)
  ([Aggressive] [Gentle]
  salesmanship)   * It's a hard; tough SELL
        (Difficult to sell)

S

It will **SELL** like hotcakes   *   A **SELL**-out
(Be very popular)   (A betrayal)
([Every seat] [All merchandise] is sold])

He'll **SELL** us
down the river   *   Don't **SELL** yourself short
(Betray us)   (Don't undervalue yourself)

He'll **SELL** it for a song   *   **SEND** it in the clear
(For very little money)   (Uncoded)

We'll give him a **SEND**-off   * **SEND** him packing
(A farewell celebration)   (Tell him to leave)

SEND him up [for a stretch]   *   My sixth **SENSE**
(Send him to jail)   (My intuition)

Come to your **SENSES**!   *   A **SERIOUS** amount
(Try to think rationally!)   (A large amount)

He'll do **SERIOUS** time   *   **SERVES** you right!
(Be jailed for a long time)   (You deserve the
treatment you are getting)

He'll pay lip **SERVICE** to...
(Note a problem but do   * Nervous in the **SERVICE**
nothing about it)   ([In doubt] [Fearful])

Have a bull **SESSION**   * I **SET** about...   * All **SET**?
(Talk; tell stories)   (Began; started...)   (Are you ready?)

A **SET**back   * It **SET** me back...   * I **SET** my cap for her
(A disappointment)   (It cost me...)   (I'm wooing her)

S

I'm dead **SET** on... * **SET** eyes on... * My heart is **SET** on...
(I'm determined)   (Observe)   (I want it very much)

SET the stage for... * **SET** store on... * **SET** him straight
(Prepare for...)   (Trust...)   (Clarify things for him)

It **SET** my teeth on edge   *   We had a **SET**-to
(It made me nervous; tense)   (An argument)

It's a **SET**-up   *   I've been **SET** up
(An arrangement to embarrass   (Put into an embarrassing
  or compromise someone)   position by trickery)

SET them up! * The **SET**-up * **SET** the world on fire
(I'm buying (The structure; scheme) (Do great things)
  the drinks!)

     * **SETTLE** down! * Things will **SETTLE** down
SETTLE   (Relax!)   (Become more stable)
  [his hash]
  [an old score]   *   **SETTLE** up!
  ([Punish him] [Have revenge])   (Pay what you owe)

Wait until the dust **SETTLES**   * At sixes and **SEVENS**
(Until conditions are stable)   (Drifting; undecided)

I'm in **SEVENTH** heaven   * ...**SEVERAL** times over
(I'm very happy)   (Many times)

He's **SEVERAL** bricks short of a load * It's all **SEWED** up
(Not very smart)   (All arranged)

SEWING his wild oats   *   It's a **SHADE**...
(Using his time/energy for pleasures)   (A bit; a little...)

S

He'll **SHADE** the truth
(Not tell the whole truth)

    *   Afraid of his **SHADOW**
    (Fearful; timid)

A **SHADY** character
(A person of bad reputation)

    *   They'll **SHAFT** me
    (Betray; treat me badly)

SHAGGY dog stories
(Humorous but long,
boring stories)

    *   I want a better **SHAKE**
    (A more favorable share)

    *

A fair **SHAKE**
(An equitable; honest
arrangement)

    A **SHAKE**down
    ([An arrangement to gain
resources by extortion/deception]
[Tests to find and resolve problems])

SHAKE [a leg] [it up]!
(Hurry!)

    *   A major **SHAKE**-[out] [up]
    (Many personnel or other
    changes were made)

How did it **SHAKE** out?
(What was the result?)

    *   More than you can
    SHAKE a stick at
    (More than you can count)

It [will **SHAKE** you]
[**SHOOK** me] up
([Trouble you] [Troubled me]
very much)

    *   Wait a **SHAKE**!
    (Wait briefly)

A mover and **SHAKER**
(One who has power
and uses it)

    *   It's no great **SHAKES**
    (It's not exciting)

    *   I [have the **SHAKES**]

In two **SHAKES** of a
lamb's tail
(Very quickly)

[am **SHAKING** in my boots]
(I'm frightened)

    * A crying **SHAME**
    (A sad situation)

S

For **SHAME**!
  (You behaved badly)

*   He put me to **SHAME**
  (He [behaved] [performed]
       better than I did)

SHANGHAI him!
  (Kidnap him!)

* In [apple pie] [ship] [tip-top] **SHAPE**
  (In excellent condition)

Bend him out of **SHAPE**
  (Force him to [do] [not]
  do something)

*   I'm in tough **SHAPE**
  (My [condition] [situation]
       is bad)

SHAPE up! [or ship out!]
  ([Get in proper condition!]
  [Follow the rules or leave!])

* It will **SHAPE** up [as...]
  ([Develop satisfactorily]
  [Take the form of...])

Whip it in **SHAPE**
  (Make it effective)

* The [elephant's] [lion's] **SHARE**
  (The biggest amount)

A card [**SHARK**] [**SHARP**]
  (A card player who cheats)

* He has **SHARP** elbows
  (He is very aggressive)

SHARP eyes
  (Keen vision)

* Look **SHARP**!
  (Be alert!)

* He has a **SHARP** nose
  ([He is good at finding things]

SHARP practice
  (Dishonest methods)

  [He has keen smell])

*   **SHARP** as a tack
  (Very alert; intelligent)

He has a **SHARP** tongue
  (He speaks bitterly; harshly)

* A [**SHARPIE**] [**SHARPY**]
  (An alert; keen person)

It was a close **SHAVE**
  (Trouble was barely avoided)

* Little **SHAVER**   * **SHAVE**tail
  (A little boy)   (A new lieutenant)

S

The whole **SHEBANG** * **SHED** light on...
([Everything] [Everyone] involved) ([Investigate] [Reveal] it)

Take him out to the wood**SHED** * The black **SHEEP**
([Criticize] [Punish] him) of the family
(The family embarrassment)

By **SHEER**...
(By simple; pure...) * A rap **SHEET** * A swindle **SHEET**
(Criminal record) (A statement of
claimed expenses)
Three **SHEETS** to
the wind * Off the **SHELF**
(Drunk) (Available; in stock) * On the **SHELF**
(Retired; out of action)

It has a short **SHELF** life
(It won't last long) * Playing a **SHELL** game
(Operating fraudulently)

SHELL out! * **SHELLACK** them!
(Pay!) (Beat them!) * **SHENANIGANS**
(Foolish pranks)

SHIFT gears * **SHIFT** for yourself!
(Change pace; strategy) (Provide for your own support)

Don't **SHILLYSHALLY** [around] * A **SHINDIG**
(Be decisive; forthright) (A big party)

Rain or **SHINE** * Take a **SHINE** to...
(In all weather) (Be attracted to; like)

My time to **SHINE** * A **SHINER**
(To [perform] [be acclaimed]) (A bruised eye)

No monkey **SHINES** * Make hay while the sun **SHINES**
(No foolishness; tricks) (Act when conditions are favorable)

S

Hang out your **SHINGLE**   * My knight in **SHINING** armor
(Advertise your skills/   (My hero)
   services)   * My **SHIP** will come in
                (I'll be successful)   * Jump **SHIP**
SHIP shape   (Desert; quit)
   (In good condition) * Shape up [or **SHIP** out!]
                (Get yourself in proper condition)
I run a tight **SHIP**   ([Follow the rules or leave!])
(Direct the operation firmly)

                         *   Hold your **SHIRT**!
                                    ([Wait!] [Go slower!])
I'll lose my **SHIRT**
(Lose a lot of money)

                         *   Keep your **SHIRT** on!
                                      (Be patient!)
He's a stuffed **SHIRT**
(He's aloof; too formal)

                    *   A **SHIRT**-tail relative
                                (A distant relative)
It gives me the **SHIVERS**
(It frightens me)
                * Sticker **SHOCK** * Waiting for the other
If the **SHOE** fits,   (The shock of   other **SHOE** to drop
   wear it   a high price)   (Something else bad
(If that describes   to happen)
   you, acknowledge it)   * Gum**SHOE**
                   (A detective) * The **SHOE** is on the
He is [old] [real] **SHOE**   other foot
([Easy to be with]   (The matter is seen
   [A fine person; gentleman])   from another perspective)

No one can fill his **SHOES**   * A goodie two-**SHOES**
(Can replace him adequately)   (A person who is too
                               correct and proper)

I would like to be in his **SHOES**
(Be [what] [where] he is)

                                                    S

She wears the **SHOES** in the family   *   He operates on
(She is the boss)   on a **SHOE**string
                    (With few resources)

SHOO!   *   I'm a **SHOO**-in
(Go away!)   (I'll win easily)   *   All **SHOOK** up
                  (Very disturbed; troubled)

SHOOT the [breeze] [bull]
(Talk; tell stories)   *   A crap**SHOOT**
                  (A gamble)

SHOOT [for it] [the works]!
([Use all available resources!]   *   He'll **SHOOT** himself
[Gamble everything!])   in the foot
                  (Blunder)

SHOOT from the hip   *   **SHOOT** his mouth off
(Act without thinking)   (Talk too much)

I'll **SHOOT** my wad   *   A straight**SHOOTER**
(Use all my money)   (A candid; honest person)

It's like **SHOOTING**   *   The whole **SHOOTING** match
   fish in a barrel   ([Everything] [All of it])
(Very easy to do)

       *   Sure as **SHOOTING**   *   **SHOP** it
Talk **SHOP**   (It's certain)   (Gather views about it)
(Discuss business)

      *   He'll **SHORT**change you *   [Come up]
Cut him **SHORT**   (Cheat you)   [Fall] **SHORT**
(Interrupt him)   (Inadequate)

Take a **SHORT**-cut   *   ...for **SHORT**
([A route of less distance/time]   (As abbreviated)
[Do less then the full requirements])

S

I'll get the **SHORT** end of the
   [deal] [stick]
   (Be treated unfairly)

                  *   I'm **SHORT**-handed
                    (My staff is too small)

          * In **SHORT**,...   * He's several bricks

That's the long and   (In brief,...)   **SHORT** of a load
  SHORT of it   (He's not very smart)
  (That tells the whole story)

                *   It's **SHORT** on...

In **SHORT** order   (It lacks...)
  (Soon)   * Don't sell yourself **SHORT**
                 (Don't undervalue yourself)

It has a **SHORT** shelf life
  (It won't last long)   *   Give him **SHORT** shrift
                (Give him little attention)

Hi, **SHORT** stuff!
  (Greeting to s small child)   *   **SHORT** and sweet
                 (Brief; quick)

In a **SHORT** time   * We're **SHORT** of time
  (Briefly)   (We lack time)   * Don't be **SHORT**
                 (Curt; impatient)

Make **SHORT** work of it
  (Do it quickly)   * I'm **SHOT**   * A **SHOT** in the arm
        (Very tired)   (A thing that renews

Give it your best **SHOT**   spirit; strength)
  (Make your best effort)

          *   He's a [big] [hot] **SHOT**

A cheap **SHOT**   (A high-ranking person)
  (A petty; needless   (A [star] [very talented] person)
  insult or comment)

      * A **SHOT** in the dark   * The day is **SHOT**

Give it a **SHOT**   (A guess)   (It is ending)
  (Try it)

349

A SHOTgun marriage
(A forced marriage)

* Ride SHOTgun with…
(Go with and protect…)

Have a SHOT at it
([See what you can do with it]
[Try it])

* Go like a SHOT out of hell
(Very fast)

*   It's a long SHOT
(It has only a small chance)

A mug SHOT
(A police picture of
a jailed person)

*   It's a one-SHOT thing
(A one-time activity)

Call the SHOTS
(Be the boss)

* He has a chip on his SHOULDER
(He's angry and belligerent)

Give him the cold SHOULDER
([Ignore] [Reject] him)

* Put your SHOULDER
to the wheel
(Assist; help)

Straight from the SHOULDER
(Candid; very frankly stated)

* He has big SHOULDERS
(He can carry a big load)

Head and SHOULDERS above…
(Clearly superior)

* Lay it on his SHOULDERS
([Give him the responsibility]
([Blame him])

I rub SHOULDERS with…
(Associate with…)

SHOVE it!
([Forget it!]
[I won't do it!])

* SHOVE off!
(Leave!)

* When push comes
to SHOVE
(If absolutely necessary)

SHOVE it down his throat
(Force him to [accept] [do] it)

*   SHOWboating
(Trying to attract attention
by conspicuous actions)

S

He'll **SHOW** his true colors
(Reveal his real character)

A **SHOW**down
(A confrontation)

Don't **SHOW** your hand
(Don't reveal your intentions)

Just for **SHOW**
(For decoration only)

He [is a no-**SHOW**]
 [didn't **SHOW** UP]
(He didn't come)

Get this **SHOW** on the road!
(Start moving!)

He'll stop the **SHOW**
(Thrill the audience)

He'll **SHOW** his teeth
 [in his eyes]
(His [anger] [resolve])

SHOW him up
([Perform better than he does]
 [Humiliate him])

He's no **SHRINKING** violet
(He is not shy)

* **SHOW** him the door!
(Dismiss him; tell him to leave)

* It goes to **SHOW** you that...
(It confirms that...)

* **SHOW** him your heels
(Get ahead of him)

* **SHOW** what you are made of
(Demonstrate what you can do)

* **SHOW** your nose at...
([Appear at...] [Come to...])

* A **SHOW**-off
(One who likes to display
his [abilities] [clothes] etc.)

* **SHOW** [your stuff]
[what you are made of]
(Demonstrate your abilities; strengths)

* **SHOW**time! * It didn't **SHOW** up
(Time to perform) (It wasn't evident)

* Give him short **SHRIFT**
(Give him little attention)

* A **SHRINK**
(A psychiatrist)

S

You are **SHUCKING** me
(You are [lying to]
[trying to deceive] me)

*   **SHUCKS** no!
([No!] [It's not true!])

*   [Oh] **SHUCKS**!
([I forgot] [It's nothing])

Lost in the **SHUFFLE**
(Forgotten; neglected)

* [SHHHH!] *   It's an open
SHUT eye   [SHUSH!]   and **SHUT** case
(Sleep)   (Be quiet!)   (The facts are clear)

A **SHUT** out   * [SHUT up!] [Keep your trap **SHUT**!]
(One team never scored)   ([Be quiet!] [Say nothing!])

Put up or **SHUT** up!   *   A **SHUTTER** bug
(Do what you should do,   (One who likes taking pictures)
or be silent!)

* **SHY** away from... *   I'm gun-**SHY**
I'm **SHY** some...   (Avoid...)   ([Afraid] [Distrustful])
(Missing some...)

* He'll take **SICK** * Cover your back**SIDE**
I have a blind **SIDE**   (Become ill)   (Act to avoid blame)
(An insensitivity)

*
That's the [down] [up] **SIDE** of...   Look on the bright **SIDE**
(The [bad] [good] part of...)   (Be optimistic)

*
Which **SIDE** of the fence is he on?   Do it on the **SIDE**
(Which position does he support?)   ([Secretly] As a
second activity)

Get on his good **SIDE**   *   Who is your **SIDE**kick?
(Seek his approval)   (Your associate)

S

352

SIDE[line] [track] him   *   Turn it upSIDE down
([Take him out of action]   (Search it thoroughly)
[Divert him])

                                          *   I'm on your SIDE
Go by the waySIDE   (I support you)
(Be discarded)

                        * Knock him SIDEways! * It seems SIDEways
Don't get on   (Really hurt him!)   (Odd; strange)
his wrong SIDE
(Don't antagonize him)   *   Don't get up on the
                                                   wrong SIDE of the bed
I was blind-SIDED   I split my SIDES   (In a bad mood)
(Surprised)   (Laughed hard)
                                          * A SIGHT for sore eyes
Don't lose SIGHT of...   (A pleasure to see)
(Don't neglect to consider...)

                                          *   Out of SIGHT!
Take in the SIGHTS   (Wonderful!)
(Tour; see things)   * Give him the high SIGN
                        (Send him a signal)   * I'll SIGN off
SIGN on [the dotted line]   (End my message)
(Participate) [Indicate your approval])

                                          *   I'm bored SILLY
I'll...you SILLY!   * I'm tickled SILLY   (Life is boring)
(Daze; stun you)   (I'm very pleased)

It has a SILVER lining   * I'll get it on a SILVER platter
(An unexpected value)   (Without effort)

He was born with a   *   SIMMER down!
  SILVER spoon in his mouth   (Quiet yourself!)
(His family is rich)

                                                                    S

SIMOLEON   * SIMPLE-minded   * Pure and SIMPLE
($ 1.00)   ([Foolish] [Simple])   (That's it; nothing else)

Guilty as SIN   * Ugly as SIN   * He'll SING
(Very guilty)   (Very unpleasant to look at)   (Tell what
                                                    he knows)

SING for your supper   *   SING a different tune
(Earn your support by   (Change what you are saying)
 doing good things)

                                    * SINGING the blues
It will SINK in   (Depressed and telling
(Be understood better)   his troubles)

Everything but the kitchen SINK   *   I went for it hook,
(Nearly everything is included)   line, and SINKER
                                        (Without reservation)

SIT on him!   * SIT on [it] [your hands]
([Control him!]   (Do nothing)   * SIT it out
[Keep him quiet!])   (Don't participate)

It doesn't SIT [right] [well] with...   *   SIT a spell
(It is not accepted)   (Relax briefly)

I won't SIT still for it! * SIT tight   * He's SITTING
(I won't tolerate it!)   (Don't [move]   on his butt
                          [do anything]) (He's inactive; lazy)

It's a SITTING duck
(Exposed; undefended)   * He's SITTING on the fence
                                (Neutral; indecisive)

I'm SITTING pretty   * SIX bits
(My situation is good)   ($ .75)   *   Deep SIX it!
                                          ([Get rid of it!]
                                            [Sink it!])

S

It's **SIX** of one and a
half dozen of the other
(It makes very little difference)

* Examine it **SIX** ways from Sunday
(Very thoroughly)

*   At **SIXES** and sevens
(Drifting; undecided)

My **SIXTH** sense
(My intuition)

*   Cut him down to **SIZE**
(Reduce his influence; role)

That's the **SIZE** of it
(That explains it)

*   Try it on for **SIZE**
([Put it on] [Consider it])

He's a cheap**SKATE**
(He is very stingy)

*   I have no **SKELETONS**
in my closet
(There are no bad things
about me kept secret)

A thumbnail **SKETCH**
(A brief description)

SKIDADDLE!   *   Grease the **SKIDS**   *   He hit the **SKIDS**
(Go away!)   (Reduce the obstacles)   (On his way to ruin)

He'll **SKIN** you [alive]!
(Punish you)

*   No **SKIN** off my [back]
[hide] [nose]
(It means nothing to me)

There is more than one
way to **SKIN** a cat
(Various means may be
used to reach a goal)

* It's **SKIN** deep
(Shallow)

*   A **SKIN**flint
(A stingy person)

...by the **SKIN** of
your teeth
(Barely; narrowly)

* Save your**SKIN**
([Escape!]
[Protect yourself!])

* I'm scared out
of my **SKIN**
(Very frightened)

He'll get under your **SKIN**
([Annoy] [Interest] you)

* He has a [thick] [thin] **SKIN**
(He [can manage criticism]
[is easily offended])

S

SKIP [camp] [out] [town]   *   A hop, SKIP, and a jump
([Leave quickly] [Disappear])   (Very near)

SKIP it!   * A SKIRT   * I'm bored out of my SKULL
(Forget it!)   (A woman)   (Life is boring; tiresome)

Get it through your SKULL   *   He's out of his SKULL
(Try to understand it)   (Crazy)

They'll SKUNK us   *   Out of a clear, blue SKY
(Defeat us badly)   (Without warning)

The SKY is the limit   *   Pie in the SKY
(No restrictions)   (Unrealistic)

Reach for the SKY!   * I'm reaching for the SKY
(Put your hands up!)   (Seeking a possibly unrealistic goal)

Cut me some SLACK!   * SLACK off * A SLACK off
([Let me rest!]   (Reduce your effort) (A lazy person)
[Give me more space/time])

                        * It will SLACK off * SLAMMER
My SLANT   (Become less busy)   (Jail)
(My view)

          * Put my SLANT on it * What's the SLANT?
SLAP dash   (Present it in ways (The theme; direction)
(Fast but   that help me)
Careless)   *   SLAP happy
                                  ([Reckless][Weary])

A SLAP on the wrist   * A clean SLATE
(A small punishment;   (A fresh start) * You SLAY me!
rebuke)   (You [amaze]
                                       [amuse] me)

S

356

A **SLEAZE**ball
(A dishonest person)

* It's [**SLEAZE**] [**SLEAZY**]
([Cheap] [Shoddy])

[Rough] [Tough] **SLEDDING**
(Things are difficult)

* I **SLEEP** like a [log] [top]
(Very deeply; soundly)

SLEEP on it
(Think about it
for a while)

* Put it to **SLEEP**
(End; kill it)

* **SLEEP** tight
(Get a good rest)

* I didn't **SLEEP** a wink
(I had no sleep)

Let **SLEEPING**
dogs lie
(Don't stir up
old problems)

* **A SLEEPER**
(A problem, issue,
or factor that becomes
or could become critical)

* The ace up my **SLEEVE**
(My secret advantage)

I wear my heart on my **SLEEVE**
(I don't hide my feelings)

* He'll laugh up his **SLEEVE**
(Be privately amused)

Roll up your **SLEEVES**
([Do your share] [Start working])

* **SLEIGHT** of hand
(Deception; tricks)

Anyway you **SLICE** it
(However you calculate it)

* He's **SLICK**
([Crafty] [A calculating
person, not to be trusted])

I got away **SLICK** as a whistle
(I escaped unnoticed)

That's **SLICK**
(Wonderful!)

* He's all **SLICKED** up
(Well dressed and combed)

He's a city **SLICKER**
(An urban person)

* He's **SLICKER** than
a greased pig
(Too clever to be trusted)

S

He **SLICKERED** us   *   **SLIM** chance!   *   **SLIM** pickings
(Fooled; swindled us)   (Little hope   (Little of any worth)
      of success)

My [butt] [rear end]
  [tail] will be in a **SLING**   *   Give him the **SLIP**
(I'll be in trouble)   (Escape from him)

SLIP him a Mickey [Finn]   *   A **SLIP** of the tongue
(A drugged drink)   (An unintended comment)

Don't **SLIP** up   *   A pink **SLIP**   *   He's no **SLOUCH**
(Don't make errors)   (A job termination   (He is very able)
       notice)

I did a **SLOW** burn   *   **SLOW** [down] [up]
(My anger grew slowly)   ([Relax!] [Go slower!])

He's **SLOW** on the [draw] [uptake]   *   Take it **SLOW**!
(He [learns slowly] [is not smart])   (Goodbye!)

SLUG it down!   *   I did it on the **SLY**   *   **SMACK** dab on
(Drink it)   (Secretly)   (On the exact spot)

They'll go **SMACK**   *   **SMACK** him [one]!
(Become worthless)   (Hit him!)

SMACKER[oo's]   *   Hi, **SMALL** fry!   *   **SMALL** fry
([$ 1.00] [Dollars])   (Greeting to   (Unimportant people)
     a small child)

In the **SMALL** hours...   *   A big fish in a
(The first hours   **SMALL** pond
  after midnight)   (One who is more important
      in a small [organization] [place])

S

A **SMALL** potato   * The **SMALL** print   * **SMALL** talk
(An unimportant   (Obscure but   (Conversation to
person)   critical details)   fill time)

It's a **SMALL** world!   * A **SMART** [aleck] [mouth]
(What is said when strangers   (A bright but
find they know the same people   annoying person)
or come from the same place)

                   * A **SMART** [cookie] [dude] [Joe]
Don't get **SMART** with me!   (A bright person)
(Impudent; sassy)

                *   You look **SMART**
Do it right **SMART**   (You are dressed very attractively)
(Immediately)

              *   You are so **SMART**!
SMART as a whip   (Fool, you think you know it all!)
(Very bright)

        * He's street-**SMART** * He has no **SMARTS**
SMARTY pants   (A survivor of   (He's dumb)
(Someone   urban street life)
annoyingly clever)   * A **SMASH** [hit]
                      (A great success)

SMASHED   * That **SMASHES** it!
(Drunk)   (That destroys; ends it)   * **SMASHING**!
                       (Outstanding!)

You look **SMASHING**!
([Beautiful!] [Very attractive!])   * They **SMELL** blood
              (Sense [opportunity] [weakness])

I **SMELL** a rat
(I'm suspicious)   * It's coming up **SMELLING** like roses)
             (Developing surprisingly well)

He'll blow **SMOKE**
([Boast] [Talk uselessly])

S

Chain **SMOKE**   *   **SMOKE**-filled room
(Smoke continuously)   (A place where a small
                               group is negotiating)

Where there is **SMOKE** there is fire
(A hint of trouble may indicate   *   I **SMOKE** like a fish
   real trouble)   (Continuously)

SMOKE him!   *   **SMOKE** and mirrors   *   **SMOKE** it out
(Kill him!)   (False display to   (Try to expose it)
          disguise something)

Put that in your
   pipe and **SMOKE** it   *   **SMOKE** screen
(I said it, and I'm   (Something used to deceive)
   not sorry I did)

          * It went up in **SMOKE** * A **SMOKING** gun
Don't **SMOOTH**   (It [burned] [failed])   (Evidence directly
   talk me!   linked to a crime)
(Don't try to   *   A **SMOOTH** talker
   flatter; fool me)   (One who captivates others by talk)

SMOOTH the way   *   A **SMOOTHIE**
(Remove or reduce problems)   (A charming, but
                        perhaps insincere person)

SNAFU
(A confused, failed activity)   *   A **SNAKE** in the grass
                          (A treacherous person)

It's **SNAKE** oil
(Worthless)   *   He sells **SNAKE** oil   *   It's **SNAKED**
         (He's a cheat; swindler)   (Plagued by bad luck)

It's a **SNAP**
(It's easy)   *   A **SNAP** judgment
             (Quick decision, without much thought)

S

SNAP out of it   *   **SNAP** to!   *   **SNAP** it up!
(Come back to reality)   (Be alert!)   (Move quickly!)

SNAP it up   *   A whipper**SNAPPER**
(Get possession of it quickly!)   (One who is insignificant
                                       but presumptious)

Make it **SNAPPY**!   *   It's **SNAZZY**!
(Hurry)   (Wonderful!)   *   It's nothing to
                                [SNEEZE] [SNIFF] at
A little **SNIP** of a...   (It has real value)
(A small, presumptuous person)

                        *   He's in a **SNIT**
A SNITCH   (He's agitated; angry)
(One who reveals secrets)

            * **SNITCH** it   * **SNOCKERED**
He **SNOCKERED** me   (Steal it)   (Drunk)
(Took advantage of me)

            *   **A SNOOP**   * The **SNOOT**
He has a **SNOOT** full   (A detective)   (Nose)
(He's drunk)

            *   We took it on the **SNOOT**
He's **SNOOTY**   *   It's a **SNOOZE**   (We lost)
(A snob)   (It's boring)

                   *   Take a **SNOOZE**
A SNORT   *   I'm **SNORTED** [up]   (Go to sleep)
(A drink of alcohol)   (Drunk)

                      *   A rip-**SNORTER**
It will **SNOW**ball   *   **A SNOW** job   (A powerful; wild...)
(Increase rapidly)   (A deceptive
                sales effort)   *   I'm **SNOWED** under
He'll **SNUB**   (Overburdened by work)
  [his nose at] me
(Reject; scorn me)

S

361

He **SNUCK** [in] [up on us]   *   It's not up to **SNUFF**
([Entered] [Approached]   (It is not what is required)
  secretly)

                                  *   **SNUG** as a bug in a rug
I'm afraid **SO**   *   **SO** be it!   (Very comfortable)
(That's it; it's true)   (That's the
                      way it will be!)   *   **SO** far **SO** good
...and **SO** [forth] [on]   (No trouble yet)
(...and more follows)   *   **SO** long!
                            (Goodbye!)   *   Make it **SO**!
Rightly **SO**!   (Do it!)
([I agree!]   *   I have the say-**SO**
 [That's correct!])   (I make the decisions) * It's **SO SO**
                                                  (Tolerable)
...**SO** to speak   *   **SO** there!
(One way of saying it)   (If you don't like it, I'm sorry!)

SO? [what!]   *   ...in **SO** many words
([What's important about that?]   (I'm summary,...)
 [What does it mean?]
 [Who cares? It's not important!]) * Go **SOAK** your head!
                                        (I don't care what
He's a **SOAK**   you say or do!)
(An alcoholic)
                              * **SOAK** the rich
                                  (More taxes on the rich)

He'll **SOAK** us
(Overcharge us)   *   He's on his **SOAP**box
                                    (Giving his views)

No **SOAP**!   * Soft **SOAP**   * A **SOB** story
("No!")   (Flattery)   (A story told to arouse sympathy)

I'm [cold] [stone] **SOBER**   *   **SOCK** it away
(Completely alert)   (Save it)

S

SOCK him with it * SOCK [it to] him!
(Get him to pay it) (Hit him!)

SOCK it to them * SOCKED in * I almost dropped
(Beat them!) (Covered by fog) my SOCKS
(I was very surprised)

Knock his SOCKS off * SOFT in the head
([Beat him badly] (Insane) * A SOFT heart
[Hit him hard]) (A forgiving person)

SOFT pedal it * A SOFT [place] [spot]
(Deal with it quietly) in my heart for...
(A special affection for...)

A SOFT sell
(Gentle salesmanship) * SOFT soap * A SOFT touch
(Flattery) (One who gives/lends

He's a SOFTY money easily)
([Gentle] [Not tough])

* I'm SOLD * I'll do you a SOLID
He's in SOLID (Convinced) (A good thing for you)
(He's accepted)

* SOLID! [man!] * We're SOLID
He's a SOMEbody (Wonderful!) (We are close)
(A person of rank)

* Get in SOME... * SOMEhow or another
You've got (Find time to...) (By some means)
SOME nerve!
(You are impudent; rude) * ...and then SOME
(...and even more)

SOME tomato!
(An attractive woman) * SOMETHING is
[afoot] [doing] [up]!
(Something is happening)

S

He's carrying on
SOMETHING awful
(He is very agitated)

* He is **SOMETHING**! [else!]
(Very different; special)

* ...**SOMETHING** fierce
(With great intensity)

SOMETHING has to give
(Must adjust; change; move)

Throw **SOMETHING** on
(Put on some clothes)

* They have **SOMETHING** going
(They are romantically linked)

He's **SOMEWHERE** else
(His mind is on other things)

* Whip **SOMETHING** up
(Prepare something fast)

* A **SON** of a gun
(An unpleasant person)

Don't give me that **SONG** and dance
(Don't try to charm/fool me)

A swan **SONG**
(A final effort)

* He'll sell it for a **SONG**
(For very little money)

* I would as **SOON** as...
(I prefer to...)

Our **S.O.P.** (Standard Operating Procedure)
(The way we do things here)

* He's **SORE** [at] [on] me
(Angry)

A sight for **SORE** eyes
(A pleasure to see)

* A **SORE**head
(An angry; mean person)

It will stick out
like a **SORE** thumb
(It's different and
won't look right)

* He is drowning his **SORROWS**
(Dealing with grief by drinking)

* He feels **SORRY** for himself
(His situation discourages him)

He's a **SORRY** one
(He's pathetic)

S

364

Out of **SORTS**   *   The life and **SOUL** of...
(Angry; sullen; troubled)   (The key person in...)

SOUND off!   *   Safe and **SOUND**   * It's duck **SOUP**
(Give your views)   (All right)   (Easy; simple)

In the **SOUP**   *   From **SOUP** to nuts   *   **SOUP'S** on!
(In trouble)   (It includes everything)   (Dinner is ready!)

His comments were **SOUR** grapes   *   **SOUP** it up
(He disparaged something he   (Give it more power)
couldn't have or do)

                         * **SOUR**puss   *   A **SOUTH**paw
SOWING his wild oats   (Scowling person)   (Left-handed)
(Using his time/energy
for pleasures)   * I need **SPACE**! * **SPACED** out
                         (Back away!)   (Dazed by drugs)

Spic and **SPAN**
(Clean/orderly)   * [Brand] **SPANKING** new   * **SPARE**
                   (Never used before)   no effort!
SPARKS are flying   (Do everything possible!)
(Tension is great)

                              *   **SPEAK** of the devil!
                                  (We talk about you,
SPEAK your [mind] [piece]!   and you appear)
SPEAK [out] [up]!
(Say what you think!)

                          * Nothing to **SPEAK** of
...so to **SPEAK**   (Not worth mentioning)
(One way of saying it)

                          *   God **SPEED**!
That's my **SPEED**   ([Goodbye!] [Good luck]!)
(It's [all I'm able to do]
[of great interest to me])

He's not up to **SPEED**
([Not feeling well]
[Not ready])

* **SPELL** me [off] [for a while]
(Perform my job temporarily)

* Sit a **SPELL**
(Relax briefly)

* It **SPELLS** trouble
(There will be trouble)

SPIC and span
(Clean/orderly)

* **SPIFF** it up
(Make it look better)

* **SPIFFY**
(Elegant; beautiful)

SPILL [the beans]
[your guts] [it]!
(Reveal what you know!)

* Don't cry over **SPILLED** milk
(Don't grieve about what
cannot be undone)

Put my **SPIN** on it
(Present it in ways
that help me)

* Take it for a **SPIN**
(A brief ride)

* We'll **SPIN** yarns
(Tell stories)

He'll **SPIN** his wheels
(Do nothing; waste time)

* A free **SPIRIT**
(An unrestrained person)

SPIRIT him away
([Kidnap] [Lure] him away)

*

A **SPIT** in the bucket
(A tiny amount)

SPIT it out!
([Talk!]
[Say what you want!])

*

SPIT and polish
(Well drilled and trim)

*

A **SPIT** in the wind
(A useless effort)

He's the **SPITTING** image of...
(He closely resembles...)

* Make a **SPLASH**
(Get attention)

A **SPLASHY** affair
(Extravagant party)

* **SPLICED**
(Married)

* **SPLIT** the difference
(Compromise halfway)

He'll **SPLIT** a gut
(Become very angry)

Don't **SPLIT** hairs
(Don't argue over details)

Let's **SPLIT**
(Leave)

Lickety **SPLIT**
(Quickly)

In a **SPLIT** second
(Very quickly)

I **SPLIT** my sides   * We **SPLIT**   * **SPOIL** him rotten
(Laughed hard)   (Separated; divorced)   (Pamper him)

A **SPOILER**
(One who causes trouble)

He's **SPOILING** to do it
(Anxious to do it)

Is she **SPOKEN** for?
(Already pledged to marry)

He's plain**SPOKEN**
(Candid; frank; simple)

He's well-**SPOKEN**
(He speaks well)

Throw in the **SPONGE**
(Give up the fight)

He [is a **SPONGER**] [**SPONGES** on...]   *   **SPOOF**
(He survives on gifts/charity   (A hoax)
  rather than work)

* He's **SPOOFING** us   * **SPOOK** him
SPOON   (Deceiving; fooling us)   (Frighten him)
(Kiss)

*   I was **SPOON**-fed
A greasy **SPOON**   (Given [wonderful service]
(A cheap restaurant)   [only limited information])

He was born with a silver   * I'll **SPORT** a ...
  SPOON in his mouth   (Wear a...)
(His family is rich)

* He's a [bad] [poor] [good] **SPORT**
(He behaves [poorly] [well even] if he loses)

S

A **SPORTING** [chance] [proposition]   *   It's not a
(A reasonable gamble)   **SPORTING** question)
                                              (It's not fair)

A blind **SPOT**   *   **SPOT** cash
(An insensitivity)   (A quick cash payment)

A soft **SPOT** in my heart for...   * Hire him on the **SPOT**
(A special affection for...)   (Immediately)

It will hit the **SPOT**   * He's Johnny on the **SPOT**
(Be perfect)   (Always there when necessary)

The **SPOT**light is on...   *   X marks the **SPOT**
(All attention is on...)   (The place of interest)

It's a **SPOT** of...   * I'm [on the] [in a tight] **SPOT**
(A little bit of...)   ([On the scene] [The focus of attention]
                          [In a crisis] [Under pressure to act])

A ten **SPOT**
($ 10.00)   *   I'll **SPOT** you...
                          (Give you an advantage in a wager)

A big **SPREAD**
([A big estate] [A feast])   *   **SPREAD** it on thick
                                         (Exaggerate)

SPREAD by word of mouth
(By each person telling others)   * I'm no **SPRING** chicken
                                    (I'm not young)

I'll **SPRING** for it
(Pay for it)   *   **SPRING** him from jail
                              (Get him out of jail)

SPRING it on him
(Surprise him)   *   Hello **SPROUT**!
                          (A greeting to a young person)

S

It will **SPROUT** wings
(Move very quickly)

SPRUCE [it] up
(Make it neat and trim)

I'm **SPRUNG** on it
(I love it)

* **SPUR** of the moment
(Suddenly)

SQUARE it away
([Get it done]
[Fix it])

* A **SQUARE** deal
(An honest arrangement)

*

[Fair and] [Four] **SQUARE**
(Honest; impartial)

He's **SQUARE**
([Very formal] [Not stylish])

* **SQUARE** it with him
([Make sure he understands]

A **SQUARE** meal
(A substantial meal)

[Apologize and gain his forgiveness])

They'll **SQUARE** off
(Prepare to fight)

* He's not on the **SQUARE**
(He is dishonest)

Back to **SQUARE** one
(To the beginning)

* We're **SQUARE**
(We owe each
other nothing)

* It doesn't
SQUARE with...
(It is contrary to...)

Eat three **SQUARES** a day
(Eat well)

*

He does diddly **SQUAT**
(He [does nothing]
[is useless])

I'll **SQUEAK** [by] [through]
(Barely [succeed] [survive] [win])

*

A [tight **SQUEAK**]
[**SQUEAKER**]

I'm **SQUEAKY** clean
(No one can make
any charge against me)

([A narrow escape]
[A difficult decision])

He'll **SQUEAL** on you
(Reveal your secrets)

* You can't **SQUEEZE**
blood out of a turnip
(It won't yield anything)

I'm in a **SQUEEZE**
([In a crisis] [I need money])

* I'll **SQUEEZE** in...
(Find time to...)

The **SQUEEZE** is on
(Great pressure is being applied)

* It's a **SQUEEZE** play
(Great pressure is being
used to gain a goal)

Put the **SQUEEZE** on him
(Put pressure on him)

* She's my **SQUEEZE**
(My girlfriend)

SQUIRREL it away
(Hide it)

* A little **SQUIRT**
(A small, pompous person)

* Take a **STAB** at it
(Try to do it)

I'll blow
my **STACK**
(Become very angry)

* **STACK** the deck
(Prearrange the result)

How does it **STACK** up?
(How do you evaluate it?)

* It's **STACKED** against us
(Conditions are unfavorable for us)

She is **STACKED**
(Her body is well-formed)

* I'm **STAGE**struck
(I want to be on stage)

STAKE a claim to...
(Assert a right to...)

* Grub**STAKE**
(An investment to start an activity)

STAKE him out
(Watch him)

* Pull up **STAKES**!
(Leave!)

* **STAMP** it out!
(Crush; get rid of it)

He'll rubber **STAMP** it
(Give it a routine approval)

* My old **STAMPING** ground
(My old neighborhood)

S

STAND by!   *   An old STANDby
([Wait a moment!] [Attention!])   (A reliable thing used before)

I won't STAND [by and...]   *   I can STAND it
   [still] [for it]   (Endure; tolerate it)
   (I won't [tolerate it]
   [remain quiet])   *   Don't STAND on ceremony
                              (Don't be too formal)

I don't STAND a chance of...
   (I have no hope of...)   * STAND down! * STAND easy!
                    (Leave your [duties]   (Relax!)
STAND on your own   [post])
  two feet
  (Be self-reliant)   *   What does he STAND for?
                           (What are his beliefs?)

STAND [your ground] [pat]!
(Stay firm and resolute!)   * Your hair will STAND on end
                           (You will be scared)

It will STAND you in good stead
(It will serve you well)   * I'll STAND on my head
                       (Make a great effort)

A STAND-in   *   I don't have
(A substitute)   a leg to STAND on   * A STAND-off
          (My arguments are   (No one is winning)
STAND them off!   not supported)
(Resist them!)   STAND for office
             * STANDoffish   (Be a candidate)
A one-night STAND   (Distant and aloof)
(A single [appearance]
  [sexual experience])   * A STAND-out   * It will STAND
               (An exceptional   to reason
STAND on your record   person)   (Be logical)
(Be judged by your deeds)

S

371

It will **STAND** you in good stead   *   Take a **STAND**
(It will serve you well)   (State your views firmly)

He'll **STAND** tall * He'll **STAND** you up * **STAND** up for...
(Be outstanding)   (Not keep his   (Defend; support)
       appointment with you)

It will **STAND** up   * A **STAND**-up guy
([The facts will support it]   (A courageous, loyal person)
[It is strong and will endure])

       * I'm **STANDING** on my ear
Grand-**STANDING**   (I'm extremely busy)
(Trying hard to get attention)

      *   It's **STAR**-crossed
A **STARE** down   (It always has problems)
(A confrontation)

     * **STARK** [raving] [staring] mad
He'll see **STARS**   (Insane)
(Be stunned)

      *   Off to a flying **START**
It gave me a **START**   (A [fast] [good] beginning])
(A surprise)

      *   Jump **START** it
START [from scratch]   (Apply special energy
[with a clean slate]   to start it)
[from the top]
(From the beginning)   *   As a **STARTER**,...
       (As a first step,...)

It's a non-**STARTER**
(It has no future)   * **STASH**   * **STATE** of the art
      (Money)   (Best technology in use)
STAY [cool [loose]!
([Goodbye!] [Keep relaxed!]   *   **STAY** on him
[Don't get involved])   (Watch him closely)

S

372

STAY on it
(Keep doing it)

* **STAY** put! *
(Stay where you are!)

STAY in tune!
(Goodbye!)

STAY tuned
(Stay involved;
continue listening)

* I should have **STAYED** in bed
(Better that I should have done nothing)

We go **STEADY**
(We go out only
with each other)

* It will stand in you in good **STEAD**
(It will serve you well)

* He'll **STEAL** you blind
(He's a crook)

A **STEAL**
(A fine bargain)

* He'll **STEAL** my
[lunch] [thunder]
(Get credit for my [work] [ideas])

Full **STEAM** ahead!
(Move vigorously!)

* [Blow] [Let] off **STEAM**
(Ease tension by yelling)

It will pick up **STEAM**
(Gain energy; speed)

* **STEAMED** [up]
(Very angry)

* A **STEEL**
trap mind
(A rigid mind)

It's very **STEEP**
(Very expensive)

* A bum **STEER**
(Bad advice)

* **STEER** clear of…
(Avoid…)

From **STEM** to **STERN**
(From one end
to the other)

* I'm **STEP** ahead of him
(I anticipate his actions)

STEP on the [gas] [it]
(Hurry!)

* Don't **STEP** on his toes
(Don't antagonize him)

Watch your **STEP**!
(Be careful!)

* He'll dog my **STEPS**
(Pursue me closely)

S

We're even **STEVEN**   * In a **STEW**   * **STEWED**
(We [have the same score]   (Angry; excited)   (Drunk)
  [are equal])

    * Let him **STEW** [in his own juice]
What is he **STEWING** about?   (Remain angry; troubled)
(What bothers him?)   ([Suffer the trouble he caused])

STICK around   * He'll **STICK** you with the [bill] [job]
(Don't go away)   (Leave it for you to [pay] [do])

The charge will **STICK**   * It will **STICK** in my craw
(It will remain valid)   (Really bother me)

STICK it in your ear!   * Get [off] [on] the **STICK**!
(I completely disagree with you!)   (Start moving!)

STICK to your guns!   * **STICK** to your knitting!
(Maintain your position!)   (Focus on your own affairs!)

A **STICK** in the mud   * **STICK** your neck out
(One who [destroys enthusiasm]   (Take chances; risks)
  [opposes change])

    * **STICK** your nose out and...
He'll **STICK** his nose into it   (Go outside and...)
([Interfere] [involve himself] in it)

    * **STICK** [it out!]
Food that will **STICK** to your ribs   **STICK** [to] [with] it!
(A substantial, satisfactory meal)   (Endure; persevere!)

More than you can   * I'll get the short end of the **STICK**
  shake a **STICK** at   (Be treated unfairly)
(More than you can count)

S

STICK it to them!   * It will **STICK** out like a sore thumb
(Defeat; punish them!)   (It's different and won't look right)

[**STICK** 'em up!]   * **STICK** up for him * He'll **STICK**
[This is a **STICK** up!]   (Defend him)   it to us
(This is a robbery)   (Cheat; take
                        * Fiddle**STICKS**!   advantage of us)
STICKER shock   (Nonsense!)
(The shock of high price)   * Out in the **STICKS**
                                              (In the rural areas)

A **STIFF**   * I'm bored **STIFF**
(A corpse)   (Life is dull for me)   * Keep a **STIFF** upper lip
                                          (Be brave; resolute)

A lucky **STIFF**
(A fortunate person) * Scared **STIFF**   * He'll **STIFF** us
                        (Very frightened)   ([Cheat] [Reject] us)

I'm a working **STIFF**
(I work to support myself)   * I won't [hold] [sit] [stand]
                                                STILL for it)
I'm **STILL** kicking   (I won't [be quiet]
(I'm alive)   * Make a **STINK**   [tolerate it])
                  (Complain; create trouble)

It's a **STINKER**   * Cause a **STIR**
(It's awful; very bad)   (Create [excitement] [problems])

STIR crazy   * In **STIR**   *   **STIR** him up
(Troubled by confinement)   (Jail)   (Get him angry; excited)

He hasn't a **STITCH** on   * A **STITCH** in time saves nine
(He's naked)   (Act now to avoid trouble later)

He's in **STITCHES**   * Clear out, lock, **STOCK** and barrel!
(Laughing hard)   (Go, and take everything!)

Put **STOCK** in...   *   Let's take **STOCK**
([Rely upon...]   (Assess our situation)
 [Give value to...])

            * **STOCKING** stuffer   * **STOGIE**

I'm **STOKED**   (A small, inexpensive, useful gift) (Cigar)
(Excited; happy)

        * My eyes were bigger than my **STOMACH**

I have butterflies   (I took too much to eat)
 in my **STOMACH**
(I am anxious; fearful)   * I have no **STOMACH** for it
                           (I can't cope with it)

It turns my **STOMACH**
(It makes me sick)   *   I'm **STONE** broke
                           (I have no money)

Keep your nose to the grind**STONE**
(Stay busy)   *   A mill**STONE**
                          around his neck
I'm **STONE** sober   * A **STONE'S** throw (A troublesome
(Completely alert)   (A short distance)   burden)

Leave no **STONE** unturned   *   **STONED**
(Do everything possible)   ([Drugged] [Drunk])

STONEwall   * It will fall between the **STOOLS**
(Delay; evade; obstruct)   (Be neglected; unnoticed)

I won't **STOOP** to that   *   His face would
(I won't do that kind of thing)   **STOP** a clock
                          (He's very ugly)

A dead **STOP**   * Pit **STOP**
(A complete stop)   (Toilet)   * He'll **STOP** the show
                          (Thrill the audience)

S

376

STOP him in his tracks!
(Stop him where he is!)

STOP your yammering!
(Stop talking!)

Pull out all the **STOPS**
(Make a full effort)

Mom and pop **STORE**
(Small, family-owned)

Don't tell **STORIES**!
(Don't lie to me!)

STORM it!
(Try to overwhelm it)

The **STORY** doesn't
  [check out] [hold up] [ring true]
  ([The facts don't support it]
  [It's false])

A [fish] [tall] **STORY**
(An exaggerated story)

Leak the **STORY**
(Deliberately give
  information prematurely)

That's the **STORY**
(Those are the facts)

* **STOP** the traffic!
(Wait a minute!)

* The buck **STOPS** here
(I take full responsibility)

* I'm minding the **STORE**
(I'm in charge)

* Set **STORE** on... * Shaggy dog
(You can trust...) **STORIES**
(Humorous, but long,
boring stories)

* He'll **STORM** about
(Move wildly) * A brain **STORM**
(A brilliant idea)

* He...up a **STORM**
(Made a great effort) * Weather the
STORM
(Survive and continue)

* A cover **STORY**
(A story to obscure the
true nature of something)

* Hang the **STORY** on...
(Base the story on...)

* A sob **STORY**
(A story told to arouse sympathy)

* What's the **STORY**?
(What is happening?)

S

A **STOUT** fellow
(A good, loyal person)

* **STOW** it!
(Be quiet!)

* A **STRAIGHT** arrow
(An honest person)

Keep a **STRAIGHT** face
(Remain serious;
don't smile)

* Get this **STRAIGHT**!
(Listen carefully!)

Go **STRAIGHT**
(Operate honestly)

* Give it to him **STRAIGHT**
(Be honest with him)

Be **STRAIGHT** [out] [up]
(Candid; honest)

* On the **STRAIGHT** and narrow
(Operating honestly)

STRAIGHT-laced
(Very proper; conservative)

* I said it **STRAIGHT** [out] [up]
(Clearly and unambiguously)

Go **STRAIGHT** to the point
(To the key fact/point)

* Play it **STRAIGHT**
[down the middle]
([Be truthful] [Don't take risks])

A **STRAIGHT** shooter
(A candid, honest person)

* The **STRAIGHT** scoop
(The facts)

STRAIGHT from the shoulder
(Candid; frankly stated)

* Take it **STRAIGHT** up
(Not diluted)

[Set him **STRAIGHT**!]
[**STRAIGHTEN** him out!]
([Clarify things for him!]
[Get him to behave correctly])

* **STRAIGHTEN** [out] [up]
and fly right!
(Act properly)

A **STRANGE** bird
(An odd; unusual person)

* **STRAINING** at a gnat
(Using much energy for
an unimportant purpose)

S

378

Passing **STRANGE**
(Mysterious)

* Don't be a **STRANGER**
(I hope to see you again soon)

Boot**STRAP** yourself
(Rely upon your own resources)

* I'm **STRAPPED** for funds
(I have no money)

The **STRAW** that will break
the camel's back
(The decisive factor)

* It's the last **STRAW**
(No more will be tolerated)

A **STRAW** in the wind
(A hint of the future)

* A **STRAW** man
(An [argument] [candidate]
set up to be easily defeated)

[Clutching] [Grasping]
at **STRAWS**
(Desperate)

* He talks a blue **STREAK**
(Very fast)

* He has a mean **STREAK**
(At times, he is mean)

A [losing] [winning] **STREAK**
(A series of [losses] [wins])

* It's on **STREAM**
(Proceeding well)

He's on [easy] [leisure] **STREET**
(He is wealthy)

* It hit the **STREET** * Man on the **STREET**
He is **STREET** (Became public) (An ordinary citizen)
[-smart] [-wise]
(A survivor of * It's a two-way **STREET**
urban street life) (I help you; you help me)

I'll **STRESS** out
(Suffer great tension)

* On the home **STRETCH**
(Near the end)

By any **STRETCH** [of imagination] * **STRETCH** your legs
(No matter how you imagine it) (Take a walk)

S

Not by a long **STRETCH**
(Hardly any chance at all)

Over the long **STRETCH**
(For a long time)

A **STRETCH** out
(A delay in schedule)

STRETCH a point
(Go beyond what may be justified)

Take a **STRETCH**
(Relax)

He's up for a **STRETCH**
(He's in jail)

He's **STRETCHING** it
(Not being truthful)

Take it in your **STRIDE**
(Do it in a routine way)

STRIKE a deal
(Make an agreement)

STRIKE while the [fire] [iron] is hot
(Act when it is most timely)

The candidate hopes that
lightning will **STRIKE** him
(That he'll be the surprise choice)

He'll **STRIKE** out
(Fail)

STRIKE me pink!
(I'm amazed!)

It doesn't **STRIKE** me [right]
[the right way]
(It doesn't seem sound)

A ten-**STRIKE**
(A wonderful idea; result)

It **STRIKES** me that...
(It appears to me that...)

STRING him along
(Keep him in doubt)

I'll **STRING** along with you
([Go with you] [Support you])

You can't **STRING** me
(You can't fool me)

The latch **STRING** is out
(Guests are welcome)

STRING it out
(Prolong it)

S

380

My **STRING** has run out
(My good fortune is gone)

* I operate on a shoe**STRING**
(With very few resources)

STRING him up!
(Hang him!)

* I have the world on a **STRING**
(Things are going well for me)

Tied to his mother's
  apron **STRINGS**
(Dependent on his mother)

* No **STRINGS** attached
(No limiting conditions)

Control the purse **STRINGS**
(Control the money)

* Pull **STRINGS**
(Use influence)

A **STROKE** of genius
(A brilliant idea)

* Pull his heart **STRINGS**
(Appeal to his emotions)

I had a **STROKE**
(Became very agitated; excited)

* A **STROKE** of luck
(An unexpected good development)

STRONG arm him
(Force him)

* He needs **STROKING**
(Special soothing attention)

Mighty **STRONG**
(Very strong)

* It's going **STRONG**
(Operating very well)

It **STRUCK** a chord
(An emotional response)

* My **STRONG** suit
(My special strength)

I **STRUCK** out
(I failed)

* It's who **STRUCK** John
(Useless debate about who hit first)

I'm **STRUNG** out
([Overextended] [Addicted to drugs])

* I'm stage**STRUCK**
(I want to be on stage)

S

381

[Do] [Show] [STRUT] your STUFF   * I'll STUB my toe
(Show what you can do)   (Make mistakes)

STUCK on go   *   I'm STUCK on her
(Unable to proceed)   (Infatuated with her)

STUCK [on himself] [up] * STUD * A quick STUDY
([Aloof] [Conceited])   (Young man) (A fast learner)

...and STUFF   * Don't give me [that] [a lot of] STUFF!
(...and other things)   (No [lies] [nonsense]!)

Hot STUFF   * STUFF it! * I know my STUFF
([Stolen goods]   (Be quiet)   (I'm well qualified)
[Very popular])

                * A lot of STUFF and [such] [nonsense]
He has the right STUFF   ([Lies] [Foolishness])
(Ability; courage; firmness)

                        *   Hi, short STUFF
STUFF them   (Greeting to small child)
(Stop; beat them)

                    *   A STUFFED shirt
A stocking STUFFER   (An aloof; overly formal person)
(A small, inexpensive gift)

                * Beat the STUFFING out of him
I'll STUMBLE [across] [on] it   (Really punish him)
(Find it by chance)

                        *   A STUMBLEbum
STUMP for office   (Clumsy; inept person)
(Be a candidate)

                *I'm [up a STUMP] [STUMPED]
I'll cramp his STYLE   (Baffled; puzzled)
(Limit what he can [do] [say])

S

382

SUCK it in!   *   He'll SUCK you in
(Flatten your stomach)   (Entice you to participate)

He'll SUCKER you   * It SUCKS   * All of a SUDDEN
(Betray; deceive you) (It's terrible)   (Without warning)

SUDS   SUFFERING catfish!
(Beer)   (Expression of amazement or frustration)

Give me some SUGAR!   *   SUGARcoat it
(I want a hug!)   (Make it look better than it is)

In my birthday SUIT   *   My [long] [strong] SUIT
(Naked)   (Special strength)

SUIT yourself!   * SUITS me!   * My [day] [moment]
(Do it your way!) (It's agreeable to me)   in the SUN
                               (My brief time of publicity)

Make hay while the SUN shines
(Act when conditions are favorable) * It's no SUNDAY picnic
                                    (It's very difficult)

Examine it [five] [six] ways to SUNDAY
(Very thoroughly)   *   A SUNDAY punch
                                   (A devastating blow)

Not in a month of SUNDAYS!
(It never will be!)   * I'm SUNK   * SUPER!
                          (Ruined)   (Wonderful!)

Sing for your SUPPER
(Earn your support   *   I'm [dead] [pretty] SURE
 doing good things)   ([Very] [Almost] certain)

SURE [enough] [thing]!   *   SURE enough?
([I agree!] [It's true!])   (Is that a fact?)

S

SURE enough,...
(And then, as expected,...)

* It's a SURE enough...
(A genuine...)

It's SURE [-fire] [as shooting]!
(It's certain)

* That's for SURE!
([I agree!] [Certainly!])

[Oh] SURE!
(I don't believe it!)

* It doesn't scratch the SURFACE
(It barely touches the subject)

SWAG
(Money)

* I'll be horn-SWAGGLED!
(Expression of amazement)

SWALLOW your fears
(Be brave)

* I can't SWALLOW it
(I can't [accept] [believe] it)

SWALLOW your pride
(Do the right thing even if
it lowers your self-esteem)

* A SWAN song
(A final effort)

* A SWANK[Y] place
(Elegant; expensive)

He SWEARS by it
(He has great [faith]
[confidence] in it)

* SWEAT [blood] [bullets]!
(Work very hard!)

Don't SWEAT it!   * No SWEAT!
(Don't worry!)   (No problem!)

* SWEAT it out!
(Be patient!)

SWEAT tacks   * Tell it to SWEENEY!
(Be really anxious) (I don't believe it!)   * A clean SWEEP
([A complete victory]
SWEEP her off her feet   [A total removal of...])
(Charm; overwhelm her)

* SWEEP it under the rug
(Hide the problem)

S

384

I'm **SWEET** on her * Short and **SWEET** * Don't **SWEET**
(I love her) (Brief; quick) talk me!
(Don't try to charm me!)

Take your own **SWEET** time
(Don't do it quickly) * I have a **SWEET** tooth
(I like sweet food)

He's my **SWEETIE** * A **SWELL**
(My sweetheart) (A fine gentleman) * He has a
SWELL head
That's **SWELL**! (He is conceited;
(Very good!) impressed with himself)

He's not too **SWIFT** * Get into the [SWIM] [SWING]
(Not very smart) (Into the routine of activities)

It's going **SWIMMINGLY** * A **SWINDLE**sheet
(Operating very well) (A statement of claimed expenses)

I'll **SWING** a deal * I'll **SWING** for it
(Make an agreement) ([Die by hanging] [Be in trouble])

In full **SWING** * I can **SWING** it
(Very active) ([Manage it] [Make it happen])

[Take] [Try] a **SWING** at it * A **SWINGER**
(Try to do it) (One who has an active
[night] [sex] life)

SWIPE it * Asleep at the **SWITCH**
(Steal it) (Not alert) * Flip the **SWITCH**
(Turn the switch)

SWITCH gears
(Change pace; strategy) * That's a **SWITCH**
(A reversal of circumstances)

S

Chapter T

He has it down to a **T**   *   It fits me to a **T**
(He knows it thoroughly)   (It's perfect for me)

On the QT   *   On the **TAB**   *   Pick up the **TAB**
(Secretly)   (On credit)   (Pay the cost)

Keep **TABS** on... * I'm at the **TABLE** * My cards are
(Watch...)   (I'm participating)   on the **TABLE**
                                              (I revealed my situation)

It's [off] [on] the **TABLE**
(It [won't] [will] be discussed) * Pay him under the **TABLE**
                                                   (Secretly)

Turn the **TABLES** on him   *   Sharp as a **TACK**
(Put him in your situation)   ([Very alert] [Intelligent])

TACKLE it * Get down to brass **TACKS** * Sweat **TACKS**
(Do it)   (To fundamentals)   (Be tense; worried)

It's **TACKY**   *   A **TAD** more   *   **TAG** along
(Not stylish;   (A little more)   (Go with me)
in bad taste)

                * The [TAG] [TAIL] end   *   **TAHDAH!**
It's a bear   (The last section)   (See, I did it like magic!)
by the **TAIL**
(A very difficult problem)   *   I'll bust my **TAIL**
                                               (Work very hard)

The **TAIL** will wag the dog
(A small factor will control
the larger outcome)   * I'm dragging my **TAIL**
                                          (I'm very tired)

Get on his **TAIL**!　*　I have it by the **TAIL**　*　I can't make
(See that he　　　(I control it)　　　head nor **TAIL** of it
　does the job!)　　　　　　　　　　(It is confusing to me)

High**TAIL** it out!　*　Move your **TAIL**!　*　　My **TAIL**
([Run!] [Escape!])　　(Hurry!)　　　　　(My buttocks)

It will **TAIL** off　*　I'm on his **TAIL**　*　In two shakes of
([Become unclear]　　(Following him)　　a lamb's **TAIL**
　[Diminish; shrink])　　　　　　　　　(Very quickly)

Shave**TAIL**　　*　Shirt-**TAIL** relative　*　My **TAIL** will
(New lieutenant)　(Distant relative)　　　be in a sling
　　　　　　　　　　　　　　　　　　(I'll be in trouble,
Turn **TAIL**　*　Work your **TAIL** off　and it will hurt)
(Flee)　　　(Very hard)
　　　　　　　　　　　　　*　I have the world by the **TAIL**
Bright-eyed and bushy **TAILED**　　　(Things are going
(Fresh and ready to go)　　　　　　　well for me)

TAKE it into account　　　　　*　　　**TAKE** after him!
(Consider it)　　　　　　　　　　　　(Chase him!)

I **TAKE** after him　*　**TAKE** him apart!　*　**TAKE** it back!
(I resemble him)　　(Punish him!)　　　(Apologize!)

You can **TAKE** it to the bank　　*　　I'll **TAKE** a bath
(It's reliable; worthy)　　　　　　　(Lose a lot of money)

TAKE your beef out on...　*　**TAKE** the bull by the horns
(Focus your complaints on...)　(Accept the challenge and act)

T

387

You **TAKE** the cake!
(You [are unbelievable!]
[win the prize!])

TAKE [care of] him!
([Punish!] (Kill him!])
[Capture him!])

TAKE a crack at [him] [it]
([Attack; criticize him])
([Try to do it])

I **TAKE** a dim view of it
(I'm dubious; skeptical of it)

TAKE him down!
(Remove; kill him)

TAKE it easy!
([Calm yourself!] [Relax!]
[Go slow!] [Be careful!] [Goodbye!])

TAKE the [fall] [rap]
(Take blame for someone else)

TAKE a flyer
([Try it] [Gamble])

TAKE a gander!
(Look at that!)

TAKE the gloves off
(Stop being gentle)

* I can **TAKE** it [on the chin; nose]
([Endure hardship] [Be tough])

*   **TAKE** care! [of yourself!]
([Expression of goodbye]
[Be careful!])

* He'll **TAKE** us to the cleaners
([Cheat] [Ruin] us financially)

*   It didn't **TAKE**
([It wasn't accepted]
[It didn't adhere])

* It will **TAKE** some doing
(A big effort will be needed)

*   I did a double**TAKE**
(Surprised, I looked
twice to be sure)

*   **TAKE** it easy on him
(Be gentle with him)

* **TAKE** five! * **TAKE** the floor
(Relax!)   (Rise to speak)

*   What do you **TAKE** me for?
(Do you think I'm a fool?)

* ...give or **TAKE** * Give-and-**TAKE**
(Approximately)   (Lively debate)

T

388

TAKE it with a grain of salt   *   **TAKE** it for granted
(Be skeptical)   (Assume it is true)

TAKE a hand   * **TAKE** him in hand   * **TAKE** it off
([Join] [Participate])   (Control him)   my hands
                                       (Take responsibiity for it)

TAKE matters into your own hands
(Move to control the situation)   *   Hard to **TAKE**!
                              ([Such a sacrifice!] [It's wonderful!])

TAKE heart!
([Be encouraged!]   * **TAKE** it to heart * **TAKE** the heart
[Have hope!])   (Consider it seriously)   out of him
                                  (Demoralize him)

TAKE the heart out of it
(Remove its key feature)   *   **TAKE** the heat
                             (Accept responsibility
TAKE heed!   and its consequences)
(Be careful!)   * **TAKE** to your heels!
              (Retreat!)   *   **TAKE** it from here
TAKE a [hike]   (Take responsibility now)
[powder] [walk]
([Leave!] [Go away!])   * We didn't **TAKE** to him
                          (We didn't like him)

It will **TAKE** hold
(Be accepted)   * The **TAKE**-home message is...
           (The key point to remember is...)

TAKE it in
(Make it smaller)   *   He won't **TAKE** me in
                (He won't fool; trick me)

Can you **TAKE** us in?
(Give us shelter)   *   I'll **TAKE** in...
             (My cash receipts will be...)

T

TAKE it as is   *
(In its present condition)

TAKE it from me
(Listen to me)   *

I'll **TAKE** to it
(Accept; adapt; adjust to it)

TAKE your [bumps] [knocks]
[licks] [lumps]

TAKE his measure
(Judge what he can do)

TAKE your medicine
(Your earned punishment)

TAKE it to mind
(Note; remember it)

TAKE [it in] [in the sights]
([Observe it carefully])
([Tour; see things])

I **TAKE** it that...
(I assume that...)

TAKE it to them!
([Attack] [Beat] them!)

We **TAKE** in each
other's laundry
(We [keep each other busy]
[help each other])

* If I **TAKE** a mind to...
(If I decide to...)

* I'll **TAKE** it on the neck
(Be the one blamed)

I'll **TAKE** a notion to...   * **TAKE** off!   * It will **TAKE** off
(Have a sudden urge to...   (Leave!)   (Become successful)

It's a **TAKE**-off on...   *   It will **TAKE** him off
(It's closely resembles...)   (He will die)

Don't **TAKE** off on me!   * I won't **TAKE** that off you!
(Don't criticize me!)   (I won't tolerate your conduct; remark)

TAKE him on!   * He's on the **TAKE** * **TAKE** it on
(Fight; challenge him!)   (He's stealing)   (Do the job)

T

What's his **TAKE** on it?   *   What's the **TAKE** on it
(His ideas; reactions)   ([The income] [What is it all about?])

Don't **TAKE** on like that   *   Don't **TAKE** on any more
(Don't react; behave that way)   (Don't [agree to do more]
    [hire more workers])

Don't **TAKE** it on yourself
(Don't blame yourself)   *   **TAKE** the opportunity to...
    (Use the opportunity to...)

TAKE out after him
(Chase after him)   *   It will **TAKE** it out of you
    (Exhaust; tire you)

He'll **TAKE** it out on me
(Focus his attack on me)   *   **TAKE** him out!
    (Kill him!)

TAKE her out
(Go out socially)   *   **TAKE** over the...
    ([Gain control of...]
TAKE a page out of his book   [Have full use of...])
(Imitate him)

    * **TAKE** pains to...   *   **TAKE** part in...
TAKE his part   (Make a special effort)   (Participate in...)
(Defend him)

    *   **TAKE** him down a peg [or two]
TAKE the plunge   (Reduce his overconfidence)
([Try it] [Begin])

    * **TAKE** a powder   *   **TAKE** no prisoners!
TAKE the rap   (Leave fast!)   (Be ruthless!)
(The blame)

    * **TAKE** a rest   *   **TAKE** him for a ride
TAKE to the road   (Sit down)   ([Take advantage of him]
(Leave!)   [Kill him!])

T

TAKE a back seat   *   TAKE a seat   *   TAKE a look see
(A secondary role)   (Sit down)   (Examine it)

He'll TAKE a shine to...   *   TAKE sick   *   TAKE it slow!
(Be attracted to...)   (Become ill)   (Goodbye!)

TAKE a snooze   *   TAKE it for a spin   *   TAKE a stab at it
(Get some sleep)   (A brief ride)   (Try to do it)

TAKE a stand   *   Let's TAKE stock   *   TAKE it straight up
(State your   (Assess our situation)   (Not diluted)
views firmly)

           *   TAKE a stretch   *   TAKE it in your stride
TAKE your   (Relax!)   (Do it in a routine way)
sweet time
(Don't do it quickly)   *   TAKE it from the top
                                   (From the beginning)

It will TAKE a turn for the
    [better] [worse]   *   TAKE a turn with me
    (Its condition will   (A brief ride)
    [improve] [deteriorate]

          *   TAKE turns with me
TAKE it up   *   TAKE up for him   (Regularly change
(Shorten it)   (Defend him)   positions with me)

TAKE up with...   *   TAKE it up with him
(Associate; join with...)   (Ask him to consider it)

TAKE him up on it   *   TAKE it to them!   *   TAKE a walk!
(Accept his challenge)   (Conquer them!)   ([Resign!] [Leave!])

What will it TAKE?   *   What's the TAKE?
(What is required?)   (The income)

T

TAKE the wind out of his sails
(Discourage; slow him)

* **TAKE** him under your wing
([Care for] [Teach] him)

TAKE him out to the woodshed
([Punish] [Criticize] him)

* **TAKE** my word [for it]
(Believe me)

I was **TAKEN** aback
(Surprised) (Offended)

* He has **TAKEN** to drink
(He is an alcoholic)

He's **TAKEN** with…
(Attracted to…)

* I'm **TAKEN** with it
(Impressed by it)

I've been [**TAKEN**] [**TAKEN** in]
 [Also, see **TOOK**]
([Cheated] [Fooled; misled])

* I've **TAKEN** to…
(Become interested in…)

* It's well-**TAKEN**
(It's a valid point)

It **TAKES** two to tango
(It couldn't be done by one person)

* I have what it **TAKES**
(Spirit; stamina to
[survive] win])

Do what it **TAKES**
(Whatever is necessary)

A [fish] [tall] **TALE**
(An exaggerated story)

* There hangs the **TALE**
(That's the key to the story)

Don't tell **TALES** out of school
(Don't reveal our secrets)

* He'll **TALK** an arm
and leg off you
(He won't stop talking)

No back **TALK**!
Don't **TALK** back!
(Don't [argue!]
 [say anything]!)

* He'll **TALK** behind your back
(Speak about you, not to you)

T

TALK is cheap
(It's easier to talk than act)

* Don't **TALK** down to me!
(Don't patronize me!)

TALK to him like a Dutch uncle
(Advise him in a stern way)

* Don't fast-**TALK** me!
(Don't try to persuade
me by deceptive talk)

A heart to heart **TALK**
(A serious, confidential talk)

* **TALK** him [into] [out of] it
([Convince] [dissuade] him)

You **TALK** my language
(We think the same)

*   **TALK** it over
(Discuss   it)

They **TALK** past each other
(Neither responds to what
the other is saying)

* **TALK** [shop] [turkey]
(Discuss [business] [what is essential])

Small **TALK**
(Conversation used to fill time)

*   Straight **TALK**
(Honest; frank discussion)

Don't [smooth] [sweet]-**TALK** me
(Don't try to [charm] [flatter] me

*   **TALK** it up
(Promote it)

Walk the way you **TALK**
(Your actions should
match what you say)

* A smooth **TALKER**
(A person who captivates
others by talk)

My feet are **TALKING** to me
(They ache; are tired)

*   He's **TALKING**
through his hat
(He is confused; wrong)

I got a real **TALKING** to
(My behavior was strongly criticized)

* He's like **TALKING**
to a wall
(He won't listen)

T

Now, you are **TALKING**!
(That's much better!)

He **TALKS** a blue streak
(Very fast)

It's a **TALL** order
(A tough challenge)

He'll stand **TALL**
(He's outstanding)

The **TANK**
(Jail)

TANKED
(Drunk)

TAP out!
(Quit!)

What's on **TAP**?
(What's next?)

I'm **TAPPED** out
(Impoverished; overcommited)

What in **TARNATION**?
([What is that?]
[Expression of amazement])

It won't be **TEA** and crumpets
(It won't be easy)

It's not my cup of **TEA**
(I don't prefer it)

TEAR into him
(Attack; criticize him)

* Money **TALKS**
(Money gives one power)

* I'm in **TALL** cotton
(I'm prosperous)

* A **TALL** [story] [tale] [yarn]
(An exaggerated story)

* Tan his **HIDE**!
(Punish him!)

* It takes two
to **TANGO**
(It couldn't be done
by one person)

* He'll get the **TAP**
(Be named; chosen)

* Red **TAPE**
(Official requirements)

* [Beat] [Whale] the **TAR**
out of them!
(Beat them badly)

* It leaves a bad **TASTE**
in my mouth
(It bother; troubles me)

* He'll **TEAR** his hair
(React with grief)

* A **TEAR**jerker
(A very sad story)

T

He's on a **TEAR**　*　Crocodile **TEARS**　*　That **TEARS** it
　([Very busy]　　(False sorrow)　(I have no more patience)
　[Acting wild;
　　destructive])　　*　Hoop**TEEDOO**　*　Armed to the **TEETH**
　　　　　　　　　(Excitement)　　　([Carrying many weapons]
The bit is in　　　　　　　　　　　　[Very well-prepared])
　my **TEETH**　　*　I cut my **TEETH** on...
　(I have the　　　　(I had my first training; experience on...)
　responsibility)

　　　　　　　　　　*　　It set my **TEETH** on edge
I would give my　　　　(I became very anxious; tense)
　eye**TEETH** for...
　(Make great sacrifices for...)　*　I'm [fed] up to my **TEETH**
　　　　　　　　　　　　　　(I can't tolerate more)

Get your **TEETH** into it
(Become actively involved)　　*　Scarce as hen's **TEETH**
　　　　　　　　　　　　　　(Very rare)

It has no **TEETH**
(It's powerless; weak)　　　*　Like pulling **TEETH**
　　　　　　　　　　　　　(Very difficult)

He'll show his **TEETH** [in his eyes]
(His [anger] [resolve])　　*　...by the skin of his **TEETH**
　　　　　　　　　　　　(Barely; very narrowly)

TELL me about it!
(I've had that experience)　　*　Blood will **TELL**
　　　　　　　　　　　(Family　[characteristics]
　　　　　　　　　　　[loyalties] will dominate)
Do **TELL**!
(Is that so?)
　　　　　　　　　*　I **TELL** [it to] you for a fact
TELL him where to　　　　(It's the truth)
　[get off] [head in]
　(Tell him what you think of him)　*　I hear **TELL** that...
　　　　　　　　　　　　(I understand that...)

T

396

You **TELL** ['em] [him]!   *   **TELL** it to the marines!
([Say it again!] [You're right!])   ([I don't believe it!]
                                                   ([Nonsense!])

He'll **TELL** on us   *   Don't **TELL** stories!
(Betray us)   (Don't lie!)   *   Don't **TELL** tales
                                           out of school

Only time will **TELL**   (Don't reveal our secrets)
(We won't know for a while)

                         *   There's no **TELLING**
It's a **[10] TEN**!   (It's unpredictable)
(It's perfect!)

          *   A **TEN** spot   *   **TEND** to your knitting
A TENDERFOOT   (A $ 10.00 bill)   (Focus on your
(An untested beginner)   own affairs)

TENDERhearted   *   A **TEN**strike   *   It goes with the
(Compassionate;   (A wonderful   **TERRITORY**
  caring)   idea; result)   (It's part of the job)

The acid **TEST**   *   **TEST** the water   *   At the end
(The critical   (Experiment; try it)   of my **TETHER**
 proof needed)   (I have no more
                         [resources] [strength])

THANK you kindly!
(Thank you very much!)   *   I'll **THANK** you to...
                     (I'm warning you, don't...)

I have you to **THANK** for that
(You are the one I blame)   *   **THANKS** a [bundle]
                     [heap] [whole lot] [million]!
No **THANKS**! [to you]!   ([That's not very helpful!]
 ([Sorry, but "No!"]   [I appreciate your help very much!])
 [You didn't help at all!])

                                           T

397

THANKS [just the same!]   *   How's **THAT?**
  [but no **THANKS!**]   (What did you say?)
(Thanks, but I don't
wish to [do] [have] it)   *   Just like **THAT!**
                   ([Easily] [Quickly])
THAT'S THAT!
  ([It's final!])   *   On top of **THAT,...**
  [I have no more patience!])   (In addition,...)

To a fare-**THEE**-well   *   [Every] Now and **THEN**
  ([To an extreme] [Too much])   (Occasionally)

...and **THEN** some! * Not all **THERE**   * I'm **THERE**
(...and even more!) (Not fully sane) (I'm very interested)

THERE you [are!] go!]   *   I'll be **THERE** for you
(See, as I predicted!)   (I'll help; support you)

I've been **THERE** [before]   *   I'll get up **THERE**
  [done that] [too]   (in higher [age] [income] [rank])
(I had that experience)

               *   **THERE** you go! [again!]
Don't go **THERE!**   (You see, as I predicted)
(Don't [talk] [think] about that!) (You [did] [said] it again!)

Hang in **THERE!** * Hang out **THERE**   * Neither here
(Persevere!)   (Be there)   nor **THERE**
                        ([Indecisive]
Put here **THERE!** * So **THERE!**   [Irrelevant])
(Shake hands) (If you don't like
           it, I'm sorry)   * How is the weather
THICK and fast   up **THERE?**
(Quickly; in great numbers) (Joking greeting to tall person)

T

THICK as [fleas] [flies]
(Very numerous)

He [has a **THICK** head]
[is very **THICK**]
(He's stupid)

In the **THICK** of it
(In the middle of it)

[Lay] [Spread] it on **THICK**
(Exaggerate)

He has a **THICK** skin
(He [is tough]
[can manage criticism])

They're **THICK** as **THIEVES**
(Closely associated)

Through **THICK** and **THIN**
(In good and bad times)

The plot **THICKENS**
(Things are becoming
more complicated)

He'll vanish into **THIN** air
(Disappear)

I don't have a **THIN** dime
(I have no money)

He's on **THIN** ice
(He doesn't have good
preparation or support)

He has a **THIN** skin
(He is easily offended)

I have a **THING** about...
(A special concern or
interest)

Big **THING**!
(Nothing to get excited about)

Do your **THING**
(Your special function;
skill)

Hold every**THING**!
(Wait!)

He has a finger
in every**THING**
(He is very busy;
involved)

A fool **THING** to do
(Stupid; unwise)

He has a **THING** for her
(He is attracted to her)

It's a [kid's] [men's]
[women's] **THING**
(It has special meaning to...)

T

The **THING** of it is…   *   I know a **THING** or two
(The main point is…)   (I have experience)

Sure **THING**!   *   Of all **THINGS**!   *   I bottle **THINGS** up
(I agree!)   (It's amazing)   (Hide my concerns/emotions)

THINGS will break for him   *   **THINGS** are clicking
(His fortunes will improve)   (Working well)

Hold **THINGS** down   *   Don't do **THINGS** by halves
(Take care of things   (Do things with enthusiasm)
   while I am away)

                     *   In the nature of **THINGS**
THINGS will pick up   (The way things are)
(Become more active)

               *   I have the run of **THINGS**
Get into the swing of **THINGS**   (I [have full access to…]
(Into the rhythm of activities)   [control things])

What do you **THINK**   *   He'll **THINK** better of it
   of those apples?   (He'll change his views)
(What is your reaction to…?)

              *   Come to **THINK** of it,…
You have another **THINK** coming!   (I also remember that…)
(You have misjudged)

               *   **THINK** twice about it
I **THINK** the world of…   ([Don't act too quickly]
(I greatly admire…)   [Consider it carefully])

A free **THINKER**   *   Give him the **THIRD** degree
(One who doesn't think   (Question him carefully)
   in ordinary ways)

T

400

THIRD rate   *   **THIRTY** lashes with a wet noodle
(Poor quality)   (A meaningless punishment)

A doubting **THOMAS**   *   Food for **THOUGHT**
(A skeptical person)   (Something to consider)

Lost in **THOUGHT**   *   Perish the **THOUGHT**
(Preoccupied)   (Don't think of it)

Don't give it a second **THOUGHT**   *   Train of **THOUGHT**
(It's not important)   (Process of thinking)

Penny for your **THOUGHTS**   *   Having second **THOUGHTS**
(What are you thinking?)   (Reconsidering)

Don't lose the **THREAD**   *   Nice **THREADS**
(Stay focused)   (Clothes)

THREE sheets to the wind   *   Eat **THREE** squares a day
(Drunk)   (Eat well)

[Cram] [Ram] [Shove] it   *   [Crawl] [Jump] down
down his **THROAT**   his **THROAT**
(Force him to [accept] [do] it)   (Criticize him)

I have a frog in my **THROAT**   *   My heart **THROB**
(My voice is hoarse)   (The one I love)

THRONE room   *   Bulldog it **THROUGH**
(Toilet)   (Push it until done)

Carry it **THROUGH**   *   Come **THROUGH** for me!
(Finish the job)   (Help me!)

T

It will come **THROUGH** in the clear
(Uncoded)

* Come **THROUGH**
with flying colors)
(Meet the test; succeed)

It will fall **THROUGH**
([Fail] [Not happen as expected])

* Get **THROUGH** to him!
(Make him understand!)

It will go **THROUGH**
([Be accepted] [Reach the goal])

* Go **THROUGH** with it
(Do [the job] [what was planned])

Heard **THROUGH** the grapevine
(From rumors)

* I've been **THROUGH** the mill
(I have a lot of experience)

Get it **THROUGH** your noodle!
(Try to understand!)

* Put him **THROUGH** his paces
(Test how he performs)

Pull **THROUGH**
(Survive)

* He'll railroad it **THROUGH**
([Get it done quickly]
[Push it hard])

See it **THROUGH**
(Finish the job)

* I see **THROUGH** you
(I understand your motives)

I'll squeak **THROUGH**
(Barely [succeed]
[survive] [win])

* **THROUGH** thick and thin
(In good and bad times)

Whip **THROUGH** it
(Examine it quickly)

* I'm **THROUGH** with you
(I'll no longer relate to you)

I've been **THROUGH** the wringer
(I've had a lot of trouble)

* Don't **THROW** out the baby
with the bathwater

THROW a big [blowout] [shindig]
(Have a big party)

(Don't let small
problems defeat large goals)

T

THROW him a bone
(Make a small
concession to him)

He'll **THROW** it [in my face]
[up to me]
(He'll remind me of it)

THROW a fit
(Become very angry)

He'll **THROW** up his hands
(Quit in frustration)

THROW it in
(Add it at no cost)

I let it **THROW** me
(Overwhelm me)

THROW him over
([Desert] [Jilt]
[Get rid of] him)

A stone's **THROW**
(A short distane)

THROW your weight around
(Use your influence to
gain your objective)

He'll **THUMB** his nose at me
(Scorn; not respect me)

* **THROW** the book at him
(Punish him to the fullest degree)

* **THROW** him a curve
(Surprise him)

* **THROW** the fight
(Act defeated and quit)

* **THROW** down the glove
(Give a challenge)

* **THROW** him for a loop
(Stun; surprise him)

* **THROW** in with us
(Join; ally with us)

* **THROW** something on
(Put on some clothes)

* **THROW** in the [sponge] [towel]
(Quit; give up the fight)

* **THROW** up
(Vomit)

* **THROW** cold
water on it
(Discourage it)

* What's its **THRUST**?
(Its basic idea; message)

* **THUMB** a ride
(Seek a ride from passing vehicle)

A rule of **THUMB**
(A useful guideline)

*

THUMBnail sketch
(A very brief description)

It will stick out like
a sore **THUMB**
(It's different and
won't look right)

*

He's under my **THUMB**
(I control him)

It's **THUMBS** [down] [up]!
(It's [rejected] [accepted]!)

*

All **THUMBS**
(Very clumsy)

Twiddle my **THUMBS**
(Sit idle)

*

THUMBS up!
(Have confidence!)

He'll steal my **THUNDER**
(Get credit for my work; ideas)

*

By **THUNDER**!
(Expression of [amazement]
[determination])

What makes it **TICK**?
(What [explains his behavior?]
[is his character; essence?])

*

Make it **TICK**
(Get it to function)

I have a bum **TICKER**
(My heart is weak)

* I'm **[TICKED!]** [T'd] off
(Angry)

Our meal **TICKET**
(Our financial supporter)

*

A [big] [hot] **TICKET** item
(A [costly] [popular] item)

Write your own **TICKET**
(You can have what you want)

*

That's the **TICKET**!
(It's exactly right!)

A rib-**TICKLER**
(A funny story)

* I'm **TICKLED** [to death]
[pink] [silly]
(Very pleased)

* **TIDE** me over
(Help me get through this emergency)

404

The **TIDE** will turn * Can you **TIE** that?
(The situation will change) (Can you [equal] [believe] that?)

TIE up the loose ends * **TIE** into him!
(Settle all details) (Attack him!)

TIE on the nose bag * **TIE** the knot * **TIE** one on
(Eat) (Get married) (Get drunk)

Fit to be **TIED** * My hands are **TIED** * Hog-**TIED**
(Very angry) (I have no choice) (Helpless)

TIED to his mother's * I'm **TIED** up * **TIED** up in knots
apron strings (Very busy) (Unable to act)
(Dependent on his mother)

* He's a paper **TIGER**
TIGHT * We're **TIGHT** (All bluster; little action)
(Drunk) ([Closely associated]
[Successful]) * A **TIGHT** argument
I'm **TIGHT** (A carefully reasoned argument)
[with the buck] [-fisted]
(I hate to spend up money) * I run a **TIGHT** ship
(I direct my operation firmly)

Sit **TIGHT**! * Sleep **TIGHT**
(Don't move (Get a good rest) * In a **TIGHT** spot
or do anything!) (In a crisis)

A **TIGHT** squeak * [Up **TIGHT**] [**TIGHTER** than a drum]
(A narrow escape) (Very tense)

TIGHTwad * **TIGHTEN** your belts
(One who hates to spend money) (Economize)

T

TIME and again   *   Ahead of TIME   *   Beat his TIME
(Repeatedly)   (Earlier then expected)   (Court his girlfriend)

For the TIME being   *   It's big TIME!
(For the present time)   ([A great amount] [Wonderful!]
([Very important!])

I'm having a big TIME
(A wonderful experience)   *   He's in the big TIME
([Famous] [A leader in his field])

He has TIME to burn
(A lot of time)   *   He won't give us the
TIME of day
He'll do TIME   (He won't help or even see us)
(Be in jail)

*   In no TIME flat   *   TIME flies
[All] In good TIME   (At once)   (Goes by quickly)
(Eventually)

*   He's a good-TIME Charlie
I have TIME on my hands   (A fun-loving person)
(I'm not busy)

*   He'll do [hard] [serious] TIME
Give him a hard TIME   (Be in jail [for a long time])
(Make trouble for him)

*   High TIME!   *   Kill TIME
[The TIME of my life]   ([Overdue]   (Stall; wait)
[A whale of a TIME]   [Finally it's
(A wonderful experience)   happening])   *   Long TIME
no see!
Make TIME with her   *   Make TIME for me   (A greeting)
(Court her)   (Reserve time for me)

In the nick of TIME   *   The TIME is ripe
(At the right moment)   (It's ready now; timely)

T

In the nick **TIME**
(At the right moment)

The **TIME** is ripe
(It's ready now; timely)

My **TIME** to shine
(To [perform]
[be acclaimed])

In a short **TIME**
([Soon] [Briefly])

Show **TIME**!
(Time to perform!)

Take your own sweet **TIME**
(Don't do it quickly)

Only **TIME** will tell
(We won't know for a while)

From **TIME** to **TIME**
(Occasionally)

Turn-around **TIME**
(Time to prepare
to act again)

He'll two-**TIME** you
(Be unfaithful)

For the [umpteenth]
[umpty-umph] **TIME**
(Many times before)

An old-**TIMER**
(An old person)

He has a **TIN** ear
(He [doesn't listen carefully]
[isn't sensitive])

He's a **TIN** horn
(He's false; not genuine)

Not worth a **TINKER'S** dam
(It has no value)

I got a **TIP** from...
(Advance information; a warning)

Don't **TIP** your hand
(Reveal your intentions)

It's the **TIP** of the iceberg
([Much more is hidden]
[It's just the beginning])

The **TIP**-off
(An advance signal; indication)

It will **TIP** the scale
(Be the decisive factor)

It's on the **TIP** of my tongue
(I almost can remember it)

T

In **TIP**-top [condition] [shape]   *   At my finger **TIPS**
(I almost can remember it)   (Easily available)

Dog-**TIRED**   *   He's **TITTLED**   *   They're in a **TIZZY**
(Exhausted)   (Drunk)   ([Anxious] [Confused])

Snap **TO!**   *   A **TOE** hold   *   **TOE** the line!
(Be alert!)   (A first step)   (Obey the rules)

I'll stub my **TOE**   *   Go [head] [**TOE**] to **TOE**   * He's on
(Make mistakes)   (Fight bitterly)   his **TOES**
                                                        (He's alert)

Don't step on his **TOES**   *   He has [his act]
(Don't antagonize him)   [it] [all] [**TOGETHER**]
                                      (He is confident; well-organized)

Get your [act] [brain]
  TOGETHER!   *   A get-**TOGETHER**
([Organize yourself better]   (A meeting; gathering)
[Think more carefully])

                            *   They are going **TOGETHER**
Let's [hang] [put our heads]   (They are romantically linked)
  TOGETHER
(Collaborate)   *   Pull yourself **TOGETHER**
                                      (Get control of yourself)

By the same **TOKEN**
  (Equally; similarly)   *   All **TOLD**   * Some **TOMATO!**
                    (Counting everything)   (Attractive woman)
TOMORROW is
  another day   *   We went at it hammer and **TONGS**
(Resume work tomorow)   (We fought fiercely)

[Bite] [Hold] your **TONGUE!**   *   The cat has his **TONGUE**
(Keep silent)   (He won't speak)

T

I said it TONGUE in cheek
(I was [teasing] [not sincere])

* A TONGUE-lashing
(Severe critcism)

He has a loose TONGUE
(He talks too much
and indiscreetly

* He'll lose his TONGUE
(He won't talk)

* He has a sharp TONGUE
(He speaks bitterly; harshly)

A slip of the TONGUE
(An unintended comment)

* It's on the tip of my TONGUE
(I almost can remember it)

TOO bad!
([I'm sorry!] [Who cares?])

* You're TOO much!
([You're really unusual!]
[You overwhelm me!])

TOOdahloo!
(Goodbye!)

We've been TOOK!
(Cheated)

* I TOOK [off] [out of there]
[out after...]
(I [left quickly] [chased after]...)

I TOOK it on the snoot
(I lost)

* TOOL along *
([Cruise] [Move easily])

TOOT your horn
(Promote yourself)

He's on a TOOT
(He's drunk)

* Fight TOOTH and nail
(Fiercely)

* Examine it with
a fine-TOOTH comb
(Very thoroughly)

I'm clean as a
hound's TOOTH
([I'm innocent] [There is
no evidence against me])

* He's long in the TOOTH
(Very old)

I have a
sweet TOOTH
(I like sweet food)

* Darn TOOTING!
([Indeed!]
[That's the truth!])

* My TOOTSIES
(My feet)

T

The **TOP** [banana] [dog] [man] * I'll blow my **TOP**
(The boss) (Become very angry)

TOP brass * Deal from the **TOP** * Pay **TOP** dollar
(The bosses; of the deck (The highest price)
leaders) (Be honest)

* **TOP** [drawer] [flight]
Off the **TOP** of my head (High quality)
(My guess is...) * **TOP** of the line
(Highest cost and quality)

A mountain-**TOP** experience
(Once in a lifetime) * **TOP** notch * ...off the **TOP**
(High quality) (Ahead of all; before)

To **TOP** it off,...
(Even more important,...) * On **TOP** of that,...
(In addition,...)

I'm on **TOP** of it
(I have [it under control] * I sleep like a **TOP**
[focused on it]) (Very soundly)

[Start] [Take] it from the **TOP** * What could **TOP** this?
(From the beginning) (Be better than this)

Tip-**TOP** [condition] [shape] * I **TOPPED** him * It's **TOPS**
(Excellent condition) (Beat him) (The best)

It's **TOPSY**-turvy * I carry a **TORCH** for...
([Confusing] [Revolutionary]) (I still love...)

I'll **TOSS** my cookies * I'll **TOSS** it off * It's a **TOSS** up
(Vomit) ([Recover quickly] (It could go
[Give it little thought]) either way)

T

TOT it up   *   **TOTALED**   *   Low man on the **TOTEM** pole
(Total it)   (Destroyed)   (The lowest ranking person)

It's not so hotsy-**TOTSY**   *   **TOUCH** base with...
(There are problems)   [Be] [Get] in **TOUCH** with...
                       (Communicate with...)

It's **TOUCH** and go
(The outcome is uncertain)   *   He has the **TOUCH**
                         (A special skill)

[Just] A **TOUCH** of...
(A small amount of...)   *   I'm losing my **TOUCH**
                           (My skill)

I'm [not in] [out of] **TOUCH**
([Not in communication with...]   *   I'm a soft **TOUCH**
[No longer closely informed])   (One who gives/lends
                           money too easily)

He's [TETCHED] [TOUCHED] in the head
(Insane)   *   He's **TOUCHY**
                         (Very sensitive)

TOUGH [bounce] [luck]!
([Bad luck] [I don't care] [Sorry])!   *   [**TOUGH** cookie]
                         [**TOUGH** as nails]

A **TOUGH** Customer   (A strong, enduring person)
(Someone difficult to
[persuade] [sell to])   *   It's a **TOUGH** go
                         (A difficult challenge)

Hang **TOUGH**!
(Persevere!)   * I look **TOUGH**   * **TOUGH** it out!
           (In poor condition)   (Persevere!)

It's a **TOUGH** sell
(It's difficult to sell)   *   I'm in **TOUGH** shape
                 (My [condition] [situation] is bad)

TOUGH sledding   * [That's] TOUGH!   * A cook's TOUR
(Things are   (Sorry, I can't help)   (Many things are
  difficult)   seen briefly)

He's in TOW   * KowTOW to...   * Have an eye
(He's going   (Bow; defer to...)   TOWARD...
with us)   (Show concern for...)

Throw in the TOWEL   * I'll [blow] [skip] TOWN
(Give up the fight)   (Leave town)

The only game in TOWN   * Get out of TOWN!
(Where the main activity is)   ([I don't believe you!]
                            [You're joking!])

I hit TOWN at...   * A jerkwater TOWN
(I arrived at...)   (A small remote settlement)

He's out of TOWN   * Piant the TOWN [red]
(He is not alert)   (Celebrate and get drunk)

Skip TOWN!   * Kick over the TRACES
(Leave quickly!)   ([Break away; escape!]
       [Radically change your life style])

Off the beaten TRACK
([Not easily found] [Remote])   * Off the TRACK
                           (Wrong)

It's [back] on TRACK
(Moving again, as planned)   * He has a one-TRACK mind
                 (He thinks only of one thing)

His TRACK record is...
(His performance over time is...)   * SideTRACK him
                 (Divert him)

T

412

I'm off on the wrong **TRACK**
(I made a poor start)

* Cover your **TRACKS**
(Camouflage your actions)

Make **TRACKS**!
(Hurry!)

* Stop him in his **TRACKS**!
(Stop him where he is!)

He's from the wrong side
of the **TRACKS**
(An area and background
considered undesirable)

* A jack-of-all-**TRADES**
(A person who has many skills)

* Stop the **TRAFFIC**!
(Wait the minute!)

Hit the **TRAIL**
(Leave!)

* I'll pick up the **TRAIL**
(Discover it)

* A gravy **TRAIN**
(A source of profits/gains)

TRAIN of thought
(Process of thinking)

* Hands-on **TRAINING**
(Learn by actually using/doing things)

Close your **TRAP**!
(Be silent!)

*

He's flapping his **TRAP**
(Talking too much)

Build a better mouse**TRAP**
(Improve the product)

* Keep your **TRAP** shut!
(Be silent!)

He has a steel **TRAP** mind
(He is rigid; stubborn)

* He'll **TRASH** us
([Hurt] [Ruin] us)

A fellow **TRAVELER**
(A sympathizer)

* **TRAVELING** at a [fancy] [fast] clip
(Very fast)

He **TRAVELS** in the fast lane
([Aggressive, he has advanced quickly]
[He parties and spends a lot])

* How's the world
TREATING you?
(A greeting)

T

He'll bark up the wrong **TREE**
(Waste time on
the wrong thing)

* He's out of his **TREE**
(Crazy)

* Up a **TREE**
(Abandoned; isolated)

* **TRENDY**
(The lastest style)

A **TRIAL** balloon
(A test to get
first reactions
to an idea/plan)

* It will [do] [turn] the **TRICK**
(Produce the desired result)

He doesn't miss a **TRICK**
(He's alert to opportunities)

* That's the **TRICK**
(The secret of how to do it)

Dirty **TRICKS**
(Actions to
confuse; deceive)

* How's **TRICKS**?
([A greeting]
[How are you?])

* He's up to his
old **TRICKS**
(Doing what he
usually does)

TRIM your sails
(Reduce your expectations)

* **TRIP** the light fantastic
(Dance)

He's on a guilt **TRIP**
(He blames himself
for everything)

* Don't lay that **TRIP** on me!
(Don't blame me!)

* He's on a **TRIP**
(He has lost his sense of reality)

Don't **TRIP** out on me
(Don't lose your sense of reality)

* He's a real **TRIP**
(An unusual person)

It's a real **TRIP**
(A wild experience)

* **TRIP** him up
(Foil him)

* I **TRIPPED** up
(I failed)

I'm hot to **TROT**
(Ready to go)

* Don't [borrow] [look for] **TROUBLE**
(Don't seek problems)

T

414

A [heap] [pack] of **TROUBLE**   * I'm having **TROUBLE**
(A lot of problems)   fixing my mouth
                                    (Trying to decide what to say)

That spells **TROUBLE**
(There will be trouble)   *   Don't **TRUCK** with me!
                                         (Don't cheat me!)

Have no **TRUCK** with him
(Don't [associate] [deal] with him!)   *   I'm **TRUCKING**
                                      (Making good progress)

TRUE blue
(Very loyal)   *   Show your **TRUE** colors
                                 (Reveal your real character)

It doesn't [hold] [ring] **TRUE**
(It's false; not supported by facts)   * ...and yours **TRULY**
                                              (...and me)

A brain **TRUST**   * He'll shade the **TRUTH**
(A source of ideas; wisdom)   (Not tell the whole truth)

Give it a **TRY**   *   **TRY** your [hand] [luck]
(Attempt; test it)   (Try to do it)

TRY it on [for size]   *   **TRY** out for...
(Put it on) ([Consider it])   (Audition; seek to qualify for...)

He's very **TRYING**   * What are you **TRYING** to pull?
(He exasperates people)   (To do by possibly devious tactics)

The boob **TUBE**   * Go down the **TUBE** * Nip and **TUCK**
(Television)   (Go bankrupt; fail)   (A close contest)

My best bib and **TUCKER**   *   [Plum] **TUCKERED** out
(Clothes)   (Very tired)

T

TUG-of-war
(A struggle between two
groups for supremacy)

             *   I didn't **TUMBLE**
    (I didn't understand; realize)

       *   Give me a **TUMBLE**
    (Let me court you)

Rough and **TUMBLE**
([Wild] [Very competitive])

        *   Call the **TUNE**
    (Be the boss)

Change your **TUNE**
(Change your views)

       *   [In] [Out of] **TUNE**
   ([In] [Not in] harmony with...)

To the **TUNE** of...
(in the amount of...)

        *   **TUNE** him out!
    (Stop listening to him!)

Sing a different **TUNE**
(Change what you are saying)

        *   Stay in **TUNE**!
    (Goodbye!)

I'm not **TUNED** in
(I don't know what is happening)

        *   Stay **TUNED**

There is light at
the end of the **TUNNEL**
(We may have success soon)
   (Stay involved; continue listening)

        *   A **TURKEY**
   ([An undesirable person] [A failure])

A cold **TURKEY**
(An aloof; unfriendly person)

   *   Quit cold **TURKEY**
    (Suddenly)

Let's talk **TURKEY**
(Discuss what is essential)
  * **TURN** it around
   (Make it successful)

TURN around time
(Time needed to be ready
again for action or service)
  * Don't **TURN** your back on...
   (Don't reject...)

T

416

It will take a **TURN** for
the [better] [worse]
(Its condition will
[improve] [deteriorate])

TURN a deaf ear
(Pretend not to hear)

TURN a dollar
(Earn; get money)

A [flat] **TURN** down
(A rejection)

TURN it upside down
(Search it thoroughly)

It gave me a **TURN**
(It startled me)

He won't **TURN** a hand
(He won't [help] [work])

You can **TURN** his head
(He can be influenced by
[flattery] [success])

TURN in!
(Go to sleep!)

TURN him in
(Report him to the authorities)

* **TURN** a blind eye to it
(Pretend it's not there)

* It will **TURN** the corner
(Become more successful)

* It can **TURN** on a dime
(Change directions quickly
in a small space)

* Done to a **TURN**
(Done perfectly)

* A down**TURN**
(A decline in activity)

* That's a ...**TURN** of events
(A change in circumastance)

* He didn't **TURN** a hair
(He showed no
[concern] [interest])

* **TURN** up the heat
(Apply more pressure)

* High **TURN**over
([Personnel] [Stock]
is replaced quickly)

* **TURN** over a new leaf
(Start fresh)

T

TURN it over [in your mind]
(Consider it)

TURN him off!
(Stop him from talking)

TURN it off
(Stop doing it!)

He'll **TURN** on you
(Betray you)

How will it **TURN** out?
(What will be the result?)

TURN out for...
(Show support for...)

He can **TURN** a phrase
(He is creative in using words)

TURN your stomach
(Make you sick)

TURN tail
(Flee)

He'll **TURN** up at...
(Be present at...)

The tide will **TURN**
(The situation will change)

* Don't **TURN** up your
nose at it
(Don't reject it)

* It will **TURN** him [off] [on]
([Repel] [Attract] him)

* It's a **TURN**-off
(It is not liked)

* **TURN** him out
([Vote him out of office]
[Get rid of him)

* The **TURN** out
(The attendance)

* **TURN** the page
([Move on] [Start fresh])

* **TURN** a profit
(Have more income than expenses)

* **TURN** the tables on him
(Put him in your situation)

* It will **TURN** up
(Be found; located)

* Take a **TURN** with me
(Take a brief ride with me)

T

418

It will **TURN** the trick
(Produce the desired result)

He's **TURNED** on
(Very active; excited)

He is well **TURNED** out
(Well [equipped] [dressed])

Leave no stone un**TURNED**
(Do everything possible)

The worm has **TURNED**
(Things are different)

A real page **TURNER**
(An interesting book)

You can't squeeze blood
out of a **TURNIP**
(It won't yield anything)

Take **TURNS** with me
(Regularly change positions
with me)

It's topsy-**TURVY**
(Confusing; revolutionary)

It's catch-**TWENTY-TWO** (22)
(I can't win either way)

Think **TWICE** about it
([Consider it carefully]
[Don't act too quickly])

I'll **TWIDDLE** my thumbs
(Sit idle)

TWINGE of conscience
(Troubled conscience)

TWIST his arm
(Force him to [do] [not do] something)

With a **TWIST**
(Done in a special way)

A new **TWIST**
(Something different)

I have a **TWITCH** on her
(I'm attracted to her)

All a**TWITTER**
(Very excited)

A **TWO**-bit crook
(An unimportant thief)

TWO bits
($ .25)

It isn't worth **TWO** bits
(It has little value)

Get your **TWO** cents in
(Make your comments)

T

For **TWO** cents, I...
(For almost nothing,...)

TWO-by-four
(A very small place)

I don't give **TWO** hoops and a hollar
(It's not important to me)

Hotter than a **TWO**-dollar pistol
(Very popular)

He'll **TWO**-time you
(Be unfaithful to you)

A **TWO**-way street
(I help you; you help me)

No **TWO** ways about it
(It's certain)

* **TWO**-faced
(Treacherous)

* A goody **TWO**-shoes
(A person who is too
correct and proper)

* I'm of **TWO** minds
(I see two alternatives)

* I know a thing or **TWO**
(I have experience)

* I put **TWO** and **TWO** together
(The facts led me
to a conclusion)

T

Chapter U

UGLY as sin   * **UH** huh   *· For the **[UMPTEENTH]**
(Very unpleasant   ([Yes]   **[UMPTY-UMPH]** time!
  to look at)   [I'm listening])   (Many times before)

It's **UNBECOMMING**!   *   Cry **UNCLE**!
(It's [not good manners!]   ([Quit!] [Surrender!]
  [unsuitable; poor taste!])

          * Talk to him like a Dutch **UNCLE**
Knock him **UNCONSCIOUS**   (Advise him sternly)
(Make him lose all sensation)

          *   **UNDER** his breath
He'll [buckle] [knuckle] **UNDER**   (In a whisper)
([Quit] [Surrender])

          *   He hides his light
Hot **UNDER** the collar   **UNDER** a bushel
(Very angry)   (Hides his abilities; deeds)

It's **UNDER** cover   * Go **UNDER**   * **UNDER** the gun
(A hidden; secret   ([Fail]   (Under great pressure)
  activity)   [Become bankrupt])

          * **UNDER**-handed
Keep it **UNDER** your [hat] [lid]   (Dishonest)
(Don't tell anyone)

          *   I'm out from **UNDER**
Sweep it **UNDER** the rug   ([No longer subject to...]
(Hide the problem)   [My debts are paid])

He'll get **UNDER** your skin   * I'm snowed **UNDER**
([Annoy] [Interest] you)   (Overburdened by work)

Pay him **UNDER** the table
(Secretly)

* He's **UNDER** my thumb
(I control him)

UNDER the weather * **UNDER** the wire * **UNDER** wraps
(Ill)   (Within the time limit)   (Still secret)

Go **UNDERGROUND**
(Hide)

* It will [UNDO] [UNGLUE] him
(Confuse; disorient him)

It's **UNHEARD** of
(There are no precedents)

* He's an **UNKNOWN** quantity)
(Little is known about him)

I **UNLOADED** on him)
(I told him what
I thought [of him])

* I gave him **UNSHIRTED** hell
(I severely criticized him)

*   **UNTIL** that day rolls around
Wait **UNTIL** the cows come home   (Until that time)
(For a very long time)

* Leave no stone **UNTURNED**
I'm **UP** and about   (Do everything possible)
([I recovered]
[I'm awake and active])

*   He'll act **UP**
(Cause problems; misbehave)

It doesn't add **UP**
(It doesn't make sense)

*   I'm **UP** against it
(I'm in trouble)

UP in arms   * Back him **UP**
(Angry; aroused)   (Support him)   * He's our back-**UP**
(Our person in reserve)

His back is **UP**   * I'm backed **UP**
(He's angry)   (Behind in my work)   *   I must play
catch-**UP** ball
(I'm losing and must work hard to win)

U

I [balled] [goofed] [screwed] [slipped] **UP**   * It's balled **UP**
(Made errors)   (It's a mess)

A bang-**UP** job   * [Bear] [Hold] **UP**!   * Beat **UP**
(Excellently done)   (Endure; preserve)   (Hurt)

UP beat   * Beef it **UP**   * I went belly **UP**
(Confident)   (Strengthen it)   (Bankrupt)

Belly **UP** to the problem   *   My blood is **UP**
(Confront it)   (I'm angry; defiant)

A blow **UP**   * I bottle things **UP**   * Bottoms **UP**!
(A big argument) (Conceal my emotions) (Empty your glass)

Break it **UP**! * It will break him **UP** * He'll break me **UP**
([Disperse]   (Be a blow to him)   (Make me laugh)
[Stop fighting!])

                    * We'll break **UP**   * Bring him **UP**
Do it **UP** brown   (End our association)   (Provide him
(Get it done with style)   care and education)

Brush **UP** on...   *   Buck him **UP**
(Renew skills; knowledge of...)   (Cheer; encourage him)

I'll burn **UP**   * Butter him **UP**   * [Button] [Dry] **UP**!
(Get angry) (Get his interest by flattery)   (Be silent!)

[Button] [Wrap] it **UP**   *   He's buttoned **UP**
([Finish; complete it]   ([Very disciplined]
[Put it into a secure position]   [Conservative])

U

Hard **UP** for cash   * Hit him **UP** for...   * I'll catch **UP**
(Without funds)   (Ask him for...) (I won't be behind)

I'm caught **UP** with...   *   Get a check-**UP**
(Very involved with...)   (A physical examination)

Check **UP** on him   *   Keep your chin **UP**!
(Investigate him)   (Have courage!)

Clam **UP**!   *   I'll clean **UP**
(Be silent!)   ([Make money]
[Wash and refresh myself])

Clear it **UP**
(Resolve the problem)   * It will go clear **UP** to...
(All the way to...)

It will come **UP** roses
(Develop unexpectedly well)   * Come **UP** short
(Inadequate)

Cook up a...
(Develop; prepare a...) * Coop him **UP**! * Cough it **UP**!
(Limit his freedom) (Give it to us!)

Crack **UP**
(Lose control; go crazy)   *   He'll crack me **UP**
(Make me laugh)

It will crack **UP**
(Become a wreck)   *   It will crack him **UP**
(Be a major blow to him)

It's not what it's cracked **UP** to be
(It's not equal to its reputation) *   I'm **UP** a creek
[without a paddle]
(In trouble)

Did anything crop **UP**?
(Did anything happen?)   ([with only poor options])

U

Don't crud it **UP**   * A cut **UP**   * My dander is **UP**
(Don't lower quality)   (A funny person)   (I'm angry)

UP-to-date   * It's an **UP** day   *   Dish it **UP**!
(Current; fresh)   (A good day)   ([Talk!] [Serve it])

Dish **UP** a…   *   [Doll] [Gussy] it **UP**
(Create; develop; produce a…)   (Make it look better)

A dust **UP**   * **UP** to my ears in…   * He'll eat it **UP**
(An argument; fight)   (Very involved in…)   (Greatly enjoy it)

Keep your end **UP**   * He doesn't know which end is **UP**
(Carry your share)   (He is ignorant; inexperienced)

Face **UP** to it   * I'm fed **UP**!   *   Fess **UP**!
(Confront realities)   (I can't tolerate more)   (Tell the truth!)

[Figure] [Tot] it **UP**   *   He's all fired **UP**
(Total it)   ([Angry] [Enthusiastic])

It will fold **UP**   *   Don't foul it **UP**
(Go out of business)   (Don't make a mess of it)

Don't foul **UP**   * He's a foul-**UP**   * Free one **UP**
(Don't make mistakes)   (A failure)   (Make one available)

He's **UP** front with…   *   The game is **UP**!
(Candid; truthful)   (You are [beaten] [discovered]!)

They'll gang **UP** on us   *   Gear **UP**!
(Combine and overwhelm us)   (Get ready to move!)

U

425

A lot of get-UP and go   *   Get UP for it
(Energy and initiative)   (Prepare yourself)

My get-UP   * Get UP a party   * Gin UP a...
(My clothes; costume)   (Plan a party)   (Quickly prepare a...)

Give UP[!] [?]   *   Give it UP!
([Surrender!] [Do you surrender?])   ([Stop it!])
               (Don't [do] [say] it again!)

It's a goof-UP
(A mistake)   * It's UP for grabs   * Don't gum it UP
             (Anyone can [take]   (Don't ruin it)

My hackles are UP   [win] it)
(I'm angry)

       * Hamming it UP   *   A hand UP
Hand him UP   (Being theatrical in   (Help given in a
(Surrender him)   exaggerated ways)   way that promotes
                            self-reliance)

Hang it UP!   * A hang-UP
([Stop it!] [Quit!])   (A delay)   * He has a hang-UP about...
                  (A problem; special concerns)

Hard UP for cash
(Without funds)   * Hatch UP a...   *   Heads UP!
              (Plan a...)   (Be [alert] [careful]!)

Play heads UP ball!
(Be alert, effective players!)   *   A heads-UP person
                     (An able; confident person)

A higher UP   * It's UP hill
(Of higher rank)   (Difficult)   *
                   Hit him UP for...
                   (Ask him for...)

Hold UP!   * What's the hold UP?
([Wait!] [Stop!])   (The delay)
                   *   A hold-UP
                     (A robbery)

U

426

The story doesn't hold **UP**   *   We'll hook **UP**
(The facts don't support it)   (Meet)

Hopped **UP**   * He's hung **UP**   * Hurry **UP**!
(Excited [by a drug])   (Delayed; stopped)   (Move faster!)

Hush it **UP**   *   He'll jack **UP** his prices
(Keep it from becoming known)   (Suddenly increase them)

The jig is **UP**   *   It will kick **UP**
([I've been caught; discovered]   (Become troublesome)
[It's over; finished])

   *   Kick **UP** a [fuss] [storm]
Kiss **UP** to him   (Create a disturbance)
(Falsely praise him)

   * Laid **UP**   * He has a leg **UP** on us
[Let] [Lighten] **UP**!   (Ill; incapacitated)   (He is ahead of us)
(Relax!)

   * Listen **UP**!   * Lit **UP**   * Live it **UP**!
Live **UP** to it   (Listen carefully!)   (Drunk)   (Enjoy it!)
(Do what is required)

   * Lock-**UP**   * It's [all] locked **UP**
Look him **UP**   (Jail)   (Arranged; certain)
(Try to find him)

   * Things will look **UP**   * Loosen **UP**!
He's made **UP** to...   (Conditions will improve)   (Relax!)
(Disguised to
  look like...)   * Make it **UP**   * We'll make **UP**
   ([Invent a story]   (Be reconciled)
Make it **UP** to me   [Recover the time lost])
(Repay what you owe)   * Measure **UP**!
   (Meet requirements!)

U

Don't mess **UP**   * **UP**-to-the-minute   * Mix it **UP**
(Don't make errors)   (Current; fresh)   (Argue; fight)

It's a [mix] [screw] **UP**   *   I'm mixed **UP** with...
(A confused mess)   (Involved with...)

Mixed **UP**   * Mop **UP**   * My number is **UP**
([Confused]   (Get is all done)   (I'll [be caught] [die])
[Troubled])

                    * I'm one **UP** on...   *   Own **UP**!
It's not **UP**   (I'm [ahead] [leading])   ([Tell the truth!]
to [par] [snuff]   [Admit it!])
(It's below standards)   * My ears will perk **UP**
                                (I'll listen carefully)

It will perk **UP**
(Revive; improve)   * A pick-**UP**   *   A pick-me-**UP**
                    (A stranger met   (Something to provide
It's a pick-**UP**... and socialized with)   quick energy)
(Informal; not
arranged earlier) * I didn't pick it **UP** * Pick **UP** a ride
                    (I didn't detect it)   (Get a ride
Things will pick **UP**   from someone)
(Become active)   * I'll pick up the trail
                       (Discover it)   * A pick-**UP** vehicle
UP a tree   A small cargo
(Abandoned; isolated)   vehicle)

Trip him **UP**   * I tripped **UP**   *   It will turn **UP**
(Foil him)   (I failed)   (Be found; located)

Pipe **UP**!   * Play it **UP**   * Play heads-**UP** ball
(Give your views!) (Give it attention)   (Be an alert,
                                          effective person)

U

Pony **UP**
(Contribute)

* It will pop **UP**
(Appear suddenly)

* Pull **UP**
(Stop!) (Wait!)

Pumped **UP**
([Angry] [Excited]
[Highly motivated])

* Punch it **UP**
(Make it stronger)

* Put **UP**
a [good] front
(Behave confidently)

Put **UP** fruit
(Cook and store
fruit for later use)

* A put-**UP** job
(The outcome is
arranged in advance)

* Put him **UP**
(Provide lodging)

* Put them **UP**!
(Hold your
hands up!)

Put **UP** or shut **UP**!
(Do what you should
do or remain silent!)

* I put **UP** with you
(I tolerate you)

Rev it **UP**!
(More speed; power!)

* Put him **UP** to it
(Encourage him to do it)

* Read **UP** on it
(Brief yourself)

*

It's right **UP** my alley!
([It's perfect for me!]
[I'm very qualified for it])

Don't rile him **UP**
(Don't make him angry)

Ring him **UP**
(Call him)

* **UP** the river
(In jail)

* Run **UP** a bill
(Accumulate a debt)

The first runner **UP**
(The second winner)

* Rustle **UP** some
(Locate some)

* Saddle **UP**!
(Prepare to move!)

Save **UP** for...
(Accumulate funds for...)

*

He's a screw **UP**
(He makes errors)

Send him **UP**
[for a stretch]
(Send him to jail)

* I've been set **UP**
(Put into an embarrassing
position by trickery)

* Set them **UP**!
(I'm buying the
drinks)

U

The set-UP   *   Settle UP!   *   It's all sewed UP
(The structure; scheme)   (Pay what is owed)   (All arranged)

Shake it UP!   *   A major shake-UP
(Hurry!)   (Many personnel or other
                             changes were made)

It [will shake you] [shook me] UP
([Trouble you]   *   It will shape UP as...
[Troubled me] very much)   ([Develop satisfactorily]
                          [Take the form of...])

Shape UP or ship out!
([Get yourself in a proper condition!]   *   It didn't show UP
[Follow the rules or leave!])   (It wasn't evident)

He didn't show UP   *   Show him UP   * Shut UP!
(He didn't come)   ([Perform better than he does]   (Silence!)
                 [Humiliate him])

He's all slicked UP   *   Slow UP
(Well-dressed and combed)   (Go slower)

Snap it UP!   *   I'm snorted UP
([Get possession of it and quickly]   (Drunk)
[Hurry!])

                *   He snuck UP on us
He's not UP to [it] [snuff] [speed]   (Approached secretly)
(He's not ready)

             *   Soup it UP
Speak UP!   (Give it more power)
(Say what you think!)

        *   [Spiff] [Spruce] it UP
It will shape UP [as...]   (Improve its appearance)
([Develop satisfactorily]
[Take the form of...])

U

It will stand **UP**
([The facts will support it]
[It is strong and will endure])

*

Stand **UP** for...
(Defend; support)

*

He'll stand you **UP**
(Not keep his appointment
with you)

Steamed **UP**
(Very angry)

Stick **UP** for him
(Defend him)

* [Stick 'em **UP**!] [This is a stick **UP**!]
(This is a robbery!)

Stir him **UP**
(Get him angry;
excited)

* He....**UP** a storm
(Made a great effort)

* Be straight **UP**
(Candid; honest)

* Take it straight **UP**
(Not diluted)

* Straighten **UP**
and fly right
(Control yourself
and act properly)

He's **UP** for a
stretch
(He's in jail)

* String him **UP**!
(Hang him!)

Stuck **UP**
([Aloof] [Conceited])

*

I'm **UP** a stump
(Baffled; puzzled)

Take him **UP** on it
(Accept his challenge)

* Take **UP** for him
(Defend him)

* Take it **UP**
(Lift; shorten it)

Take **UP** the subject
(Consider it)

*

Talk it **UP**
(Promote it)

Throw **UP**
(Vomit)

* Thumbs **UP**!
([Have confidence!]
[It's accepted!])

*

I'm tied **UP**
(Very busy)

He's **UP** tight
(Very tense)

*

It's a toss **UP**
(It could go either way)

U

UP a tree
(Abandoned) (Isolated)

* He's UP to his old tricks
(Doing what he has a
reputation for doing)

It will turn UP
(Appear; be found)

* Don't turn UP your nose at it
(Don't reject it)

It's on the UP and UP
(It's [honest] [legitimate])

* Use it UP
(Consume it all)

It's UP to you
([You are the key person]
[You make the choice])

* Wait UP!
(Wait briefly)

Wait UP for me
(Stay awake until I return)

* A wake-UP call
(An alert; a warning)

A warm-UP * Washed UP * What's UP?
(A rehearsal) (Defeated; finished) ([What's happening?]
[A greeting])

What is he UP to? * Whip UP something
(What is he (Prepare something fast) * [Whip]
[doing] [plotting]?) [Whomp] UP...
([Create...] [Arouse; stir up...])

I'll wind UP as...
(Finally become a...)

* Wind it UP
(End; finish it)

How did it wind UP?
(What was the final result?)

* He's really wired UP
(Excited)

Wise UP!
([Be realistic!] [Don't be stupid!])

* Work him UP
(Make him agitated)

U

All wound **UP**
(Very tense)

I had a good **UPBRINGING**
(I was taught good manners
and had a good education)

The **UPPER** crust
(The rich; elite class)

Keep a stiff **UPPER** lip
(Be brave; resolute)

It's **UPSCALE**
([High price] [Stylish])

Turn it **UPSIDE** down
(Search it thoroughly)

Kick him **UPSTAIRS**
(Promote him to possibly
unwanted duties)

UPSY daisy!
(Get up!)

USE it to death
(To the fullest degree)

He's not **USED** to it
(He is not familiar with it)

* That wraps it **UP**
(That's the end of it)

* I feel put **UPON**
(Exploited; overburdened)

* He'll get his come**UPPANCE**
(Be humbled)

* Get the **UPPER** hand
(Gain control)

* **UPS** and downs
(Good and bad times)

* He **UPSET** the applecart
(Foiled the plans)

* That's the **UPSIDE**
(The good part)

* He has nothing **UPSTAIRS**
(He is dumb)

* He's [fast] [slow] on the **UPTAKE**
(He learns [fast] [slowly])
(He is not smart])

* **USE** it up
(Consume it all)

U

Chapter V

The better part of **VALOR** is to...
(It would be smarter to...)

* Its face **VALUE** is...
(Its evident value is...)

VAMOOSE!
(Go away!)

* **VANISH** into thin air
(Disappear)

* The garden **VARIETY**
(Common; ordinary)

A pick-up **VEHICLE**
(A small, cargo vehicle)

* He has ice in his **VEINS**
(He has no compassion)

With a **VENGEANCE**
(With great energy)

* I know it chapter and **VERSE**
(I memorized it)

Play it close to the **VEST**
(Be secretive)

* We have good **VIBES**
(We relate well)

I take a dim **VIEW** of it
(I'm dubious; skeptical)

* A point of **VIEW**
(An opinion)

A worm's eye **VIEW**
(A low level perspective)

* It's ends**VILLE**
([It has no future] [A remote place])

It will die on the **VINE**
([Be neglected] [Wither])

* Full of **VINEGAR**
(Energy; spirit)

I'm no shrinking **VIOLET**
(I'm not shy)

* **VIP**
(A very important person)

VISITING fireman
(An important guest
treated with honor)

* A **VOICE** in the [dark]
[wilderness]
(Someone heard
but not heeded)

* An edge in his **VOICE**
(A tension)

V

Chapter W

[WACKO] [WACKY]
[Also WHACKY]
(Crazy)

* WAD *
(Money)

[Blow] [Shoot] my WAD
(Use all my money)

* A tight WAD
(A person who hates
to spend money)

The tail will WAG the dog
(A small factor will
control the larger outcome)

* It had a bandWAGON effect
(It caused a lot of people
to change their thinking)

Fix his WAGON
([Harm] [punish] him)
(Make problems for him)

* I'm [off] [on] the WAGON
(I'm [drinking] [sober] again])

I'll WAIT with baited breath
(Anxiously)

* WAIT until the cows come home
(For a very long time)

WAIT [a bit] [a minute]
[on me] [a shake] [up]!
(Wait [I'm not sure!] [briefly!]

*

WAIT it out
(Be patient)

WAIT up for me
(Stay awake until I return)

* WAITING in the wings
(Available; ready to act)

A WAKE-up call
(An alert; a warning)

*

I'll WALK on air
(Be very happy)

It's a cakeWALK
(Very easy)

* Cock of the WALK
(Master of the situation)

* I WALK on eggs
(I have to be
very careful)

WALK a fine line
(Be [very careful]
[impartial])

* A WALKover
(An easy victory)

He'll **WALK** the plank   * [Take a **WALK**!] [He'll **WALK**]
(Die)   ([Leave; resign!] [Be found not guilty])
(Be [punished] [sacrificed])

                                    *   **WALK** the way you talk
I won [in a **WALK**]   (Your actions should
   [**WALKING** away]   match what you say)
(Very easily)

                                    *   I got my **WALKING** papers
[I'm against] [My back is to]   (I was fired; lost my job)
   the **WALL**

(I [am trapped] [have no good options])   * He'll drive you
                                              up the **WALL**
Go to the **WALL**   (Aggravate; bother you)
(Become bankrupt) (Fail)

                          * The handwriting is on the **WALL**
A hole in the **WALL**   (The [situation is] [facts are clear])
(A very small place)

                        * Off the **WALL**   *   Stone**WALL**
He's like talking   (Very unusual; wierd)   ([Be evasive]
   to a **WALL**   [Delay; obstruct])
(He won't listen)

                                *   He packs a **WALLOP**
Don't **WANG** on me!   (He hits hard)
(Don't criticize me!)

                        * A **WANNABEE**   * I **WANT** out
What do you **WANT**   (Someone who wants   (I quit!)
   out of me?   to be famous; rich)
(What do you expect   * I **WANT** it in
   from me?)   * A **WAR** horse   the worst way
                          (A long time fighter) (Very much)
I'm on the **WAR**path
(Very angry)   * A tug-of-**WAR**
                (A struggle between two groups for supremacy)

W

Bend over back**WARDS** * You're **WARM**
(Make a special effort) (Close to...)

I'll **WARM** to it * A **WARM**-up * A house**WARMING**
(I'll like it more) (Rehearsal) (Celebration at a new home)

It **WARMS** my heart * I'm a worry**WART** * It's a **WASH**
(Makes me feel good) (I always worry) ([It won't work]
[No gain or loss])

It will all come * I **WASH** my hands of it
out in the **WASH** (I'm through * Hog**WASH**!
(The truth will with it) (Nonsense!)
be revealed)

* Don't **WASH** our dirty linen in public
A **WASH**out (Don't discuss our problems in public)
(A failure)

* **WASH**room * It won't **WASH**
WASHED up (Toilet) (It's not acceptable)
(Defeated; finished)

* I'm chief cook and bottle **WASHER**
Don't **WASTE** your breath! (I'm the manager here)
(It's useless to say more)

* **WASTE** him!
Not on my **WATCH** (Kill him!)
(Not while I'm in charge)

* **WATCH** [it] [out] [your step]!
WATCH over it (Be careful!)
(Guard; take care of it)

* He's a clock-**WATCHER**
A lot of **WATER** has (Always anxious to leave work)
gone under the bridge
(Much has happened since...) * **WATER** closet
(Toilet)

W

Like **WATER** off a duck's back * He carries **WATER** for...
(It has little impact) (He does chores for...)

[Pour] [Throw] cold * It's **WATER** over the dam
WATER on it (Old history; not relevant now)
(Discourage it)

* Dead in the **WATER** * I'm in deep **WATER**
Dull as [dish] (Stalled) ([Beyond my capacities]
[ditch] **WATER** [In real trouble])
(Very plain; uninteresting)

* **WATER** it down
He's a fish out of **WATER** (Dilute; weaken it)
(Not right for the job)

* I cover the **WATER**front
Come hell or high **WATER** (I have many responsibilities)
(Despite many problems)

* It won't hold **WATER**
I'm in hot **WATER** (It's false; not supported by facts)
(In trouble)

* A jerk**WATER** town
It makes my mouth **WATER** (A small, remote place)
(I want it very much)

* Test the **WATER**
We're on the same **WAVE**length (Experiment; try it)
(We think the same way)

* Don't make **WAVES**!
Mind your bee's **WAX**! (Don't [cause trouble]
(Don't interfere in [try to change how things are done])
other's affairs)

* **WAX** him! * I'm in a bad **WAY**
I'm **WAY** behind (Kill him!) (I'm [in trouble]
(I'm lagging in my work) [Sick])

W

438

By the **WAY**,...
(Incidentally,...)

Every which **WAY**
([Everywhere]
[In all directions])

I had my **WAY**
(I got what I wanted)

No **WAY** [in Heaven!]
([I won't do it!]
[No chance at all!])

Go by the **WAY**side
(Be discarded)

It's a two-**WAY** street
(I help you; you help me)

I went by **WAY** of...
([Through...] [Via...])

He has a **WAY** with words
(He uses language very well)

It will rub you the wrong **WAY**
(Really bother you)

Knock him side**WAYS**!
(Really hurt him)

*   He comes off that **WAY**
(He is perceived that way)

* It will give **WAY**   * Give **WAY**!
(Collapse)   (Abandon the effort)

*   **WAY** [to go] [out]!
([Wonderful!] [Perfect!])

*   He and his highfalutin **WAY**
(He tries to appear very important)

* It doesn't strike me the right **WAY**
(It doesn't seem correct; sound)

*   Smooth the **WAY**
(Remove or reduce problems)

*   Uphill all the **WAY**
(Very   difficult)

* That's the **WAY** the wind blows
(That's the situation)

* I want it the worst **WAY**
(Very   much)

* I examined it [five] [six]
WAYS to Sunday
(Very thoroughly)

*   No two **WAYS** about it
(It is certain)

W

He's **WEAK** in the knees
(He lacks courage; firmness)

* I **WEAR** my food well
(I drop food on my clothes)

I **WEAR** my heart on my sleeve
(I don't hide my feelings)

* **WEAR** next to nothing
(Almost naked)

If the shoe fits, **WEAR** it
(If it describes you,
acknowledge it)

* I'm no worse for the **WEAR**
(I survived in good condition)

* She **WEARS** the [pants] [shoes]
in the family
(She is the boss)

Keep a **WEATHER** out for …
(Watch carefully for…)

I'll **WEATHER** the storm
(Survive and continue)

* Under the **WEATHER**
(Ill)

How is the **WEATHER** up there?
(Joking greeting to tall person)

* **WEIGH** in!
([Participate!] [Give help!])

Give it great **WEIGHT**
(Consider it very important)

* He's a light **WEIGHT**
(He has little brains; influence)

Pull your **WEIGHT**
(Carry your part of the load)

* Throw your **WEIGHT** around
(Use your influence to gain
your objective)

WELL-[fixed] [to-do] [heeled] [off]
(Wealthy)

* …to a fare-thee-**WELL**
([To an extreme] [Too much])

I wear my food **WELL**
(I drop food on my clothes)

* Let **WELL** enough alone
(Don't disturb things)

WELL put
(Stated very well)

* It won't sit **WELL**
(It won't be accepted)

W

440

He's **WELL**-spoken　　　　　*　　　It's **WELL**-taken
(He speaks well)　　　　　　　　　(It's a valid point)

He's **WELL**-turned out　　*　I **WENT** [blank] [cold]
(Well-[dressed] [equipped])　　　(I couldn't think)

I **WENT** for it　　*　I **WENT** off　*　...as it **WERE**
(I [was fooled]　　(Angry, I yelled)　(As if it were so)
[thought it was so])

　　　　　　　　　　　　　　*　　　As you **WERE**!
He's all **WET**　　　　　　([Relax!] [Keep doing what
(Misinformed; wrong)　　　　　　you are doing!])

He'a **WET** blanket　　　　*　His feet aren't **WET** yet
(He's negative; unenthusiastic) (He's inexperienced; untested)

Madder than a **WET** hen　　　*　　　Thirty lashes with
(Very angry)　　　　　　　　　　　　a **WET** noodle
　　　　　　　　　　　　　　(A meaningless punishment)

WET your whistle
(Have a drink)　* Out of **WHACK**　* **WHACKED** out
　　　　　　　　(Not functioning)　　(Exhausted)

[WHACKO]
[WHACKED]　　　　　* **WHALE** the tar out of them
(See also **WACKED**)　　　　(Beat them badly)
(Crazy)
　　　　　　　　　　*　　　A **WHALE** of a time
A got a double **WHAMMY**　　　(A wonderful time)
(I was hit from two sides)
　　　　　　　　　*　**WHAT** [in] [the] blazes?
WHAT on earth?　　　　(An expression of surprise)
(An expression of amazement)

W

I'll give you **WHAT** [for] [have you]
(Heavy criticism; punishment)

* **WHAT** goes?
([What is happening?]
[A greeting])

...or **WHAT** have you
(...or what else may be involved)

* **WHAT** are you in for?
(What offenses got you in jail?)

WHAT are we in for?
(What may we expect?)

* **WHAT** is [it] with
you [anyway]?
(What is your problem?)

WHAT'S it to you?
(What is your interest in it?)

* **WHAT** is more,...
(In addition,...)

[So] **WHAT'S** new?
(A greeting)

* ..., and **WHAT** not
(...and other things too)

WHAT nots
(Various things) * Say **WHAT**?
(Repeat what you said)

* So **WHAT**?
([Who cares?]

WHAT'S [up?]
[**WHAT**?]
([What is happening?]
[A greeting])

[What does it mean?])

* I know **WHAT'S WHAT**
(I am informed; experienced)

It's a **WHATCHAMACALLIT**
(A thing whose name I can't recall)

* A big **WHEEL**
(A high-ranking person)

A fifth **WHEEL**
(A useless role)

* He [will **WHEEL** and deal]
[is a **WHEELER** dealer]

Put your shoulder to the **WHEEL**
(Assist; help)

(He likes to
manipulate; make deals)

W

442

Free **WHEELING**
(Operating without
[a plan] [restraint])

WHERE'S the beef?
(Where is what is important?

WHERE do I come in?
(What is my [role] [share]?)

The whys or **WHERE**fores of…
(The reasons for…

Every **WHICH** way
([In all directions]
[However you think of it])

Spell me for a **WHILE**
(Do my job temporarily)

WHIP it into shape
(Make it effective)

WHIP something up
(Prepare something fast)

[WHIP] [WHOMP] up a…
([Create] [Stir up] a…)

I **WHIPPED** it
(I did the job)

* He'll spin his **WHEELS**
(Waste time; do nothing)

* Say **WHEN**?
(Tell me when to stop
filling your glass)

* **WHERE'S** the fire?
(Don't go so fast!)

* That's **WHERE** its
[at] [happening]
(Where the action; excitement is…)

* Lay out for a **WHILE**
(Be absent; away for a while)

* I had the **WHIP** hand over…
(Control over…)

* Smart as a **WHIP**
(Very bright)

* **WHIP** [through] it
([Examine it quickly]
[Conquer; master it])

* I got **WHIPPED**
(Defeated)

* A **WHIPPER**snapper
(An insignificant but presumptious person)

W

I won't be your **WHIPPING** boy
(Be blamed for your actions)

* Give it a **WHIRL**
(Try it)

...by a **WHISKER**
(By the smallest amount)

* It's the cat's **WHISKER**!
(Wonderful!)

Hang by a **WHISKER**
(Barely survive)

* Blow the **WHISTLE**!
(Reveal the facts)

* He can **WHISTLE** for it
(He'll never get it)

I'm clean as a **WHISTLE**
(There is no evidence against me)

* I got away slick as a **WHISTLE**
(I escaped unnoticed)

Wet your **WHISTLE**
(Have a drink)

* With bells and **WHISTLES**
(With many fancy things added)

WHISTLING in the dark
(Acting naively, hoping
things will be all right)

* In black and **WHITE**
(In clear language)

A **WHITE** elephant
(An unprofitable, unwanted thing)

* I have **WHITE** knuckles
(I'm scared)

I told a little **WHITE** lie
(A lie told to shield
someone from unpleasant truth)

* A **WHIZ**bang
(A remarkable performer)

WHO cares?
(I don't care!)

* From [giddap] [giddyap] to **WHOA**
(From beginning to end)

A **WHO**-done-it
(A mystery story)

* The **WHOLE** [bit] [shebang]
([Everything] [Everyone involved])

W

He'll go [for] [at] it **WHOLE** hog
([He'll be completely fooled]
[Without reservation] [Greedily])

* Thanks a **WHOLE** lot!
(That's not helpful!)

* On the **WHOLE**
(Considering everything)

The **WHOLE** nine yards
(Everything)

* I'll **WHOMP** you!
(Hit you)

* **WHOMP** up a...
([Create] [Stir up] a...)

WHOOP it up!
(Have a wonderful time)

* A **WHOPPER**
(Really large)

* **WHOPPING** mad
(Very angry)

WHUP him!
(Beat him!)

* A **WHOPPING** story
(An exaggerated story)

* **WHY** on earth?
(For what reason?)

The **WHYS** [or
wherefores] of...
(The reasons for...)

* Give him **WIDE** berth!
(Avoid him)

From far and **WIDE**
(From many places)

* Yay **WIDE**
(That wide)

* A big **WIG**
(A high-ranking person)

Don't flip your **WIG**!
(Don't get angry; excited)

* Get a **WIGGLE** on!
(Hurry!)

WIGGLEroom
(Space to maneuver)

* I'm **WILD** about her!
(I love her!)

In the **WILD** blue yonder
(The distant sky)

* The **WILD** card
(The unpredictable factor)

A **WILD** goose chase
(A useless errand)

* He's hog **WILD**
(Crazy; out of control)

He's sowing his **WILD** oats * **WILL** do!   * It **WILL** do
(Spending his time and   ([I agree!] (It's satisfactory)
  energy seeking pleasures) [I'll do it!])

                    * ..., at **WILL**
A [cry] [voice] in the **WILDERNESS** (When one desires)
([A lonely, hopeless appeal]
[Someone heard but not heeded]) * It gives me the **WILLIES**
                    (It makes me nervous)

I'll do it **WILLY** nilly
(I have no other choice) * He's [a **WIMP**] [**WIMPING** out]
            (Weak; cowardly] [Losing his resolve])

WIN her hand
(Get her to marry you) * **WIN** out * **WIN** him over
           (Survive; triumph) (Convince him)

It's a [no **WIN**]
[**WIN-WIN** situation)   *   A **WIND** bag
([There is no way to win] (Someone who talks too much)
[Everyone gains])

         * That's the way the **WIND** blows
I'll get **WIND** of it   (That's the situation)
(Learn about it)

        *   It's in the **WIND**
Take the **WIND** out (Being [considered] [rumored])
  of his sails
(Discourage and slow him) *   Second **WIND**
            (Renewed energy)

He's three sheets to the **WIND**
(Drunk)   * A spit in the **WIND**
        (A small, useless effort)

A straw in the **WIND**
(A [clue] [hint] of the future) * **WIND** it up!
        (End; finish it!)

W

446

I'll **WIND** up as a…
(Finally become a…)

A **WINDOW** of opportunity
(A limited [time] [chance]
to do something)

You make a better door
than a **WINDOW**!
(You are blocking my view!)

[Waiting] In the **WING**
(Available; ready to act)

A **WING**ding
(A big party)

Clip his **WINGS**
(Reduce his role;
influence; power)

He'll hood**WINK** you
(Fool; mislead;
take advantage of you)

Catch forty **WINKS**
(Get a little rest)

A **WINNING** a streak
(A series of wins)

He gives away ice in **WINTER**
(He gives away what no one needs/wants)

* It's **WINDOW** dressing
(A display designed to make
something look better than it is)

* It's out the **WINDOW**
(It won't be considered further)

* Scatter to the four **WINDS**
(In all directions)

* **WING** him! * I'll **WING** it
(Wound him) (Perform
without preparation)

* Take him under your **WING**
([Care for] [teach] him)

* My **WINGS** * It will sprout **WINGS**
(My arms) (Move very quickly)

* In the **WINK** of an eye
(Very quickly)

* I didn't sleep a **WINK**
(I had no sleep)

* The bread**WINNER**
(The family money earner)

* A cold **WINTER** in hell
(A very rare occasion)

W

A **WIPE** out   * It will **WIPE** me out   * Down to the **WIRE**
(A bad defeat)   ([Exhaust me]   (Uncertain to the end)
       [Bankrupt me])

He'll go **HAY**wire   * A hire **WIRE** act
(Crazy; out of control)   (Very risky)

A live **WIRE**   *   Under the **WIRE**
(A very active person)   (Within the time limit)

He's really **WIRED** [up]   * Our **WIRES** were crossed
([He has influential   (We had poor comunications)
relationships] [Excited])

               *   A **WISE**[acre] [guy]
I can't get in a word   **[WISENHEIMER]**
edge**WISE**   ([A bothersome, sarcastic person]
(It's difficult to get   [One who seems to know everything])
into the discussion)

       * He's street**WISE** * A word to the **WISE**
[Get **WISE**!]   (A surviver of urban   (Take my advice)
[**WISE** up!]   street life)
([Be realistic]   *   He's **WISE** to us
[Don't be stupid!])   (He understands our
                     motives; our plans)

WISHY-WASHY   * Get **WITH** it!
(Weak; indecisive)   ([Pay attention!]   * Get it over **WITH**!
           [Be more up-to-date]   (Do it now!)
Go **WITH** it   [Be more in style])
(Support it)   * I'm **WITH** you!
                     (I agree!)

WITHIN a hair * Keep your **WITS** about you!
(Very close)   (Think carefully!)

W

448

I'm at **WIT'S** end
([I'm frantic!]
[I don't know what to do])

A lone **WOLF**
(One who prefers to act alone)

It's a **WOMEN'S** thing
(It has special meaning to women)

I **WON** [going away] [hands down]
[in a breeze] [in a walk] [walking away]
(Easily)

We **WON** by a nose
(By a tiny amount)

Saw **WOOD**
([Keep working] [Sleep; snore])

A babe in the **WOODS**
(An untested, naive person)

I'm not out of the **WOODS**
(My problem is not yet solved)

They came out of the **WOOD**work
(As though from hiding)

Dyed in the **WOOL**
([Genuine] [A loyal believer])

* The **WOLF** is at the door
(Many debts; no money)

* Don't cry **WOLF**
(Don't give false alarms)

* A **WOLF** in sheep's clothing
(A hostile person who
tries to appear friendly)

* We **WON** the
whole nine yards
(We won everything)

* Knock on **WOOD**!
(A superstitious saying, to ward off
evil or encourage good things to happen)

* Don't take any
WOODEN nickels
(Don't get cheated)

* In my neck of the **WOODS**
(My home area)

* Take him out
to the **WOOD**shed
([Criticize] [Punish] him)

* Pull the **WOOL** over his eyes
(Confuse; deceive him)

W

He'll break his **WORD**
(Fail to keep his promise)

Buzz**WORD**
(A word that gains temporary popularity)

I can't get a **WORD** in edgewise
(It's difficult to get into the discussion)

Get out the **WORD**
(Tell everyone about it)

The **WORD** will get out
(The information will be revealed)

Give us the **WORD**
(Tell us)

From the **WORD** go
(From the beginning)

I'm as good as my **WORD**
(I'm honest and dependable)

What's the good **WORD**?
(A greeting)

Put in a good **WORD** for me
(Say something helpful to me)

Have a **WORD** with him
(Talk with him)

The last **WORD** in...
(The most advanced version of...)

Spread by **WORD** of mouth
(By each person telling others)

Mum's the **WORD**
(Keep silent)

Pass the **WORD**
(Tell others)

Take my **WORD** [for it]
(Believe me)

A **WORD** to the wise
(Take my advice)

I'll eat my **WORDS**
(Regret what I said)

Those are fighting **WORDS**
(Provocative)

I had **WORDS** with...
(I [argued] [talked] with...)

You took **WORDS** out of my mouth
(You said what I intended to say)

In so many **WORDS**,..
(In summary,...)

W

450

He has a way with **WORDS**
(He uses language very well)

* **WORK** him around
(Change his thinking)

WORK your [butt] [head] [tail] off
WORK [like a dog] [like mad] [your fingers to the bone]
(Work very hard)

* It will go off like clock**WORK**
(According to plan)

WORK the crowd
(Greet people; seek their support)

* My **WORK** is cut out for me
(I know what I must do)

All in a day's **WORK**
(The normal routine)

* Dirty **WORK**   * Fancy foot**WORK**
([Dishonest activity] (Careful preparation)

Get to **WORK**!
(Start work!)

[Work none want to do])

Do the ground **WORK**
(Prepare well)

* I'll get off **WORK**
([Be excused from work]
[Finish work for the day])

WORK on him
(Try to influence him)

* Knock off **WORK**
(Stop working)

WORK out the bugs   * **WORK** it out   * It will **WORK** out
(Solve the problems)   (Resolve it)   (Succeed; be resolved)

A **WORK**-out
(An exercise; a drill)

* **WORK** him over
(Beat; punish him)

I **WORK** for peanuts
(For very low wages)

* He's a [nasty] [real]
piece of **WORK**
(A [really bad]
[unusual] person)

WORK to the rules
(Do no more than the rules require)

W

Make short **WORK** of it
(Do it quickly)

* **WORK** him up
([Agitate] [Stir] him)

Get a **WORK**-up on him
(A report on his status)

* They came out of
the wood**WORK**
(As if from hiding)

I'm **WORKED** out
(Exhausted)

* I'm a **WORKING** stiff
(I work to support myself)

[Bet] [Shoot] the **WORKS**!
(Commit everything)

* It **WORKS** like a charm
(It functions very well)

I'll get the **WORKS**
([Be killed] [Gain it all]
[Be given the finest treatment])

* It **WORKS** for me!
(I [agree!] [understand!])

It's in the **WORKS**
(Being developed)

* He'll screw up the **WORKS**
(Ruin things)

For all the **WORLD**,...
(In every way,...)

* Dead to the **WORLD**
(In deep sleep)

Set the **WORLD** on fire
(Do great things)

* It will do me a
WORLD of good
(Be good for me)

He's lost to the **WORLD**
([Preoccupied] [In deep sleep])

* Never in the **WORLD**!
(I will never agree!)

Out of this **WORLD**!
([Bizarre; very unusual]
[Wonderful!])

* It's a small **WORLD**!
(What is said when strangers realize
they know the same people or come
from the same place)

W

452

I have the **WORLD** [on a string]
  [by the tail]
  (Things are going well for me)

How is the **WORLD** treating you?
  (A greeting)

A **WORMS'S** eye view
  (A low level perspective)

It's a can of **WORMS**
  (It's full of problems)

I'm a **WORRY**wart
  (I always worry)

I'm no **WORSE** for the wear
  (I survived in good condition)

If **WORSE** come to **WORSE**
  (If there is no other choice)

For all it's **WORTH**
  (For its full value)

A bird in the hand is **WORTH**
  two in the bush
  (A thing one has is more valuable
  than a thing promised)

It's **WORTH** a go
  (It should be tried)

* I think the **WORLD** of...
  (I greatly admire...)

* The best of both **WORLDS**
  (A gain either way)

* I'm a book **WORM**
  (I love to read)

* The **WORM** has turned
  (Things are different now)

* **WORN** to a frazzle
  (Very tired)

* It's [going from bad to]
  [a turn for the] **WORSE**
  (The situation is deteriorating)

* I want it the **WORST** way
  (Very much)

* Not **WORTH** a [hill of beans]
  [darn] [plugged nickel] [two bits]
  (Worthless)

* I'm **WORTH** big bucks
  (I'm very wealthy)

* It's **WORTH** a bundle
  (A lot of money)

W

It isn't **WORTH** a hoot [in hell]   * It's not **WORTH** a lick
(It's worthless)   (It's useless)

He's **WORTH** a pretty penny   * He's not **WORTH** his salt
(He's rich)   (He's a worthless person)

All **WOUND** up   * **WOW** them!   * It's a **WRAP**
(Very tense)   (Thrill them!)   (It's done; finished)

Put a **WRAP** on it!   * **WRAP** it up!   * He's all **WRAPPED**
(End it!)   (Finish it!)   up in himself
                                              (He thinks only of himself)

That **WRAPS** it! [up!]
(That's the end of it)   *   Under **WRAPS**
                                              (Still   secret)

It's a monkey **WRENCH** in our affairs
(It complicates; spoils things)   * He'll **WRING** his hands
                                              (Be anxious; worried)

I've been through the **WRINGER**
(I've had a lot of trouble)   *   A new **WRINKLE**
                                          (A new [development] [problem])

A slap on the **WRIST**
(A small punishment)   * Nothing to **WRITE** home about
                                              (Not very good)

WRITE [him] [it] off
([He has no further value]   *   **WRITE** your own ticket
[It's worthless])   (You can have what you want)

The hand**WRITING** is on the wall   * Dead **WRONG**
(The [situation is] [facts are] clear)   (Completely wrong)

Off on the **WRONG** [foot] [track]   * Don't get me **WRONG**
(Making a poor start)   (Don't misunderstand me)

W

It went down the **WRONG** hatch
(I swallowed wrong and choked)

* I hit the **WRONG** note
(I didn't communicate well)

Don't get on his **WRONG** side
(Don't antagonize him)

* From the **WRONG**
side of the tracks
(From an area and background
considered undesirable)

Don't get up on the **WRONG**
side of the bed
(In a bad mood)

* Don't bark up the **WRONG** tree
(Don't waste time on the wrong thing)

It will rub you the
WRONG way
(Really bother you)

* I **WROTE** the book on...
(I'm the expert on...)

He's a **WUSS**
(Timid; not willing to be tested)

W

Chapter X

The X factor
(The unknown factor)

* **XMAS**
(Christmas)

* X-rated
(Rated as obscene)

X marks the spot
(The place of interest)

Chapter Y

YAK YAK YAK
(Talk, talk, talk)

* Stop your **YAMMERING**
(Stop talking)

Close your **YAP**!
(Be quiet!)

* The whole nine **YARDS**
(Everything)

A tall **YARN**
(An exaggerated story)

* Spin **YARNS**
(Tell stories)

* It's **YAY** wide
(That wide)

Oh **YEAH** [!] [?]
([I don't agree!]
[Is that so?])

* **YEP**!
([Yes!] [I agree!])

* **YEAR** in **YEAR** out
(Year after year)

Hither and **YON**
(This way and that way)

* A **YES**-man
(One who always agrees without
giving his real views)

In the wild blue **YONDER**
(In the distant sky)

* You forget **YOURSELF**
(You have lost your sense
of proper conduct)

YONDER a piece
(Over there some distance)

X, Y, and Z

Help **YOURSELF**!
([Serve yourself!]
[Take what you want!])

YUMMY!
(It [looks] [tastes]
very good)

*

YUP!
(I agree!)

[**YUCKY**!] [**YUK**!]
(Disgusting!)

We had a good **YUK**
(A good laugh)

* **YUPPIES**
(Young upward mobile persons)

Chapter Z

From A to **Z**
(It covers everything)

* **ZAP** them!
(Shoot them)

* **ZERO** in on...
(Focus on...)

ZERO it out
(Reduce it to zero)

* It's **ZILCH** to me
(It's nothing)

* It has **ZING**
([It has spirit]
[It's stimulating])

[**ZIP**] [**ZIPPO**]
(Nothing) (Zero)

* **ZIP** your lip!
(Say nothing!)

I'll lose my **ZIP**
(My energy, power, strength)

*

I **ZONKED** out
(Went into deep sleep)

He's getting his **ZZZ's**
(He is sleeping)

PART II
Special Chapters

458

AMERICAN EXPRESSIONS TO SAY:

HELLO AND GOODBYE

Americans have many ways for saying "Hello" and "Goodbye."
Mostly such expressions are friendly; occasionally, they are
not. The same expression may be used either way, with the
difference reflected in the tone of voice or manner of speaking.
The few unfriendly expressions for "Hello" and "Goodbye" are
grouped separately below. Sometimes, these expressions are
questions, but, usually, no answer is expected, especially if the
gretting person is in a hurry. The purpose is to say "Hello" or
"Goodbye" quickly without taking time. Many of the expres-
ssions are found also in the alphabetical chapters in Part I.

HELLO

Friendly Ways of Saying "Hello"

Good [afternoon!] [day!] [evening!] [morning!]

As I live and breath!   *   Give me five!   *   Greetings!

[Hey] [Hi] there! * Hi [dude!] [partner!]

How are [things?] [you?]   *   How be [things?] [you?]

How have you [Hahyah] been?   *   How is by you?

How do you do? * How you doing? * Howdy? [do?] [doody!]

How's it [going?] [with you?]   *   How's [life] [tricks?]

Hello/Goodbye

How's the weather up there? (Joking greeting to tall person)

How's [life] [the world] treating you?   *   Long time no see!

Look who's here! * Pleased to meet you!   * Put her there!

Put her there partner!   *   Take care! [of yourself!]

What [cooks?] [goes?] * [So] What's new? * What's with you?

What's [cooking?] [doing?] [gives?] [going on?] [the good
news?] [the good word?] [happening?] [up?]

Unfriendly Ways of Saying "Hello"

Look what the cat dragged in!   *   Look who's here!

GOODBYE

Friendly Ways of Saying "Goodbye"

Bye! [Bye Bye!]   * Be seeing you!   *   Catch you later!

I'm checking out!   * Farewell!   *   God speed!

Good [afternoon!] [day!] [evening!] [night!]

Have a good [day!] [one!] * Got to [go now!] [leave!] [scoot!]

Later! [on!] * Must [go now!] [run!]   *   I must run [along!]

460

I'm off! * I'm out of here! * See you! [around!] [in church!] [later!] [in the funny papers!]

See you soon!   * So long!   *   Don't be a stranger!

Stay loose   * Stay in [touch!] [tune!]

Take care! [of yourself!]

Take it [easy!] [slow!] * Too-dah-loo! * You all come back!

Unfriendly Ways of Saying "Goodbye"

Beat it! * Blow! * Bug [off!] [out!] * Butt out! * Bye Bye!

Byee!   * Clear out!   * Drop dead!   *   Flick off!

Get [going!] [lost!] [moving!] [on your way!] [out of here!]

Git!   *   Hit the [road!] [trail!]   * On your [horse!] [way!]

Push off!   *   Scram!   *   Shoo!   *   Shove off!

Show him [the door!] [out!] * Skidaddle! * Take a [hike!] [powder!] [walk!]

Take off!

EXPRESSIONS FOR SAYING "YES" AND "NO"

Many expressions are used to show agreement or disagreement with other people. Some expressions are simple alternatives to "Yes" or "No." Others are used to provide greater emphasis when agreeing or disagreeing.

YES/AGREEMENT

And how!   *   I agree!   *   Agreed!   *   It's A okay!

I'm all for it!   *   By all means!   *   All right!

You bet [your life!]   *   You better believe it!   *   I'll buy that!

Can do!   *   That's for [certain!] [sure!]   *   Check!

I check on that!   *   I concur!   *   You're cooking with gas!

Could be!   *   Darn [right!] [tooting!]   *   You're [dead] right!

It will do!   *   I'll do it!   *   Deal!   *   It's a [done] deal!

Deal me in!   *   That does it for me!   *   Done!   *   Fair enough!

Fine and dandy!   *   I'm for it!   *   I give in!   *   It's [a] go!

[I'll] Give it go!   *   [I'll go] [I'm] with you!   *   [I'll] Go for it!

Go ahead!   *   I'll go along! [for the ride!]   *   I'll go with it!

Good enough!   *   You got it!   *   Gotcha!   *   I gotcha!

YES/NO

462

Granted! * I grant you that! * Great! * Guess so!

[Heck] [Hell] yes! * It's hunky-dory! [with me!]

You talk my language! * Neat! * Okay! * O.K. [with me!]

You're on! * Right! [on!] [you are!] [as rain!] * Righto!

You're right! * Roger! * You can say that again!

I'll say! [so]! * You said a mouthful! * Shoot for it!

I'll sign! [on!] * Yes siree! * So be it! * I'm sold!

[To be] Sure! * Sure [enough!] [thing!] * Swell!

Now, you're talking! [my language!] * You tell him!

That's it! * Thumbs up! * Uh huh! * Yah! * Yeah!

Yep! * Yes! [indeed!] * Yup! * Way to go! * Why not!

Will do! * It works for me!

NO/DISAGREEMENT

Baloney! * I don't buy it! * I disagree! * I won't do it!

It won't do! * Drop dead! * You're [dead] wrong!

My [elbow!] [eye!] [foot!] * Forget it! * Get lost!

[Heck] [Hell] no! * Hold [your horses!] [on!] [the phone!]

I don't hold with you! * Impossible! * Nah! * Naw!

Negative! * Never! [in a million years! [in the world!]

Nix! [on that!] * It's nixed!

No! [can do!] [deal!] [dice!] [go!] [how!] [never!] [sale!]
[siree!] [soap!] [thanks!] [way!] [way hosea!]

Nonsense! * Nope! * Not! [in my book!] [on your life!]
[Not a prayer!] * Nothing doing! * Nuts! [to you!] [to that!]

Says you! * Shucks no! * Take a hike! * Thumbs down!

It's a turn down! * Uh uh! * Whoa! * It won't do! * Yuck!

EXPRESSIONS OF AMAZEMENT OR FRUSTRATION

Some American expressions evolved in response to experiencing amazement or frustration. Most have no other purpose.
Some are uttered as exclamations; others as questions. Also.
some have evolved as ways of softening swear words uttered
in response to amazement or frustration (See next section).
Many amazement/frustration expressions are explained in Part
I (Alphabetical Chapters).

My aching back!   *   Ah hah! * Awesome!   *   Bad news!

Oh beans! * That beats all! * Bogus! * In all my [born] days!

Boy o'Boy! * Aw [come] [go] on! * Criminy! * For crying
   out loud!   *   Darn! [darn!]

I'll be [darned!] [hornswaggled!] [switched!]   *   Dear me!

I declare! * Fantastic! * Your father's mustache!

Fiddlesticks! * Galloping ghosts! *   Gee [whiz!] [willigers!]
   [wizigers!]   *   [Oh] Get out!   *   I can't get over it!
   Go away! *   Golly!

Good [golly!] [gracious!] [grief!] [heavens!] [Lord!] [night!]

Great [Caesar's ghost!] [day in the morning!] [guns!] [Scott!]

Hang it [all!] * I'll be hanged! * Heavens [to Betsy!] [forbid!]

The heck you say!   *   Hold you horses!   *   Honest? [!] [to
   goodness? [!] [to Pete? [!]

Honestly? [!]   *   Hot [diggity] dog!   *   How about that? [!]

How do you like that? [!]   *   Huh?   *   Jeepers! [creepers!]

Jimney crickets! * Jumping [catfish!] [Jehoshaphat!]   *   You are [joking? [!] [kidding? [!]

Land [sakes!] [of Goshen!] * Leaping lizards! * As I live and breath!

For the love of [mercy] [Mike!] [Pete!] * Man o'Man! Mercy me!

I'm a monkey's uncle!   *   My [eye!] [aunt Fanny!] [foot!]

No [fooling? [!] [kidding? [!]   *   Oh [boy!] [brother!] [man!] [my!] [oh!] [phooy!] [pooh!] [puey!] [shucks!] [stuff and such!] [yeah!]

Really? * Sakes alive! * You don't say! * Son of a gun!

Strike me pink! * Suffering catfish! * I swear! * Do tell? [!]

Of all things! * Thunder and lightning! * Uh oh!

Well, I'll be! * What on earth? [!]   * What the...? [!]

What in the Sam Hill? * What do you know? [!]

What about that? [!] * Whooey! * Wow!

Ye gods! * Yuck!

Amazement/Frustration

466

EXPRESSIONS USED TO AVOID MENTION OF "GOD"

The third of the biblical Ten Commandments forbids taking the name of God in vain. Some have extended this prohibition to references to Jesus Christ. Many expressions have evolved to avoid such references. They also have many other uses.

The [Lord] Almighty!   * Oh [balls] [beans!] [boy!] brother!]

Bless [my soul!] [you!]   *   Blessed be He!   *   Doggone it!

The Eternal! * Eternal one! * Father in heaven! * By George!

Glory be! [praised!] * Godfrey! * Goll darn! * Golly! [be!] [gee!]

By golly!   *   Good [golly!] [grief!] [heavens!] [Lord!] [night!]

[My] [Oh] Lord!   *   Goodness! [gracious!] [knows!] [me!]

[By] [My] [Oh my] gosh! * Gosh [no!] [yes!] * Great [guns!] [Scott!]

By gum! * He * Him * So help me! [Hannah!] * Heaven [forbid!] [knows!]

Heavens [above!] [to Betsy!]   *   In heaven's name!   *   In the name of heaven!

Heavens [no!] [yes!]   * Oh my heavens!   * Thank heaven!

In his name! * Holy [cats!] [cow!] [gosh!] [mackerel!] [moley!] [Moses!] [smokes!] [Toledo!]

Mention of "God"

Honest to [goodness] [gosh] [Pete] [?] [!}   *   Jehovah

By Jove!   *   Jupiter!   *   Jiminy [Christmas!] [crickets!]

Land [of Goshen!] [sakes!]

Lord in heaven!   *   Lord [help] [protect] me!

Lord knows! [how!] [when!] * Lordy lordy!

For [Lord's] [Pete's] sake! * For the love of [Mike!] [Pete!]

The man upstairs * For pity's sake!   * Saints be [praised] [with us!]

My stars!   * By sugar! * I swear...!   *   By thunder!

My word!   *   Oh Zeus!

Mention of "God"

EXPRESSIONS TO AVOID OR SOFTEN SWEAR WORDS

Both religious teachings and good manners oppose use of swear words. Some words, like "Hell," are considered swear words by some but not by others. Often, the swear meaning comes from the context in which the expressions are used. Below are expressions that avoid swear words or soften them.

...as all get out! * My aunt Fanny! * Oh baloney sausage!

Oh beans! * It scared the bejeebers out of me! * Blast [it!] [you!]

Dad [blast] [burn] it! * What in [blue] blazes! * Go to blazes!

It's hotter than blazes! * The blooming... * That's [a lot of] bull!

Raise Cain! * Confound it! * For crying out loud! * Dadgum [it!] [it all!]

Dagnab it! * Damnation! * Hot dang! * [Dang] [Darn] [it!] [it all!]

Gosh darn! * I'll be darned! * Darn tooting! * It's not worth a darn!

[You're] Darned right! * Darned if I do; darned if I don't!

I declare! * What the deuce! * The deuce it is! * How the devil? * The devil you say! * To the devil with you!

Raise the devil] * What the devil! [?]

I caught the dickens! * Full of the dickens * Like the dickens I will!

What the dickens? * I'll be doggone! * [Doggone] [Drat] it!

I don't give a [fig!] [hang!] [hoot!] [rap!] * He's so all-fired...

Son of a gun! * See you in Hades! * What in hades? * Hail Columbia!

Hang it! [all!] * I don't give a hang! * You can go hang!

I'll be hanged! * What in heaven? * Oh heck! * Heck no!

To heck with it! * He's a heck of a guy! * What the heck? [!]

The heck you say! [?] * H.E. double toothpicks with shoes on!

Hells bells! * What [in] [the] Sam Hill! * Holy [catfish!] [hell] [moley!] [Toledo!]

I'll be hornswaggled! * Horse [feathers!] [manure!] * He's madder than [a wet hen!] [hops!] [you know what!]

Oh mischief! * Who in mischief are you? * [Oh] shoot!

Sure as shooting! * Shucks! * He's a so and so! * I swear!

I'll be switched! * [What in] Tarnation? * [How in] Thunderation! [?]

Soften Swear Words

EXPRESSIONS USED TO REFER TO JAIL OR PRISON

Being in Jail or Prison
or Being Arrested

Behind bars * Doing hard time * Put away * Sent up [the river]

Doing a stretch

[Arrest] [Book] [Bust] [Charge] [Cuff] [Detain] [Hold] [Nab] him! * Take him in

Other Names for Jail/Prison

Big house * Cage * Clink [Klink] * Cooler * Correctional institution

Detention * Freezer * Hoosegow * Joint * Jug * Keep

Lock-up * Penal institution * Penitentiary * Pokey

Slammer * Stir * Tank